Teaching and Learning

ARABIC

as a Foreign Language

Teaching and Learning

ARABIC

as a Foreign Language

A GUIDE FOR TEACHERS

KARIN C. RYDING

Foreword by Roger Allen

Georgetown University Press
Washington, DC

Library of Congress Cataloging-in-Publication Data

Ryding, Karin C.
  Teaching and learning Arabic as a foreign language: a guide for teachers
Karin C. Ryding.
      pages cm.
  Includes bibliographical references and index.
  ISBN 978-1-58901-657-6 (pbk.: alk. paper)
1. Arabic language—Study and teaching—Foreign speakers. 2. Arabic language—
Textbook for foreign speakers. 3. Second language acquisition. I. Title.
  PJ6066.R95 2013
  492.7'80071—dc23

                                                                          2012049965

This book is printed on acid-free paper meeting the requirements of the American National Standard for Permanence in Paper for Printed Library Materials.

15 14 13   9 8 7 6 5 4 3 2 First printing

Printed in the United States of America

Contents

We need to embark upon a whole series of experiments in the teaching and learning of Arabic, approaching the process of curricular planning and innovation with enough flexibility to incorporate within our goals the wonderfully varied features of the Arabic language that should serve as a constant challenge to our own pedagogical creativity.

Roger Allen
Higher Level Language Skills in Arabic

Foreword

It would be no easy task to think of a scholar in Arabic linguistics who is more qualified to write a detailed study of the teaching of the Arabic language than Karin Ryding. Already the author of a major study of modern Arabic grammar (*A Reference Grammar of Modern Standard Arabic* [Cambridge: Cambridge University Press, 2005]), she has recently retired after a lengthy career teaching language and linguistics at Georgetown University, with a long and illustrious history of research, teaching, and publication in and about Arabic. The names of Richard Harrell and Wallace Erwin, Ryding's own mentor (as she herself duly notes), have long been respected by all those who have a concern for pedagogical methodology as it pertains to Arabic. Ryding's own experience, of course, goes beyond the academic sector to include a period spent at the US government's Foreign Service Institute, the institution from which have emerged over the course of the last half century so many ideas and practices with regard to the oral and aural dimensions of language teaching and learning that have come to be introduced and applied in colleges and universities throughout the United States and beyond.

The Arabic-speaking world as we know it today, which is often depicted as mostly coterminous with the problematically named "Middle" East ("Middle" implying between what and what else?), began to take its current shape in the wake of the demise of the Ottoman Empire and decisions made by colonial powers (especially Britain and France) after the First World War. However, it was after the second of those world conflicts (1939–45), and as a consequence of contacts with indigenous peoples in North Africa and greater Syria, that both the United States and Britain became aware of the strategic dimensions of language competence in Arabic, among other non-Western languages. While governments and their diplomatic arms were the first to realize this and implement new programs of instruction, the trend gradually but inevitably moved into the academic sphere. The National Defense and Education Act of 1958 in the USA and the Hayter Report in Britain (1961) referred to the importance of non-Western language competence within their reviews of a new entity dubbed "International Studies." The move now began from the grammar-translation approach long favored by Classical and Semitic (biblical and ancient Near East) studies to a "modern languages" approach and a greater emphasis on the modern and even contemporary.

In Arabic language teaching terms, these changes were exemplified by the publication in 1968 of a new syllabus for Arabic, *Elementary Modern Standard Arabic* (EMSA), prepared by a group of professors of Arabic language and linguistics under the leadership of Peter Abboud of the University of Texas (with Wallace Erwin as one of the team's members). This new curriculum and the subsequent *Intermediate Modern Standard Arabic* (IMSA) served for many years as the standard syllabus for Arabic classes that introduced students to the written language of the modern Arabic-speaking world. In 1979 came the report of the Carter Commission, named for President Jimmy Carter, on international studies and foreign languages that termed the nation's so-called language readiness "scandalous," and advocated a much closer relationship between the goals of government language schools—with their emphasis on oral competences—and academe. Thence was born the so-called proficiency movement in which I was heavily involved for some twenty years. The emphasis in Arabic language teaching and learning now gradually shifted to a four-skills approach—listening, speaking, reading, and writing—the development of descriptors for each skill and a number of different "levels," and a quest for materials that were "authentic" (or even "simulated authentic") examples of native-speaker behaviors (with concomitant debates on precisely who a "native speaker" might be and what behaviors were involved). In subsequent decades a series of new syllabi and textbooks has emerged, and, to add to the current general scenario for Arabic language teaching and learning—including the events of September 2001 through 2011—the number of learners of Arabic has increased. Karin Ryding's work, taking up, as it does, many of the debating points connected with issues that I have raised here, is thus not only timely but also a much-needed study of a continuingly and increasingly exciting and complex topic.

The focus of this book is on teaching and the teacher. Ryding begins by citing a single tenet: "the acknowledged heterogeneity of spoken and written Arabic requires methodological aware-ness and pluralism." A few pages later, that is translated into another basic question: "What to teach?" From the outset of establishing basic principles, Ryding's text offers practical advice: Of ten identified initial statements of principle, all of them useful, the cardinal one for me (based on years of observing Arabic being taught in a variety of institutions and through a variety of meth-ods) is that "the textbook is not the whole course." And, if this initial chapter seems to focus on practical basics, then the one that follows it provides an excellent summary of the development of pedagogical theory over the course of the last half century. What is already obvious from what is presented in the early chapters is Ryding's specific concern for the individual teacher and his/her own learning process; each chapter closes with a set of posed questions to consider and a topic-specific bibliography.

Following the opening section on fundamentals (including a third chapter on the profession itself), there follow six more sections. The virtues already noted are still present: The principles involved are explained (different teaching methods and approaches, for example, in part II), and then their implementation is explored through multiple illustrations and examples, along with some sage advice based on the author's own experience. From a third section devoted to programmatic issues—goals, materials, and assessment (with a subsection on the all-important role of study-abroad programs)—she moves to a series of specific investigations devoted to classroom issues, including the complex topic of heritage learners, and the pedagogy of more specific comprehen-sion and production skills. A final section discusses what Ryding terms "core competencies": vocabulary acquisition, the role and place of grammar, and, in the context of a quest for authen-ticity and the use of the native-speaker model, the important status of culture and sociopragmatic competence.

Among the things that impressed me the most is the emphasis she gives in the chapters on com-prehension to the need for specific strategies in encouraging its development in learners. Chapter 13 on reading discusses not only different types of text but also different types of reading itself, which is a significant factor when one is dealing with a culture such as that of the Arabo-Islamic world, in which reading out loud to a group of listeners has been and still is a frequently encoun-tered phenomenon. Listening itself, the topic of chapter 14, has long been acknowledged as a skill, the teaching and testing of which brings its own complexities. It is clearly a topic that merits much more attention than it normally receives in the curricular planning and its implementation in the language classroom itself, even though it is a crucially important aspect of a teaching and learning program that concentrates on the four-skills approach and the need for their integration within a logically organized and sequenced curriculum.

The discussion of the productive skills allows Ryding to show her expertise in linguistics. That emerges initially in the section on pronunciation where phonemic differences are explained and illustrated. Beyond that, I have already noted the amount of attention that has been paid by the Arabic-teaching community in recent decades to the speaking skill, and especially how to test it and to train teachers in assessment procedures such as the Oral Proficiency Interview (OPI). With that in mind, Ryding's concentration in the chapter on speaking on the basic question as to "what to teach"—in other words, the decision as to whether to teach learners to speak modern standard Arabic, a dialect, or a combination of both, and in which order—allows her to bring her linguis-tic expertise to bear on the complex series of issues that need to be addressed in making such a curricular decision, one indeed that has frequently been "ducked" by Arabic language programs at many colleges and universities. By contrast, the development of the writing skill has, if anything, been relatively neglected as a topic of research and experiment. It is thus a welcome feature of this book to find an entire chapter devoted to it, beginning with the development of good script (a prized asset in the Arabic-speaking world) and including valuable sections on note-taking and the gradual development of more cursive writing practices.

In part VII, Ryding takes on two issues that are central and crucial to the process of learning to use Arabic in contemporary contexts and thus to those teachers who would organize the learning process for their students. Chapter 18 discusses grammar, a term that has traditionally been used to describe a system that examines the morphology and syntax of a language (and often also a textbook that illustrates those features in a graduated fashion). But, in the context of more modern approaches that lay greater emphasis on the development of communication and reception skills, grammar has come to be represented by the organization of a pedagogical quest for accuracy. The chapter provides not only a discussion of the meanings associated with the various terms involved, but also goes on to provide valuable discussion of the stages and levels in the learning process and the role that accuracy may play within them. In this connection I can remember pointing out at any number of language-teaching workshops that "Me Tarzan, You Jane" does communicate a certain (very basic) message, but its "accuracy" leaves something to be desired (and developed). The final chapter broaches a topic that has tended to be downplayed in discussions of teaching and learning strategies, namely, the role of culture. There is a considerable focus in this chapter on the definition and role of "area studies." However, beyond the academic sector itself, the process of introducing learners of Arabic to sociopragmatic skills alongside linguistic ones and the all-important issue as to what is culturally appropriate and, if anything more important, inappropriate in the different regions of the Arabic-speaking world, is shown by the contents and contexts covered in this chapter to be as crucial to the teaching and learning process as the more easily identifiable "four skills."

While every chapter in this book contains useful information and discussion, teachers of Arabic—and particularly those who are beginning the process of becoming teachers—will find the appendices and bibliography at the end of the volume to be a rich and comprehensive resource on virtually every aspect of the profession—its history, its methodologies, and its aspirations. The reference materials are thus a clear reflection of Ryding's career in the field and the close attention that she has paid over the years to the ever-increasing volume of publications on language teaching in general and those devoted to Arabic in particular.

The past forty or so years during the course of which I have had the privilege of observing and participating in the Arabic language teaching enterprise have witnessed a sea change in methods, goals, testing, and, perhaps most significant of all, learner numbers and identities—all of which have had a major impact on pedagogy and on those who either practice or aspire to practice it. By any yardstick one wishes to apply, the number of students now studying Arabic has increased exponentially in the last decade. Arabic has been added as a language-learning option, more often than not for the first time, at an increasing number of colleges and universities as well as at the precollege level. National standards have been developed and new syllabi have been thoroughly pretested and then published. All of this development has demanded and continues to demand the increased availability of teachers of Arabic, indeed, more teachers who are qualified to teach, and, even beyond that, more qualified than heretofore.

Therein lies the challenge for the present and into the future. Ryding's book cannot, nor does it, replace the need for the kind of teacher-training workshops that are regularly offered by the National Middle East Language Resource Center (NMELRC) based at Brigham Young University in Utah, and the American Council for the Teaching of Foreign Languages (ACTFL). However, what it does offer to both incipient and experienced teachers of Arabic is a wealth of research, information, advice, and insight on the complex and totally rewarding career of the Arabic language teacher. This book is a great tribute to the commitment of a distinguished and devoted scholar and pedagogue of the Arabic language.

ROGER ALLEN, University of Pennsylvania (Emeritus)

Acknowledgments

I am deeply indebted to Hope LeGro, director of Georgetown Languages at Georgetown University Press, for her constant encouragement and valuable feedback during the preparation of this book, and to her predecessor, Gail Grella, with whom I originally developed the concept. My colleague Terrence Potter also generously provided support and advice on key points.

I thank my husband Victor Litwinski for his affectionate tolerance of my preoccupation with all things TAFL during the production of this manuscript, and for his eagle eye in editing.

I hope this book will honor the spirit of my Georgetown mentor and consummate Arabic linguist, the late Wallace M. Erwin.

Abbreviations and Acronyms

AATA	American Association of Teachers of Arabic
ACTFL	American Council for the Teaching of Foreign Languages
AIM	Army Intensive Method
CALL	computer-assisted language learning
CBI	content-based instruction
CLAC	cultures and languages across the curriculum
CL	counseling-learning
CLL	community language learning
CLT	communicative language teaching
CV	consonant + short vowel
CVC	consonant + short vowel + consonant
CVCC	consonant + short vowel + consonant + consonant
CVV	consonant + long vowel
CVVC	consonant + long vowel + consonant
DL	distance learning
DLI	Defense Language Institute
EMSA	*Elementary Modern Standard Arabic*
ENS	educated native speaker
ESA	educated spoken Arabic
FDH	fundamental difference hypothesis
FonF	focus on form
FSA	formal spoken Arabic
FSI	Foreign Service Institute
FTF	front the familiar
H	"high" or formal Arabic
i + 1	input + one level beyond learners' interlanguage
ILR	Interagency Language Roundtable
L	"low" or colloquial Arabic
L1	first or native language
L2	second or foreign language
LAC	languages across the curriculum
LCTL	less commonly taught language
LRC	language resource center
MESA	Middle East Studies Association
MLA	Modern Language Association
MSA	Modern Standard Arabic
NA	the natural approach
NCOLCTL	National Council of Less Commonly Taught Languages
NS	native speaker

OPI	oral proficiency interview
PT	processability theory
RSA	regional spoken Arabic
SLA	second language acquisition
TAFL	teaching Arabic as a foreign language
TBLT	task-based language teaching
TL	target language
TLA	teacher language awareness
UG	universal grammar

Introduction

With each passing year it grows more obvious that colleges must prepare Americans to deal more competently with people from other parts of the globe.

Daniel Yankelovich

The language major should be structured to produce a specific outcome: educated speakers who have deep translingual and transcultural competence.

Modern Language Association

As American students increasingly acknowledge that what happens in Europe, Asia, Africa, or the Middle East may ultimately impact on their well-being and security, they have turned more and more to the study of languages and cultures that, until twenty years ago, were little studied and rarely taught. Arabic is one of those languages. Important as an official language in the United Nations, as the liturgical language of Islam, and as the official language of twenty nation members of the Arab League, Arabic also offers an extensive literary and documentary tradition stemming from widespread literary activity in Arabic during the era of the Islamic empire, from approximately the seventh to thirteenth centuries. As a key component of Mediterranean cultural heritage, and as a rich resource for the study of Islamic culture, Arabic invites learners to experience the many facets of literary and spoken discourse that create Arab identity and Arabic cultural cosmopolitanism.

In many respects, and in almost every mode, Arabic instruction differs from teaching a Western language or an Asian language. Therefore, research done on second or foreign language learning in those areas is only partially applicable to Arabic. Although it is useful and even necessary to be aware of key research findings through research on other languages, it is equally necessary to compare and contrast those findings with Arabic and its particular social, cultural, popular, and literary environments. This work deals with the basics of Arabic language instruction from both theoretical and practical points of view. It is intended as a resource for teachers of Arabic as a foreign language, as a place where they can find information about curricula, methods, goals, testing, and research. It is not intended as the last word about teaching techniques or as a proposal for using any one particular approach. Nor is it intended to describe the Arabic language itself. It is meant to serve as an introduction to pedagogical practice and as a reflection of my own perspective on difficult but central issues that constantly demand attention, such as application of second language acquisition theories, clarity of concepts, definitions and terminology, and particular challenges for Arabic pedagogy. It reviews, describes, and discusses traditional and contemporary methodologies and specific aspects of foreign language teaching such as classroom management, teaching grammar and vocabulary, teaching about culture, and other key topics. As an attempt to compile fundamentals and provide a roadmap of important topics for a rapidly growing field, this work is necessarily limited in its scope, but it is also exploratory in its reach and in its observations, aiming to foster an intellectual framework for the pedagogy of Arabic as a foreign language. This book provides groundwork information and principles to guide teachers of Arabic and to formulate

Arabic-specific pedagogical paradigms. Those paradigms need to be broad enough to allow a range of interests and perspectives to flourish, and solid enough to build on for the future.

The central tenet of this book is that the acknowledged heterogeneity of spoken and written Arabic requires methodological awareness and pluralism. A range of key theories and practices can provide a foundation for thoughtfully creating learning situations according to institutional curricular goals and design. Although it is important to avoid "unprincipled eclecticism" (a random or ad hoc sampling of procedures and tactics), with a knowledge of contemporary theory and hypotheses, instructors can be ready to define their professional practice. They can make and defend informed choices about a range of curricular options and materials, syllabus designs, and classroom procedures. The present work aims to pull together information about the major aspects of instruction in Arabic as a foreign language in one place and to provide a baseline reference for teachers-in-development throughout the profession. I do not hesitate to express my own convictions based on many years of research and experience, even when those convictions may differ substantially from contemporary consensus on second language acquisition and Arabic language teaching. Also, given the abundance of research on second language acquisition and the depth of complexity in Arabic language instruction in particular, there is much that had to be omitted from this study in order simply to complete it in a reasonable period of time. Readers may well find lacunae in certain areas, but I hope that by compiling this initial study, a sense of the field as a whole may evolve and that areas of particular interest to Arabic learning will undergo further examination and elaboration.

Each chapter of this book addresses specific aspects of foreign language learning and teaching, especially as they pertain to Arabic. Each chapter also contains a list of suggested further readings and questions for study and reflection. By pulling together the various strands of teaching experiences and traditions, and by connecting those strands with contemporary research, it is my hope that this book will provide a solid base for teachers-in-training (both native and nonnative speakers), a springboard for discussion of theory and application, and a framework for conceiving more effective models of Arabic communicative instruction. Although the chapters are of necessity sequential, the topics they cover are not related linearly, but interrelated in multiple ways.

The Rising Interest in Arabic Language and Culture

An interconnected world with ever-increasing international links and interests, as well as key economic and political concerns at the global level, have raised the public profile of Arabic language and literature, Arab society and culture, and the Arab world in general. Increased academic attention to and marked interest in Arabic distinguish a new stage in the conceptualization of Arabic teaching and learning, expanding the study and discussion of a culture with ancient roots, complex histories, and fine-grained sociocultural diversity. The burgeoning of Arabic studies in the United States has already taken place to a great extent. Recently established Arabic courses and programs reflect responses to both pragmatic and academic needs in a wide range of disciplinary and interdisciplinary curricula. The rapid expansion of programs, however, also inevitably discloses points of weakness and incompleteness in program design and in professional preparation.[1] Thoughtful consideration of ways to strengthen and refine professional resources is required, especially as the need for those resources continues to grow.[2]

Expanded access to foreign languages and cultures to counteract the "acute isolation of educated Americans from the conversations of the world at large" has been noted by both individuals and professional organizations (MLA 2008, 291). These same authors advocate developing integrated curricula situated "in cultural, historical, geographical, and cross-cultural frames" that "challenge students' imaginations" and intellects through various forms of language study that lead learners to higher levels of "critical language awareness, interpretation and translation, historical and political consciousness, social sensibility, and aesthetic perception" (290). Approaching these goals through the teaching of Arabic language and culture will require the broad regrounding of pedagogical principles and practice, articulation of clear professional standards, and the creation of multiple paths to translingual competence and intercultural literacy. Moreover, developing an ethos of professional engagement with Arabic language studies and a distinct tradition of research and teaching requires that teachers be integrally involved with the intellectual work of this field.

The Role of the Teacher

It is assumed that those engaged in teaching a language will have two sets of skills: They will have declarative knowledge about Arabic structure and use (sometimes referred to as "teacher language awareness," TLA), and they will have procedural knowledge that informs their management of classroom instruction.[3] This book is aimed primarily at developing procedural knowledge, but in language teaching, procedural knowledge and content knowledge are interwoven because of the need to use the L2 as the primary vehicle of instruction as well as for the objective of instruction. For Arabic teaching in particular, teachers need to have an extensive knowledge base not only in literary Arabic, but also in the ways that written and spoken Arabic interrelate, and what that implies for communicative language teaching. Interweaving this complex knowledge with the procedural knowledge needed for effective instruction is a central professional challenge.

Starting Off in Arabic: Key Themes

Teachers and teaching assistants starting out in the Arabic profession may be faced with quandaries and questions about procedures and principles but may find few sources of reliable information. Myths about Arabic language complexities have engendered reluctance to examine objectively the sociolinguistic realities of Arabic, and they have often discouraged learners. Choosing to be a teacher of Arabic as a foreign language, therefore, means choosing to teach in a field that is complex, extensive, and abounding in competing choices and even in paradox.[4] Arabic teachers face an array of challenges and choices: curricular, developmental, methodological, and linguistic. Diversity in professional background, philosophy, and training leads to different paths for Arabic teaching, different sets of materials, and sometimes strong disagreement about principles and procedures for developing professional norms. Key pedagogical issues in Arabic include spoken and written variants, literacy and word recognition, and the role of grammar.

Spoken and Written Variants

Arabic is at once a classical language and a modern language, with literary traditions that span a millennium, a lively and sophisticated practice of contemporary journalism, and widely differing, vibrant spoken vernaculars. Formal classroom instruction in Arabic does not often take into account the realm of natural, everyday spoken Arabic. It is relatively easy in formal classwork to sidestep exposure to the language of daily existence and to focus only on literacy skills.[5] This lack of attention to everyday language, however, hinders access to serious study and acquisition of "performance fluency" as well as normal discourse skills—from speech acts such as requesting, apologizing, complaining, suggesting, and inviting, to more advanced speech activities such as negotiation, argumentation, and debate. It also blocks the potential for one modality to enrich the other, and the opportunity to develop full linguistic competence. Developing genuinely interactive skills, therefore, needs greater attention in Arabic instruction, even though the calibration of teaching those skills in one curriculum is a substantial challenge. This traditional dichotomy between spoken and written Arabic is a reflection of widespread ideological concern in the Arab world, contrasting the unifying value and importance of Arabic literacy with potential fragmentation, alienation, and local social and cultural values that are typically keyed to regional spoken vernaculars. Some Arab scholars have even equated valorization of vernaculars with colonial efforts to divide and weaken the Arab world.[6] This issue is a thread of discussion throughout this book.

Recent studies have shown that for learners of Arabic as a foreign language, the Arabic system of orthography presents cognitive challenges that seriously affect speed and depth of learning. This finding has important implications for organizing the teaching of reading and enriching the depth of textual experience for learners. This is discussed at greater length in chapter 13.

The Role of Grammar

The communicative approach to teaching that has been prevalent in recent years has emphasized acquisition of language structures primarily through indirect and intuitive means, rather than through direct presentation and practice of language skills. This has led to the belief among many teachers and teacher trainers that grammatical rules should not be explicitly taught, discussed, or tested. More recent research, however, has shown that adult language acquisition can be accelerated and strengthened by systematic, effective explanation and practice of grammatical structures to improve skills and enrich performance. How to implement grammatical awareness and accuracy for learners is a central issue in Arabic pedagogy, especially for those learners aiming at advanced levels of proficiency. For further discussion, see chapter 19 on Arabic pedagogical grammar.

Arabic Today: Unity and Diversity

The Arabic language is highly flexible. In fact, this flexibility is one of its distinguishing features. Written and spoken Arabic, though distinct from each other, are closely interwoven components of all Arabic speech communities. The continuum between the sacred and secular Arabic literary canon on one hand, and the lively, creative, always edgy forms of colloquial Arabic popular culture on the other, fuse the richness of the past with the vibrancy of the new.

Arabic speakers have a vernacular Arabic mother tongue (ʕāmmiyya) as well as literacy skills built through education in standard Arabic (fuṣḥā). The regional variation of Arabic vernaculars is extensive and substantial, whereas the written language acts as an anchor to link Arab countries closely with each other and with their shared past. The dual, side-by-side existence of vernacular Arabic for primary (informal) discourse functions and modern standard Arabic (MSA) for secondary (formal) discourse is known by the English technical term "diglossia" (in Arabic, izdiwājiyya lughawiyya).[7] The key to being a functional Arabic speaker is flexibility and interconnectedness: The ability to operate at all levels, and, even more important, to be able to navigate between them as required by different social contexts.[8] Those who learn Arabic as a foreign language, therefore, face a daunting challenge: competence in a full spectrum of language varieties. In most cases, training programs as well as educational programs in the United States have chosen to focus on MSA, in keeping with the generalized cultural notion in the Arab world that the written language is superior to the spoken, and in keeping with the myth that vernacular Arabic is easily acquired outside the classroom, in-country, with no formal instruction. Everyday spoken Arabic is rarely a significant component of an academic curriculum, even in the first two years of study.[9]

Of all the key issues in Arabic as a foreign language instruction, therefore, the most salient and defining one is *what* to teach. Which forms of language—spoken or written—meet the goals of language instruction in a particular school, institute, or department? How will learner needs be determined and analyzed? If more than one variant of Arabic will be taught, how will they be blended into an effective curricular structure? How will communicative competence be measured? It is difficult enough to address the qualitative differences between primary and secondary discourses in a language where the spoken and written variants are essentially alike (such as French); it is far more complex to address those differences in the Arabic classroom setting when the language variants diverge substantially in lexicon, morphology, and syntax.

Despite the importance of what to teach, however, the fact is that key questions about how to teach arise quickly as well. Faced with a prescribed curriculum or textbook, many Arabic teachers find that they are expected to know how to teach MSA to Americans (or Westerners) in "communicative" ways—ways that differ substantially from how they themselves were taught, and ways that in some respects make little sense when teaching a primarily written language.

Pedagogical Norms

MSA dominates as the instructional medium and instructional goal of most Arabic as a foreign language program. If a legitimate goal of instruction is to attain a language skill repertoire reasonably similar to that of native speakers of Arabic, however, then the role of colloquial or vernacular Arabic has to be part of the constitutive matrix of Arabic language acquisition. But—and this is a big "but"—spoken Arabic is challenging to teach because of the lack of explicit spoken Arabic norms.[10]

In applied linguistics research, the concept of "pedagogical norm" or "target model" has been developed to help teachers and materials designers deal with native-speaker use of spoken variants, inasmuch as a "fundamental aspect of all educated native speakers' language competence is stylistic variation, or the ability to adjust speech register to situational formality" (Etienne and Sax 2009, 584). Such a norm enables even first-year learners to engage in authentic usage for basic communicative functions, and can be calibrated according to learners' levels "so that more native-like variation . . . [is] gradually introduced as a student progresses" (598).[11]

A key conversation for the Arabic profession to have, therefore, is on the topic of spoken Arabic norms. For Arabic in particular, these norms may need to be plural and flexible in order to ground our teaching in responsible educational principles and practice. This book approaches this issue, but for overall professional effectiveness, the concept of pedagogical norms for Arabic needs to be carefully explored and evaluated on a number of levels. Equally important are questions of curricular logistics. As is well known, the question of "which colloquial" (out of the geographical range of spoken Arabic varieties) has often stopped curriculum planners in their tracks. Selection of one particular form of colloquial Arabic seems to exclude other forms of colloquial and to severely limit learner options. Does this need to be the case? In the opinion of this author, the question of "which colloquial" is not an insurmountable obstacle; it is a hurdle to be cleared. What is needed is a distinct, well-defined range of choices motivated by both academic and pragmatic requirements.[12]

Changing Norms and Learning Objectives

In the past when travel to the Arab world was not as common, strict academic focus on literary Arabic could lead students to advanced levels of written language knowledge without attending to concepts such as "communicative competence," in the expectation that few students would actually need to speak or understand Arabic in daily interaction. Now interest in the Arab world has been revitalized, careers in government and international agencies abound, and many Arabic students eventually study, live, and work in the Arab world. Oral proficiency testing is standard for many programs across the country and decisions need to be made about what an oral Arabic norm (or norms) should be. Objective reassessment of the contested relationship between spoken and written Arabic needs to be undertaken in order to develop wider options for curricula and realistic proficiency goals that meet student needs as well as educational aims.

A Web of Competencies

With respect to designing curricula for Arabic, it is important to remember that competence in one's native language or in another language does not develop in a linear fashion even though expressions used for describing levels of achievement or development usually imply a linear progression, for example, the terms "elementary, intermediate, advanced," or proficiency levels 1, 2, 3, 4, 5 as used in the Interagency Language Roundtable (ILR) skill-level descriptions.[13] Expressions of sequence borrow from a linear metaphor that is useful for classification and measurement but that is not identical with actual processes of learning and acquisition. Advanced language skills are not formed simply by additive measures focusing on higher-level literary, public, and formal discourse functions; they are part of a wide web of competencies that need to be developed for multiple functions and in multiple ways. A normal language skill-level profile represents a web of interconnected sectors, strategies, and types of knowledge that articulate with and reinforce each other. Growth in communicative competence is not a linear process; it is an expanding, carefully rehearsed network of social, cognitive, and linguistic skills that interact to form a wider as well as higher range of functional ability and confidence, and that also assist learners in improving their performance.

To become functionally competent in the full range of language skills in Arabic is not impossible. But it entails reconfiguration of priorities and expectations as well as reconsideration of how curricula are structured from the perspective of learner needs, programmatic requirements, and best instructional practices. Whether a program chooses to focus on literacy only, on the study and analysis of canonical literary texts, on contemporary Arabic genres such as media Arabic, or on a combination of spoken and written skills, curricular planning needs to take into account the implications and contexts of linguistic variation as they impact departmental objectives.

⬡ Proficiency

The concept of "proficiency" as applied to language learning stemmed originally from government agency attempts (started in the 1950s) to measure foreign language ability on a scale of 0–5 in order to identify actual language capabilities of job holders and job candidates. Candidates were originally measured in speaking (S) and reading (R), and received an S/R rating, for example, S-2+/R-3. Speaking and reading are still the central categories for skill-level testing and descriptions, but official skill descriptions exist for listening and writing as well. As a result of concern about overall mediocre levels of competence reached in foreign language instruction at both the high school and university levels in the United States, the idea of measuring actual performance rather than solely measuring classroom achievement began to take effect in the 1980s with the development of the American Council on the Teaching of Foreign Languages (ACTFL) proficiency guidelines. These guidelines were developed to bring what has been called "a common yardstick" to the measurement of language proficiency in American schools along the lines of the government (ILR) measurement system.

The impact of proficiency testing on both philosophy and methodologies of language teaching has been significant, encouraging and underscoring the importance of communicative competence and the idea that proficiency is not an end result but a stage in a trajectory of development toward a specific outcome that more and more closely resembles the competence of an educated native speaker of the foreign language.[14] These concepts are analyzed in greater detail in chapter 8; for present discussion, it should be noted that the concepts of spoken proficiency and usage-based language learning have significantly impacted curricular decisions to teach only MSA. Although Arabic-specific ACTFL guidelines were published in 1989, the emphasis at that time was on speaking MSA for almost all purposes, and the role of vernacular Arabic was attended to only at higher levels, the opposite of the natural functions of these forms of Arabic. Revised ACTFL Arabic guidelines updated to reflect Arabic linguistic reality are now available via the ACTFL website: http://actflproficiencyguidelines2012.org/arabic/.

⬡ Standards for Teaching Arabic

The advent of standards for language teaching in the 1990s introduced a set of five curricular components to which foreign language teaching programs were encouraged to adhere in order to develop full communicative competence. These broad-based components were goal-directed concepts around which proficiency-based programs could be constructed, taught, tested, and administered. They were functionally based and stated in terms of desired terminal behaviors.[15] The five concepts are: communication, cultures, connections, comparisons, and communities (often referred to as "the five Cs"). Each of these concepts specifies typical content knowledge as well as functional capabilities; for example, for the communication standard, a primary requirement is that "students engage in conversations, provide and obtain information, express feelings and emotion, and exchange opinions" or, for the culture standard, "students demonstrate an understanding of the relationship between the practices and perspectives of the culture studied."[16] A summary of "the five Cs" is found in appendix E.

The most important aspect of implementing a standards-based curriculum is the careful and thoughtful calibration between language structures and the requirements of the standards. Vocabulary and grammar need to be optimally geared to learner levels as well as to the standards themselves. It is essential to understand that the standards do not provide a methodology for application in the classroom; they provide an educational framework within which to build language and culture skills. The Arabic-specific standards, published in 2006, can be found in *Standards for Foreign Language Learning in the 21st Century,* compiled by the National Standards in Foreign Language Education Project (pp. 111–55).

✧ Terminology: Key Terms, Concepts, and Metalanguage

Terminological precision is an essential factor in developing concepts and avoiding confusion in any field. Yet few studies exist that focus explicitly on key terms for teaching Arabic as a foreign language. Therefore, one aim of this text is to introduce conceptual and terminological clarity and to provide working definitions of key terms. It is, of course, important to recognize that the Arabic grammatical tradition developed its own sophisticated terminology, and one of the most important issues for Arabic professionals is not only to be aware of that tradition, but also to be fully aware of the differences between those terms and contemporary English linguistic terminology. This will lead to a richer, more reliable, and more comprehensive bilingual model of Arabic methodology and language acquisition. Key concepts, terms, and definitions are central components of this text. A set of basic terms used in Arabic and in applied linguistics is provided in appendix C.

One of the most important competencies for teachers of any language is to know, understand, and use metalanguage effectively. Metalanguage is language used to talk about language; it is the terminology that is needed to describe language phenomena accurately. Metalanguage includes terms such as *verb, noun, preposition, syntax, morphology, phonology.* Some metalanguage is straightforward, but under certain circumstances it can also become highly technical. The Arabic language has a metalanguage of its own that is used to describe its structure and features, and so does English. Arabic technical grammar terms are key components of professional Arabic teaching terminology but rarely have exactly the same semantic field or reference points as their English equivalents. For example, the term *ḥarf* in Arabic is polysemic and difficult to render adequately in English except as separate terms: "letter of the alphabet," "(grammatical) particle," "edge." Sometimes, English terms describing Arabic structures are translated from Arabic (e.g., *kān-a* and her "sisters"), sometimes they are established terms in Western linguistics or philology (e.g., "accusative" or "subjunctive"), and sometimes they are coined as new terms to apply specifically to Arabic (e.g., "modern standard Arabic"). With regard to the teaching of Arabic to speakers of English, however, it is useful to keep in mind that in some cases there are no exact, one-word equivalents for certain concepts, and that on the other hand, there may be many ways to interpret a particular term.

The control of English/Arabic metalanguages is important because many teachers and learners will be moving between languages in a regular, consistent, bilingual manner. Even if a course is conducted solely in Arabic, it is crucial for English-speaking learners to understand concepts clearly in order to contrast or compare them with their L1 concepts, especially where semantic boundary lines differ from one language to the other.

A further reason to study nomenclature and technical linguistic terminology is for reading and discussing professional materials on foreign language pedagogy, applied linguistics, and second language acquisition. Language-teaching professionals need to periodically refresh and deepen their knowledge of both applied and theoretical concepts in order to maintain their professional skills, standing, and stature. Arabic as a foreign language needs to be part of the larger discussion of foreign language learning and second language acquisition, which is largely conducted in English. In this book a certain amount of technical terminology is used when discussing language pedagogy in general and when describing Arabic linguistic phenomena. Essential technical terms in the text appear in **bold**, and a list of basic terms is provided in appendix B.

 ## This Book

Arabic instruction is complex in many ways. Those who choose the profession of Arabic teaching will not find ready answers to questions of curricular goals, norms, or methods but must work them out for themselves through reading, research, and reflection on principles and procedures and in discussion of professional practices and standards. The scarcity of published research on Arabic as a second language results in two calls to action: Teachers need to engage in the intellectual work of the profession and share their knowledge; and publications on a wide range of linguistic research and practice need to be consulted on a regular basis in order to keep developing insights and ideas applicable to the Arabic language classroom.

This book is organized into seven parts dealing with various aspects of Arabic teaching and learning: pedagogy fundamentals, different approaches and methods, programmatic issues, management of classes, comprehension skills, production skills, and the teaching of core competencies such as grammar, vocabulary, and culture. Each part is composed of chapters focusing on specific topics, and each chapter contains not only a summary of research, but also advice and ideas about Arabic pedagogy in particular, as well as study questions and suggestions for further reading. Thematic threads recur throughout the text: the importance of teaching authentic Arabic skills (spoken as well as written), the need for classroom-based research about Arabic learning, the importance of practice and review, and the central importance of both vocabulary and grammar.

 ## Study Questions and Activities

1. Do you believe that literacy goals are approximately the same for native and nonnative Arabic speakers? If not, how do they differ?
2. List and describe three "norms" for teaching spoken Arabic.
3. What is an accurate way to describe the relationship between spoken and written Arabic? Is it static? Functional? Blurred? Shifting? Solid? Strained?
4. Do you think it is more pedagogically effective to keep spoken and written Arabic separate or blend them in some way? If blended, how can this be done? If separate, how can this be managed?
5. Do you believe that spoken modern standard Arabic (i.e., speaking the written language) is a useful skill? Please discuss your reasons.

 ## Further Reading

American Council on the Teaching of Foreign Languages (ACTFL). 2012. *ACTFL Proficiency Guidelines: Speaking, Writing, Listening, and Reading.* Arabic annotations and samples. Available at http://actflproficiencyguidelines2012.org/arabic/.

Andrews, Stephen. 2007. *Teacher Language Awareness.* Cambridge: Cambridge University Press.

Loewen, Shawn, and Hayo Reinders. 2011. *Key Concepts in Second Language Acquisition.* Houndsmills, Basingstoke, Hampshire, UK: Palgrave McMillan.

National Standards in Foreign Language Education Project. 2006. *Standards for Foreign Language Learning in the 21st Century*. Lawrence, KS: Allen Press, Inc.

Richards, Jack C., and Richard Schmidt. [1985] 2010. *Longman Dictionary of Language Teaching and Applied Linguistics*. Harlow, England: Longman.

VanPatten, Bill, and Alessandro G. Benati. 2010. *Key Terms in Second Language Acquisition*. London: Continuum.

⬡ **Notes**

1. In this respect I appreciate the observation of Lawrence Buell that with regard to fields of study, "to burgeon is not necessarily to mature or to prevail" (Buell 2005, 1).

2. This situation does not affect Arabic alone; other less commonly taught foreign languages face similar demands on limited resources, reflecting a catch-up mentality based on the misguided idea that little or no professional preparation is needed to rapidly extend foreign language instructional capacity.

3. See Andrews 2007 for a thorough analysis and discussion of teacher language awareness.

4. Regarding the relationship of standard Arabic to other varieties, one author states that the vernaculars, "though they may be practically dominant, [do] not theoretically receive any formal or even informal recognition or endorsement as local standards. This may sound paradoxical, but it is factual" (Abd-el-Jawad 1992, 261).

5. This is sometimes rationalized by what I term "the acquisition fallacy:" that spoken or vernacular Arabic is easy to acquire once a student is in an Arab country, and that it is not a complex or demanding linguistic task.

6. A general unease with legitimization of vernacular Arabic has been associated with divisive policies of colonialist powers to the point where many believe that the effect of "Western colonizing countries . . . on language was obvious in the implementation of imperial language policies which ultimately aimed at suppressing the use of SA [standard Arabic] and at the same time imposing the colonizing language and/or promoting the formal use of the colloquial dialects" (Abd-el-Jawad 1992, 265).

7. Ferguson 1959a is the foundational work for this concept in English. See Boussofara-Omar 2006 for an overview of diglossia.

8. "Arabic native speakers shift from the High variety to the Low variety and vice versa in well-defined contexts. This indicates that native speakers not only have grammars of both varieties but that they also internalize the rules that govern the switch from one variety to the other" (Farghaly 2005, 29).

9. Exceptions at the university level include Brigham Young University, Western Michigan University, Georgetown University, University of Texas at Austin, and Cornell University, all of whom introduce spoken Arabic in the undergraduate curriculum using different curricular models.

10. One definition of "norm" is "that which is considered appropriate in speech or writing for a particular situation or purpose within a particular group or community" (Richards and Schmidt 2010, 398). A pedagogical norm "consists of a neutralized variety of the language conceived for pedagogical purposes" (Etienne and Sax, 2009, 598). Regarding Arabic norms, Abd-el-Jawad states, "we are using many varieties in our daily lives, yet we do not want to recognize them as norms or let them have any normative values" (1992, 261).

11. This topic has been especially important for French, where focus on what has been termed "hypernormal" correctness has long shaped both teacher preparation and materials, but whose pedagogical effectiveness and validity is now increasingly interrogated by scholars who underscore the pervasive stylistic variation used by French speakers in day-to-day conversation, or "le français ordinaire." This does not at all mean abandonment of "le bon français;" what it does is introduce pragmatic balance into language teaching approaches and materials. There are useful parallels here for Arabic instruction.

12. Prestige regional variants such as educated spoken Jordanian or educated spoken Egyptian may offer forms of the vernacular that can be used in a wide range of situations and serve learners well. See Ibrahim 1986 and Badawi 1985.

13. Interagency Language Roundtable skill-level descriptions can be found at www.govtilr.org.

14. For an overview of the concepts of communicative competence and proficiency in foreign language teaching, consult Hadley 2001, 1–50.

15. See Hadley 2001, 34–41, and National Standards 2006, 9–15.

16. See National Standards 2006, 9.

Part I

Fundamentals of Foreign Language Pedagogy

Some Pedagogical Principles

The acquisition of another language is not an act of disembodied cognition, but is the situated, spatially and temporally anchored, co-construction of meaning between teachers and learners who each carry with them their own history of experience with language and communication.

Claire Kramsch

Language learning is developmental, requiring repeated exposure to target language data in multiple ways and from multiple angles, as well as deliberate practice. This chapter outlines some general principles that apply to language teaching and to Arabic teaching in particular. These principles are provided both for use as a springboard for discussing related topics and as fundamental concepts that one can return to over and over again in one's teaching. That is, they apply widely to teaching situations, be they with beginners or advanced learners. They center on the relationships between teacher and learners, on what Kramsch calls the "co-construction of meaning between teachers and learners," and how learning and teaching at every step co-determine each other and enrich our experience.

Making Pedagogical Decisions

At almost every turn, an Arabic teacher is faced with crucial professional and procedural choices. If you are a native speaker of Arabic, how do you understand the perspectives and problems of nonnative-speaking learners? Where do you start? How do you connect with everyone in the class? For a nonnative speaker, you have to assure your students that you know Arabic well and that you know what you are doing in the classroom. How can you do this effectively and build their trust from day one forward? Does one speak Arabic all the time in the classroom? If so, what kind of Arabic should be used—colloquial, literary, or something in between? How will meaning get across? Can English be used at all? If so, when, how, and what for? Is there a dependable formula for this? How can errors be corrected without discouraging learners? How much homework should be assigned? How, how often, and when should I test students?

Where Does One Start?

With so many choices, concerns, and limited selection of materials, where does one start? For this chapter, ten basic principles have been selected for examination as a way of beginning a professional discussion of Arabic language instruction. Most of them are what is termed "high-leverage practices," in that they "increase the likelihood that teaching will be effective" (Teachingworks 2012). These are certainly not the only principles that exist for Arabic language teaching but they are based on research, learning theory, and my own practical experience as a teacher and trainer. These principles and topics often surface as issues in teacher evaluation, in methodology courses, and in Arabic teacher training.

Ten Basic Principles for Discussing How to Teach Arabic

1. Have high expectations of students and build their confidence.
2. The textbook is not the whole course.
3. Speak Arabic as much as possible in the classroom.
4. Keep it lively and interesting.
5. Provide learners with extensive deliberate practice, especially on "the hard parts."
6. Front the familiar; use what students already know as a springboard.
7. Assign written homework regularly.
8. Prepare a range of specific learning activities before every class.
9. Keep a file of teaching resources.
10. Build in time for regular, consistent review.

---

1. Have High Expectations of Your Students and Build Their Confidence.

Most teachers hold the door to Arabic language wide open and help their students through it; some hold it only a little bit open and tell their students that it is going to be difficult or impossible for them to get through it. Students often fulfill the prophesies of their instructors. A teacher's attitude is an essential factor in the success or failure of Arabic language acquisition, and bolstering student confidence is key to their progress. In fact, one of the central factors in good learning experiences is high expectations on the part of the teacher.

This seems like a very straightforward concept, but it is complicated by certain attitudes on the part of both instructors and learners. Here are some common negative attitudes or misconceptions that have been expressed by teachers of Arabic:

- American students will have major difficulties learning Arabic.
- Difficulties in pronunciation are too great for American students to master, so there is no point in requiring accurate pronunciation.
- The system of Arabic noun plurals is so complex that it should be delayed in presentation.
- Arabic grammar is extremely difficult and should not be directly taught or explained because it will discourage and confuse learners. And conversely, Arabic grammar is so difficult that it needs extensive and repeated explanation.
- Students do not need to write Arabic script accurately; it is too demanding to expect them to write fast and clearly. Handwriting must be taught very slowly, if at all.

All of these attitudes reflect profound underestimation of the capabilities of English-speaking students. Some of these misconceptions can severely undermine learner confidence and delay or discourage effective learning. Teachers are a guide and an inspiration as well as a source of information for the learners. Arabic is a complex language and yes, it demands a great deal of study and practice, but it is definitely possible for learners to make substantial and rapid progress as long as they believe they can, and as long as the teacher upholds that belief. As a general rule, it is better to overestimate students' capabilities as long as one periodically checks with them to make sure they are not feeling overwhelmed.

Another aspect to developing student confidence is to show them that you are well prepared and qualified to bring them along to high levels of performance. On the first day of class, you should briefly introduce yourself and talk about your professional background, including where you have taught, how long you have taught, your experience abroad, and your professional credentials. This is not showing off, rather, it is informing your class that you have deep experience and you know what you are doing. It should not take more than five minutes, but it is a very important step in presenting yourself as a professional. This is especially true if you are a nonnative speaker, a new teacher, or a graduate student (or all three).

2. **The Textbook Is Not the Whole Course.**

The course consists of all the learning activities, assignments, events, and tests that are planned and practiced both inside the classroom and out. The textbook may provide a sequence of lessons to follow, but it is often the case that texts require supplementation with other, more specific exercises and tasks that are devised by you to fill gaps or to reinforce particular points.

Moreover, a course period should not consist solely of working on textbook material. At some point in every class the instructor should tell the students to close their books and lead them into new and different language work that is not textbook-based. It can be dictation, working with pictures, rapid oral quiz, small group work, a learning game, sending them to the chalkboard, work with realia, working with specific sets of items such as numbers or colors, or a special task. The point is to create a different pace, a different perspective, alertness, and greater interaction among the learners as they use the language for specific purposes. This means that for every class, the instructor should prepare one or two learning activities that do not require textbook use. These activities should be based on what the students have already been exposed to, extend and stretch their language abilities, and reinforce their knowledge base.

3. **Speak Arabic as Much as Possible.**

Communicative language teaching involves and requires oral performance on the part of learners, and this is built from the beginning by the use of spoken Arabic as much as possible in the classroom. Some teachers believe in speaking Arabic 100 percent of the time even from the very first day. Others use oral Arabic much less. I believe in being pragmatic about Arabic language use; the key point being to get one's meaning across without using up too much class time and without mystifying the students. There are ways to communicate that use language plus gestures, pictures, drawing on the board, and even writing an English equivalent on the board if necessary. If a grammar point requires brief explanation in English, then use English, but limit it.

As a general rule, at least 75 percent of classroom language use, even from day one, can be in Arabic. This means that you must prepare students for the uses of classroom language by introducing them to predictable use items such as functional phrases, numbers, and normal classroom expressions so that most classroom communication can easily be done in Arabic and communicative skills are built up rapidly. Key factors in using the target language include calibrating classroom language to the level of the learners, stretching learners' understanding but not frustrating it (in keeping with Krashen's principle of **i + 1**), keeping language practical, and testing learners regularly to make sure they have grasped and understood the Arabic used in the classroom.

4. **Keep It Lively and Interesting.**

This principle goes along with principle number 2, "the textbook is not the whole course." One of the most important factors in foreign language acquisition is learner attention. In any class, attention can wander or fade, but in a foreign language class it is particularly important for learners to be alert and attend to what is being said and done, especially since performance is required on the part of everyone. Activities that involve vivid or memorable language experiences are easier to recall; shifting of pace re-alerts students to new information and to new uses of language.

This element of pacing requires that you have planned out almost every minute of the class ahead of time and that you have at least one or two activities that are not textbook-based that will serve to enrich the learning situation. It is always better to be over prepared than to run into a block of time where there is little to do. The teacher thus choreographs the entire class session, whether it is 50 minutes, 60 minutes, 75 minutes, or longer. In order to do such careful choreography, it is essential that you keep a resource file of activity types and add consistently to that file. Some teachers keep track of successful and unsuccessful exercises by recording immediately after class notes about what worked and what didn't, as well as any ideas that occurred to them during the activities. The notes can be placed in the textbook, in a file, or anywhere where they are easily accessible when needed. As your teaching experience increases and your resource file grows, you will be able to spend less time on activity development and more time thinking creatively about improving the learning experience in different ways.

5. **Provide Learners with Extensive Deliberate Practice.**

   Speaking, writing, reading, and listening are the four core modalities of foreign language function that need to be attended to in communicative classrooms. For each of these modalities, practice is a key path to competence, and the concept of "deliberate practice" is one that works well for language learning.[1] Sustained engagement with a disciplined activity facilitates learning and performance, something well known to musicians and dancers, for example. Because language acquisition requires performance, the better prepared and rehearsed learners are, the more easily and fluently they can use language with attention to meaning. In addition to general practice and review, it can be useful to focus on what educator David Perkins calls "the hard parts" (2009, 79).[2] Structures, usage, pronunciation, and vocabulary words that students are unsure of or find difficult are sometimes glossed over, but in order to provide a chance for improvement, these structures need to be singled out and practiced on their own. Then they must be reintegrated into the learners' interlanguage where they fit naturally and where they form part of a continuous whole.

   Practice in this context does not consist of mindless repetitive drilling, but refers to a range of carefully thought-out language exercises that involve language use in many different ways.[3] They may be exercises borrowed directly from another textbook or modified by the teacher, exercises designed by the teacher, or exercises that involve creative design by the students. I strongly advise Arabic teachers to consult textbooks other than the ones being used for a particular course in order to examine and evaluate a range of different activities that can elaborate and enrich the learning experience. For example, even if you are teaching MSA, textbooks on spoken Arabic vernaculars can provide models of speaking activities that can be adapted for use in the MSA classroom.[4]

6. **Front the Familiar; Use What Learners Know.**

   Many learners confront Arabic with a sense of bewilderment at the vast vocabulary and grammar that they will be expected to assimilate, as well as an unfamiliar culture, and this challenge can block or undermine their progress, especially at the start of language study. Even the most common classroom items have names and plurals that are hard to remember (*kitāb/kutub* book/books; *daftar/dafātir* notebook/notebooks).

   One successful and proven practice for launching language skills for new learners of Arabic is "fronting the familiar" (FTF), that is, using vocabulary and concepts that are already familiar to the students so that they have less of a "learning burden" at the start, can readily comprehend, and can more easily express themselves. FTF is a principle for accelerating familiarity with Arabic pronunciation, vocabulary, and structure, and for encouraging transparency in communication at the earliest points in the learning experience.[5]

   For example, one way to focus student attention on correct pronunciation as well as to build their vocabulary at early stages of study is to introduce the Arabic names of countries, land forms, and persons that they may already know or have heard about, such as the Red Sea, Qatar, the Nile, Syria, Lebanon, Bahrain, Tunisia. Most of these Arabic names have closely related equivalents in English, so the meaning of these terms is not burdensome.[6] Learning how to pronounce and spell them accurately in Arabic does two things: It gives the students a sense of achievement by knowing the "real" pronunciation, and it allows learners to practice language in context, in a lesson on geography, for example. The learners already know about these things, but they don't know how to talk, read, or write about them in Arabic yet. This kind of exercise does three things: (1) it reduces learner anxiety and affective barriers, (2) it allows time and energy to focus on target language forms because meaning is largely understood, and (3) it reinforces knowledge of a particular area or region of the Arab world.

A second FTF approach to building proficiency is to provide Arabic texts about American culture, American history, American music, or any topic with which the students are highly familiar. Texts about familiar topics written from an Arab point of view are useful cultural springboards for discussing comparative cultures and for cross-cultural understanding. In addition, texts in Arabic translated from English may offer a rewarding form of reinforcement for early learners (one of my advanced students read *Harry Potter and the Sorcerer's Stone* on his own, in Arabic, and vowed that it helped him greatly to expand his Arabic vocabulary). These texts may not be prime examples of canonical Arabic literature or style, but they are highly practical and engaging materials for teaching vocabulary and structure at early stages of Arabic language learning.

7. **Assign Written Homework Regularly.**

This is an area where many teachers' expectations are low. Written homework should be a daily component of instructed learning and it should be read, graded, and handed back with brief comments as soon as possible. If the homework is unreadable or if the handwriting is sloppy, require the student to resubmit the assignment. Shoddy or partial work is not acceptable. Make it clear in writing on the first day of class what the homework expectations are and how they affect the learners' grades or performance evaluations. Written homework provides a constant stream of individualized feedback to learners and gives the teacher insight into both individual and general learning problems and strengths. Corrected writing assignments provide focused feedback on errors and help learners become aware of what they may not know. Writing assignments can be as simple as copying out an exercise or a basic text or completing a written drill, or as complex as writing an essay. It is up to the teacher to determine what learners need and are ready for, as well as to take time restrictions into account. As a general rule, it is practical to intersperse easier homework assignments with more complex or difficult ones.

8. **Prepare a Range of Specific Learning Activities before Every Class.**

Nothing signals an amateur teacher like the need to search or scramble for things to do during a class. That is a waste of class time and undermines student confidence in the professionalism of the teacher. Instructors need to devote a specific period of time for preparation for every class, not just to rely on working through a textbook or engaging in ad hoc discussion, but developing what I call "elaboration activities" related to what is being studied. As a general rule, you should be overprepared and line up a sequence of activities that exceeds the time of the class period. This means that you should have prepared a set of explicit learning activities designed to fill class time, and more. Sometimes a well-prepared activity goes fast and smoothly and you may be faced with the need for additional activities. Other times, a learning activity fails miserably ("bombs"), and you will need quickly to shift to another type of practice.

For example, if I am working on a particular chapter in *Al-Kitāb* or *Elementary Modern Standard Arabic* (EMSA) with students, I will devote at least half an hour of prep time for every class, designing small-group activities, communication tasks, short quizzes, or games that can be used to practice vocabulary, enhance grasp of grammatical structures, and support the development of communicative competence. An important subprinciple here is changing the pace, that is, knowing when and how to shift the nature, cognitive demands, speed, and content of exercises in the classroom in order to keep the level of learner attention high. It is an art in itself.

The key caveat about this topic is never simply to resort to what is called "free conversation." This can deaden a class as students struggle to find random things to talk about with their limited knowledge of the L2. Besides, most students will realize this for what it is—a substitute for teaching—and it will undermine your professional credibility with them. Conversation practice at the beginning and intermediate stages needs to have clear pedagogical relevance; it should be meaningful, structured, and guided carefully by you. In other words, both you and the students need to be prepared for conversation activity in order to make it pedagogically useful.

9. **Keep a File of Teaching Resources.**

Your teaching resource file is your best friend. When you are tired or feeling unimaginative but need to have a set of activities for your next class, turning to tried and tested materials, realia, games, maps, tasks, or strategies will save you time and earn the attention and respect of your students. As you know, the course is not the textbook. Students may feel comfortable with the textbook, but they need to get away from it on a regular basis and engage in other forms of learning and communicative interaction. Calibrate your teaching resource files with the central textbook for your course so that the learning activities you plan mesh smoothly with the students' level of vocabulary and grammar, their "interlanguage." The idea is for these files to provide you with ways to improve upon a text (if it needs it) or to supplement the text with activities that will deepen learner understanding and build their confidence as well as keep their attention.

I have two file drawers filled with two sections of folders: The first section is organized by chapters of textbooks that I use and includes supplementary exercises on the content of those chapters. This may include flashcards purchased or drawn by me to work on vocabulary through card games such as Concentration; it may hold exercises in translation flexibility—going from and into Arabic using various structures in various ways for small-group work, or exercises on particular topics that I have copied from other textbooks or designed myself. The second section is organized by general topic: numbers, maps, artwork, economics, colors. This allows me to have materials for introducing subject matter outside the text but relevant to learners' interests and needs, or it may help supplement a lesson on a particular topic.

10. **Build in Time for Regular, Consistent Review.**

Review should be a regular part of every class. Five minutes spent on review in every class yields greater learning and confidence and allows for questions to arise from students about previously studied material. A weekly review of vocabulary in the form of a 10–15 minute written quiz will help learners study and retain what they have been working on. The importance of recycling, reviewing, and reinforcing previously studied material is central to the processes of building memory and long-term retention.

✷ Study Questions and Activities

1. In the list of principles of Arabic teaching, which do you think are the two most important? Why?
2. If you could add another principle to the list, what would it be?
3. In "front the familiar" exercises, what would be some areas of knowledge that would be shared by the students and that could yield useful learning activities?
4. Do you already have a file of teaching resources? If so, what are some of the most useful items in it? What would you like to have that you don't?
5. Reflect (in writing or in discussion) on the role of expectations and how it affects your own teaching.

6. What are some regular review routines you have found to be successful as classroom activities?

7. Perkins stresses the need to focus on "the hard parts" in a concentrated way. What is your experience with "hard parts," either as a learner or teacher? If you are a native speaker of Arabic, what were the hardest parts about learning English? If you learned Arabic as a second language, what were the hardest parts for you?

Further Reading

Bain, Ken. 2004. "What makes great teachers great?" *Chronicle of Higher Education*, April 9, 2004, B7–B9.

Bartlett, Thomas. 2003. "What makes a teacher great?" *Chronicle of Higher Education*, December 12, 2003, A8–A9.

Al-Batal, Mahmoud, ed. 1995. *The Teaching of Arabic as a Foreign Language*. Provo, UT: American Association of Teachers of Arabic.

DeKeyser, Robert M. 1998. "Beyond focus on form: cognitive perspectives on learning and practicing second language grammar." In *Focus on Form in Classroom Second Language Acquisition*, edited by Catherine Doughty and Jessica Williams, 42–63. Cambridge: Cambridge University Press.

Hammoud, Salah-Dine. 1996. "A survey of current classroom practices among teachers of Arabic." *Al-Arabiyya* 29: 95–128.

Stevick, Earl W. 1980. *A Way and Ways*. Boston: Newbury House.

Notes

1. "Deliberate practice is effortful practice with full concentration and includes a mechanism by which the results of the practice can be evaluated and improved upon in future sessions. Often a coach or master teacher oversees the deliberate practice, chooses individualized training tasks, and evaluates the results" (Single 2009).

2. See also chapter 9 in this book.

3. Perkins calls attention to the concept of "études," the French word for "studies," but which in music are "pieces of music deliberately written to strengthen particular technical elements, say scales and arpeggios, without simply playing them over and over" (Perkins 2009, 105). That is, the difficult parts are contextualized into a form that makes their rehearsal and practice more interesting, into actual music, and therefore more likely to retain attention.

4. The many well-designed textbooks for teaching English as a foreign language can also offer ideas about activities that can be adapted for use in the Arabic language classroom.

5. As Swaffar notes in her classic 1999 article, "The case for foreign languages as a discipline," a basic feature of foreign language curriculum design is that the use of "familiar topics, genres, and rhetorical usage will facilitate students' comprehension" (1999, 161).

6. There are of course, many exceptions to this cross-linguistic similarity: the name of Egypt, *miṣr*, for example, or the Syrian site of Palmyra, *tadmur*.

Theory and Practice

CHAPTER

2

Instructors need a bridge between research and practice, between teaching and learning.

Ambrose et al., *How Learning Works*

The art of teaching involves the deep interplay of theory and praxis. To the extent that practice is effective, it is connected with theory, whether explicitly or implicitly. To the extent that theory stimulates creativity and precision in practice, a familiarity with various theories is useful and even empowering. This is not to say that straightforward techniques used in the classroom are ineffective unless rooted directly in theory, but that theory may help to build out practice and to develop and refine techniques. A question that professional Arabic programs may want to ask is: Can there be one underlying theory or model for dealing with the pedagogy of the multiple varieties of Arabic? If so, then how can it be investigated and tested? Several key language acquisition theories are introduced in this book as touchstones for further discussion, for research in the Arabic classroom, as analytical tools, and as directions for further development of teaching skills. The theories presented in this chapter are by no means the only ones, but they will give novice teachers an idea of where SLA theory development has been and how it is developing.

⬡ Foreign Language Learning Theory

Foreign language pedagogy is usually seen as closely related to the field of second language acquisition (SLA). Researchers in SLA focus, however, not on teaching methods or on pedagogical options but on the learners themselves and their internal representation and development of target language skills as measured through their performance and, especially, through study of their **interlanguage**.

> Second language acquisition research is concerned with the process by which children and adults acquire (learn) second (third or fourth) languages in addition to their native language and learn to speak and read these languages in transactions of everyday life—whether they acquire these abilities in natural settings (by living in the country in which the language is spoken) or in instructional settings (classrooms or individual tutoring of various kinds, including virtual environments). (Kramsch 2000, 315)

Another prominent researcher notes, SLA is "the study of how learners create a new language system with only limited exposure to a second language" (Gass and Selinker 2001, 1). SLA research

A distinction made between "foreign" language learning and "second" language learning is that foreign language learning takes place in foreign language classrooms in the L1 (first language) environment (such as studying Arabic in the United States), whereas second language learning takes place in the L2 (second language) environment (such as studying Arabic in an Arab country), both in and outside the classroom. That said, "foreign" and "second" language learning are often used synonymously in both public and informal discourse about language learning.

is not divorced from pedagogical concerns, but those concerns are seen primarily through the prism of learners' progress.[1] Theories of second language learning, often based on studies of first language acquisition, have influenced many contemporary approaches to language teaching. However, the connection between theory and practice in language learning is not direct, and it can become a vexing issue.[2] It is often unclear how the findings of research can impact classroom instruction, and there is no familiar formula that converts research findings into classroom practice. In response to the gap between theory and practice, a subfield within SLA research emerged in the 1980s centered on the relation between theory and practice: Instructed SLA (ISLA). ISLA focuses on "the degree to which external manipulation (e.g., instruction, self-directed learning, input manipulation) can affect development" (VanPatten and Benati 2010, 6). Nevertheless, despite some progress on the part of researchers, even ISLA findings can be indeterminate, conflicting, or limited in scope.

Major differences between first and second language acquisition, such as cognitive development and complex psychological factors, have stimulated further examination of the nature of adult or adolescent learning as opposed to that of infants. The **fundamental difference hypothesis (FDH)** explicitly states that "first language acquisition and adult second language acquisition are fundamentally different in a number of ways" (VanPatten and Benati 2010, 89). The main difference is that the point of "ultimate attainment" in a foreign language for adult learners varies greatly, whereas ultimate attainment for infants in their L1 is normally full, native competence.

Classroom research in second language acquisition is an important component in defining and determining procedures that will aid in language acquisition at the adult stage. Unfortunately, aside from some specialized studies of learning Arabic in Israel, little research has been done on the acquisition of Arabic as a foreign or second language, and no central framework has been proposed or investigated for Arabic as distinct from other languages.[3] The opposing demands of traditional teaching and communicative objectives in the Arabic language classroom are intensified by the existence of diglossia and complicated by the lack of a theoretical framework for conceptualizing curricula and methods. This chapter reviews some of the basic theories that have evolved with respect to foreign language learning and teaching, and relates these to specific issues in Arabic language teaching.

Theories, Models, and Constructs

VanPatten and Williams, in their discussion of the nature of language acquisition theories, point out that the terms "model" and "theory" often get confused or are used interchangeably. Theories, according to the authors, answer the question "why," whereas models answer the question "how," and "do not need to explain why" (2007, 5). Theories "ought to account for and explain observed phenomena and also make predictions about what is possible and what is not" (4). Models, on the other hand, are more illustrative and concerned with the way components of theories interrelate. Key features of a theory are called "constructs" (6); that is, they are definable concepts upon which a theory relies, such as "phoneme" in phonology, or "germ" in biology. As VanPatten and Williams point out, SLA abounds in constructs that need agreed-upon definitions; the pedagogy of Arabic as a foreign language is no different. Definitions of key terms are essential in order to formulate theories, build reliable and informative models, and provide a clear and level field for the discussion of topics that, if undefined, may trigger resistance or misunderstanding rather than fruitful interaction. Topics such as Arabic dialect teaching, for example, need to be studied with objective clarity, despite occasional instinctively negative reactions to the idea.

Hypothesis

A hypothesis is a proposed possible idea. Stated within a particular paradigm, or theory, it provokes research to prove or disprove it. Krashen's **input hypothesis** (that learners will acquire a target language more fully and rapidly if they are exposed to intensive language input) is one example that has triggered a great deal of classroom research. The **critical period hypothesis** (that the ability to acquire a foreign language is closely related to—perhaps even determined by—the age at which language study is initiated) is another. Richard Schmidt's well-known **noticing hypothesis** (that learners need to notice or pay attention to language forms in order to internalize them) is an important consideration in SLA, as is the popular **interaction hypothesis** (sometimes characterized as a theory, as will be discussed), which posits that language learners acquire the L2 from interacting with others, primarily in conversations. Hypotheses are generally interesting and sometimes intuitively based proposals that are seeking empirical validation or refutation. It may be the case that a hypothesis is partially but not entirely true. As classroom teachers, an awareness of current hypotheses about foreign language learning informs our ability to think critically about the learning process and to observe patterns in learners as they progress in their knowledge of the L2.

For the field of Arabic language pedagogy, the implications of the critical period hypothesis and the fundamental difference hypothesis are crucial because of the nature of Arabic first language acquisition. This difference between first and second language acquisition has direct relevance to the ways that Arabic is taught to foreign learners in three respects:

1. The first language or Arabic mother tongue of native speakers is colloquial Arabic;
2. Arab children start studying literary Arabic only after developing a strong, fluent colloquial base;
3. Arabic speakers continue to use colloquial Arabic for daily communication throughout their education experience and thereafter.

In other words, native Arabic speakers are surrounded by colloquial language throughout their lives and bring a very different skill set and cognitive background to formal learning of literary Arabic than do foreign learners. Moreover, native Arabic speakers' literacy skills are developed in tandem with increased proficiency and skill in their mother tongues, the Arabic colloquials. This is a key factor in evaluating the type and sequence of instruction for learners of Arabic as a foreign language because it indicates that the starting points for literacy studies for native speakers and for nonnative speakers differ greatly. Many of the traditional constructs for TAFL rely strictly on teaching literary language (as would be the case for native speakers) while omitting what the nonnative speaker crucially requires: authentic communicative competence in spoken Arabic.

❁ Some Key Theories in Language Learning

Theory development is central to any discipline, and it is constantly evolving. Foreign language teaching is an interdisciplinary effort that borrows theories and components of theories from behavioral and educational psychology, from cognition and neuroscience, as well as from linguistics.

Therefore, the theories that are cited here are all related to language learning, but have emerged out of different disciplinary traditions. It may be helpful to see the strands of influence plucked out of their home discipline and highlighted in order to see where ideas in language learning and teaching originated. The theories mentioned here include behaviorism (Skinner), universal grammar (UG) (Chomsky), monitor theory/input hypothesis (Krashen), skill development theory

> "Each branch of linguistics starts from more or less the same pretheoretical notion of what language (or a language) is and, according to its own viewpoint and the alliances that it forges with other disciplines (psychology, sociology, anthropology, literary criticism, etc.), practices its own kind of abstraction and idealization in the construction of its own model of the underlying language-system" (Lyons 1990, 17).

(DeKeyser), processability theory (Pienemann), interaction theory, focus on form, and the noticing hypothesis.[4]

Behaviorism

The school of thought known as behaviorism emerged as the dominant psychological theory in the United States in the 1930s and 1940s. This theory regards objective and accessible facts of behavior or activity of humans and animals as the only subject for psychological study and explains that behavior "solely with reference to external factors in the environment" (VanPatten and Williams 2007b, 18). It focuses on the impact of environment on any organism, particularly stimulus and response (S-R) actions. From such observations, behaviorism reaches the conclusion that all behavior is learned behavior, even language.

In the behavioralist approach there are two essential ways of modifying behavior: conditioning reflexes and reinforcement. Conditioning reflexes are well known through Pavlov's famous experiments conditioning the behavior of dogs to salivate first upon getting food, then while getting food and hearing a bell ring, and then salivating merely at the ringing of the bell. This is called a "conditioned reflex" or "classical conditioning."[5] Reinforcement, meanwhile, refers to the shaping of behavior through reinforcement, such as feeding an animal every time it performs the right action. This is referred to as "operant conditioning" or "behavioral conditioning." B. F. Skinner was the leading US proponent of the theory (see, for example, his *Science and Human Behavior*). A third component of behaviorism is frequency; that is, "each time the response is made to the stimulus, the association between them is strengthened. . . . Continuous repetition therefore, is an important factor in developing new behaviors" (VanPatten and Willliams 2007b, 18). Generalized to humans, conditioning and reinforcement are seen as ways to develop new behaviors or habits through imitation, repetition, and reinforcement to the point where actions are "overlearned" and become automatic, requiring no prior thought process. This theory was the basis of the Army Intensive Method (AIM) for foreign language training during World War II, which then planted the seeds of the audiolingual method of teaching (see chapter 4 in this book).

Postbehavioralism: Generative Theory and Universal Grammar

Generative linguistic theory, especially as a reaction to extreme behavioralist speculations on the nature of human language acquisition and use, is associated with Noam Chomsky and is outlined in a series of his books beginning with *Syntactic Structures* (1957) and *Aspects of the Theory of Syntax* (1965).[6] In these books (and subsequent ones), Chomsky departs radically from behaviorism by devising formalized and precise accounts of how human language works as a system to generate all the grammatical and none of the ungrammatical sentences in a language. "More generally," Chomsky states in *Syntactic Structures*, "linguists must be concerned with the problem of determining the fundamental underlying properties of successful grammars" (2002, 11), that is, the cognitive processes that characterize the human language function. Rather than focusing on a particular language, Chomsky focuses on language in general and its universal properties.

Chomsky's concerns are with language as cognitive process rather than language as external behavior. In distinguishing between the two he uses the terms "competence" and "performance." Competence is the internal, conscious or unconscious model of language in a speaker/hearer's head: "the knowledge of the language that provides the basis for actual use of language" (Chomsky 1965, 9). A generative grammar is a theory of the speaker's competence. Performance, on the other hand, is the actual use of language—how one uses rules and models in the performance of real-world language tasks. Performance is measurable and is often used as a yardstick to measure competence, but much of human language competence is tacit, unconscious knowledge that is hidden from view and even from introspection.

Chomsky proposed that there is an innately given schema in the mind for interpreting the world of human experience and the fundamental categories of human experience. The human mind applies this schema to sense-data in order to construct cognitive systems, so these systems are to a significant extent not learned but, instead, activated. Their basic properties constitute preconditions for learning. An abstract system of inherent, incipient structures and rules is latent in the human brain, determining an infinite range of sound-meaning correspondences referred to as "grammar." Furthermore, grammaticalness (Chomsky's term) is determined not by meaning but by abstract, underlying syntactic structures. Chomsky uses the now-famous example of the sentence: "Colorless green ideas sleep furiously" (which is grammatical but nonsensical) to show that grammaticalness lies not in word meaning but in syntax. He states: "I think that we are forced to conclude that grammar is autonomous and independent of meaning" (1957, 17). The term "universal grammar" (UG) is used to refer to Chomsky's basic idea that humans (and only humans) share an innate capacity to acquire language, no matter where one is born or what one's native language environment is. "In a highly idealized picture of language acquisition, UG is taken to be a characterization of the child's pre-linguistic initial state" (Chomsky 1981, 7). As a counterpart to the existence of language learning readiness in humans, Chomsky also proposes that "all languages share similar abstract qualities" (Loewen and Reinders 2011, 171). Thus, the fit between maturing humans and their language environment is precise and complementary; the potential for developing grammar is triggered by the distinguishing features of a particular language (called "parameters") and incorporated into the child's cognitive systems.

One of the concepts in Chomsky's UG theory derives from the fact that normal children learn a first language fluently by the age of five, despite the limited nature of the input or what has been termed the "poverty of the stimulus" (the limited amount of language children hear or that is directed toward them). Thus, in their language development children are thought to be (unconsciously) constantly generating and trying out rules, rejecting the ones that do not work, and settling finally on the ones that do. Because all humans acquire language intuitively, in regular steps, making systematic rather than random errors (such as generalizing the past tense {-ed} morpheme using, for example, "digged" for "dug"), Chomsky early on proposed that human brains have what he then termed a "language acquisition device" (LAD) that is activated at birth. This device is highly active during what is called "the critical period"—a period of child maturation that extends into adolescence, but not after puberty.[7] Once the critical period is over, it is much more difficult to acquire language.[8]

The foregoing applies to the acquisition of one's first language, one's native language. It was only subsequently that some aspects of UG were applied to second language acquisition. Cook provides a concise summary of possible implications of UG for foreign language teaching, as follows:

1. Teaching as the provision of input. This is a key role of the teacher in foreign language learning.
2. The importance of vocabulary. UG theory maximizes the importance of vocabulary acquisition over the learning of syntax. "Teaching may be seen as most effectively building up this mental lexicon in the student" (1994, 46).
3. The role of "core grammar." UG operates primarily within a highly abstract domain called "core grammar." Outside this domain each language has its own "parameters" of use and application. Cook states that "teachers must look elsewhere for ideas for teaching these" (1994, 46). That is, language specifics are not part of what UG has to offer.
4. Language as mental knowledge. As Cook states, "Teaching in the 1980s was primarily concerned with language as social behavior. Whatever the goals of language teaching, it still has to aim to create the mental knowledge that underpins this behavior" (1994, 46).

Perhaps one of the clearer connections among UG, generative grammar, and second language learning is within the concept of interlanguage, which describes learners' mental representations of language at various stages of second language learning. The learners' version of the target language or L2 is not native-like but changes over time as the learner develops both conscious and unconscious mental representations of the L2 that inform his or her ability to use it in performance.

Interlanguage—referring to both the cognitive and communicative competence of the learner—is neither L1 nor L2, but somewhere in between. It is sometimes also referred to as the learners' "developing system, approximate system, learner language" (VanPatten and Benati 2010, 100). Corder refers to it as "transitional competence" (Corder 1981, 69). The important thing to understand about interlanguage is that it may contain errors and be piecemeal or inadequate, but it shows evidence of systematic cognitive processing and growth.[9]

Monitor Theory and the Input Hypothesis

Whereas Chomsky developed his ideas in the realm of theoretical linguistics, Steven Krashen approached theory development from the perspective of applied linguistics and language teaching. Described as "one of the most ambitious and influential theories in the field of SLA" (VanPatten and Williams 2007b, 25), monitor theory (later known as the "input hypothesis") is composed of a number of constructs that have had wide impact on SLA.[10] "Its broader success rests in part on its resonance with the experience of language learners and teachers. An understanding of this theory is crucial to understanding the field of SLA theory and research as a whole" (ibid.). Krashen lists five sub-hypotheses that constitute the whole input hypothesis:

1. The acquisition-learning distinction
2. The natural order hypothesis
3. The monitor hypothesis
4. The input hypothesis
5. The affective filter hypothesis. (Krashen 1985, 1–2)

Learning and acquisition   Krashen made several crucial and intuitively appealing observations. First of all that there are (at least) two different cognitive processes for acquiring a foreign language: learning (formal) and acquisition (informal). They have the following characteristics:

Learning	Acquisition
formal	informal
conscious	unconscious
logical; analytical	intuitive; instinctive
rule-oriented	tacit competence
classroom	nonclassroom

Making a key distinction, Krashen states that learning is what provides structural accuracy, whereas acquisition provides both fluency and the ability to initiate utterances. Learning is more adult-based, whereas acquisition is more instinctive and draws on our ability to access childlike states of openness and absorption. Learning, Krashen declares, is used primarily as a **"monitor"** of learner L2 efforts—a conscious correctness check and rapid consultation of rules that apply when one is using the L2. Use of the monitor requires the following conditions, however: time, focus on form (how something is said, not what is said), and conscious knowledge of the rules of grammar. Krashen points out that these conditions appear mainly when taking discrete point grammar tests in the classroom, and not in situations where one must use the L2 interactively under the pressure of time and context. In the latter case, acquisition skills kick in, providing learners with the ability to generate reasonably appropriate language.

All adults have access to strategies of acquisition as well as learning, and most of us have a preference for one learning style or strategy over another. Acquisition is a subconscious means of internalizing linguistic generalizations that in many respects resembles the way a child intuitively gains control over language. Learning, in the specific way in which Krashen uses it, is a conscious process of "knowing about" language and having a conscious awareness of linguistic generalizations. Krashen's theoretical model of adult second language ability predicts that acquisition and learning are interrelated in a definite way, and that acquisition is far more central than learning in second language performance. Specifically, says Krashen, speakers initiate utterances using acquired competence for normal second language performance, and their fluency in using a foreign language comes from what they have acquired, not from what they have learned.

The monitor Learning plays a role, albeit a minor one. It is used as a filter, or monitor, a conscious mental checklist of rules that need to be observed in using a second language. That is, when one is engaged in expressing oneself in a foreign language, there are certain "automatic" responses and utterances one makes without thinking at all, and to a certain extent one can express oneself spontaneously without paying attention to form. But when the going gets tougher, when learners have to express themselves in new ways or deal with less familiar or more complex grammatical structures, they have fewer acquired skills and tend to rely on their knowledge of rules to express themselves accurately. When speaking, learners usually slow down, speak carefully, quickly search their memories for expressions, and mentally review rules of structure as they speak.

The natural order hypothesis Inspired by the findings of natural order of acquisition in first-language studies of children, this hypothesis states "that we acquire the rules of language in a predictable order, some rules tending to come early and others late. The order does not appear to be determined solely by formal simplicity and there is evidence that it is independent of the order in which rules are taught in classes" (Krashen 1985, 1). This is an intuitively appealing concept, and is verifiable in terms of experience with language learners who may never "acquire" certain rules in their interlanguage, despite having studied them extensively. Little work has been done on this topic when it comes to the acquisition of Arabic as a foreign language, however. Nielsen's and Al-Hawary's work on order of acquisition (discussed later in this chapter) and processability theory has provided an opening for the study of natural order of acquisition in Arabic, but much more remains to be done.

The input hypothesis and comprehensible input As Krashen states, "the input hypothesis claims that humans acquire language in only one way—by understanding messages, or by receiving 'comprehensible input'" (1985, 2). In order to make input to learners "comprehensible," teachers and others need to be aware of the interlanguage stage the learners have reached, and to provide "**input + 1**" or **i + 1**, that is, input that is understandable but that stretches the comprehension skills of learners because it is just slightly beyond their full range of comprehension. Krashen sees comprehensible input as necessary to the natural order of acquisition, in that it provides a way for learners to progress in understanding and to form their own interlanguage rules as they gradually grasp both meaning and structure. Krashen calls comprehensible input "the essential environmental ingredient" for language acquisition (1985, 2).[11] Input can be in either spoken or written form. In fact, Krashen encourages extensive reading for language learners as a way to increase their acquired proficiency.

The affective filter Combining multiple aspects of language learner psychology including defensiveness and resistance, Krashen proposes the term **"affective filter"** to represent the bundle of features that characterize language learners who block out, or filter, much of what they hear and see, thus preventing both acquisition and learning. It has been described as "a metaphorical barrier that prevents learners from acquiring language even when appropriate input is available" (Lightbown and Spada 2006, 37). The filter may exist in all learners, but sometimes it is high, preventing intake of all kinds, and sometimes (ideally) it is low, allowing for intake, processing, and progress in language acquisition and learning. Krashen summarizes his overview of second language acquisition as follows: "People acquire second languages only if they obtain comprehensible input and if their affective filters are low enough to allow the input 'in'" (1985, 4).

Taken as a whole, one can see that Krashen's input hypothesis and its components have been key elements influencing the original direction of SLA research and theory and that this pedagogically based group of hypotheses has found resonance with many language professionals. Ellis notes that "it affords a set of very general illuminative ideas that are applicable to a wide range of instructional settings" (2010, 187).

The Relative Contribution Model

The relative contribution model was formulated by Theodore V. Higgs and Ray Clifford in articles published in the early 1980s. In a 1985 article, Higgs reviews various methodologies and observes that "most 'methods' fail because they are self-limiting, adhering strongly to one set of principles and not allowing for other principles or procedures" (8). Although Higgs does not treat pedagogical procedures as such, he proposes that at different levels of study or proficiency, different approaches or foci are needed. He notes that specific subskills are listed as components of proficiency ratings and that "every new level in the ACTFL or ILR level definitions represents a new constellation or interrelationship of the factors of content, function, and accuracy. In addition, the relative contribution of specific language subskills—pronunciation, vocabulary, grammar, fluency, and sociolinguistic appropriateness—changes from level to level . . . when the relative contributions of the subskills are graphed, they peak at different levels" (Higgs 1985, 5–6).

At the Novice level (ILR 0), for example, vocabulary and pronunciation play the greatest roles in proficiency as charted on the graph. Therefore, Higgs suggests, "at the most elementary level the lexicon must be the focus of instruction . . . [and] what is needed is a lexical syllabus. Nothing else could reasonably be asked to pick up the students where they are and move them onward" (1985, 5). For the intermediate level (ILR 1), in referring to the graph that shows "hypothesized relative contribution" (6), vocabulary and pronunciation are still near their peaks in importance but in addition, the "grammar curve, though still well below its peak, is ascending sharply" (7). The advanced plus/superior level borderline (ILR 2+/3), "finds the grammar curve at its peak. This means that all the basic grammatical structures of the target language must be under control," and that "a grammatical syllabus is not only defensible, it is indispensible" (ibid.).

In other words, Higgs advocates shifting pedagogical focus and strategies at different levels of instruction rather than adopting one particular methodology or "syllabus" for all levels. He is careful to point out that this does not imply a radical limitation of approaches, but that "the association of a particular approach with a particular level of instruction simply identifies the major pedagogical focus for that time. A lexical syllabus does not mean that vocabulary is taught to the exclusion of other skill areas. A functional/notional syllabus depends on pronunciation, vocabulary, morphology, and syntax. A grammatical syllabus presents communicative functions in believable, relevant contexts" (Higgs 1985, 8). The relative contribution model therefore advocates calibration and recalibration of instructional focus according to the proficiency level being taught.

Processability Theory

Processability theory (PT) was introduced by Manfred Pienemann as a way to account for sequences in second language acquisition. As he states, "at any stage of development, the learner can produce and comprehend only those second language (L2) linguistic forms that the current state of the language processor can handle" (2007, 137). The "language processor" is a component of human cognition and has a certain "architecture" that is responsible for different "developmental trajectories" in language learners. The constituents or models of Pienemann's theory are "based on Lexical-Functional Grammar (LFG)" (2007, 139), and assert that the teachability of language is constrained by what the learner is ready to acquire. That is, if a learner does not have a certain conceptual readiness to take in L2 information, it will not stick.

In his 1989 article Pienemann supplied empirical evidence (experiments and longitudinal studies) to bolster the hypothesis that most language learning is actually acquisition, that overt teaching of specific language phenomena is only effective when learners have reached a specific psychological stage at which they are able assimilate the incoming information, and that formal instruction is only effective if calibrated to learner readiness. The details of the theory are fascinating, and I refer interested readers to his 2003 and 2007 articles as well as to his book, *Language Processing and Second Language Development: Processability Theory* (1998).

There have been two key contributors to the study of PT as it applies to Arabic word order and morphosyntactic features: Alhawary (2009a, b, and c) and Nielsen (1994–2009). The authors particularly focus on Pienemann's assertion that "given the hierarchical nature of the processability hierarchy none of the processing procedure constraints in the hierarchy can be skipped because every lower procedure constitutes a prerequisite for the next higher one. Therefore frequency cannot override the constraints of the hierarchy" (Pienemann 2007, 152).[12] Alhawary and Nielsen have shown through careful experimentation that the concept of cognitive "readiness" depends largely on L1 or previous L2 knowledge preparing the way for similar concepts in Arabic, that is, that language transfer plays a key role. Moreover, the idea that frequency plays no role in acquisition of Arabic was not validated.

Skill Acquisition Theory

The concepts of deliberate practice and skill acquisition as components of L2 learning have received considerable attention in the past few years. Whereas the idea of deliberate and extensive drilling of language structures had largely fallen out of favor when communicative language teaching emerged, the problems of skill practice, acquisition, and proceduralization remain issues that teachers and learners need to deal with in order to accelerate and assure fluent and accurate L2 use. One basic claim for skill acquisition theory is that "the learning of a wide variety of skills shows a remarkable similarity in development from initial representation of knowledge through initial changes in behavior to eventual fluent, spontaneous, largely effortless, and highly skilled behavior, and that this set of phenomena can be accounted for by a set of basic principles common to the acquisition of all skills" (DeKeyser 2007b, 97).

DeKeyser notes that technical terms regarding skill development vary. "Generally speaking," he writes, "researchers have posited three stages of development, whether they call them cognitive, associative, and autonomous . . . ; or declarative, procedural, and automatic . . . ; or presentation, practice, and production" (2007b, 98). Each of these stages shifts the learner toward greater ease and effectiveness of performance, and each set of three identifies the second stage as central, wherein practice acts as the bridge to the third stage, autonomous functioning with automatic control of L2 skills needed for production.

These stages of learning are key constructs in instructed language learning. DeKeyser describes a "central concept" in this developmental sequence as "the power law of learning" (2007b, 99, and 2007a, 3), which specifies that "regardless of the domain of learning, both reaction time and error rate decline over time according to a very specific function that is mathematically defined as a power function" (2007a, 3). It is this law that teachers and learners see in action as they progress through multiple exercises that allow students to practice what they have been taught and to rehearse these skills in meaningful contexts. For further discussion of skill acquisition and the notion of practice, see chapter 13.

Input Processing

"Input," as Gass and Mackey have put it, "is the *sine qua non* of acquisition" (2007, 177). L2 input, especially comprehensible input, "is a critical variable as it is a major data source for the language learner" (VanPatten and Benati 2010, 36). Input processing refers to the idea that language acquisition is essentially a product of comprehension of the L2 and of "how learners come to make form-meaning connections or parse sentences" (VanPatten 2007, 127). If learners do not understand what they hear, it will make no impact on them; input must be comprehensible (see this chapter's earlier discussion of Krashen's work) in order to constitute "intake" upon which learners can base their own judgments about how form and meaning connect in the L2. As VanPatten and

Benati observe, "the idea behind input processing is this: Acquisition is input dependent. Learners get data during the act of comprehension. Comprehension involves extracting meaning from the input" (2010, 97).

VanPatten has devised a set of principles for input processing that are based on the fact that learners tend to take certain strategies for processing input in particular ways. These principles are discussed more extensively in chapter 12 of this book.

The Interaction Hypothesis

This hypothesis is somewhat related to input processing and is based on the observation that "conversational interaction is an essential, if not sufficient, condition for second language acquisition" (Lightbown and Spada 2006, 43). Learners come to understand and use the L2 primarily through interactions with others, including teachers and fellow students. "Interaction, simply put, refers to the conversations that learners participate in" (Gass and Mackey 2007, 178). Interaction is seen as central to acquisition because learners using the L2 in this way will become more accurately aware of their communicative strengths and weaknesses when talking with others and getting the immediate feedback that conversation allows. "The emphasis is on the role which negotiated interaction between native and non-native speakers and between two NNSs plays in the development of a second language" (Gass 2003, 234). Note that it is called a hypothesis, not a theory, but that it includes elements of hypothesis testing, elements of a model, and elements of a theory, which is defined as "a set of statements about natural phenomena that explains why these phenomena occur the way they do" (Gass and Mackey 2007, 176). Core beliefs about the interaction hypothesis center around the idea of the "communicative pressure" of a situation and the need for learners to use their interlanguage—whatever stage of L2 they have acquired—in order to get meaning across. Learners with even rudimentary skills can try to negotiate meaning with each other and with teachers, but the demands of the learning situation have to be calibrated with the interlanguage capabilities of the learners. This situation requires both "forced output"—talking before one is sure of how to say something—and, often, adjustments or modifications by the teacher in order to make the input understood.

For teaching Arabic as a foreign language, the interaction hypothesis complicates the acquisition of MSA, because MSA is not a variant of Arabic normally used for conversation, and conversation lies at the core of the interaction hypothesis. The kinds of conversation normally engaged in for basic interactional purposes would be in vernacular Arabic, not literary Arabic. Vernacular Arabic has linguistic systems (including lexicon and morphology) in their own right that may or may not match up with MSA. Research on the effectiveness of interactions has been done primarily for languages whose written and spoken variants are essentially the same and can reinforce each other (mainly English); no published research yet exists on this topic as it applies to Arabic teaching. Some programs use MSA for all purposes, even conversation, and increase learner abilities in MSA, but it is clear that if an Arabic program chooses to implement the interaction hypothesis as part of its approach, then decisions need to be consciously made and agreed upon as to the nature of language use for spoken interaction. A rich field of potential research exists in testing the effectiveness of the interactional approach in different types of Arabic instruction.

Focus on Form (FonF)

The concept or practice of **"focus on form"** (FonF) that originated with Michael Long in the early 1990s was at least partially motivated by the interaction hypothesis as mediated through the accomplishment of "pedagogical tasks" (Long and Robinson 1998, 22–23). FonF is a procedure that involves attention to target language structures as they occur spontaneously during interactive, meaning-oriented classroom activities. As noted by Long and Robinson, "focus on form often consists of an occasional shift of attention to linguistic code features—by the teacher and/or one or more students—triggered by perceived problems with comprehension or production" (23).

It is thought that when target language structures occur in a meaningful context, they will be more memorable for language learners, and that teachers can take the opportunity to focus on form as particular forms arise. It is a way of engaging learners in communicative activities and at the same time calling their attention to particular aspects of usage and grammar. FonF is a broad-based procedure that has attracted a large number of practitioners and researchers because of its utility in communicative language teaching. It does require, however, that instructors be highly tuned to accuracy within learner performance, even as learners are using the target language in meaningful activities. If errors are allowed to persist, then learners may develop resistance to correction. Thus, the FonF scenario is one where the instructor needs to monitor target language performance, bring learners' attention to incorrect forms, and devise follow-up exercises in order to practice those forms. In an ideal situation, both instructor and students participate in identifying areas where accurate performance requires correction, explanation, further practice, and attention.

Attention and the Noticing Hypothesis

One of the key areas of research undertaken to understand second language acquisition is in the area of attention and awareness studies. This has arisen through questioning of the role of unconscious acquisition (in Krashen's terms) as compared to conscious learning of the L2, and the relationship between the two in instructed language learning. Schmidt's **noticing hypothesis** claims that awareness at the point of learning is essential in order for students to learn, and that "**input** does not become **intake** for language learning unless it is noticed, that is, consciously registered" (Richards and Schmidt 2010, 401; emphasis in original). Schmidt also notes that "one important role of instruction is helping learners to pay attention to, notice, and understand L2 phenomena that they are unlikely to notice by themselves" (1994, 1). This may involve students' "noticing the gap" between authentic L2 and their own interlanguage, and comparing "their own output to that of others" (Schmidt 1994, 19). In their article on attention and cognitive science, Tomlin and Villa provide a "fine-grained analysis" of three factors involved in attention: (1) alertness: general readiness to deal with incoming data; (2) orientation: the focusing or alignment of awareness; and (3) detecting: the discernment of specific bits of information and "cognitive registration of sensory stimuli" (1994, 190–193).

These studies and others point to the importance of instructors' highlighting key features in the L2 so that they do not escape the attention of learners. The term coined for this process is **input enhancement**. This enhancement may take many forms, from highlighting certain terms or structures in reading assignments (e.g., using a different font, a different color, underlining), to using intonation and stress for spoken language features. The essential point is to make key features salient for learners so that they notice them and focus their attention on them. For example, an Arabic teacher may want to focus on the *iḍāfa* structure by underlining all of the *iḍāfas* in a particular segment of text. Subsequently, she may ask the students to underline all the *iḍāfas* in another text.

Many more theories and hypotheses exist that relate to second language acquisition. The ones chosen for discussion here have shown relevance to or potential for application to teaching Arabic as a foreign language. In the discussion section that follows, you are asked to apply what you know about Arabic teaching and learning to some of the ideas presented in this chapter. Some may seem logically suitable for Arabic, others may not, but the discussion raises key questions about SLA theory and Arabic second language acquisition, and pedagogy of Arabic.

⬡ Study Questions and Activities

1. Discuss the intersection of research and practice as it relates to Arabic language teaching. Do you think that theoretical proposals are important to what is done on a daily basis in the classroom? Why or why not?
2. Discuss the fundamental difference hypothesis and its implications for TAFL.

3. What part of monitor theory/input hypothesis do you find most interesting or most validated in your experience either as a learner or as a teacher?
4. There are, as noted, complicating factors in applying the "interaction hypothesis" in the Arabic language classroom. What do you think is the most effective way or ways to approach this complexity?

⬡ Further Reading

Chomsky, Noam. 1957, 2002. *Syntactic Structures*. 2nd ed. Berlin: Mouton de Gruyter. (Chomsky's first major book; well-written and a good start for those interested in the history of his ideas.)
____. 1959. A review of B. F. Skinner's *Verbal Behavior*. *Language* 35, no.1:26–58. (A definitive overall statement of the issues between behaviorism and cognitive theory.)
Krashen, Stephen D. 1981. *Second Language Acquisition and Second Language Learning*. Oxford: Pergamon.
____. 1985. *The Input Hypothesis: Issues and Implications*. London: Longman.
VanPatten, Bill, and Jessica Williams, eds. 2007. *Theories in Second Language Acquisition*. New York: Routledge/Taylor & Francis.

⬡ Notes

1. "The field of SLA grew out of concerns of pedagogy so much so that in the past and to some extent, today, the fields are erroneously seen as one" (Gass 2006, 21).
2. Despite the abundance of SLA research and the development of linguistic theory, one must be aware, as Larsen-Freeman notes, that "research/theory can inform, but not substitute for, a theory of second language teaching" (1990, 262).
3. See Brosh 1993 and Brosh and Olshtain 1995 for TAFL in Israel, for example. Also note Garrett's comment on SLA research that "to the extent that SLA theorists and researchers have explored the acquisition of other languages, the focus has been to a great extent on Spanish and French. . . . SLA theory has to a much smaller extent considered the acquisition of languages that are very different from English, especially those that are highly inflected" (2009, 720).
4. For a useful overview of SLA theories see VanPatten and Williams 2007a.
5. As another example, anyone who has a cat knows that the cat will appear as soon as he hears the cat food can opening or the crinkling sound of a bag of treats, having associated those sounds with food.
6. For a detailed exposition of Chomsky's particular critique of Skinnerian behavioralism as applied to language, see his review of B. F. Skinner's *Verbal Behavior* (1959).
7. "Some researchers suggest that 'critical period' is too narrow, implying a cut-off point. They argue instead that a 'sensitive period' may be a better description, allowing for a wider range of ages. Finally, some researchers reject a critical period at all" (Loewen and Reinders 2011, 46).
8. For more on UG the critical period and the critical period hypothesis, see VanPatten and Benati 2010, 78–79, and as applied to foreign language teaching, Cook 1994.
9. For more on UG and interlanguage, see White 2007.
10. Monitor theory was sometimes called the "monitor model," and later the "input hypothesis" (see Krashen 1985).
11. See chapter 9 in this book on "caretaker speech."
12. See Ryding (2013) for a more detailed analysis of Al-Hawary's and Nielsen's research.

Professionalism and Professional Standards

CHAPTER
3

Good teaching cannot be reduced to technique; good teaching comes from the identity and integrity of the teacher.

Parker J. Palmer, *The Courage to Teach*

Professionalism in Arabic teaching requires not only teacher language awareness (TLA) and a sophisticated knowledge of pedagogical procedures, but also an understanding of oneself and of professional standards, as well as contact with other professionals. That is, it requires knowing how and what to teach, and also figuring out ways to communicate, grow, and improve. Cultivating one's own professionalism wisely through one's actions may involve, for example, joining professional organizations; attending seminars, workshops, and conferences; getting an advanced degree; reading professional journals; subscribing to an online discussion group such as Arabic-L; starting a discussion group with colleagues; or thinking about and planning professional goals.

Reflective Teaching Practice

"Effective Arabic teachers systematically reflect on their practice retrospectively and introspectively and learn from experience" (Alosh, Elkhafaifi, and Hammoud 2006, 416). In order to develop professionally, it is wise to be both flexible and analytical about direct classroom experience. The act of reflection upon what you do, think, or feel is crucial to objective evaluation of your performance. Within the teaching profession, reflective action refers to practitioners thinking objectively and critically about their choices and what they do, as well as a readiness to engage in regular self-appraisal and evaluation. Sometimes this involves only quiet self-reflection; sometimes you may engage others in a discussion of mutual self-appraisal. This reflective act in and of itself helps to construct your own professional viewpoint and your own theory of best practices in pedagogy, because it involves monitoring your actions, planning, acting, data collection, and renewed evaluation and experiment. Reflective teaching involves a kind of calibration between experience and observation, between theory and practice.

Reflective teaching has been influenced by a distinction in types of knowledge: the distinction between received knowledge (built on data, theory, and accepted facts) and experiential knowledge (built up through everyday practice in making decisions, judgments, and adjustments). Teachers use a mix of received knowledge and experiential knowledge to build their own practice of teaching and to develop professionally. As a teacher who is also a scholar of teaching, I believe it is necessary to examine your experiential knowledge. Document it, write about it, keep a journal with observations, analyze it. As long as one's knowledge remains experiential only, it may not connect with the experience of others or with any particular cognitive theory. But if you seek patterns in your experience, then those patterns may connect with others and lead to a better understanding of how we teach and how we learn.

Keeping a Teaching Portfolio

A key resource in documenting your professional skills and growth is a teaching dossier or **portfolio** that shows evidence of your experience, achievements, academic credentials, and creativity. A teaching portfolio is "a coherent set of materials including work samples and reflective commentary on them compiled by a faculty member to represent his or her teaching practice as related to student learning and development" (Hutchings 1994, 3). Increasing numbers of teachers are doing this online as well as on paper. For example, you may want to keep a file for each course that documents your ideas about how to change the course to improve it. It could contain your observations about teaching a particular course in a particular semester with recommendations for changes in the future, such as spending more or less time on a particular topic, or with ideas that occurred to you after the course was over. This can be an effective way to keep track of strengths and weaknesses in any class and to deal with them over time. Note whether you have been involved in curriculum development, materials development, proficiency testing, or teaching and research.

You may also want to keep a record of some of the outstanding achievements or projects of your students—or projects that required your intervention as an advisor, and how you managed that intervention. If you contribute to a conference by making a presentation, chairing a panel, or participating in a discussion group, document it in your portfolio. You may also want to document any in-service training or new credentials that you earn. Keeping such a portfolio not only helps you develop a dynamic perspective on your own career, it also serves as key evidence for promotion or other well-earned bonuses. As Hutchings comments, "aim to develop an argument, a case, a coherent picture—not just a collection of stuff—with entries as evidence" (1994, 10).

It is important to note that expectations for teachers vary depending on their professional position. Teachers at secondary schools need to maintain their professional credentials in education; teachers at government institutes need to maintain their effectiveness and sophistication in methodology, testing, and materials development; teachers at a community college will want to document advanced training or other credentials; teachers who are also publishing scholars at a university are required to be active in terms not only of publishing in refereed journals, but also in terms of service to their department, their university, and their profession at large. Wherever you teach Arabic, it is important to be clear about what is expected from you not just on a day-to-day basis, but in terms of being a valuable member of your academic community.

 ## Communities of Practice

Just as learners may improve their understanding and use of the L2 through scaffolding and interaction within the zone of proximal development (see chapter 9), teachers also need interaction and the stimulation of working with and observing others in action. Teaching can be a deeply solitary activity; your concerns and practices cannot always be effectively shared with those who are not co-practitioners. But often, in both informal and formal faculty groups, discussion will lead to learning and progress in your own practice. That is why it is important not only to concentrate on your own performance, experiences, and successes, but also to situate yourself within a community of practice where spontaneous discussions of craft can arise. "In a community of practice, participants share a common mission. . . . Social contact among them creates opportunities for the exchange of craft. Participants naturally talk about what's most on their mind, what they need to

> Involvement in a community of pedagogical discourse is more than a voluntary option for individuals who seek support and opportunities for growth. It is a professional obligation that educational institutions should expect of those who teach (Palmer 1998, 144).

know today or tomorrow, or what they found out yesterday or the day before that seemed especially helpful" (Perkins 2009, 181). In addition to the context of situated learning that can be organized among peers, there is also the practice of what Perkins calls "legitimate peripheral participation," which is a type of apprenticeship period where preprofessionals "make no attempt to tackle the hard problems, but watch and help out with the simpler aspects of the enterprise" (Perkins 2009, 182). This, of course, is the pattern followed by graduate assistants who are mentored by a professor, assume some of the more routine aspects of teaching, and observe the professor in action as ways of developing their own skills and eventually becoming professionals themselves. This legitimate peripheral participation is all the more effective if it is associated with an organized study group (of co-practitioners, both senior and junior) where apprentices or novice teachers can bring questions, observations, reactions, and ideas about their craft.

Professional Organizations and Publications

The nature of language teaching means not only that one benefits from contact with professionals in one's own specialized field (e.g., Arabic, German, or French), but also that one can benefit greatly from being a member of a larger group such as ACTFL, the MLA, AATA, or NCOLCTL, where many different perspectives on pedagogy, research, and teaching are represented in their publications, on their websites, and at their conferences. One of the most important elements in professional development is learning by analogy—seeing how someone else has solved a problem, experimented with a new idea, or made an important breakthrough, and comparing that strategy to what you can do in your own situation. This is particularly applicable to Arabic language teaching because the range of research and applications of theory are much more extensive in western languages than in Arabic, and the heralded insights from some of these successful experiments may or may not apply to the Arabic pedagogy situation. Sometimes, excellent food for thought is provided by such work, and other times, one can immediately see that a certain application would be of limited use for Arabic. It is up to the reader to judge, but if you do not read and attend conferences, you will be unaware of the extent of research in instructed SLA that is available and how it might relate to and possibly improve your position and practice.

Professional Standards

Standards of professionalism in language teaching involve ethical conduct, objectivity, qualifications, responsibility, and good judgment. A strong knowledge of Arabic is a *sine qua non*, but is not the only component of high standards. Knowledge of educational psychology, pedagogy, assessment models, and applications are also key components of professionalism. In their 2006 article on professional standards for teachers of Arabic, Alosh, Elkhafaifi, and Hammoud take a careful look at the elements of professionalism in the field. They organize their observations into "professional knowledge," "conceptual framework," "a reflective approach to teaching," "action research," and "achieving professionalism." Under the first category, "professional knowledge," are the following subcategories: proficiency, psychological/cognitive theory, culture, pedagogy and curriculum design, assessment, and professional development. Altogether, the authors list 61 points under these subcategories, all worth examination, discussion, and evaluation. Under the rubric of "conceptual framework," they list 18 points of professional competence that are again worth serious study and discussion. Under "achieving professionalism," the authors provide six final points:

- Teachers should seek certification.
- Teachers should collaborate with their colleagues.
- Teachers should create networks with other teachers to share views, materials, and techniques.

- Teachers should seek small grants to develop materials and tests.
- Teachers should seek opportunities to present to peers strategies they use, materials they have developed, and research they are involved in at professional meetings.
- Teachers should participate in mentoring programs if and when available or sponsored by electronic listservs or organizations, such as AATA. (Alosh, Elkhafaifi, and Hammoud 2006, 416)

This particular article can serve as a centerpiece for departmental discussion of pedagogy and professional development, and should certainly have a wide readership within the field of Arabic teaching.

Applying for Grants

Among the most underused professional development opportunities are the seeking out of granting agencies and the crafting of grant proposals. Proposals do not always have to be extensive, but they usually do require a final product or demonstrable end result. Sometimes there are grant opportunities for specific things, such as acquiring technology, or for travel to attend conferences. Many universities open requests for proposals for summer research grants or for professional development grants. If you have a chance to participate in a larger grant proposal operation (such as a Title VI proposal), volunteer to do it. Even if you do not make major contributions to the final grant proposal, over the course of the discussions and the drafting activities you will learn a great deal about the process and what it involves in terms of time, planning, coordination, and energy. Universities and colleges normally have offices that coordinate grants and grant proposals, and they often provide information for grant seekers. If you teach in a high school, states usually have education grant opportunities. Go online to websites of organizations such as CARLA, MLA, NCOLCTL, and ACTFL to see if they offer grants or stipends to offset your expenditures to attend workshops or annual meetings. Be alert to requests for proposals (RFPs) that appear online such as in the Arabic-L discussion list. In particular, check the website of the Department of Education (www.ed.gov/fund/grants-apply.html) and foundations such as the National Endowment for the Humanities (NEH), the Mellon Foundation, or the Pew Charitable Trust. Do not be overly concerned if your first grant proposal fails; you can always apply again, and grant writing is an acquired skill.

Study Questions and Activities

1. Make a list of your own professional qualifications for teaching Arabic. Turn this into a formal statement by making it a part of a letter of application for an academic or training position in which you present yourself and your qualifications. You can make up the position or choose one that is being advertised. When you have your materials together, submit them to your professor for feedback, and/or share with others in the class to compare statements.
2. Is there anything in particular that you think would enhance your professional skills (such as attending a conference, going to a workshop, or time off for a research project)? What is it, and how can you go about making it happen?
3. Do you have a teaching portfolio? If not, start accumulating documentation of your professional achievements and organizing them into a narrative of your professional development.
4. Have you ever applied for a grant? Investigate sources of funding for development or projects that you would like to undertake. Report your findings to the class and share information.
5. As a class, read the Alosh, Elklhafaifi, and Hammoud article (2006) and comment on it. In your opinion, what are some of the most important points or elements of the article? Are there items there that you were not aware of before? Write a two-page reaction paper on this article, describing its strengths and weaknesses and discussing how it might be improved or updated.

⬡ Further Reading

Alosh, Mahdi, Hussein M. Elkhafaifi, and Salah-Dine Hammoud. 2006. "Professional Standards for Teachers of Arabic." In *Handbook for Arabic Language Teaching Professionals in the 21st Century*, edited by Kassem Wahba, Zeinab Taha, and Liz England, 409–417. Mahwah, NJ: Lawrence Erlbaum Associates.

Antonek, Janice L., Dawn E. McCormick, and Richard Donato. 1997. "The Student Teacher Portfolio as Autobiography: Developing a Professional Identity." *Modern Language Journal* 81, no.1:15–27.

Edgerton, Russell, Patricia Hutchings, and Kathleen Quinlan, eds. 1991. *The Teaching Portfolio: Capturing the Scholarship in Teaching*. Washington, DC: American Association for Higher Education (AAHE).

Modern Language Association (MLA). 2001. Final Report: MLA Ad Hoc Committee on Teaching. *Profession 2001*, 225–238.

Rivkin, Benjamin, ed. 2001. *Mentoring Foreign Language Teaching Assistants, Lecturers and Adjunct Faculty*. Boston: Heinle & Heinle.

Part II

Approaches to Foreign Language Teaching

Traditional Approaches and Methodologies for Language Teaching

CHAPTER 4

The interesting thing to me is that if you take ten excellent teachers they will all teach differently.

Kathryn Watson

In most language teaching methodology courses, methods used through the 1970s and 1980s are described as "traditional." They are not often given in-depth attention in the literature because they are not based on contemporary second language acquisition theory and are considered to be old-fashioned, or pretheoretical. These methods, or components of them, however, continue to be used by many teachers and institutions, and they can still be valid, effective approaches to language learning if one takes into account the specific goals at which they aim. Moreover, elements from any of these traditional teaching methods may be blended into communicative teaching settings and adapted for use in all modalities: speaking, writing, listening, and reading. Such a recombination of practices allows for saving what works and for valuing the successes of past practice. Part of our responsibility as language professionals is to recognize and define points of success in traditional methodologies and to find ways to incorporate successful procedures into contemporary communicative approaches.

Approach, Method, and Technique

Writers on the topic of methods in language teaching often make a distinction among the terms "approach," "methodology," and "technique." To clarify, I would like to summarize these distinctions as defined by experts. **Approach** is an umbrella term that includes a basic philosophy, a "set of assumptions about the nature of learning and teaching" (Stevick 1982, 203), and a "set of theoretical principles" (Hadley 2001, 91). It is the broadest level of theoretical statements. **Method,** on the other hand, is a more explicit term for classroom organization, what Hadley calls "a procedural plan for presenting and teaching the language" (ibid.), or, as Stevick states, "a set of techniques which fit well together and which are consistent with some approach or other" (1982, 203). Finally, **techniques** of teaching involve "strategies for implementing the methodological plan," (Hadley 2001, 93), or "simply something that we do" in the classroom, according to Stevick (1982, 203).[1]

A distinction should also be drawn between methodology and pedagogy. As one author states, "the essential difference between methodology and pedagogy is that methodology is more narrowly focused . . . whereas pedagogy has broader educational goals, is influenced by a wider range of theories and curricular influences and tensions, and is more rooted in and responsive to the practical realities of a particular classroom" (Adamson 2006, 605). The approaches/methods most often considered to be traditional include grammar-translation, the direct method, the army intensive method, and the audiolingual method.

The Grammar-Translation Approach

This classic approach to foreign language pedagogy has most often been used for teaching dead languages or those used only in writing. The grammar-translation approach was used in Europe for teaching Latin and Greek throughout the Middle Ages and even into the 20th century. It has also been widely used for teaching other literary languages such as biblical Hebrew, Sanskrit, and classical Arabic. Its effectiveness as a learning experience can be very powerful, especially with regard to the development of analytical thinking, pattern recognition, and synthesis. Grammar-translation is based on "an emphasis on writing, on grammar, on accuracy, and on the ultimate aim of enabling its students to read the literary classics of the language they were learning" (Cook 2010, 9). Major objectives of this approach include:

- The ability to read in the target language (with the help of a dictionary, if needed);
- The ability to translate both ways, both from and into the target language (with reliance on reference grammars and lexicons, if needed);
- Appreciation of the target language culture, especially its literary and cultural heritage;
- Understanding of grammatical theory, including its technical terms and morphological and syntactic rules and structures;
- Through the development of rigorously disciplined language analysis, the ability to think critically and analytically (through close, detailed focus on grammatical theory and the explanation of grammatical relations).

When applied to living languages such as French, for example, the grammar-translation approach, with its stress on written language, accuracy, ability to translate, and appreciation of literary works, does not prepare learners for immediate use of spoken language in day-to-day conversation. It is focused on developing literacy rather than on well-rounded proficiency. And whereas this can be a logical goal for students of dead languages or for older written variants of languages (such as Old French), it falls substantially short in equipping learners for real-world language-in-use.

Features of the grammar-translation approach   As can be seen from the objectives of this teaching method, grammar-translation focuses on rational thinking, syntactic puzzle solving, and developing an appreciation for literary texts. It is highly cognitive and analytic, aiming at theoretical knowledge of language structure but not at direct or immediate grasp of spoken language. In terms of values, literary language is considered superior to the spoken or vernacular language.

Some of the teaching techniques used in the grammar-translation approach include:

- Memorization of lists and paradigms: vocabulary words, rules, conjugations, declensions;
- Close reading and analysis of canonical texts
- Translation of sentences or literary texts and answering questions on texts (in writing in the target language or through discussion in L1)
- Explanation of grammar points in L1
- Practice with dictionary structure and use
- Deductive method of explanation: Teacher introduces grammar rules, gives examples, and illustrates how the rules apply
- Using words in context: Students construct sentences to show that they know how to use new words and rules.

Other techniques may, of course, be employed in this approach—for example, reading out loud to develop correct pronunciation—but the central idea is that grammar and vocabulary are the core of language, and manipulating these two components in various ways strengthens students' understanding of language both in theory and in written use.

Arabic grammar-translation texts   In general, grammar-translation-type textbooks consist of overtly grammar-based lessons with short sentences or texts in the target language, translation exercises both to and from the target language, and substantive grammatical explanations. An excellent example of this approach applied in an Arabic textbook is *An Introduction to Modern Arabic* by Farhat Ziadeh and R. Bayly Winder, first published in 1957 by Princeton University Press.

An Introduction to Modern Arabic has many strengths, among them complete, extensive, and explicit grammar explanations in English, a detailed and comprehensive set of Arabic derivational and inflectional paradigms in appendix I, and a special glossary of "Arabic verbs and their prepositions" in appendix II. Another classic Arabic grammar-translation textbook is David Cowan's *Modern Literary Arabic* (1964). It is a tightly packed, informative, clearly written introduction to written Arabic in the grammar-translation tradition.

Drawbacks of grammar-translation Because of its strict focus on declarative knowledge, translation, and grammatical accuracy, learners taught through the grammar-translation method develop strengths in written skills, but are unprepared for real-life spoken functions in living languages such as French or German. Moreover, the emphasis on strict accuracy can make learners afraid to make mistakes, and trying to learn to speak a living foreign language without making mistakes is almost impossible. If learners want to try to speak and understand everyday language, they are often tongue-tied and miserable, with no experience in interactive discourse skills to guide them or prepare them for functional, everyday language use, even if the literary language and the standard spoken language are not linguistically distant from each other. Moreover, many students learn to fear the intricacies of grammatical structure because of the numerous complexities lying in wait for the unwary student, as well as the penalties imposed for making wrong choices, such as lower grades or embarrassment in the classroom.

The ability to communicate in a modern language as actually used for conversation in the foreign culture is not an aim of the grammar-translation method. However, many scholars believe that this method prepares foreign language students for rapid adjustment to real-world target language use by giving them a strong background in the most difficult and culturally valued form of the language, and that students will be readily able to pick up the spoken language when or if they have a chance to visit the country. This opinion may be valid, but it is based on the fallacy that spoken language is simpler than written. Linguistic analysis of spoken discourse shows that it is as complex as the written language, but in different respects, including interactive pragmatics. Years can be spent picking up or acquiring spoken language piecemeal and informally, and formal instruction in the vernacular can substantially accelerate spoken proficiency.

The Direct Method (Berlitz)

In the late 19th century a reaction to the highly formal study of grammar developed. Judging the academic focus on written language to be too far removed from practical concerns, a reform approach began to take shape focused on building speech repertoires for everyday foreign language situations.[2] The movement began in Europe with publications including Gouin's *The Art of Teaching and Studying Languages* (1880), Jespersen's *How to Teach a Foreign Language* (1904), and Sweet's *The Practical Study of Languages* (1899). At around the same time, in the 1880s, Berlitz schools were established in the United States, focusing on many of the same goals as the Direct Method and aiming to prepare learners in a fast and functional way to handle practical situations in foreign languages. As Cook states, "the relation between the [European] Reform Movement and the Berlitz methods is not a straightforward one" (2010, 7), but they had much in common, and have, to some extent, become identified with one another.

Goals and theoretical bases of the direct method The goals of the direct method are functional and pragmatic, focusing particularly on speaking and listening. Especially important is the idea of developing direct mental connections between meaning and use without the need to pause and mentally translate from the L1 to the L2, and vice-versa. A list of goals might include:

- Speaking and comprehending readily in the target language
- Interactive use of everyday language
- Learning to think in the target language and make immediate connections between language and situations
- Developing a direct bond between language and experience

Underlying the goal of building language resources for direct experience in the target language is the idea that explicit or declarative knowledge of grammar is not necessary for language acquisition, and that humans possess an innate ability to acquire language through systematic situational exposure and exercises. Moreover, such direct experience enables learners to accelerate their acquisition of proficiency by avoiding the L1 completely and omitting conscious practice of translation and language analysis.

Characteristics and techniques Characteristics of the direct method include the following:

- Modeled after first language acquisition
- No use of L1; a monolingual classroom
- No translation work
- "Situational reinforcement" of target language structures and vocabulary through experiencing meaningful situations
- Vocabulary emphasized over grammar
- Speaking and listening emphasized
- Intensive exposure to L2
- Literacy skills (reading and writing) are used to reinforce interactive skills (speaking and listening).

Specific classroom practices are based on the core concept of direct contact with meaningful situations in the target language, without translation. Some of these include:

- Enacting situations, role-playing
- Questions and answers
- Associating meaning and target language directly by means of doing and saying at the same time, for example, "Now she is opening the door," "My hand is in my pocket."
- Use of pictures, props, various forms of realia, items to talk about
- Grammar explanations only when absolutely necessary
- Dictation
- Reading aloud.

In many respects the direct method continues to exercise influence on foreign language teaching, even in educational situations where proficiency in academic language is the ultimate goal, rather than solely pragmatic conversational ability. One can readily perceive vestiges of the direct method in communicative language teaching, for example, which is the most prevalent contemporary approach to language instruction.

The Army Intensive Method (AIM)

The acute and pressing need for foreign language skills during World War II accelerated development of pragmatic approaches to foreign language acquisition that combined the presence of a native speaker of the target language with a trained linguist who could explain and describe language use and structures to learners. Influenced by behaviorist theory in psychology as well as the direct method and more traditional teaching approaches, the Army Intensive Method was developed on the basis of cognitive grasp of structural features reinforced repeatedly and strongly through habit formation, memorization, mimicry, and overlearning.[3] The goal was communicative competence, primarily in conversational type discourse.

Characteristics and Techniques The characteristics of the AIM method include:

- Grammar explained in L1
- Use of linguist and native speaker/informant together
- Practical conversations

- Mimicry-memorization
- Very intensive
- Reading and writing secondary to listening and speaking.

The techniques for using AIM include:

- Memorize and rehearse typical conversations
- A great deal of repetition
- Drills to develop automatic control of phonology and grammatical structures
- Practice in the target language with a native speaker
- Grammar study with a linguist

Drawbacks of the Army Intensive Method Although this method found success during wartime, its application outside military or government institutions was hindered by the need for two instructors, one a native speaker with whom students practiced in the target language exclusively, and the other a professional linguist qualified to explain language structure in all its detail. Moreover, the Army Intensive Method's goals were focused on immediate performance in an assigned military or diplomatic role. Its objectives did not include familiarity with literature, with formal written language, or with language and culture. After WWII this approach evolved into the audiolingual method as a way of applying the successes of this training method to academic situations.

Audiolingualism

The audiolingual approach made substantial progress after WWII as Army-trained linguists returned to the workforce, prepared materials, and trained new recruits. The appeal of audiolingualism was its practicality, and the challenge was to develop materials and methods that would suit academic environments. Compared to traditional grammar-translation methodology, the audiolingual method promised livelier classrooms and more competence in interactive language situations. As with the Army method, audiolingualism was based on behaviorist theory, on conditioning reflexes through reinforcement. Language was seen primarily as a set of habits that gradually become second nature to speakers. In order to operate effectively in a language, the set of habits must be built up piece by piece and over-learned in order to become automatic so that the learner can operate without needing to pay attention to form and with full attention on meaning. This outcome was called "full linguistic performance."

In addition, the role of linguistics came at this time to be extremely important in structuring the learning processes and ordering material. A knowledge of structural linguistics allowed the teacher and materials developer to systematize language presentation, to predict problem areas, and to develop exercises to overcome the most challenging elements. Because foreign language learning was seen essentially as forming new habits, comparison between the two languages—L1 and L2—could show where the differences were and allow learners to focus on mastering these differences. The study of these interlanguage differences is called contrastive analysis. Contrastive analysis helped the teacher to identify areas where the L2 diverged from the L1 and to explain patterns, rules, units, and features of language.

The goal of audiolingualism: Full linguistic performance (FLP) Audiolingualism tackles all four modalities: speaking, listening, reading, and writing. Speaking is considered the hardest challenge, so the emphasis is on developing speaking skills because the reasoning goes that if one can speak the L2 accurately, the other skills will follow more easily. In terms of fluency the goal is to be able to speak about 100–250 words per minute, essentially equivalent to a native speaker. In reading and listening the goal is to be able to grasp meaning without the need for translation. In other words, the goal of audiolingual methodology is to engage in language use at normal speed with attention on the message, not form. Language skills or modalities are categorized as either active or receptive, as follows:

Active Skills	Receptive Skills	Time Element
Speaking	Listening	More Time Pressure
Writing	Reading	Less Time Pressure
(Output)	(Input)	

That is, when speaking or listening in the L2, time pressure is a key element in performance. When reading or writing, time pressure is greatly reduced.

Some audiolingual principles

- Partials: In order to reach full linguistic performance, partial goals are to be identified and used to build a solid base of language habits. This applies to pronunciation, vocabulary, grammar, and fluency in conversation. Proponents of the method believe that breaking things down into smaller parts will yield more immediate control of L2 components. The aim is to build up slowly using materials that have a gradation of difficulty level. This focus on partials provides a gradual, systematic way to develop complex skills.
- Contrastive analysis: Contrastive analysis is a system for comparing languages, evaluating where and how they differ, and to what degree. Where substantial contrasts are seen, these can be used as a basis to predict problem areas, for learners of the L2. This approach is sometimes referred to as "teaching the problems." For example, in contrasting Arabic and English sound systems, one can readily see that they are not identical. In particular, the pharyngeal consonants of Arabic (/ʕayn/ and /ħaʔ/) are not present at all in the English phoneme inventory. That would lead to the conclusion that learners may have more difficulty acquiring those sounds than others that are present in English, such as /kāf/ or /bāʔ/. In terms of grammatical structures, there are two features of Arabic that contrast significantly with English: (1) the category of dual nouns, adjectives, pronouns, and verbs and (2) the category of humanness in nouns. Learning to think of the dual as a category separate from plural takes English-speaking learners some time; learning that the quality of humanness in nouns affects their agreement patterns in the plural also takes considerable time (*tullāb judud* 'new students' as contrasted with *kutub jadīda* 'new books'). It is one thing to describe these categories and their rules of agreement to learners; it is quite another for them to acquire these distinctions as part of their procedural skills in Arabic.
- Role for linguistics: The audiolingual method ideally requires a solid knowledge of structural linguistics in both the L1 and the L2. This permits instructors to systematize language presentation, predict problems through contrastive analysis (in phonology, morphology, syntax, and semantics) and practice the problem areas. A knowledge of linguistics also helps instructors sequence L2 materials for systematic progression from basic to complete language structures and, finally, a knowledge of linguistics helps instructors identify and explain patterns, rules, units, and features of the target language.
- Primes and transforms: Primes and transforms are categories of cognition. "Primes" are items that come to mind immediately, bypassing any thinking process, such as: $2 + 2 = 4$; $3 \times 3 = 9$; $5 \times 5 = 25$. "Transforms" are items or puzzles that need conscious thought in order to be processed, for example, $29 - 13 = 16$. In language learning, the audiolingual method encourages learners to form "primes" in the L2 and to develop as much L2 as possible to the level of automatic, unconscious skill.

Basic audiolingual features   These features include dialogue memorization, use of audiotapes, explanation of grammar, a focus on all four skills, and rapid oral drill, including pattern practice.

- Dialogue memorization: The memorization of dialogues and routine conversation sequences is thought to provide learners with chunks of language that they can manipulate easily in context. These chunks allow learners to have solid footholds in the language that can reliably form a foundation for developing autonomous speaking skills. Although dialogue manipulation may seem artificial at first, it ultimately helps learners perform naturally. Moreover, within each dialogue are key grammatical structures and vocabulary whose contextualization makes them easier to recall.

  At a very basic level, conversational routines can be practiced and internalized to provide learners with common courtesy expressions and a foundation for interactive skills. As learners advance, more complex interactions can be worked on and variations of situations introduced. These dialogues are rehearsed in many ways, learned by heart, and then elaborated upon under the guidance of the instructor. Memorization and dialogues become less central at the more advanced levels, where reading and the study of more abstract grammar concepts shift to prominence. Some key memorization techniques of the audiolingual approach are as follows:
- Backward buildup: This kind of exercise focuses on memorizing sentences aloud by starting at the end and building up control of the sentence in reverse order. The technique can be illustrated by writing one word on the board and having students repeat it, then prefixing another word, and so on, repeating each time until a whole sentence is built from the end backward. By the time the first word of the sentence is introduced, the students have already repeated the rest of the sentence many times and it will start to be easy to say and remember. For example, if there is a sentence such as: *maktab al-mudarris hunāk* ('The teacher's office is there'), the teacher would start out with the word *hunāk*, have the students repeat it several times, then add *al-mudarris* to it: *al-mudarris hunāk*, again having the students repeat several times. Finally, the teacher would add the word *maktab* to the sentence: *maktab al-mudarris hunāk*. The reason that backward buildup works for memorization is that it takes the memory load off the end of the sentence, as that part becomes the most familiar and most easily accessible. This helps learners gain confidence with their ability to form complete statements.
- The vanishing technique: In this form of memorization practice, the teacher has a copy of the dialogue on the board. Gradually, one by one, she erases words from the dialogue and has the students (either chorally or one by one) say full sentences aloud (including the erased bits), building up their ability to remember words from context. The words are usually erased in random fashion, a word here and a word there—not beginning at the end and working forward or vice versa. At the end of the exercise, she might ask if two people are ready to volunteer to do the dialogue on their own. If not, then she knows that more work is needed.
- Repetition: There are several ways to undertake repetition in the classroom. Obviously, it is done to help memorization, but it also aids in fluency and accurate pronunciation. Repetition is sometimes seen as a rather mindless exercise, but it can also be a way of relaxing the class as a break from a more strenuous activity or as an introduction to more cognitively demanding work. In audiolingual methodology choral repetition is used a great deal for the following reasons: Everyone gets to participate and, therefore, practice, and no one is called to be "on the spot" if they are not ready. Normally the teacher will model a sound, a word, a set of words, or a phrase (depending on what is being practiced) two or three times and students repeat two or three times. This is often done when introducing new vocabulary or a new dialogue.

A warning about repetition: do not overdo it. It is useful at certain points in the classroom, but it is not communicative in any sense. It is a way of building partial communication skills, but is certainly not an end in itself and is tedious and a waste of time if overdone.

- Listening to recorded dialogue: One of the breakthroughs of audiolingual technology was the use of audiotapes. In the 1950s and 1960s audio was recorded on large spools of reel-to-to reel tape that could only be accessed in a language laboratory, where students would sit in a booth and listen using earphones. It was clunky and cumbersome technology, but it at least introduced a way for learners of foreign languages to obtain input outside the classroom—a key factor in increasing time-on-task.
- Reading, writing, repeating: In addition to listening in the language lab, learners were encouraged to read out loud to themselves, and to write and repeat vocabulary, phrases, and sentences from the text being studied. Tying reading and writing to pronunciation was yet another way to reinforce the connection between sound and script, and it also helped to tie auditory memory to written language.
- Say it out loud: All of the above activities reinforce the ideas of speaking the L2 out loud and of repeated articulatory practice. Students in the grammar-translation tradition hardly ever spoke the target language, so this procedure was in direct contrast with traditional academic approaches to language learning.[4]

When working with oral practice for dialogue memorization in the classroom, it is advisable to have students say lines chorally at first, and then ask for volunteers who would like to try lines out on their own. This is a less threatening approach that still allows for class participation. At some point, the assigned dialogue has to be recited or acted out. You may assign half the class to act one role and half another, the men and women may be assigned different roles, or everyone may be assigned to memorize the entire dialogue. These kinds of decisions are usually determined by the length and content of the dialogue. Once the students are very familiar with the text, you should stretch their ability to use the dialogue as a basis for unrehearsed performance by varying the situation.

You can say lines quickly in random order and ask students for the next line. You may then vary your lines slightly and students can still use most of theirs. Finally, you may change the lines to a much greater extent such that students have to listen carefully in order to respond. For this sort of dialogue variation it is crucial that you stay within the conversational framework so that the students get input that is comprehensible but that stretches their ability to understand and form appropriate responses. You cannot engage in random variation; it must be highly controlled and keyed to student interlanguage levels.

For follow-up you can suggest a target language situation and ask students to determine what sort of "key lines" they would need in that situation—what they would have to be able to say. They may come up with these lines in English or in Arabic, and you can give the correct Arabic form of the key line. The students are assigned to learn these lines and then try them out while you act the part of native speaker of Arabic. This way students have something invested in the conversation—it isn't all imposed from outside.

Reading and writing The literacy skills of reading and writing are sometimes seen initially as backups to oral practice and as reinforcement for oral skills. For languages with non-Roman scripts, however, the need to use reading and writing is important from the beginning; reading skills need to be quickly developed in order to deal with text, and writing is necessary for taking notes and doing homework. Therefore, in Arabic classes, reading and writing, and learning the alphabet, script, and orthography conventions, are major components of classroom activity as well as goals of instruction.

Explanation of grammar Because it derived from the Army Intensive Method where linguistic structure was explained in the L1 by a professional linguist, grammar explanation in the L1 was accepted in the audiolingual approach. Students can often grasp points more easily and more quickly if they are explained in the L1. Illustrations and examples form an important part of the presentation of grammar, with the rule given first and then examples (deductive procedure) or with examples given first, and students then working out the rules from the examples (inductive procedure).

Drills and exercises Once grammatical points are taught in an audiolingual approach, drills and exercises constitute the logical next step, the middle ground between cognitive understanding of a rule and ability to apply the rule in actual speech situations. This process of proceduralization is recognized as an important bridge between declarative knowledge and automatic use of that knowledge. Drills and exercises are structured to bring short-term memory into long-term memory and to internalize language structures so that they are automatically accessible to learners.[5] The expected outcomes are short term and long term: short-term goals include being able to handle foreign language sentences under immediate memory with variations but without full cognitive control of grammar rules; long-term outcomes are to acquire full functional skill and automatic control of foreign language structures in phonology, morphology, and syntax. One way of classifying drills is by the kind of learner attention they involve, another is by the degree of control of the response by the teacher.

- Drills with conscious choice: These drills require learners to focus their awareness and consciously apply rules in order to solidify cognitive control of grammar points. Some examples of this would be:
  1. Repetition
  2. Simple substitution: This involves making one change at a time such as:

We went to the library.	ذهبنا الى المكتبة.
	dhahab-nā ilā l-maktaba.
We went to the museums.	ذهبنا الى المتاحف.
	dhahab-nā ilā l-mataāḥif.
We went to the manager's office.	ذهبنا الى مكتب المدير.
	dhahab-nā ilā maktab-i l-mudīr.
We went to Cairo.	ذهبنا الى القاهرة.
	dhahab-nā ilā l-qāhira.

  3. Transformation drills: these are more complex, requiring single or multiple changes or operations, such as changing singular to dual or to plural (e.g., changing a singular noun and its adjective to dual or to plural; changing a demonstrative phrase from singular to dual to plural, etc.):

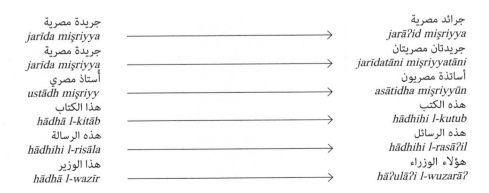

Ideally, transformation drills should be contexted, that is, put within a framework of a sentence or a narrative, for example:

We read an Egyptian newspaper every day.	We read Egyptian newspapers every day.
qara'-nā jarida miṣriyya kull yawm	*qara'-nā jarā'id miṣriyya kull yawm*
قرأنا جريدة مصرية كل يوم	قرأنا جرائد مصرية كل يوم

- Other transformative drills might be: embedding one clause into another (e.g., relative clauses, complement clauses); changing a verb from active to passive voice and making any other necessary changes in a sentence; and changing a statement from positive to negative and making any necessary changes.
- Drills with attention away from grammar point (to solidify automatic mastery of language patterns): In these types of drills, the learners engage in an activity that requires them to use their L2 knowledge, but in a subtler way. Fill-in-the-blank drills, multiple choice drills, questions and answers, and multiple transformation are some of the ways this is done. These activities may seem straightforward, but the idea is that they require the student to make changes other than just the one specified in the instructions. These changes may appear incidental to the learner, but are actually the point of the exercise.
- Drills with different levels of meaning and communication: Drills can be classified by degree of response control that the teacher has:
  - Mechanical: In a mechanical drill, there is only one correct response, and the teacher knows what it is, such as a drill in conjugating a verb, declining a noun, repetition, substitution, or transformation. Mechanical drills can be overused and can become tediously ineffective unless they are done in a snappy, enthusiastic, and animated manner, and in brief spurts of time. On the other hand, they can also be refreshing and restful if done as review, or as a break from a more cognitively demanding activity.
  - Meaningful: In a meaningful drill, the learner needs to understand the L2 in order to provide the right answer. For example, situational questions such as "What color is your shirt?" "How many books do I have?" and other classroom descriptive questions can provide a great deal of language practice. Students can describe each other's clothes, backpacks, or books. They can describe a famous person or family (such as the president and the first family). The key here is that the information is known to everyone; it is obvious. The practice involved is focused on learning how to communicate that information in the L2 and on building a basis for fast, flexible responses. There is also some need for cognitive manipulation of language but the learning burden is lighter here than it is in the next type of drill.
  - Communicative: In a communicative drill (or exercise), learners must understand fully and be creative with language, communicating something that they know or believe to others who do not know, that is, new information about the real world. The teacher does not control the content of the response but can give feedback on lexical and grammatical accuracy. Basic questions or topics such as "What color is your car?" or "What will you do tomorrow?" can lead to informative discussions between teacher and students and among students themselves. Role-playing may fall into this category; so may the description of a situation or event ("What was the film like?" Who was in it?") or the soliciting of an opinion ("Who do you think will win the election?" "Will the European Union survive?").

It is important to remember that drills are for practicing, not for testing. That is, they provide the kind of open practice that learners need to get without feeling that they are constantly being judged. Feedback during such exercises needs to be done in an impartial, nonjudgmental way. Corrective feedback is important in these situations.

The outcome of all these types of drills and exercises is for learners to be able to handle discourse situations under immediate memory with variation, even though they may not have full cognitive control of grammatical structure. If students are allowed to speak only in tightly controlled responses, they will not develop full linguistic performance. Once rules are introduced and practiced, the internalization and learning process should be embedded in a meaningful context where learners can practice and gain confidence in their ability to function in the L2.

⬡ Conclusion: Legacies

One legacy of traditional language teaching methods is clearly that of explored terrain. The methods described in this chapter have been implemented over years and even over centuries (grammar-translation) with varying results—sometimes successfully and sometimes not. They have aimed at developing different skills in different ways, and provided a partial map of language learning territory. In almost all cases it is the ingenuity and skill of the teachers that determine the success of a particular method when applied in the classroom. A second legacy of traditional language teaching is in the importance of clear, organized objectives and the development of a range of exercises that can be implemented in the classroom. That is, they provided teachers with explicit procedures for pedagogical purposes. Although some researchers have judged such explicitness as restrictive, it does not necessarily need to be so.

⬡ Study Questions and Activities

1. Of the methodologies discussed in this chapter, which are you familiar with? Is there one that you have used as a teacher or experienced as a student?
2. Of these methods, which appeals to you and why? Do you think parts of it may still provide useful tools for teaching?
3. Select one drill from a textbook that you have used and bring it to class. Hand out copies to your teacher and classmates and explain why you chose this exercise/drill. Have everyone go through the drill or even actually do it. Discuss what type of drill it is, its effectiveness, and the reasons behind that. This procedure can be done several times throughout the course.
4. One of the most challenging and exemplary exercises I have encountered is from the *Elementary Modern Standard Arabic* (EMSA) textbook.[6] Discuss its strengths and weaknesses.

Drill 9. Written. Transformation: Singular → dual → plural
Replace the underlined word with the dual, then the plural, making any necessary changes.

١. هذا هو قائد النهضة الادبية الذي قرأت مقالاته في الجريدة اليومية.

٢. الدولة ستساعد الشركة على بناء مصنع حديث.

٣. الحزب الرئيسي انتخب مرشحا اثناء مؤتمره الصيفي.

٤. هذه هي الرسالة التي كتبها الطالب.

٥. الطالب الامريكي ذاهب لزيارة ذلك البلد العربي.

(Abboud and McCarus 1983, 493)

 **Further Reading**

Brown, H. Douglas. 2001. *Teaching by Principles: An Interactive Approach to Language Pedagogy*. 2nd ed. White Plains, NY: Addison Wesley Longman. (Especially chapter 2 on the history of language teaching.)

Larson-Freeman, Diane. 1983. "Training Teachers or Educating a Teacher." *Georgetown University Round Table on Languages and Linguistics 1983*, eds. James E. Alatis, H. H. Stern, and Peter Strevens, 264–274. Washington, DC: Georgetown University Press.

Larson-Freeman, Diane, and Marti Anderson. 2011. *Techniques and Principles in Language Teaching*. Oxford: Oxford University Press. (Especially chapters 1–4.)

Notes

1. I have relied on Hadley's and Stevick's overall definitions but advise those who would like further information to consult those sources directly, as they reference further readings, authors, and ideas on these topics. Adamson makes a distinction between "methodology" and "method:" "Methodology denotes the study of the system or range of methods that are used in teaching, while a method is a single set of practices and procedures, derived from theory or theorization of practice, that impinges upon the design of a curriculum plan, resources, and teaching and learning activities" (2006, 604).

2. On the "Reform Movement" among European linguists at the end of the 19th century, see Cook 2010, 4–5.

3. Behaviorist theory emerged as a dominant theory in psychology in the 1930s and 1940s. It considers observable facts of behavior or activity in humans and animals as the sole proper subject for psychological study. Behaviorism endorsed the concepts of conditioning reflexes and shaping behavior through reinforcement ("operant conditioning").

4. For some critics, the audiolingual emphasis on repetition, memorization, and constant oral practice appeared to be an undemanding, boring, and even stultifying experience rather than a lively and stimulating approach to oral mastery. It was not considered to be in the same cognitively demanding category as old-fashioned grammar study. In contemporary approaches, there is little attention to repetition in the classroom, and some CLT critics of audiolingual methods see memorization and repetition not only as unimportant but also as a waste of classroom time.

5. On automaticity see Fukkink, Hulstijn and Simis 2005, 56–58.

6. My teaching assistant and students several years ago jokingly (and affectionately) named this exercise "the drill from hell."

Newer Methods and Approaches

CHAPTER 5

There are no new steps, only new combinations.

George Balanchine, choreographer

Newer language teaching methodologies date from the 1970s and 1980s, when a number of them emerged onto the teaching scene. Many had humanistic aims and underpinnings, representing a shift in perspective toward a focus on learners, considering them from a viewpoint that took into account not only mind and intellect, but also affect, experience, psychology, motivation, and attitude.[1] In many respects these methods reflected innovative thinking about traditional problems; they also reflected insights from fields such as psychology, counseling, and cognition studies. Some of these approaches had a lasting impact on the field of language teaching (such as Krashen's input hypothesis in the natural approach and content-based instruction), while others had a more peripheral, albeit lasting, influence (such as counseling learning/community language learning for task-based instruction and for the concept of reflective feedback).

In this chapter the major characteristics and contributions of five approaches are outlined: (1) counseling learning/community language learning (CL/CLL), (2) the natural approach (NA), (3) communicative language teaching (CLT), (4) content-based instruction (CBI) and cultures and languages across the curriculum (CLAC), and (5) task-based learning and teaching (TBLT). These five have been chosen because of their relevance and applicability to Arabic language teaching, and also because of the extent of their influence on contemporary foreign language pedagogy. The aim here is not to endorse or dismiss any approach, but to examine objectively their principal features and to put new ideas into conversation with more traditional teaching concepts. Best practices often result from a combination of experience, understanding of theory, and willingness to experiment.

Counseling Learning and Community Language Learning (CL and CLL)

Counseling learning (CL) is a broad approach to teaching based on psychological understanding facilitated by the teacher; community language learning (CLL) is CL applied to language learning situations. This approach takes a certain amount of specialized training in both listening and counseling skills. It originated with Fr. Charles A. Curran, a practicing psychologist, who noted that foreign language learning, in particular, evoked high levels of anxiety among adults because language learning involves performance, and also because language learning requires learners (at least temporarily) to relinquish their familiar ego boundaries and adapt their personal behavior to distinctly different foreign standards.[2] Language learning, therefore, cannot be a depersonalized experience; in fact, it is highly personalized in the sense that learning a foreign language requires individuals to shift their verbal behavior into a different gear, to reexamine their abilities to communicate, and to be willing to act and sound different. Curran referred to this personal tension as a "profound core of existential anxiety" (1968, 82) that emerges in language learning situations because of the particular nature and demands of the foreign language learning experience. To deal with the anxieties of change, then, is an important skill of the teacher because high levels of anxiety can block input and learning. The central concept of CL/CLL, therefore, is that the "quality and structure of personal relationships" between teacher and learners is central to learning and is prior to and more important than any particular methodology (Rardin et al. 1988, viii). In addition to being an instructor, the CLL teacher is a highly conscious model of personal and professional integrity, a trained and active listener, and a counselor. Community language learning has contributed to language teaching pedagogy over the last thirty years by identifying some of "the most profound and elusive issues in the learning/teaching experience, including: risk, trust, (in)security, the context and processes of retention, the skillful use of silence, the importance of witnessing and affirming another person's feelings, teacher and learner responsibility and integrity, interpersonal relationships, and stages of psychological growth" (Ryding 1990, 111).

All of the above elements contribute to lifting CLL out of the strict "methodology" mode and into an educational theory that has generated an acute awareness of learner affect (e.g., Krashen's "affective barrier"), spanning many methods. This awareness may well be its most important contribution to contemporary SLA theory and practice, especially for learner-centered approaches.

CLL and Humanism

Typically, CLL is referred to as a "humanistic" approach because of its focus on interpersonal relationships and personal growth. A good definition of a humanistic approach is found in Richards and Schmidt, who define it as an approach "in which the following principles are considered important:

a. the development of human values
b. growth in self-awareness and in the understanding of others
c. sensitivity to human feelings and emotions
d. active student involvement in learning and in the way learning takes place (for this last reason such methods are also said to be student centered)." (2010, 265)[3]

In addition to being humanistic and learner-centered, CLL can also be said to be task-based because it allows learners initiative in deciding upon communicative tasks in the classroom. In his seminal book on task-based teaching, Ellis states that "one of the earliest proposals for task-based teaching is that associated with *humanistic language teaching*" (2003, 31; emphasis in original). He also identifies CLL as "an attempt to construct a task-based method that incorporates humanistic principles" (32). In some ways, CLL was ahead of its time.

A General Outline of CLL Theory

Curran's writings delineate and describe certain principles that underlie a counseling approach to teaching, and how these principles relate to pedagogical procedures.[4]

> The importance of these writings resides in their ability to inform and guide teachers with respect to aspects of psychological struggle, transformation and growth which many of us experience and witness, but which we do not completely understand from a theoretical point of view, nor are we normally equipped with a framework to deal with the various manifestations of these struggles. Most importantly, Curran's writings address the elusive concept of classroom community. (Ryding 1993, 141)

I have been a practitioner of CLL for many years, and although my practice has inevitably evolved from when I was first trained in the approach in 1976, I have also come to see a theoretical core of CLL that has the following components and constructs, even though in the CLL literature they may not be stated as such. Basically, I see that CLL theory concerns various aspects of **teacher awareness.**

Teacher Self-Awareness

The first kind of awareness is teacher self-awareness. Being a CLL practitioner means that you try to understand your own motivations and behaviors in the classroom and are able to be objective about yourself. You practice control of a class rather than dominance of it, you allow for learner autonomy, and you are always aware of your own behaviors as they affect the learners. In this respect, CLL can be said to be a form of "reflective practice" for teachers. Klapper provides an excellent description of reflective teaching practice, as follows:

> The idea of reflective teaching dates back at least to Dewey (1933) and his contrast between 'routine action' and 'reflective action.' The former is shaped by such influences as authority, tradition, and habit, as well as by the expectations and norms of institutions. Routine action is inflexible and static and is therefore unable to respond easily to changing situations and needs. Reflective action, on the other hand, is characterized by a readiness to engage in regular self-appraisal and evaluation; it is necessarily flexible and analytic and entails an acceptance of the need for constant self-development. (2001, 144–145)

The same author also notes that "teachers should be researchers of their own practice and . . . their teaching and curricular decisions should be shaped by questioning their pedagogy and by collecting data about their classrooms, specific teaching methods and learners' responses" (Klapper 2001, 147). Essentially, reflective teaching examines classroom activity on many levels, including self-appraisal, with an objective eye, aiming at formulating and reformulating one's own approach. The MLA Committee on Teaching wrote in its 2001 report: "To create meaningful discourse between scholarship and the classroom, the committee believes *reflective practice* is the operative term that best describes the attitude and activities that make teaching matter" (MLA 2001, 228; italics in original).

Reflective teaching entails examination of your own experiential knowledge (built up through everyday practice) as well as your theoretical or "received" knowledge learned through study and reading. By reflecting on your own teaching in action, you can achieve a personal but objective perspective on your assets, drawbacks, and successes; can find patterns that may be worth attention; and can recalibrate practice and theory for more effective teaching in the future. Analyze your teaching, document it, write about it (even if it is just a personal journal), keep notes about it, think about it, blog about it.

Another key awareness of the teacher is that she is not the most important person in the classroom. She is a key person without whom the lesson will not take place, but she should not consistently be the center of attention or dominate all activity. The center of attention is language learners and language learning. The center of attention is humans working together to build skills, retention, and performance. Some SLA theories emphasize that learners should be the center of attention in order to shift the focus of the teacher/student relationship to one of mutual support and responsibility. This does not mean that learners determine the curriculum or that they control the learning situation. It does mean that they are considered "active participants in the language learning process" (Loewen and Reinders 2011, 107).

The term "dominate" in this context refers to the teacher being the visual and mental center of all classroom activity. In a traditional classroom, students are usually seated in rows facing the teacher, and he or she is the visual point of reference. The teacher also judges the correctness and appropriateness of classroom utterances and behaviors. Whereas this may be an adequate arrangement for lecture-type learning situations, language learning theory and newer methodologies focus on restructuring the teacher/learner relationship so that the teacher forgoes dominance or eminence while still retaining careful control of the learning situation. Teachers set the parameters for the learning experience while providing opportunities for learners to become actively and meaningfully involved; sometimes the learners may even take the lead.[5] Teachers thereby provide an atmosphere wherein both individual learner responsibility and group responsibility are allowed to develop. In educational psychology, instructors' willingness to foster learner growth and independence is referred to as their "autonomy orientation."

Teacher Awareness of Learners

As a counseling approach to learning, CLL requires teacher awareness of all learners in a class. This awareness extends to individuals and it also extends to the class as a group, a learning community.

Body language, behavior, attitude, preparedness, and many other factors enter into the mix of personalities that constitute the class atmosphere and its special character. If you have taught before, you know that each class is similar and yet different; each class develops an identity and a dynamic of its own. As a teacher with wisdom and experience on your side, you have the capability to direct and foster this dynamic and the class's sense of community. A key component of CLL involves teacher awareness of learner psychology, one aspect of which is Curran's description of five psychological **stages of development**. These stages often correlate with learners' linguistic development, but sometimes not. Nonetheless they are perceptible levels of psychological maturity that often manifest themselves in the language learning experience.

- Stage one: Dependence. This earliest stage of development is one of almost complete dependence on the teacher. Learners at this stage need all the support and scaffolding that they can get in order to start developing their L2 identities.
- Stage two: Self-assertion. At this stage, the learner slowly starts to stand on his or her own two feet and to take initial, experimental steps into the target language. The learner is still heavily dependent on the teacher for structure, feedback, setting goals, and support.
- Stage three: Separate existence. Stage three is a critical psychological threshold for foreign language learners. By this stage they may feel that they can make their way in the L2 on their own. They are functional, but on a minimal level; this is the beginning of learner autonomy. Learners' interlanguage at this stage is by no means error-free, but because they have limited autonomy, they have less motivation for improvement than before. Sometimes learners do not hear corrections or, if the corrections are heard, they do not sink in. Learners at this stage are developing confidence in communicating, but they still need help, direction, and practice in order to reach higher levels of proficiency.

    A characteristic stage-three feature is that some learners may not only resist correction; they may reject the teacher and the teacher's role. In such cases, Curran speculated that the learners at this stage have developed an immature target language "self" and find it difficult to admit that they need help. In many cases, students simply stop learning language at this stage. They have reached a pseudo-terminal developmental state, can function well enough to communicate on some level, and they show disinterest in improvement. Two terms used to describe this language stage are "fossilization" and "stabilization," meaning that learners' interlanguage has ceased to develop. It is important to note that a teacher faced with student resistance to learning or to improved performance may unconsciously want to avoid provoking anger or resistance in learners, or may fault herself for this situation. Teachers may therefore get discouraged, depressed, or angry with themselves when confronting such resistance. The key contribution of Curran is his observation that this is a predictable and even normal stage for many learners, that it is fixable, and that teachers do not have to blame themselves for this unwillingness or resistance to further development. What can be done, then, to help learners through stage three of their development and into a stage where they can once again make headway in the target language? This is where stage four comes in.
- Stage four: Role-reversal. At this point, learners need to understand the teacher's "need to teach." That is, in order to move on, learners must put the teacher at ease, respect her need to teach, and welcome her help and support. Up to this point, the teacher has led the learners and made efforts to understand their problems and their progress. Now they need to have the maturity to understand hers. This is another key step in the psychological development and progress of language learners, facilitated by CLL procedures that ultimately foster this role-reversal.
- Stage five: Independence. Stage five is where learners are able to function truly autonomously in the target language. This does not mean that their interlanguage is perfect, or that they have reached native-like proficiency, or that they have stopped learning. It means that they have reached a level of communicative competence where they can continue to learn on their own and where they are open to feedback (from teachers, peers, or native speakers).

Teacher Awareness of Principles

Six principles of CLL are contained in the acronym SAARRD, which stands for security, attention, assertion, retention, reflection, and discrimination.[6] These concepts are broad enough to apply whether or not one has been convinced of the efficacy of the entire CLL approach. To summarize the principles, Curran was convinced that emotional **security** lay at the heart of the language learning experience, and that teachers should be prepared to engage learners on many levels, not just the intellectual. By understanding the full range of learner affect and anxieties and using specific counseling procedures and tools, teachers can more effectively deal with students' concerns and facilitate their learning in constructive and effective ways. Attentive and active involvement in the learning situation attest to true investment with the subject matter and its context, accounting for the principles of **attention** and **assertion**. **Retention**, the next principle, is facilitated through learner involvement in meaningful L2 interactions. The principle of **reflection** in CLL refers to two different processes; first, the learner is given time in class to reflect upon or think about the material just covered (even 1–2 minutes of reflection works here). Second, reflection is a procedure undertaken by the teacher in order to elicit, listen to, and acknowledge the learners' reactions to the learning experience, listening and then "reflecting" or "recasting" their remarks back to the learners in a nonjudgmental, objective fashion that gives evidence that the teacher has truly heard and comprehended the learners' concerns. This procedure allows learners to know whether or not they have been correctly understood and to feel comfortable expressing their feelings, reactions and observations about the learning situation. It is this particular form of reflection that constitutes the counseling nature of the approach, and which requires explicit training in active listening and counseling. The final principle for CLL is **discrimination**, in the sense of closely analyzing and discerning L2 features, sorting them out and categorizing them. This is done by the learners as well as by the teacher in order to develop language awareness.

Within these principles lie theoretical bases for the CLL approach as well as specific guidance on how these can be applied in the classroom. Extensive discussion, description, and application of these principles are described in the CLL literature as referenced in note 4, in Ryding-Lentzner 1978 (11–14) (Arabic-specific); in Ryding 1993 (142–143); and in Stevick 1980 (100–226).

CLL and Translation

The use of translation as a learning activity is often ignored or sidelined in communicative approaches because of its tainted association with the grammar-translation method of teaching and its strict focus on declarative knowledge, writing, and structural accuracy. Nonetheless, translation itself may be a useful and highly desirable activity. In referring to CLL and Curran's approach, Cook notes that "learning activities, rather than being determined in advance, should arise from a process of negotiation between student and counsellor (as the teacher is called). True to this principle, it [CLL] allowed translation in its inevitably eclectic repertoire, and in practice made use of translation more often than not" (2010, 24). In teaching MSA, the use of translation exercises may be both appropriate and valuable. The focus on the literary language, the language of writing, can benefit from the kind of interlingual analysis and attention to form required by accurate translation and fits well with what is usually required in the study of MSA: the ability to read and comprehend morphosyntactically complex texts.

❖ The Natural Approach

The "natural approach" to language teaching/learning is based on Krashen's monitor theory and developed primarily by Tracy Terrell and Stephen Krashen.[7] It is built around the following concepts:

- Comprehension is basic and essential to language learning. This is so at the first stages of study and remains so even at advanced levels.
- Comprehension precedes production (as in the acquisition of one's L1). At the start of language learning, there is a **preproduction phase** (L2 output not required from learners)

wherein the focus is on listening (as well as reading) and comprehension of increasingly complex i+1 input. This often involves a "silent" phase where learners are not required to produce any L2 but simply focus on understanding. The key to enabling understanding is to provide substantial amounts of L2 comprehensible input. The teacher modifies his or her speech and relies on visual aids in order to get meaning across. The content or topic may be familiar, thus exploiting the learners' background knowledge, but it should all be in the L2. The effect of this focus on comprehension combined with the lack of pressure to speak results in the gradual and more "natural" spontaneous emergence of the spoken L2.

- Spoken competence emerges in stages. Forcing early speech output causes errors, particularly L1 transfer errors. Early communication in the classroom can take various nonverbal forms, for example, gestures, yes/no responses, physical action responses, and responses in both L1 and L2. Gradual emergence into one-word and two-word stages is encouraged, as are choral responses, still with massive doses of L2 comprehensible input. There is constant recycling, reinforcement, and review of material. From the preproduction/comprehension stage, or Stage I, students progress to Stage II "early production" and Stage III "production" (Terrell 1985, 1).

- Conscious focus is on meaningful communication. There should be useful, functional, and pragmatic content within the comprehensible L2 provided, such as biographies, historical information and important dates, examination of key cultural artifacts, geographical data, and map work. In addition, there should be continuous review and recycling, or spiraling, of information. Because adult learners do not come to L2 learning as blank slates, they possess worlds of information and background knowledge that can contribute to their grasp of content in i+1. As one reviewer put it,

    > Language acquirers do understand input beyond their current level of development in the target language (TL). What makes this possible is access to context: "extra-linguistic information, 'knowledge of the world,' and previously acquired linguistic competence" (Krashen 1985, 2). The IH (input hypothesis) succeeds because the acquirer does not rely only on TL input. TL input which would otherwise be incomprehensible becomes comprehensible because of the scaffolding provided by contextual sources of information. (Oller 1988, 171)

- Reduce the affective filter. In order to reduce anxiety and accelerate comprehension, responses from students in their L1 are permitted. Terrell notes that "the student should be allowed to respond in L1 or in any combination of L1 and L2. When, then, will the student begin to speak the second language? The answer must be: whenever he makes a decision to do so, i.e., whenever his self-image and ease in the classroom is such that a response in the second language will not produce anxiety" (1982, 168).

- No overt correction of speech errors. Terrell declares that "there is no evidence which shows that the correction of speech errors is necessary or even helpful in language acquisition" (1982, 165). He also notes that "error correction be done only in written assignments which focus specifically on form" (ibid.), that explanation and practice of grammatical structures be done outside of class, and that outside work "must be carefully planned and highly structured" (1982, 164).

Terrell and Krashen were convinced that the overt correction of errors during learner speech activity in class would (1) disrupt the flow and the performance of the learner, (2) possibly discourage further attempts to communicate, and (3) not result in improvement. The key word here is "overt." Instead of direct or overt correction, it was advised that "correction [be] limited to 'expansion'" (Terrell, Egasse, and Voge 1982, 174–175).[8] "Expansion" in this sense refers to covert correction through more natural feedback forms, such as using recasts, repetitions with correction, or prompting (rephrasing). This is also referred to as "modeling," that is, responding to error by providing a correct model for the learner. This kind of feedback is considered much less intrusive, and reflects the kind of corrective feedback that adults provide for small children learning their L1.[9]

Communicative Language Teaching (CLT)

The term CLT designates a broad spectrum of approaches to language teaching and learning that center around developing full communicative competence rather than specific targeted grammatical competencies. It "is seen to derive from a multidisciplinary perspective that includes, at least, linguistics, psychology, philosophy, sociology, and educational research. The focus has been on the elaboration and implementation of programs and methodologies that promote the development of L2 functional competence through learner participation in communicative events" (Savignon 1990, 210).[10] A key characteristic of CLT is that it tends to be learner-centered and responsive to learner needs, whether they be academic or pragmatic. Another key characteristic is an emphasis on building learner confidence and fluency, with a secondary emphasis on structural accuracy, at least in the initial and intermediate stages.

An environment rich in L2 contexts and multiple sources of comprehensible input was originally thought to be enough to lead to second language acquisition in a natural way without intervention from instructors to explain particular points of grammar. However, after some years of research and testing "it became clear that, while learners did achieve high levels of fluency in the L2, they did not always achieve correspondingly high levels of accuracy" (Loewen and Reinders 2011, 32). Tyler notes that "explicit grammar explanations, coupled with more communicative activities, are consistently more effective in the instructed L2 setting than solely inductive approaches in which the learner is given no explicit explanation" (2008, 457). Judicious grammar instruction is now considered a component of CLT approaches and grammatical accuracy is now acknowledged as a requirement, especially at more advanced levels of study.

Two widely known and interrelated CLT approaches are content-based instruction and task-based instruction. Both are founded on the concept of usage-based learning, which is context-embedded and context-driven communication that provides a base, a medium, and an authentic environment for using the L2.[11] One researcher notes: "Formal knowledge, such as grammar and the like, remains important but needs to be taught . . . as situated knowledge, knowledge that deals with real-world activities. In other words, the curriculum should not treat the body of conceptual knowledge to be learned as separate from the situation in which it is to be used" (Blake 2008, 40).

Both the natural approach and CLT in general assume relatively little difference between spoken and written language; engaging in authentic speaking activities is seen as reinforcing reading and writing skills, and vice versa. Extensive reading, in fact, is encouraged as the best way to increase acquisition of productive skills. To some extent this is true of Arabic as well, but the linguistic differences between authentic spoken interactions and authentic written tasks change the equation from one of straightforward equivalence to one of finely attuned differentiation.

Content-Based Instruction (CBI)

A Georgetown colleague, Heidi Byrnes, is well-known for her laconic summary of CBI: "Content from the beginning, language until the end." That is, integrate rich content into language teaching from day one, and yet never forget that language skills need to be attended to, even at advanced levels. CBI (also referred to as LAC, languages across the curriculum, or CLAC, cultures and languages across the curriculum, and as "sheltered" instruction) is an approach "in which language proficiency is achieved by shifting the focus of the course from the learning of language *per se* to the learning of subject matter" (Leaver and Stryker 1989, 270). By focusing on content or particular topics in the target language, learner attention is deflected away from specific aspects or procedures typical of instructed language learning and toward the task of mastering the subject matter. This results in language knowledge and subject matter knowledge being learned at the same time in a synergistic manner rather than sequentially (Leaver and Stryker 1997, 7).

A CBI curriculum typically adheres to three principles:

1. **Subject-matter core**

   "The fundamental organization of the curriculum is derived from the subject matter, rather than forms, functions, situations, or skills. Communicative competence is acquired through the process of learning about specific topics such as math, science, art, social studies, culture, business, history, political systems, international affairs, or economics" (Leaver 1997b, 1).

2. **Authentic language and texts**

   "The core materials," write Leaver and Stryker, such as texts, videos, realia, recordings, and visual aids, "should be selected primarily (but not exclusively) from those produced for native speakers of the language. The learning activities should be both expository and experiential in nature and focus on conveying real messages and accomplishing specific tasks" (1989, 271).

3. **Appropriate to learner needs**

   "The topics, content, materials, and learning activities should correspond to the cognitive and affective needs of the students and should be appropriate to the proficiency level of the class" (Leaver and Stryker 1989, 271).

There are no particular required procedures for applying this approach; as long as the core principles are adhered to, there are any number of creative ways that curricula can be organized and implemented. However, most instances that I know of have required considerable time and resources in order to be developed. The conception of a CBI curriculum or course idea, the course design, the planning that includes proficiency goals as well as content learning, and the materials selection and organization can take weeks, months, even years—let alone specific pedagogical procedures and refinements. CBI is one of the most promising approaches to foreign language teaching and yet its success depends on detailed and time-consuming design and, often, collaboration with colleagues.[12] That said, the time and effort spent often produce the kind of innovative courses that appeal to students and that are effective in fostering communicative competence.

Suggested procedures and models for implementing CBI and its variants are wide ranging and can be found in a number of sources (Leaver and Stryker 1989, 1997; Larson-Freeman and Anderson 2011, 131–147; Hadley 2001, 164–169; Brown 2001, 49–50, 234–236). For an Arabic approach to CBI, see Ryding and Stowasser 1997, an article based on a collaborative effort to introduce a well-articulated intersection between Arabic language and area studies at the Foreign Service Institute.

Theme-Based Instruction

One variant of CBI is a theme-based approach to course design, where "a continuous content thread across the curriculum" (Swaffar 1999, 161) is used as a means of systematically linking and articulating levels of instruction, as well as providing thematic coherence that takes advantage of the principles of recycling texts, rereading, and repeated exposure to strengthen acquisition. Swaffar suggests some "commonsense principles" to incorporate in such a curriculum:

> First, familiar topics, genres, and rhetorical usage will facilitate students' comprehension. . . . Second, a precept especially necessary with beginners but true for all stages of foreign language instruction, planners of new curricula and crossovers should allow ten to fifteen minutes for in-class reading tasks with texts or videos to introduce subject matter and treatment so that students will be alerted to the new demands placed on them. . . . Third, rereading promotes the kind of comprehension and vocabulary retention that ties language and content learning. . . . Consequently, curricular planning for upper-division courses does well to use texts read in earlier semesters or texts on similar topics (1999, 161).

Genre-Based Instruction

Another variation of CBI is genre-based instruction, wherein the selection of a particular written or spoken genre (e.g., historical narrative, interview, book review, sports reporting, business letters, biography) ties together a curriculum (on a large scale) or a course (on a smaller scale), particularly at more advanced levels. "Genre-based pedagogy allows for an integrated approach to diverse upper-level content courses in a department's curriculum. Genres which work across diverse content areas present similar intellectual and linguistic learning opportunities" (Weigert and Rinner 2005).

Genre can be defined as "a type of discourse that occurs in a particular setting, that has distinctive and recognizable patterns and norms of organization and structure, and that has particular and distinctive communicative functions" (Richards and Schmidt 2010, 245). In different cultures and different discourse communities, genres may have very distinctive and contrasting features as well as some features that are shared and familiar to learners from their L1. This is the case in Arabic as compared with English, and comparative analysis of texts and text-types is an important component in literary criticism as well as in learning to express oneself clearly and appropriately at advanced levels of competence.

Genre classification is a first step in developing a genre-based curriculum or syllabus.[13] For Arabic purposes, for example, the contrasting styles employed in media writing and broadcasting (interviews, surveys, straight reporting, editorials, advertisements, financial reports, news commentary, film reviews, cooking programs, advice programs) on their own provide a wide range of rhetorical and presentational genres for MSA. The study of legal documents—both personal and public (e.g., application forms, contracts, official position papers, treaties)—may be of interest and use to certain groups of learners. In terms of literary texts, poetry (classical and modern), biography (e.g., *Al-Ayyām*), historical narratives, chronicles, and other narratives offer an expansive selection for genre-themed coursework. And, of course, key Islamic texts from various periods of history provide a rich vein in classical Arabic genre study.

In all these cases the texts (written and spoken) are a means not only of developing advanced literacy skills and cultural understanding, but of providing calibrated reading and listening comprehension materials that can be used to develop analytical skills and critical thinking about Arabic language and culture through writing assignments and through formal classroom discussion and presentations.

Task-Based Language Teaching (TBLT)

Task-based instruction has developed into a popular but sometimes polarizing approach to foreign language learning, with some researchers taking positive stances toward it and others taking negative and highly critical positions. As with any methodology, too strict adherence to one form of interaction with learners can render it ineffective or frustrating. Nonetheless, task-based learning is highly useful in many learning environments and can respond to a wide range of student needs, especially in language training situations where the learners will be living, working, or studying abroad, or assuming professional positions abroad that require a defined subset of linguistic skills, such as Foreign Service Officers. Tasks are activities where accurate communication is needed in order to resolve the assignment successfully and activities that are representative of typical communicative functions found outside the classroom.[14] While many types of tasks are spoken and interactive, they may also take the form of written, text-based tasks that lead to improvements in literacy skills and secondary discourse in general.

The tasks involved in task-based learning can be academic or pragmatic, but they should replicate as closely as possible authentic interactions and experiences that students can learn from as they undertake them. Tasks are sometimes categorized as either "focused" or "unfocused", meaning tasks that focus on targeted language structures or vocabulary or tasks that do not. TBLT is therefore a key venue for using "focus on form" activities that emphasize highlighting and attending to particular grammatical and lexical structures as they occur in a communicative context. "In using tasks in the classroom teachers often make use of a cycle of activities involving a) preparation for a task b) task performance c) follow-up activities that may involve a focus on language form" (Richards and Schmidt 2010, 585). Preparation may involve familiarization with the topic, the vocabulary, or the cultural context of a task; follow-up activities may involve testing (of content and/or language), review work, expansion of the topic, and exploration of related topics. Some ideas for classroom tasks include interviewing a native speaker (another teacher, for example) on a particular topic and writing up the interview for publication or presentation, map reading for analysis of terrain or historical boundaries, developing a summary translation of one day's leading news articles (as for an ambassador at a diplomatic post), or reading a book or going to a film and reviewing it.

> Perhaps the most important contribution of task and task-based assessment in adult L2 programs is this: a properly conceived notion of 'task' can capture the symbiotic relation between content/knowledge and language, in L1 acquisition as well as in adult instructed L2. In that sense, 'task' is not merely an expedient replacement of grammar but a value-added notion. It fosters a heightened awareness of language as a network of interlocking options (Halliday 1985) rather than as primarily a system of rules, thereby highlighting and confronting issues of identity and voice within typified contexts. At the same time, 'task' could become an identifiable site where an otherwise all-too-vague 'language use' orientation can indeed be engaged to foster development of a sophisticated cognitive fluency in the context of situated communication, both in the L1 and the L2 (Segalowitz 2000). In that case it might replace componential notions of accuracy, fluency and complexity that rely on largely decontextualized, formal and sentence-based criteria . . . with relational, yet carefully specified statements about language performance. (Byrnes 2002b, 434)

According to Ellis, language learning tasks should have the following features:

1. A task is a workplan, a plan for learner activity
2. A task involves a primary focus on meaning
3. A task involves real-world processes of language use
4. A task can involve any of the four language skills (speaking, listening, reading, writing)
5. A task engages cognitive processes
6. A task has a clearly defined communicative outcome. (2003, 9–10)

Out of all of these, he identifies task criterion number 2, the need for a primary focus on meaning, as the "key criterion" (2003, 16). Ellis provides a great deal of detail about these criteria as well as illustrative tasks, and situates task-based teaching theory within the SLA research paradigm, especially with regard to the interaction hypothesis and to CLT in general. He also points out that there are two ways of implementing tasks in the classroom: through task-based instruction, where the "task is a pedagogical unit that can be used as a basis for designing language courses," and through "task-supported language instruction," where tasks are incorporated into other types of methodologies (2003, 27). As regards the latter, when dealing with written Arabic it is important to remember the usefulness and validity of translation as a typical real-world task. "It is outcome-oriented: a successful translation is one that works. It promotes a focus on form as an offshoot of a communicative need, rather than as an end in itself" (Cook 2010, 30).

 ## Conclusion

This chapter signals a transition from traditional to contemporary approaches to foreign language teaching. It shows in particular the different interpretations of learner-centered theory and instruction that have emerged and covers many years' worth of developments in language teaching methodology: theorization, experimentation, application, and evaluation. I have not covered every method or approach that has arisen since the 1970s, but have tried to introduce the most well-known and successful ones. In all cases I have had to abbreviate the considerable information and in-depth research available about these approaches, but I hope that by providing references to key writings on these topics I will have enabled further examination and research for those interested in pursuing them.

As Balanchine says in the epigraph at the beginning of this chapter, it is the combinations of steps or procedures that is new; not necessarily all the steps themselves. With language pedagogy as with choreography, new approaches need not eliminate the old entirely. With consideration of insights from contemporary research, useful steps from traditional methodologies can be combined into highly effective new practices.

✦ Study Questions and Activities

1. Out of the methods and approaches presented in this chapter, which one appeals to you most? Why?
2. Which method presented here intrigues you the most?
3. Aside from CL/CLL, which "humanistic" methods of language teaching have you heard of?
4. Are you currently using CLT in the classroom for teaching Arabic? If so, what do you see as its strengths and weaknesses?
5. Have you tried to use language learning tasks in your classes? If you have not yet taught a class, have you ever experienced task-based or task-supported instruction? How effective do you think it was?
6. Do you think that one of these approaches is more suitable for teaching Arabic than any of the others? Why?

✦ Further Reading

Blair, Robert W., ed. *Innovative Approaches to Language Teaching.* 1982. Boston: Newbury House. (A key compilation of articles by theorists and applied linguists.)

Curran, Charles A. 1976. *Counseling-Learning in Second Languages.* Apple River, IL: Apple River Press. (A good introduction to CLL theory and application.)

Ellis, Rod. 2003. *Task-Based Language Learning and Teaching.* Oxford: Oxford University Press. (Contains an excellent glossary of SLA terms.)

Krashen, Stephen D., and Tracy D. Terrell. 1983. *The Natural Approach: Language Acquisition in the Classroom.* Hayward, CA: Alemany Press/Oxford: Pergamon Press. (A classic.)

Larsen-Freeman, Diane, and Marti Anderson. 2011. *Techniques and Principles in Language Teaching.* Oxford: Oxford University Press. (An excellent survey of methods from traditional to contemporary.)

Leaver, Betty Lou, and Stephen B. Stryker. 1989. "Content-Based Instruction for Foreign Language Classrooms." *Foreign Language Annals* 22, no. 3:269–275. (One of the foundational articles on this topic.)

Oller, John W., and Patricia A. Richard-Amato, eds. 1983. *Methods That Work: A Smorgasbord of Ideas for Language Teachers.* New York: Newbury House/Harper-Collins. (An extensive compilation of articles by key contributors to new methodologies.)

Ryding, Karin. 1993. "Creating a Learning Community: Community Language Learning for the Nineties." *Georgetown University Round Table on Languages and Linguistics 1995,* edited by James E. Alatis, 137–147. Washington, DC: Georgetown University Press.

Ryding, Karin, and Barbara Stowasser. 1997. "Text Development for Content-Based Instruction in Arabic." In *Content-Based Instruction in Foreign Language Education,* edited by Steven Stryker and Betty Lou Leaver, 107–118. Washington, DC: Georgetown University Press.

Ryding-Lentzner, Karin. 1978. "The Community Language Learning Approach to Arabic: Theory and Application." *Al-Arabiyya* 11:10–14. (CLL as applied to Arabic.)

Stevick, Earl. 1980. *A Way and Ways.* Boston: Newbury House. (A classic.)

____. 1990. *Humanism in Language Teaching: A Critical Perspective.* Oxford: Oxford University Press. (One of the few direct discussions of humanism in language pedagogy.)

____. 1996. *Memory, Meaning & Method.* 2nd ed. Boston: Heinle & Heinle. (Another classic.)

✵ Notes

1. "Like all enlightened teachers, Curran [community language learning], Lozanov [suggestopedia], Terrell [the natural approach] . . . see the learner rather than the subject matter as central to the learning process, and the teacher and materials serving mainly to help activate this process" (Blair 1982, 102).

2. "If asked to name language teachers whose seminal contributions to language teaching . . . have influenced current thinking and practice, I would include among them the counseling psychologist Father Charles A. Curran, who brought from his collaborative work with Carl Rogers in counseling therapy a revolutionary view of education in general and of language teaching in particular, including an understanding of how to deal with the [affective] filter" (Blair 1982, 103).

3. For an in-depth treatment of humanism in language teaching and learning, see Stevick 1990.

4. See Curran 1968, 1972, 1976, 1978, and 1982a.

5. "The perception of control appears to be a significant factor affecting [students'] engagement in learning and quality of learning. When teachers are seen as emphasizing independent thinking in addition to content mastery, students are more likely to place value on using effective learning strategies." (Ames 1992, 265)

6. For a description and discussion of these principles, see Curran 1982b, 141–45; Curran 1976, 6–8; and Rardin et al. 1988, 110–122.

7. See their coauthored book, *The Natural Approach* (1983).

8. Krashen and Terrell state that "error correction should be used for what it was meant for, conscious learning, and should therefore be limited to rules and situations where Monitoring is possible and appropriate" (1983, 178).

9. See a definition of "modeling" in Richards and Schmidt 2010, 370. See also "recasts" in chapter 16 of this book and "error correction" in chapter 19. The strong stance against overt correction of speech errors in Terrell's and Krashen's work has led over the years to some overinterpretation, including the misconception that no grammatical correction should be used at all (see, for example, Sato and Kleinsasser 1999, 504–505).

10. See chapter 4 for a definition of communicative competence.

11. "Usage-based models assume language acquisition is input-driven and experiential. They assume first-person experience of language (by children or adults) during situated, communicative language use provides evidence of *patterns* in the input that carry *meaning,* and that these patterns are learned while doing something with communicative intent, like . . . exchanging currency in a foreign country" (Robinson and Ellis 2008c, 495; italics in original).

12. "As every practitioner has recognized, languages across the curriculum requires a discipline of cooperation, patience, and long-term commitment" (Adams 2007, 14).

13. See Crane 2002, 11 for a helpful analysis of steps in genre classification for advanced language and culture study.

14. Ellis defines tasks as "activities that call for primarily meaning-focused language use. In contrast, 'exercises' are activities that call for primarily form-focused language use" (2003, 3).

Part III

Programmatic Issues

Learning Goals, Curricula, and Syllabi

CHAPTER

6

The interplay among curricular structures, instructional practices, and assessment demands, when approached in persistent and iterative cycles of improvement, leads to a much richer synthetic whole.

Heidi Byrnes, Hiram Maxim, and John Norris

We form our programs in dialogue with the past. Even when we push the envelope a bit . . . we do so with the traditional curriculum clearly visible in the rearview mirror.

Nick Shumway

Language learning is cumulative but not linear. It is also incremental; it does not occur all at once but instead through repeated exposure, practice, instruction, and experimental use. The cyclical interplay and mutual reinforcement of comprehension and expression needs to be carefully considered and planned out in advance. Even if individual teachers sometimes diverge from a curriculum, the central goals and features of a well-articulated sequence of courses act as an anchor to stabilize offerings, to inform innovation, to clarify objectives, and to provide for future growth. First of all, programs need to specify their academic and communicative goals; second, they need to determine the methods of approach and accomplishment of those goals; third, they must enrich language programs with stimulating content; and fourth, programs must assess learning progress and stages of achievement. The Standards for Teaching Arabic, devised by the National Standards in Foreign Language Education Project in 2006, provide a framework for curriculum development and negotiation, but they need to be embedded in a coherent curriculum informed by research in second language acquisition, in linguistic theory, in cognition, and in the assessment of best teaching practices.[1]

Defining Arabic Instructional Goals

A number of topics suggest themselves for this chapter, but the overriding themes chosen here are suitability or appropriateness of instruction, long-term planning, and practicality. In recent years, new Arabic language programs have evolved in response to student demand and to national need, but some have done so without professional input, long-term vision, or informed planning to define learning outcomes. Many programs simply progress from first-year classes to intermediate and (sometimes) to advanced levels, relying on textbooks to provide the structure for courses and the curriculum, and relying on student demand for determining the levels offered. Moreover, the fallback position for selecting materials and the medium of instruction has been literary Arabic (MSA) because the complexities of trying to teach communicative vernacular skills demand specific materials, expertise, discussion, consensus, and clarity of objectives.[2] The context-determined nature of language functions within the Arabic speech community has an impact on goals and assessment of learning Arabic as a foreign language. Not the least of these goals is the nature of learner ultimate attainment, or the end result being targeted. Is the goal for the learner to attain proficiency equivalent to an educated native speaker of Arabic? A working proficiency to adequately perform certain professional tasks? Or situation-appropriate, advanced communicative effectiveness?[3] In a balanced or diverse curriculum, curricular sequencing of discourse types can be a central issue.

 ## Time Considerations and Arabic's Difficulty Category

A second key issue is time on task. As Jackson and Malone report, "development of functional communication in a foreign language requires extended uninterrupted study," and "languages (and cultures) that are very different from English take longer to learn for English speakers than do Western European languages. . . . This means that expectations of program outcomes should account for the considerable time needed to attain a functional level of proficiency" (2009, 17). Arabic, Chinese, Japanese, and Korean are all rated at level IV in terms of the ILR Language Difficulty Category (LDC), which is calculated in terms of time needed to reach specific levels of proficiency (US Department of State 2004, 46). Jackson and Kaplan note that "two things need to be understood about these [difficulty] categories. First, they are entirely a-theoretical, being based solely on the time it takes our [State Department] learners to learn these languages. Second, the categories do nonetheless reflect various parameters of linguistic distance" (2005, 5).

Why is Arabic at the highest difficulty level whereas Hebrew and Amharic (closely related Semitic languages, which also use non-Roman scripts) are rated at level III? It is rated differently primarily because of the range of difference between spoken and written variants of Arabic, and the need to reach professional levels of proficiency in both. For level IV languages, the number of classroom hours required ranges between 2400 and 2760 hours. That is, 80–92 weeks of full-time (30 hours a week) study (US Department of State 1973, 1). This compares with considerably lower rates of time on task achievable in academic curricula where other subjects compete with language study. For example, one 15-week semester of three credit hours of Arabic yields 45 hours; an intensive six-credit course would yield 90 hours. After four years of study at this rate, the maximum achieved would be 360 hours. This is one reason why study-abroad components of Arabic curricula are so important; they are crucial for learners to develop reasonably authentic and automatic spoken language skills.

Key considerations in Arabic curriculum development need to take into account the concept of difficulty level, and to require intensive coursework (preferably six hours a week and six credits per semester—or the equivalent). Study abroad and immersion experiences such as the Middlebury summer Arabic program should play significant auxiliary roles in curriculum development and in determining requirements for Arabic language majors and minors.

 ## Key Questions

One way to approach curriculum development involves devising key questions whose answers provide a theoretical and practical framework for a program. Subsequent to development of these questions is prioritization: Which are the central topics and themes that will guide curricular decisions and inspire both faculty and students? Framed differently, here are six questions that can be used as springboards for discussing Arabic curricula.

A department or program might start with some of these questions or might develop its own sets of questions regarding proficiency goals, intellectual content, and ultimate attainment. In the event that there are few or no experienced Arabic teaching professionals on the faculty, it may be a good idea to contact the American Association of Teachers of Arabic (AATA) to see if an experienced consultant would be willing to advise in discussions of curriculum. This is important because of the unique nature of the Arabic pedagogical tradition and the complexity of Arabic sociolinguistics. It may be useful, moreover, to consider that the development or redevelopment of

---

Six Questions for Discussing Arabic Curricula

1. What classroom approaches and materials are most effective for developing balanced proficiency in all four skills: reading, writing, listening, and speaking?
2. What forms of Arabic have maximal generality or projection value for use throughout the Arab world?
3. How exactly does the vernacular/literary split affect the acquisition of ultimate attainment in Arabic as a foreign language? Is there a way to accelerate the accurate development of interpersonal discourse as well as the acquisition of interlanguage pragmatics without compromising the learning of literacy skills?
4. What templates of study abroad programs yield the best results?
5. In proficiency testing, what is the most effective approach to identifying and analyzing problem areas, including sample ratability, tester training, interrater reliability, compatibility of different systems, and issues regarding the validity and appropriateness of Arabic register shifting and code-mixing?
6. What are best practices for teaching Arabic heritage learners? How can their linguistic and cultural backgrounds be most effectively transformed into professional-level skills?[4]

---

an Arabic curriculum is not simply an administrative task; it may be seen as an act of "programmatic inquiry," that is, "as an activity that scholars can and should embrace" (Byrnes, Maxim, and Norris 2010, 201).[5]

❖ Components of a Competence-Oriented Curriculum

If one takes communicative competence as a baseline framework for a language and culture curriculum, it is important to know the possible components of such an approach, and to decide where a particular curriculum would focus—on one component, on several, on all? The issue of communicative competence has complicated as well as enriched Arabic instruction, learning strategies, goals, and achievement, so it requires some clarification.

Communicative competence has been defined as follows: "the ability to use language in a variety of settings, taking into account relationships between speakers and differences in situations" (Lightbown and Spada 2006, 196). Savignon describes it as "the use of language in social context, the observance of sociolinguistic norms of appropriacy" (1990, 209). Canale and Swain (1980) propose four different components for communicative competence:

1. **Grammatical or linguistic competence:** knowledge of L2 linguistic forms and structure (e.g., lexicon, morphology, syntax)
2. **Discourse competence:** knowledge of how language works above the sentence level in cohesive, coherent L2 written and spoken situations[6]
3. **Sociolinguistic/functional competence:** knowledge of language use in context; ability to adjust register and formality levels depending on social context (e.g., the relationship between participants) and discourse function (e.g., apology, praise, persuasion, requesting help)
4. **Strategic/pragmatic competence:** knowledge of how to manage communication situations, especially where difficulties may arise in interactive discourse, and ability to compensate for limited language resources, such as asking for clarification, repetition, or paraphrase, and other conversation management strategies.

Brown adds a fifth component: psychomotor skills, including pronunciation (Brown 2001, 68). Handwriting would also fall under this category.

These components are now widely recognized as foundational concepts for communicative competence. They may not be complete, but they cover most of the issues involved in authentic communicative situations: not only being familiar with linguistic forms of the language, but also being aware of when, how, and with whom it is appropriate to use these forms—the system of rules for social interaction. As noted earlier, these components focus on spoken language authenticity as part of discourse competence, and raise an issue that needs to be decided within Arabic language teaching programs: the relationship between literacy and spoken language competence. In his textbook, *Teaching by Principles*, Brown notes that "the array of studies on CC [communicative competence] provides what is perhaps the most important linguistic principle of learning and teaching:

> Given that communicative competence is the goal of a language classroom, instruction needs to point toward all its components: organizational, pragmatic, strategic, and psychomotor. Communicative goals are best achieved by giving due attention to language use and not just usage, to fluency and not just to accuracy, to authentic language and contexts, and to students' eventual need to apply classroom learning to previously unrehearsed contexts in the real world. (2001, 69)

Following up on this, Jackson and Malone comment that "a competency-oriented language curriculum needs to incorporate learning opportunities that focus on language and cultural content and functional ability at all levels, from beginning to the most advanced" (2009, 18).

Limitations of Communicative Language Teaching (CLT)

It is important to distinguish between the goals of a competency-based curriculum and the CLT approach to teaching, especially for academic program designers. CLT has been criticized for undervaluing and "constraining student achievement" because of its overall focus "on oral self-expression rather than the full complexity of language and culture," with a subsequent diminishment or dilution of intellectual rigor and scope (Levine et al. 2008, 244). For academic programs, development of literacy and analytical skills is usually central to departmental mission and goals; therefore, a foreign language curriculum at the tertiary level needs seriously to consider intellectual content and sophisticated language awareness as well as oral fluency in everyday language. In this respect, the use of translation as a tool for bilingualization and smooth operation between languages is being advocated by some researchers. "Translation is a major and obvious way of using two languages together in a useful and systematic manner" (Cook 2010, 37). The use of translation as a learning process in the classroom can be seen as a means of grasping semantic equivalence in very precise ways.[7] In addition to its repression of translation, other limitations of CLT include its elaborate distancing from the pedagogy of grammar and its highly restricted use of the L1, of drills and other grammatical exercises, and of anything that seems designed to fasten explicitly and consciously upon linguistic detail. Although none of these traditional activities holds all the answers to language acquisition, it is neither productive nor professional to avoid them when they may be valuable or even critical factors in accelerating learner understanding and performance.

Proficiency and Performance

Performance within language learning situations reveals learners' communicative competence at various stages in their learning experience. Proficiency is a term used to refer to learner performance in the target language on many levels. It may be measured and scored by various means, some quite extensively developed, such as the ACTFL proficiency guidelines or the ILR skill-level descriptions. Measurement is done through a process called proficiency testing, where a learner is put into a decontextualized language situation and tested on his or her ability to deal with that situation in the target language. Resulting scores are then used to describe the learner's proficiency level. The concept of proficiency testing arose in the 1950s in government agencies such as the State Department in order to rate the skills of US employees assigned to overseas positions.[8] Since then it has become much more than a way to rate skills; proficiency testing has turned into a driving force behind communicative curriculum design and has influenced in many ways the goals of instruction, whether academic, governmental, private, or military. The main difference between proficiency testing and traditional classroom achievement testing is that classroom testing usually focuses on what are termed "discrete point" tests, where items such as vocabulary and specific grammatical points are tested in written form, and where written translation ability is assessed. The FSI proficiency test was the first to rate spoken language skills and to design skill-level descriptions for evaluating and scoring student performance according to those descriptions. Government proficiency testing has traditionally focused on speaking and reading evaluation, giving students an "S/R" score in a range from 0 to 5. Other official skill level guidelines, such as those for listening and writing, are available on the ILR website.

The American Council on the Teaching of Foreign Languages (ACTFL) has over the past 30 years or so organized a proficiency testing system to certify testers and to introduce oral proficiency testing as an objective way of evaluating student performance in academic programs. The effect of the "proficiency movement" has been to redirect the focus of language instruction at the university level from grammar-based to situationally and functionally based instruction that has as its goal the achievement of specific proficiency levels. However, it may be useful to keep in mind that the original concept of proficiency testing came into being through government training programs, and that transplanting training goals and procedures into an educational environment takes considerable discussion, planning, and evaluation.

Goals of Instruction: Education and Training

The objectives of any curriculum depend upon the needs of the learners as well as the institutional mission. That is, a university will have different and more demanding educational goals for learners than a government institution that is focused on specific training for professional job needs. To some extent the goals and methods of language education and language training overlap, but it is useful to keep the distinction in mind. Diane Larson-Freeman has pointed out the following useful differences between education and training:[9]

Education	Training
• Is individual-centered with general objectives of intellectual growth and critical thinking. • Students learn to be independent thinkers and seek their own knowledge and skills. • Focus is on the process of defining and solving problems in general. • Progress is measured in relative terms—how far the student has come, significant personal and intellectual growth.	• Is situation-specific with finite objectives. • Trainer transmits information to trainees on particular issues. • Focus is on solving specific problems posed by the trainer. • Success is measured in absolute terms on task-specific criteria.
GOAL: To prepare people to make informed, literate, intelligent choices; to teach them how to think clearly and critically.	**GOAL:** To provide skills necessary for specific task accomplishment.

Training is therefore what is usually undertaken at government schools and at private institutes that contract to teach individuals language skills for specific occupational purposes. Education is what is undertaken in academic settings for academic purposes. These approaches are not mutually exclusive; their distinctiveness does not mean that educational goals cannot be pragmatic, nor that training goals lack educational value. The two approaches are different systems for organizing curricula and pedagogy according to student needs and learning outcomes. In fact, it is important to realize that there is interplay between education and training, and to be able to take advantage of the strengths of both.

 ## Training Curricula

Any sequence of language and culture training needs to have a roadmap or plan outlining and addressing the goals of training as well as the standards, methods, and appropriate methodologies for attaining those goals. As Jackson and Malone note, "effective language learning depends on a continuous, articulated program of study and must build on previous language learning experiences" (2009, 17). The focus of classroom activities is normally language use and practice of appropriate job-specific professional communication skills. The nature of these skills needs to be carefully assessed, analyzed, and broken down into teachable/learnable sequences. Therefore, needs analysis is one of the essential tools of training curricula development, as is the conversion of such analysis into effective pedagogical materials. Moreover, adult students tend to prefer well-organized coursework where their performance is evaluated frequently and where teachers give timely, detailed feedback. Especially when the learning objective is a specific proficiency skill level (for example, an S-3/R-3 in ILR terms), regular formative assessment needs to be included in any course design effort in order to provide learners with benchmarks of progress toward their performance goals.

Typical preferences for training curricula include functional/notional course design, content-based instruction, and task-based instruction, or a combination of these approaches. These types of curricula focus primarily on the learners' ability to accomplish professional tasks using specific discourse skills. Although often unspecified, regular homework assignments are key parts of training curricula, whether they are written or are comprehension tasks in reading and listening. Training courses also aim at expanding regional and cultural knowledge in terms of area and culture studies. Often, the area studies components are taught in English, but the content is generally more deeply understood when the information provided by area specialists is also integrated into the language curriculum through specific study modules devoted to these topics. Converting such information into level-appropriate teachable activities demands considerable pedagogical effort and sophistication.[10] Simple follow-up conversation exercises after an area studies lecture, for example, rarely produce long-term control of key vocabulary or content expertise.

 ## Academic Curricula

Goal-setting for academic curricula is more complex and perhaps more vexing than designing goals for training. In an academic setting, intellectual and emotional growth, objectives measured in terms of cognitive development and achievement, are taken into account. Even though foreign language teaching is occasionally misconstrued as a skill-only discipline, it can and should be based on goals that include the development of critical thinking. The nature of judgment and analysis needed for effective language acquisition is different from the adversarial type of critical thinking: It involves curiosity, willingness to explore and take risks, objective recognition of a new linguistic reality, and the observational skills needed for noticing and analyzing difference. In particular, linguistic reasoning is often analogical reasoning, that is, the ability to perceive key relationships between language items, identify phonological, morphological, and syntactic patterns, and retrieve from memory appropriate analogies for learning new items and processes.

The 2007 MLA report, "Foreign Languages and Higher Education: New Structures for a Changed World," advocates that programs teach learners "to reflect on the world and themselves through the lens of another language and culture" (237). The development of self-reflection and objectivity about one's self and one's own culture is a key step in intellectual, psychological, and social growth that can be encouraged and accelerated through the creative incorporation of cultural content in Arabic language courses from the very beginning stages until the end.[11] Careful consideration of cultural themes to be interwoven into an Arabic language curriculum can be a springboard for creating strands of key intercultural topics, aesthetics, and values that enhance and distinguish a well-conceived curriculum.[12] "Intellectually challenging content is . . . needed at the post-secondary level, and foreign language departments are well advised to maintain a broad educational vision for their programs" (Levine et al. 2008, 245).[13]

Syllabus Rationale

Whereas the curriculum of a program, a major, or a minor provides an overarching rationale and roadmap of coursework and intellectual development, a syllabus is usually a session-by-session outline of sequenced materials, activities, assignments, themes, projects, and tests for one course. A syllabus can be described in general as "that part of a course which serves as a schematic frame of reference" and also "a schematic construct of what is to be taught" (Widdowson 1992, 501). Syllabus planning for individual teachers entails working within departmental structures to develop and teach one's own courses in an effective, systematic, and informed way, using particular methods, techniques, and materials to bring out interest and top performance in one's students. Learners especially appreciate well-organized courses where assignments and objectives are well defined, and where clear benchmarks signal specific stages of progress. A piece of valuable advice is to "use the syllabus and the first day of class to establish the course climate" (Ambrose et al. 2010, 184). The structure of the syllabus should provide a delineation of both the path and the goals of a course.

The way to approach syllabus development depends on particular course objectives as well as overall department approaches and goals. Most often, a foreign language course syllabus is anchored either in a particular methodology or in an integrated set of selected methods and techniques preferred by the teacher. Very often, a syllabus will incorporate the lesson sequence of a particular textbook, but will also include non–text-based activities. Having an explicit, carefully sequenced syllabus assures students that they will be making progress and that there are clear expectations for their performance. For beginning and intermediate classes in particular, having a day-by-day syllabus that includes specification of class coverage, homework assignments, and quizzes is a key asset for both learners and teachers. For learners it gives a systematic outline of assignments and learning outcomes; for teachers it frames the work to be done and helps in preparing for the class. A syllabus should be both explicit and flexible; it should provide a sequenced outline of activities but it should also provide for time to review and to allow for unexpected developments (such as snow days, having a special visitor in class, or having to spend more time on a project or topic than originally planned). Fortunately, syllabi are easy to revise.

Consulting Peers about Syllabi

In constructing a syllabus it is often helpful to see and discuss the syllabi of other colleagues—both in your department and in other departments—in order to develop ideas. One of the most useful faculty exercises I have experienced was in a faculty seminar titled "Teaching as Scholarship: Reflections on a Syllabus," designed and run by the American Association for Higher Education.[14] Another approach to this topic is described as follows:

> We have taught a noncredit but strongly recommended [graduate] course in which we invite departmental faculty members to share copies of syllabi and discuss their rationale for teaching certain courses in certain ways. . . . At the end of the semester, students have a stack of syllabi for virtually every course in the traditional . . . major including advanced grammar and composition, literature surveys, and dialectology. Further, the students hear successful and experienced teachers explain why they organize a course in a particular way: how they choose readings; and how they structure exams, correct student papers, and determine grades. (Shumway 2000, 1193–1194).

Shumway notes that this was a "noncredit . . . [graduate] course" but such interfaculty consultation could be constructed as a faculty seminar, symposium, or regularly scheduled discussion among peers as well as graduate students.

 ## Syllabus Types

Selecting, organizing, and sequencing the content of instruction may comprise the surface of a syllabus, but these are based on many things: particular learning theories, materials, instructional goals, methodologies, and, of course, experience. Most syllabi fall into several categories: grammar-based (structural), functional/notional (situational), content-based, or task-based. Many can be described as "communicative," focused on fostering both communicative and cultural competence.

A **grammar-based syllabus** structures learning activities and goals around grammatical structures of growing complexity. A grammar-based syllabus often is based on particular grammar-based materials. A good example of a grammar-based textbook in the grammar/translation tradition is Ziadeh and Winder's *An Introduction to Modern Arabic* (1957). Another excellent example (in the audiolingual tradition) is Abboud and McCarus's two-volume *Elementary Modern Standard Arabic* (1983 [1968]). Each of these books is carefully designed around building control of grammatical structures and the development of key vocabulary.

A **functional/notional syllabus** structures learning around situations based on the type of linguistic and social functions required in real-world experiences. For example, speaking functions might involve asking questions, greeting and leave-taking, apologizing, getting directions, clarifying, thanking, refusing/accepting an invitation, expressing condolences, or asking for help. Some listening functions might include listening for explanations, listening for information, dyadic (one-on-one) listening, listening in general conversations, or telephone listening. Reading functions could include both gisting and close reading, and reading for information of various kinds—in academic publications, in journals and newspapers, on street signs, in official documents, or in manuscripts, for example. Writing functions may include filling in official forms, writing a brief letter or an email message, reporting, presenting information, expressing thanks, expressing opinion, or taking lecture notes.[15] In this type of syllabus, attention is paid to incorporating appropriate vocabulary and structure for the accomplishment of such functions and to the process of interweaving appropriate levels of language with those functions. *Formal Spoken Arabic: Fast Course* (Ryding and Zaiback 1993) is a situation-based textbook designed to introduce rank beginners to basic interactive functions and intercultural pragmatics in Arabic. Some universities have adapted it to calibrate with *Al-Kitaab* or other MSA introductory texts in order to teach basic spoken Arabic skills.[16]

A **content-based syllabus** structures learning activities around specific content topics, often using authentic spoken and written texts as materials for study. The language medium is Arabic and the topics included depend on the course design; areas of discussion could involve culture, society, art, religion, business, politics, or geography—to name a few. Some important concepts of content-based instruction (CBI) are that language is calibrated with topic, that learning tasks are calibrated both with topic and with language level, and that vocabulary is systematically recycled throughout the course.

A **natural-approach syllabus** is similar to a functional/notional syllabus in that it focuses on contexted language use. However, in the natural approach, the course design necessarily includes massive quantities of comprehensible input (spoken and written) and works its way through various contents and situations with the aim of developing language acquisition (as distinct from language "learning").[17] These stages may include an initial silent period where learners are exposed to selected spoken and written texts but are not required to speak in the L2 until they are willing and ready. *Formal Spoken Arabic: Basic Course* (Ryding and Mehall) is designed along the lines of a natural-approach syllabus.

A **task-based, procedural syllabus** is focused chiefly on task performance as a way of fostering foreign language acquisition. Some tasks might include map reading or timetable reading in the target language, interviewing various L2 speakers to obtain information, listening to a news broadcast and summarizing it, ordering a meal by telephone, or making arrangements for a visiting speaker. In a task-based approach, there is greater emphasis on "doing" foreign language and less on learning about a foreign language. Grammar explanations play a secondary role, if any at all. It is assumed that learners will cognitively sort out the right way to use language as they involve themselves in purposeful and authentic types of task accomplishment.

A **communicative syllabus** may look very much like a syllabus for the natural approach, for CBI, for the functional/notional approach, or for a task-based approach, but it is flexible in accommodating different teaching styles and choice of technique, as long as the primary goal of communicative competence is served.

Curricular Sequencing of Arabic Discourse Types

When it comes to Arabic curricular sequencing, syllabus development, and pedagogy, the standard syllabus types encounter complexities eventuated by the sociolinguistic facts of diglossia. In a previous work I have called the traditional model for teaching Arabic as a foreign language **reverse privileging** (RP).[18] This identification is based on the distinctions between primary discourse and secondary discourse developed by J. P. Gee (1998) and elaborated upon by Heidi Byrnes (2002a, 38–49). In short, primary discourse is the kind of language that surrounds people in informal or intimate circumstances—at home, in the office, or with family and friends. Secondary discourse, on the other hand, is the language of public life, involving "social institutions beyond the family" (Byrnes 2002a, 49). Byrnes uses this distinction to point out the "the extraordinary privileging of discourses of familiarity" in classrooms using communicative approaches, while the discourses of "the professions, the academy, and civil society are largely disregarded" (2002a, 49). That is, within the tradition of European language teaching some researchers believe that the CLT approach (communicative language teaching) has shifted academic goals too far toward the vernacular and left little room for the formal and literary forms and functions of language.[19] For Arabic, the situation has been just the reverse.

One reason it has been difficult for Arabic language teaching to find firm footing in practice and to define communicative curricula is that instead of privileging everyday forms of communication, it does the reverse: Arabic language teaching usually focuses almost exclusively on competence in the written language, MSA—even to the point of teaching it as a quasi-authentic form of everyday discourse. This reverse privileging places importance fully and firmly on the literary language at the expense of attention to communicative, sociopragmatic competence in vernacular Arabic. Students of Arabic who want and expect to function in primary discourse situations—as they would do after one or two years of another language—may become discouraged by their inability to interact with Arab peers and friends in informal situations.

As noted by Wilmsen, "communicative Arabic is largely vernacular Arabic" (2006, 131). Wilmsen examines the requirements for professional translators and interpreters in Arabic in particular. Based on his own experience and research, he recommends that "the designers of Arabic programs at universities should begin to think in terms of a five-year major" as is done in some European translation programs (2006, 134). "Before students can move along to the higher cognitive skills of text analysis and production, they must first receive a firm grounding in the mechanics of their languages. For Arabic students, this grounding must include a spoken vernacular along with the formal written . . . code" (ibid.).

The five-year degree program is certainly a possible option for Arabic majors who seek the full range of communicative competence. It should include a semester or (preferably) an academic year abroad in the Arab world, as well as an immersion experience either in the United States or abroad. The fifth year could be an add-on for Arabic majors who receive B.A.s after four years, then devote a year to full-time, intensive Arabic study in return for a certificate and/or other documentation of their advanced proficiency.

Diluting Attention to Literacy Skills

Contemporary textbooks, programs, and methodology training in Arabic have tackled the RP issue by building spoken discourse goals and features into MSA courses in a kind of blanket approach. In approaches to Arabic using MSA as the only form of discourse, however, a key problem is the dilution of attention to literacy skills in order to accommodate unrealistic "communicative" type goals and activities in MSA. The focus on development of spoken discourse skills in MSA can only be done at the expense of attention to the authentic functions of literary language.[20] The blanket approach shelters Arabic students from the linguistic reality of multiple skills. This is done with the highest intent and purpose because it is widely believed that introducing learners to the complexities of diglossia will be confusing for them. However, in the long run this policy may create rather than dispel shock and confusion. It is essential for learners of Arabic to acquire sophisticated understanding of Arabic sociolinguistic reality, not only in order to communicate properly but also to build the intellectual framework for understanding key social and cultural topics such as language and identity in the Arab world. In this sense, the field of critical pedagogy may be of interest to Arabic programs. Critical pedagogy "seeks to help students gain critical understanding of how language is intertwined with social and political structures" (Leeman, Rabin, and Roman-Mendoza 2011, 481); for Arabic, this is a topic of considerable relevance.[21]

Program directors and faculty may want to reevaluate the sequencing of coursework and the content of courses, even at beginning levels of instruction, considering mixed, balanced curricula that include both literary (secondary discourse) and vernacular (primary discourse) work as legitimate learning tracks, with adequate attention to each. This may require expanding time-on-task for Arabic study, as in the five-year model proposed by Wilmsen. More flexibility in curricula would allow students to select courses that correspond with their learning needs and objectives. The multiple skills issue is central to the fundamentals of Arabic language instruction and to teacher training programs, and requires research by Arabic SLA scholars who, while learning from research in other languages, need to reformulate their assumptions in order to rethink realistic and ambitious curriculum design.[22] Arabic truly is a special case.

Learning Goals and the Arabic Standards

The Arabic learning standards published in 2006 as part of the National Standards in Foreign Language Education Project[23] acknowledge that Arabic teaching "should adopt an integrative approach that allows the learner to develop control of the communication process" (National Standards 2006, 115). They focus on the "five C's"—communication, cultures, connections, comparisons, and communities—and provide both descriptions of specific learning objectives and "learning scenarios" for different grade levels, including college courses. Among the learning goals of these standards are the ability to operate *between* languages as well as within languages; the ability to compare Arabic language and culture with their own; the ability to understand differences in meaning, mentality, and worldview; and the capacity to reflect on oneself. These constructs have been useful especially in designing programs for K-12 teaching of Arabic; however, their application to college-level Arabic curricula has been limited. As far as their use for the future of Arabic course design and content, I agree with Allen, who states that:

> It is ultimately less important whether one embraces or rejects the *Standards* than whether one takes advantage of engaging in a dialogue about what they represent—finding meaningful and coherent ways to teach FL. Considered in this way the *Standards* can be seen as an important document within a professional dialogue that has, since their publication in the mid-1990s, both continued to pursue certain ideals embodied in it and evolved as new directions have emerged in FL-learning pedagogy and research. (2009, 50)

An important factor to note with respect to the standards is that they are sets of goals rather than methodologies, and that when implemented in a particular curriculum, they need to be carefully calibrated with points of vocabulary and grammar keyed to specific levels of study and performance. That is, if the Arabic standards are adopted as part of a departmental or institutional curriculum, that is only the first step. Substantial detailed pedagogical work then needs to be done to activate the potentials of the standards in any program.

Study Abroad: Best Practices

There is no substitute for in-country experience. No matter what the language and culture being studied are, living the quality, intensity, and customs of everyday life in a foreign country is key to understanding the ways in which culture, geography, history, society, and language intertwine. In an era of global engagement and internationalization of education and business, international programs play a key role on many campuses.

All Arabic language majors should have a chance to study in the Arab world at some point in their programs—at least a semester, an academic year if possible. In most cases, Arabic learners cannot be "mainstreamed" or directly enrolled into local university classes because their proficiency levels are usually far below what is required for that level of study. Therefore, Arabic study abroad programs have developed a number of options for Arabic students, ranging from immersion language classes to carefully calibrate exposure to a variety of language levels and functions—both vernacular and academic, gradually building up their proficiency. The study abroad paradigm that has become so popular in American university education has several implications for Arabic programs and their students.

First, the study abroad experience will be infinitely richer, less stressful, and less disappointing for learners if they have already studied the regional colloquial language used at their destination. Many Arabic study abroad programs offer courses in the local vernacular language on site, but students need to hit the ground running in order to make the most of their experience abroad and to accelerate their ability to manage day-to-day situations. Learning the colloquial on site is important, but it should be a higher-level follow-on to having previously been prepared by their Arabic programs in the essentials of the local vernacular.[24]

Second, serious and even extensive predeparture preparation should be undertaken to introduce everyday culture, standards of polite behavior and courtesy, and (especially for young women) how to meet and befriend Arabs. Research has shown that young women in Arabic study abroad programs have far more difficulty meeting and interacting with native Arabic speakers than young men do (Ishmael 2010). Although this is not surprising, little has been published about the need to provide systematic predeparture advice and counsel to female students heading to Arab countries.

Third, because of the potential for culture shock, distraction, and social isolation, ongoing contact should be actively maintained with study abroad students. Mechanisms for regular contact should be coordinated between students' home departments, the study abroad office of the college or university, and the study abroad program they are attending.[25]

Fourth, predeparture planning should also include a specific long-term academic trajectory of study for reintegration during students' senior year. "Senior work, whether or not it involves a thesis, should be mapped out by students and academic advisers before departure, with the overarching goal of maximizing the opportunity for cultural field research through a mainstreamed academic experience (where possible, based on linguistic proficiency) combined with guided independent study (e.g., portfolio work) or internships" (Geisler 2008, 235).

Fifth, debriefing or reentry sessions with returned students are essential both to the home department or program and to the students themselves as a way of reflecting on their learning experiences. For both ongoing and debriefing counseling, asking students to keep journals and/or other documentation of their life abroad helps them reflect objectively about their experiences and to put them into words. The study abroad experience is one in which as much (or more) learning may take place outside the classroom as in it. However, students are rarely expected to explicitly describe or analyze those non-classroom experiences even though they may be transformative or deeply important for the student. "I continue to be amazed by students' inability to articulate what they've learned" states one study abroad official (Kowarski 2010). Research done at Michigan State University found that "many students could not explain their international experiences in a compelling way," and therefore were unable to convince potential employers that those experiences were of value (Kowarski 2010). Providing an opportunity and a framework for feedback on study abroad should be part of any ongoing program. Debriefing is also of value for building up prestudy briefings through development of key points in the study abroad experience as seen from the learners' perspectives.

⬡ Study Questions and Activities

1. Has your experience as a teacher/learner of Arabic been in a training situation, an educational situation, or both? If both, describe the differences you encountered and state the advantages or disadvantages of each approach.
2. Choose a syllabus from one of your courses or a course you have taken, or create a syllabus and make it the subject of a reflective memo (five pages or less). The memo should provide colleagues in your field with a window into the choices and rationale that underlie your syllabus. It should illustrate the thought behind your choices, the ways in which it connects with other courses in your own and other fields, as well as your experience with learner understandings and difficulties. Think about metaphors for your course as it reflects learning progress: for example, a road map, a bridge, a building, a highway, a key, a journey, a race, a landscape, a ship, a labyrinth, a country road, or a soccer game. How does your metaphor(s) illuminate central aspects of your syllabus? (Adapted from Hutchings and Shulman 1994)
3. How would you structure a curriculum that includes both vernacular and standard Arabic? How would you conceive of the goals, time on task, and methodologies? What would be the most salient problems in such a curriculum?
4. What advice would you give to an Arabic student heading for study abroad in an Arab country? What three things do you believe are the most important to know?
5. If you have been a student in a study abroad program or a teacher in one, how does your own experience compare with the topics in this chapter?
6. What suggestions do you have for long-term study abroad projects that can be accomplished by undergraduates and integrated into their senior year curricula? These might include such activities as interviews with native speakers on particular topics, visits to historical and archaeological sites, visits to manuscript collections in libraries and museums, or any number of on-site linguistic, cultural, or literary experiences.

⬡ Further Reading

Association of Departments of Foreign Languages (ADFL). 2008. "Best Practices in Study Abroad: A Primer for Chairs of Departments of Foreign Languages." *ADFL Bulletin* 39, nos. 2 and 3:89–94.

Jackson, Fredrick H., and Margaret E. Malone. 2009. "Building the Foreign Language Capacity We Need: Toward a Comprehensive Strategy for a National Language Framework." Downloaded from www.cal.org/resources/flcapacity.html.

Kuntz, Patricia, and R. Kirk Belnap. 2001. "Beliefs about Learning Held by Teachers and Their Students at Two Arabic Programs Abroad." In *Al-ᶜArabiyya* 34:91–113.

Larson-Freeman, Diane. 1983. "Training Teachers or Educating a Teacher." *Georgetown University Round Table on Languages and Linguistics 1983*, edited by James E. Alatis, H. H. Stern, and Peter Strevens, 264–274. Washington, DC: Georgetown University Press.

Palmer, Jeremy. 2008. "Arabic Diglossia: Student Perceptions of Spoken Arabic after Living in the Arabic-Speaking World." *Arizona Working Papers in SLA and Teaching* 15:81–95.

Ryding, Karin C. 2006. "Teaching Arabic in the United States." In *Handbook for Arabic Language Teaching Professionals in the 21st Century*, edited by Kassem Wahba, Zeinab Taha, and Liz England, 13–20. Mahwah, NJ: Lawrence Erlbaum Associates.

Stevick, Earl W. 1985. "Curriculum Development at the Foreign Service Institute." In *Teaching for Proficiency, the Organizing Principle*, edited by Theodore V. Higgs, 85–112. Lincolnwood IL: National Textbook Company.

Suleiman, Yasir. 1991. "Affective and Personality Factors in Learning Arabic as a Foreign Language: A Case Study." *Al-ᶜArabiyya* 24:83–110. (Especially pp. 106–108 on student reactions to Arabic study abroad.)

Wilmsen, David. 2006. "What Is Communicative Arabic?" In *A Handbook for Arabic Language Teaching Professionals in the 21st Century*, edited by Kassem Wahba, Zeinab Taha, and Liz England, 125–138. Mahwah, NJ: Lawrence Erlbaum Associates.

⬡ Notes

1. See National Standards in Foreign Language Education Project. 2006. *Standards for Foreign Language Learning in the 21st Century*, especially Arabic Standards 111–155.

2. Regarding attempts to create artificial discourse situations using *fuṣḥā*, Mitchell observes: "No reasonable man . . . is anxious to talk like a book, much less like a newspaper or a public orator" (1962, 11).

3. "Advanced language training often seeks to replicate the competence of an educated native speaker, a goal that post-adolescent learners rarely reach" (MLA 2007, 237).

4. Ryding 2013.

5. See the entire final chapter for a description and analysis of curricular change as inquiry.

6. Brown places both grammatical and discourse competence in one category: "organizational competence" (2001, 68).

7. See Cook 2010, 54–81, for an interesting discussion of the use of translation for language learning and also "as an end with its focus on discourse" (74).

8. "The term 'language proficiency' was first established at FSI. For us, it refers to the ability to use language as a tool to get things done" (Jackson and Kaplan 2005, 2).

9. Adapted from Larsen-Freeman 1983.

10. See Ryding and Stowasser 1997 for an example of Arabic area studies integration.

11. "Deep, rather than superficial, learning is presumed to occur when learners have the opportunity to grapple with authentic and complex problems . . . in that they use cognitive tools, multiple sources of information, and other individuals as resources" (Blumenfeld 1992, 277).

12. For more extensive analysis of culture and cultural studies within an Arabic language curriculum see chapter 20 in this book.

13. "The primary task of foreign language departments in this country should be to teach proficiency in the language, along with a critical understanding of important issues in rhetoric and discourse analysis . . . and as broad an understanding of the primary elements of the country's national or ethnic narrative as can be provided in four years and, when applicable, at the graduate level" (Geisler 2006–2007, 63).

14. See Hutchings and Shulman 1994.

15. For an excellent and informative list of language functions calibrated with particular learning activities see Hamilton, Crane, and Bartoshesky 2005, 185–191.

16. Based on an Arabic FAST (Familiarization and Short-Term) course (six-week intensive) developed at the Foreign Service Institute to provide language survival skills for support personnel and others who do not have time for the full year of Arabic training, this text deals with situations that many Americans are likely to encounter living and working in the Arab world. It includes transliteration as well as Arabic script. Plans are afoot to design a second edition that has considerably more Arabic script as well as more general situations (instead of Foreign Service–based ones), and updated references.

17. See chapter 3 in this book on Krashen's distinctions between learning and acquisition.

18. See Ryding 2006.

19. In a more recent commentary, it is stated that "communicative language teaching is often disparaged for focusing too heavily, and too uncritically, on everyday communication at the expense of a sophisticated exploration of the range of authentic second-language registers and discourses" (Levine et al. 2008, 245).

20. Alosh notes: "Reading is the major goal of most Arabic programs, and in no way should [developing the ability to speak Arabic] infringe on this goal" (1997, 134) as cited in Wilmsen 2006, 125.

21. For introductions to critical pedagogy, see Kincheloe 2008 and Darder, Baltodano, and Torres 2009. For a contemporary ethnolinguistic study of "Arabic, self, and identity" see Suleiman 2011.

22. Please note that in identifying the RP model, I am not indicating that it is either right or wrong. It is a pervasive framework that has long been used for TAFL based on traditional literacy goals and outcomes. The main reason I have identified it is to call attention to its features, to contrast it with models of European language training, and to query its usefulness for communicative language teaching.

23. Standards for learning Arabic K-16 in the United States. In *Standards for Foreign Language Learning in the 21st Century,* National Standards in Foreign Language Education Project, 111–155.

24. See Palmer 2008 for an in-depth overview of this issue.

25. The topic of culture shock is an important one for Arabic, and "the problem of culture shock in its specifically Arabic context needs investigation" (Suleiman 1991, 107). Adjustment to a dramatically different daily mode of life in foreign countries can cause disorientation, discouragement, and depression if not attended to early in a curriculum, both before and during a study abroad experience.

Materials, Resources, and Technology

The textbook is as necessary to language teaching as a low gear is to an automobile.

Earl Stevick

Materials form the backbone of any language curriculum, and choosing Arabic textbooks is a key responsibility within program design and development. There now exist several well-researched, well-written, and reliable textbooks for introducing Arabic language and culture, but not very many that serve for advanced training in MSA or in advanced colloquial Arabic.[1] This chapter outlines principles for selecting texts, what texts are available, how to work with textbooks, and also how to work with other important resources such as reference materials, including dictionaries and grammars. It is important to remember, however, that the textbook is not the whole course. The course consists of all the activities undertaken in the classroom, whether student-generated, teacher-generated, task-based, or textbook-based. On the other hand, a good textbook will anchor the course and provide a sequence of activities and information that will help both teacher and learners organize the learning experience across a semester or a year of work. It will also provide a point of reference for learners who want to look up particular items of vocabulary, grammar, or other information. Particularly in situations where multiple sections of one course are concerned, a good textbook can provide a coordinating link between and among classes and provide a foundation for both achievement and assessment.

Selecting a Textbook

One function for textbooks is "their role as a structuring tool" (Crawford 2002, 83). Crawford points out that language classes are social as well as academic events, "and so, inherently unpredictable." She views textbooks as key components in managing classroom "structure and predictability that are necessary to make the event socially tolerable to the participants. It [the textbook] also serves as a useful map or plan of what is intended and expected, thus allowing participants to see where a lesson fits into the wider context of the language program" (ibid.).

Choosing textbooks should ideally be done in consultation with other programs that have used the same materials in order to evaluate their strengths and weaknesses and how their design complements the goals of a particular language program. Every textbook has strengths and weaknesses—no text is perfect. However, professionally published texts have gone through very thorough editing processes and field testing that usually result in high-quality, effective materials for use in the classroom. Most publishers will send examination copies of texts to instructors or program directors who are considering their use in the classroom so that their structure, design, and content can be previewed. Most textbooks come with audio and visual support in the form of DVDs, CDs, or MP3 disks. It is important that all components be viewed and assessed together when deciding on textbook choice, since the video component often complements the written materials in essential rather than peripheral ways, as with *Al-Kitaab*, for example. (See textbook list in appendix F.)

Supplementing Materials

I do not advise preparing and using your own materials to the exclusion of others. Excellent textbooks available today cover the basics of Arabic grammar, vocabulary, and culture in systematic, effective ways, and are developed by professional linguists who specialize in pedagogy. It is rarely useful to ignore published work and spend months or years developing personal materials that cover essentially the same ground from an amateur point of view, even if you perceive gaps in available materials and you believe you have something valuable to offer. On the other hand, it can be very useful to supplement a basic textbook with creative activities and exercises of your own that are based on the learners' need to rehearse, refresh, review, or extend their knowledge in particular areas or on particular topics. These activities or resources may fall into a number of categories: "Materials development refers to anything which is done by writers, teachers or learners to provide sources of language input and to exploit those sources in ways which maximize the likelihood of intake: in other words the supplying of information about and/or experience of the language in ways designed to promote language learning" (Tomlinson 1998b, 2). As mentioned above, no textbook is perfect, and instructors may find that they want to add supplementary exercises to the material provided by the textbook. This is a good and often necessary idea, but I would advise the following principle: Supplement thoughtfully.

A teacher's resource files can be a valuable source of supplementary information, insights, and successful exercises from past classes. A set of personal files coordinated with the sequence of a particular textbook can provide extra materials that teachers have collected and found useful. What would be the bases for adding exercises or activities to what a textbook provides? One researcher states that "for materials to be valuable the learning points should be potentially useful to the learners and that the learning procedures should maximise the likelihood of the learners actually learning what they want and need to learn. It is not necessarily enough that the learners enjoy and value the materials" (Tomlinson 1998b, 3). Added activities should enrich the texture of the materials at hand, develop certain skills further, or fill essential gaps in information. It is seldom useful to elaborate on grammatical theory, but it may be very useful to produce more examples of a particularly important structure or topic. It is a good idea to keep your eye out for suitable illustrations of particular structures or vocabulary use and to keep them on file. It may also be useful to devise further activities to practice vocabulary. Keep in mind, however, that all such activities should be directly relevant to student interests and needs, complementary to the textbook, and as lively as possible.

"Authentic materials" are often advocated as key supplements to textbooks and designed course materials. "The term 'authentic' characterizes materials created by and for native speakers, in contrast to those created for pedagogical purposes" (Garrett 2009, 722). This would obviously cover all texts written by and for Arabic native speakers, ranging in difficulty from low to extreme. It is rare that an authentic text can be presented to beginning or intermediate learners without some modification, but such modification is not usually considered good pedagogy because it distorts the authenticity of the document involved. More acceptable are activities that are adjusted to the learners' levels—such as scanning for bits of information or indications of genre—rather than adjusting

---

A useful procedure for review and skill development is to do rapid oral review (ROR) of materials previously covered. For example, for the first ten minutes of a class, prepare a set of short, vivid exercises (rapid oral translation, transformation of number or gender in short phrases, vocabulary practice) and run the class through them at a good pace. The ROR is like calisthenics: It limbers up the students, reminds them of what they know or don't know, and gets the class in gear.

> One way to use currency from Arab countries for a learning activity is to bring samples of currency to class and hand them around for discussion. Have students make a chart in Arabic of the different countries and their forms of currency. This could be in the form of a list, a map, or a table. This kind of exercise reinforces numbers, counting, noun plurals (e.g., *dīnār/danānīr*), and noun-adjective expressions (*riyālāt saʕūdiyya*). Yes, all this information may be available online. But this is kind of exercise can be done early in a course before learners are ready to search online in Arabic.

the text itself.[2] Working with advance organizers can also help learners penetrate the meaning of authentic texts (see also chapter 12).

Realia

"Realia" is a term that refers to authentic contemporary artifacts of a particular culture, from the most mundane to the most sophisticated. Train tickets, menus, timetables, TV schedules, street signs, and other everyday items can be brought into class to introduce or practice particular language skills. Currency from various Arab countries is an excellent resource. Both coins and paper portray not only Arabic numerals and names of particular items of currency, but also feature national symbols and important public figures.

Calendars are another way of providing abundant input and cultural information. For Arabic learners, the western and Islamic calendars provide many opportunities to compare, contrast, and study the organization of time, holidays, days of the week, months, years, centuries, millennia, cardinal and ordinal numbers, important historical dates, and many similar concepts such as schedules, agendas, and planning. In addition, calling cards or business cards, as well as games such as chess and backgammon, can also provide opportunities not only for building vocabulary and discussing cultural traditions, but also for description, explanation, and instructions.

When to Supplement?

Supplement the textbook:

- When you see that your class is in need of extra practice on particular points of grammar or pragmatics that will help them develop automaticity and depth of understanding (e.g., grammatical support such as practicing the *iḍāfa* construction, noun-adjective agreement, singulars and plurals, or discourse conventions such as introducing themselves, asking for information, or accepting an invitation).
- When you see that there is an immediate need for specific vocabulary sets that will help your students be able to discuss everyday topics (e.g., colors, relationships, sizes, numbers, basic verbs of motion).
- If you see the need to liven up the class by getting away from the textbook and into something related, but different.
- If bringing in particular bits of realia (bus tickets, newspapers, local maps, menus) will help reinforce, reenact, and practice vocabulary, concepts, and situations.

> Menus are useful for the high density of noun phrases in them, as well as chunks of language that often go together: noun-adjective phrases (e.g., *fuṭūr khafīf, bayḍatān maslūqatān, fawākih ṭāzija*), prepositional phrases (*ḥummuṣ bi-taḥīni, qahwa maʕa ḥalīb*), construct phrases (*fākiha l-mawsim, ʕaṣīr burtuqāl*), and common phrases (*maftūḥa yawmiyyan, ḥattā ghurūb al-shams*). Try using a menu as a starting point for vocabulary-building.

Familiarize yourself with several different textbooks and borrow exercises from one to supplement another. You do not have to invent completely new drills or exercises on particular topics. Useful and well-designed supplementary material can often be found in additional Arabic texts. Being able to design activities by pulling from a wide range of available materials considerably enhances your repertoire of classroom resources.

 # Reference Works

Although many native speakers of Arabic have little need for recourse to a dictionary, a good Arabic-English dictionary is an essential and even crucial tool for learners of Arabic as a foreign language. Vocabulary acquisition is the central and probably the most time-consuming learning activity that Arabic learners undertake, and dictionaries are key sources of information about words, form classes, derivational morphology, inflectional morphology (e.g., substantive plurals), usage, and phraseology. The Hans Wehr *Arabic-English Dictionary* is an indispensable tool and the definitive dictionary of its kind for learners and researchers alike.[3] Other reference works include English-Arabic dictionaries, Arabic-Arabic dictionaries and encyclopedias, and Arabic reference grammars, such as Ryding 2005 and Wright 1967.

 # Arabic and Technology

There are at least three ways to think about technology as a key resource for foreign language programs and faculty. Technology can provide highly structured and innovative learning resources, it can provide immediate interaction with the L2 outside the classroom, and it can also provide teachers with access to information that will enhance their effectiveness and professional development. Technology as we know it is an ever-evolving, shifting, and accelerating mode of interaction between humans, computational devices, and various forms of communication. When supporting language education in the classroom, technology can be defined as "a series of electronically-based platforms and tools that support many language learning activities, from the most mechanical drill-and-kill exercises to fully communicative real-time conversations (i.e., *chat*)" (Blake 2008, 15). The difficulties of Arabic script for many years delayed development of massive amounts of new pedagogical materials online. Although that is no longer the case, the development of Arabic computer-assisted language learning (CALL) materials is still catching up.[4] Research materials, media materials, internet access, YouTube, podcasts, text messaging, Twitter, and social networking sites such as Facebook all mean that Arabic learning opportunities are now potentially available any time, anywhere. Building these tech options into progressive and coherent programs of instruction is the challenge for contemporary teachers, authors, and administrators.[5]

Why Use Technology, and When?

Integrating technology into a curriculum means thoughtful reconceptualization of how learners, teachers, and others interact, and to what degree this is helpful for language learning. One aspect that Larsen-Freeman and Anderson point out is that technology "contributes to reshaping our understanding of the nature of language: Language is not a fixed system. Instead it is always changing and being changed by those who use it" (2011, 201). Arabic, like all languages, is being transformed by its use in network-based communication and in social networking. Spoken varieties are being written in an emergent romanized script (Arabizi). Widespread code-mixing is used and to some extent even being incrementally standardized among users; MSA is still used widely, but rarely for immediate interpersonal communication. Eventually these developments may problematize the distinctions between spoken and written Arabic to an even greater extent, or they may actually smooth out and reduce the sometimes sharp differences between spoken and written Arabic.

Many websites advertise Arabic learning tools and programs, but they need to be carefully vetted because websites can make many unsubstantiated claims. Before one decides on any new technological elements for a curriculum or a course, certain issues should be kept in mind. Richards and Renandya cite five questions for consideration when adopting a new technology:

1. Does the new technology facilitate the attainment of course goals?
2. Is it cost effective? Do the benefits outweigh its cost?
3. Are the teachers ready to work with the new technology? Is any training required?
4. Does it serve the needs of the teachers and students?
5. Does it help teachers make more efficient use of class time? (2002, 361)

I would add two more questions: (1) does the technology blend well with your current resources? and (2) does your institution provide adequate tech support structure for your needs?

Blake cites "three important technological platforms that provide tools to assist language learning, in order of increasing interactivity: the web, CD-ROM or hypermedia applications, and network-based communication (i.e., e-mail, electronic mailing list, user groups, MOOs, chat programs, blogs, and wikis)" (2008, 9). Any of these types of platforms may be blended in with traditional materials and resources to enrich the Arabic classroom experience.[6]

Blended Learning

The term "blended learning" refers to the balanced incorporation of technology into learning environments along with more traditional materials. Jackson and Zeoli provide a summary of "best practices" in blended learning. They recommend using technology to:

1. Increase learners' time on task
2. Promote learners' reflection and self-monitoring
3. Provide asynchronous interaction between teacher and learner (rather than a combination of synchronous and asynchronous tools)
4. Provide asynchronous interaction between learners and their peers and other speakers of the language
5. Maximize opportunities for meaningful practice outside of the class
6. Provide focused insight and feedback for, for example, pronunciation or control of other language features
7. Focus on meaningful tasks with authentic materials
8. Provide feedback to learners. (2011, 7)

Distance Learning

Distance learning (DL) has become an increasingly sought-after mechanism for teaching Arabic in situations where classes are not offered but strong student interest exists. Blake defines distance learning as "planned learning that takes place whenever there is a distance between teacher and student in time and/or space" (2009, 824). DL may consist of an online course or of particular CALL interactions that are assigned within a regular course. As Blake points out, videoconferencing is often what comes to mind when one thinks of distance learning, but "asynchronous or online learning also has a long DL pedigree" (2009, 824). Key concerns about building DL features into regular coursework include effectiveness, timeliness and constant updating, and teacher training to make the most of CALL and DL assets.

Discussion Lists

Probably the best and most essential electronic source of information on Arabic language pedagogy and linguistics is the discussion list Arabic-L, administered through Brigham Young University. Subscription to the list can be requested by contacting arabic-l-subscribe-request@listserv.byu.edu. This active list posts announcements, questions, answers, and discussion on just about every contemporary (and noncontemporary) issue in Arabic language study, teaching, research, and other professional topics such as translation and interpretation. It serves teachers, students, professionals, amateurs, writers, researchers, and linguists.

Websites

The website of the National Capital Language Resource Center (NCLRC) is a treasure trove for Arabic teaching resources, especially at the K-12 level (www.nclrc.org). Another rich resource for Middle Eastern languages in general is the website of the National Middle East Language Resource Center, which can be found at www.nmelrc.org. For teaching Arabic phonology and for listening exercises, see the *Aswaat 'Arabiyya* website at www.laits.utexas.edu/aswaat. The Center for Advanced Research on Language Acquisition (CARLA), whose address is www.carla.umn.edu, is a title VI–funded research center at the University of Minnesota providing a wide array of conferences, workshops, resources, summer teacher training programs, and information about less commonly taught languages. The website of the American Association for Teachers of Arabic (AATA) provides a wealth of information about professional conferences, job openings, and Arabic-related topics in general (www.aataweb.org). The website of the National Council of Less Commonly Taught Languages (NCOLCTL) provides information on a wide range of professional activities in LCTLs, including Arabic (www.ncolctl.org). For the Center for Arabic Study Abroad (CASA), see their website at www.utexas.edu/cola/centers/casa/. See also the website of the Arabic Department at the University of Pennsylvania at http://ccat.sas.upenn.edu/arabic/links.htm for a useful list of additional websites about and in Arabic.

CALL resources are slowly building up for Arabic language teaching. Quality control and pedagogical applicability are key issues, however. Sites claiming to teach Arabic or to have systems that teach Arabic must be thoroughly investigated by teachers and curriculum developers before being recommended to students. The *Al-Kitaab* textbook now has extensive online teaching resources in the form of links to internet sites that directly complement and enhance the *Al-Kitaab* series, starting with *Alif Baa*. On the whole, however, Arabic CALL remains underdeveloped. A leading CALL researcher observes: "That CALL is essential to the teaching of LCTLs no one doubts, but we do not as yet have nearly enough funding for comprehensive projects of materials development in an adequate number of LCTLs, especially at the advanced levels and for specific career purposes" (Garrett 2009, 726).

❁ Study Questions and Activities

1. How are Arabic textbooks chosen in your home department? Is there experimentation with new books? If so, how does this take place? Does your department maintain a library of Arabic textbooks and reference works for you to consult?
2. What are some of the limitations of the texts you have used/are using, either as a student or as a teacher? How can these be overcome?
3. Write a two-page report evaluating the effectiveness of a textbook that you are familiar with, analyzing its strengths and weaknesses.
4. How do you find out about new textbooks on the market?
5. Sign up for the Arabic-L discussion list and have a look at the topics currently under discussion.

❁ Further Reading

Bäbler, Adriana. 2006. "Creating Interactive Web-Based Arabic Teaching Material with Authoring Systems." In *Handbook for Arabic Language Teaching Professionals in the 21st Century*, edited by Kassem Wahba, Zeinab Taha, and Liz England, 275–293. Mahwah, NJ: Lawrence Erlbaum Associates.

Blake, Robert J. 2008. *Brave New Digital Classroom: Technology and Foreign Language Learning*. Washington, DC: Georgetown University Press.

_____. 2009. "The Use of Technology for Second Language Distance Learning." In *Technology in the Service of Language Learning: Update on Garrett (1991) Trends and Issues*, edited by Barbara A. Lafford, 822–835. *Modern Language Journal* 93: Focus Issue.

Brown, H. Douglas. 2001. *Teaching by Principles: An Interactive Approach to Language Pedagogy.* 2nd ed. White Plains, NY: Addison Wesley Longman. (Especially chapter 9, "Techniques, textbooks, and technology.")

Garrett, Nina. 2009. "Computer-Assisted Language Learning Trends and Issues Revisited: Integrating Innovation." In *Technology in the Service of Language Learning: Update on Garrett (1991) Trends and Issues*, ed. Barbara A. Lafford, 719–740. *Modern Language Journal* 93: Focus Issue.

Lafford, Barbara A., ed. 2009. *Technology in the Service of Language Learning: Update on Garrett (1991) Trends and Issues. Modern Language Journal* 93: Focus Issue.

Samy, Waheed. 2006. "Instructional Media and Learning Arabic." In *A Handbook for Arabic Language Teaching Professionals in the 21st Century*, edited by Kassem Wahba, Zeinab Taha, and Liz England, 263–273. Mahwa, NJ: Lawrence Erlbaum Associates.

Tomlinson, Brian, ed. 1998. *Materials Development in Language Teaching*. Cambridge: Cambridge University Press. (See especially the glossary and the introduction for technical terms and overview.)

⬡ Notes

1. Although this is changing. See, for example, Lahlali 2008 and 2009, Samy 1999, and Frangieh 2005.

2. "Teachers prefer to adjust the difficulty of the tasks they assign, rather than the difficulty of the materials themselves" (Garrett 2009, 722).

3. For English-Arabic dictionaries and Arabic-Arabic dictionaries for learners, see chapter 18.

4. It has been pointed out that SLA research on less commonly taught languages, and consequently "the development of CALL for such languages, especially those that use a non-Roman script, has lagged far behind" (Garrett 2009, 720).

5. For example, one widely used application of technology to Arabic is the development of the "Arabic Without Walls" first-year Arabic program, coauthored by professors Robert Blake (University of California Davis, University of California Consortium for Language Learning and Teaching) and Kirk Belnap (Brigham Young University, National Middle East Language Learning Resource Center). This is a program designed around both the *Alif Baa* textbook and *Al-Kitaab Part One*.

6. See Larson-Freeman and Anderson's chapter, "Emerging Uses of Technology in Language Learning and Teaching" for a good introduction to principles and techniques for introducing technology into language learning experiences (2011, 199–218).

Assessment and Testing

CHAPTER 8

When we test for competency or elaborate standards for assessing it, we are really doing diagnosis: not measuring a thing or property as much as gauging a potential, scrutinizing behavior for the signs that we agree to accept as evidence that the condition of competency exists. We can never capture the total linguistic knowledge of a student in a test.

Haun Saussy

To maximize learning, quiz early and often.

David Glenn

The field of academic language testing has developed rapidly in the past 25 years, moving from standard grammar-based achievement tests to a range of proficiency assessments that both enable and measure communicative competence.[1] The development of academic testing rubrics and guidelines has been profoundly affected by what is referred to by some as "the proficiency movement"—that is, by measuring specific foreign language skills on a predetermined scale of performance. Inspired by government agency testing procedures—especially those of the Foreign Service Institute (FSI) and the Defense Language Institute (DLI)—the adoption of proficiency testing has had a considerable "washback" effect on academic language teaching, focusing attention on communicative abilities rather than on declarative knowledge of discrete points of grammar, vocabulary, and usage. The site of major impact has been oral L2 proficiency and its development in the classroom.

One key aspect of assessment, which involves the use of "student learning outcomes" and "outcomes assessment," is the use of testing—especially proficiency testing—in providing evidence of effective teaching and curriculum design within a department, a center, an institute, or a school. Especially for universities and schools within state systems, the provision of systematic results or learning outcomes verifies and validates methods, goals, and curriculum management, and provides the accountability that legislators and the voting public often demand. "A well-managed assessment program tells the world precisely what students learn in an FL program," and "the power of having a nationally recognized assessment standard—the ACTFL/FSI scale—cannot be overestimated" (Bernhardt 2006, 589).

The act of testing can be a highly charged one, depending on the stakes involved. Grades are of central importance to university students; promotion or job qualification may be profoundly important to government or business employees. In other words, testers or examiners may be acutely stressed, pressured to give certain grades, and challenged to change grades, in which cases they have to defend their actions. All those who test need to be prepared to discuss in detail and justify their ratings in case they are challenged by concerned stakeholders. The best way to deal with this level of challenge is to have systems and procedures in place for testing that are adhered to faithfully and fairly, including interrater reliability. As teachers and testers, you are the experts, but you should also have detailed plans and procedures for explaining and justifying your judgments in a clear, coherent, and reasonable way.

Some useful preliminary distinctions among testing terms have been provided by Norris. In his 2006 article on student learning outcomes, Norris comments that one "major stumbling block is the lack of terminological precision with which we talk about assessment and related processes" (2006, 578). He makes a "three-way distinction" that is useful in facilitating communication with researchers, teachers, and administrators:

1. **Measurement** is the consistent elicitation of quantifiable indicators of well-defined constructs via tests or related observation procedures; it emphasizes efficiency, objectivity, and technical aspects of construct validity.

2. **Assessment** is the systematic gathering of information about student learning in support of teaching and learning. It may be direct or indirect, objective or subjective, formal or informal, standardized or idiosyncratic, but it should always provide locally useful information on learners and on learning to those individuals responsible for doing something about it.

3. **Evaluation** is the gathering of information about any of the variety of elements that constitute educational programs, for a variety of purposes that primarily include understanding, demonstrating, improving, and judging program value. Evaluation brings evidence to bear on the problems of programs, but the nature of that evidence is not restricted to one particular methodology (Norris 2006, 579).

Formative and Evaluative Assessment

It has long been the case for academic Arabic language programs that periodic testing takes place to measure progress. Regular quizzes are a popular and standard way of helping learners study course materials and show the results. Midterm and final exams are key points in a language curriculum that have substantial impact on students' grades and are therefore what students prepare for in a serious and intensive way. Most of these tests are written. Most of them test reading ability, writing ability, and specific points of vocabulary and grammar.

In the literature on testing a difference is made between formative or progressive assessment and end-of-training or final assessment. Various types of formative or informal assessment can be used to provide learners feedback during a course and to help them gauge their own performance; this is testing to teach. It differs in impact and in structure from evaluative final tests that are given in order to assess or measure performance on a particular scale. The process of quizzing students regularly during a course, for example, is not simply a way to evaluate their performance; it is also a way of enhancing their retention of language. Recent research has led to the hypothesis that learners' mental effort to retrieve information actually deepens their grasp of the tested topic. "Testing not only measures knowledge but changes it" by making it "far more accessible in the future" (Carey 2010).

Formative Assessment as Teaching

Formative testing, that is, testing or quizzing often and regularly during a course and providing feedback, serves at least two purposes: (1) it alerts students to their ability or inability to judge accurately how they are doing (their metacognition), and (2) it provides a systematic review of topics covered in class. Metacognition has been defined as "a person's awareness of his or her own level of knowledge and thought processes. In education it has to do with students' awareness of their actual understanding of a topic" (Stephen Chew, in Lang 2012). Poor students are usually unaware of their inadequate grasp of material, are often overconfident, and are using inferior study habits. Formative testing brings them face to face with reality. "Formative assessments are brief, low-stakes activities that students do in order to give both themselves and the teacher feedback about their level of understanding" (ibid.).

In Arabic language teaching, in particular, low-stakes, preannounced weekly quizzes provide a way of helping learners study and provide useful feedback for review and further preparation. It also helps them learn how to write Arabic clearly and rapidly. It alleviates the pressure on students for midterms and finals because it gives them a solid idea of what they are expected to know and prepares them for higher-stakes test taking. These quizzes may be oral (although oral may take much more time) or written. They may test vocabulary, reading, grammar, writing, or listening skills. As a teacher, it is a good idea to have a set of quizzes prepared for any course, to adapt quizzes as needed, and to retain those from previous courses that were especially successful and helpful.

Administrative Assessment

For correct assignment to particular language levels, placement tests are often given. The most common purpose of these tests is to assess at which level in a language program a student belongs. Sometimes tests are given to determine whether a student places out of a language requirement (i.e., the student performs at a level at or beyond departmental, school, or university requirements). The format and conduct of such tests is determined by institutional administrative requirements and individual departments. Some language departments have to give many placement tests within a few days at the beginning of the academic year; this is a key administrative task that demands experience, time, and astute judgment. Initial placement tests are particularly important in Arabic because there is no advanced placement (AP) exam available for high school Arabic students, and because Arabic heritage learners present specific challenges for placement in university programs.[2]

Achievement Testing and Proficiency Testing

Achievement testing is done to measure how well a student has mastered the knowledge and skills covered in a particular sequence of instruction; it can test both declarative and procedural knowledge. Proficiency testing is done to assess where a student is located on a spectrum of possible levels of performance; it tests procedural knowledge only. Thus, anyone who knows a foreign language even slightly can take a proficiency test to assess where his or her skills lie along a particular spectrum, whereas an achievement test is given to measure mastery of knowledge taught within a specific context. Sometimes college-level programs measure learning outcomes by a combination of both achievement and proficiency testing.[3]

Achievement Testing and Scoring

For academic purposes achievement testing is valuable because it gives feedback on how well learners are grasping the essentials and details of a particular subject matter (including grammar and lexicon), and also because tests can be scored. Scoring tests renders them valuable and important to learners because of the ultimate impact on student grades, and because it shows where they rank in respect to their past performance and to other learners. These factors may not be particularly ideal impacts of scoring, but they are highly pragmatic ones. I endorse a few test-scoring procedures:

1. Do not always count quiz grades toward the final grade—give some leeway and let students know
2. Do announce when a test or quiz will impact a learner's grade
3. Be prepared to explain how and how much a test will impact a final grade (students will ask)
4. Grade on a number system (for example, 1–100), not a letter system. It is far easier to calculate numerical grades at the end of a course than a set of letters; also, letter scores may mean different things to different learners. Numbers have both a greater impact and provide a more fine-grained assessment. For a final letter grade you can design a system

of equivalence between numbers and letter-grade ranges, or your school may already
have a system in place

5. When you are in the process of designing a test or a quiz, include a calculation of how it
will be scored overall (e.g., part A, 20%, part B, 50% and part C, 30%). This will facilitate
final grading

 # Writing Arabic in Tests

With beginning students, insist on inclusion of short vowels when they write Arabic in exams.
If students are not highly motivated to learn Arabic word orthography, they most often will not,
especially when they see unvoweled words in most of their Arabic texts. If you want students to
master correct Arabic pronunciation, however, you need to specify that when being tested, they
must write in fully voweled Arabic script. Deduct points (or fractions of points) from their grades
if they err in the use of word-internal short vowels (ḥarakāt), just as you would deduct points for
errors in using consonants. The fact that short vowels are invisible in normal Arabic script does not
mean that beginning or intermediate learners may omit them when being tested. Full word spelling
(including short vowels) is not reinforced through reading Arabic, so learners do not receive regular or consistent detailed input for spelling. In a test, they need to demonstrate thorough control of
Arabic phonology and orthography. This requirement may appear didactic and demanding, but for
learners of Arabic as a foreign language, it is key to developing an ear and an eye for the structure
of Arabic words. If you are consistent about requiring complete orthography, students will adopt
the practices of learning word pronunciation and spelling accurately. At more advanced levels they
may be allowed to omit word-internal vowels in writing.

 # New Models for Assessment

Alongside movements that stress authentic interaction in the language classroom, newer models
of assessment focus not only on achievement but also on the cognitive, skill-based, and affective processes involved in language learning. As Liskin-Gasparro notes, these "have been called
'authentic assessment,' 'alternative assessment,' and sometimes 'performance assessment' . . .
[and] are designed to include observation and evaluation of the thinking process students use in
arriving at a response or a demonstration of knowledge and skills. Information about the processes that students use to complete tasks is valued as highly as the products the students create"
(Liskin-Gasparro 1996, 170). Among the assessment types that fall into this category are proficiency testing and learner portfolios (including learning logs and journals).

 # Proficiency Testing

Proficiency testing—especially oral proficiency testing—is a highly calibrated, explicit, and reliable procedure for assessing a learner's skill level along a particular spectrum, measured either
numerically (0–5 in the ILR system) or in terms of labels such as "novice," "intermediate," or
"advanced," used in the ACTFL proficiency guidelines. These two systems measure performance
in closely related ways and are very similar, except that the ACTFL system allows for more fine-
grained skill level grading at the lower proficiency levels.

The ILR Scale

The ILR skill-level descriptions were developed because of the US government's need to assess actual foreign language capabilities in diplomatic, military, security, intelligence and other
government personnel in order to appoint them to particular overseas duties. In the 1950s it was
determined that relying on self-assessments (e.g., "fluent German" or "excellent Italian") or relying

on transcripts documenting academic language study were not adequately informative with regard to individuals' true competence in foreign language situations. "The [Civil Service] Commission concluded that the United States government needed a system that was objective, applicable to all languages and all Civil Service positions, and unrelated to any particular language curriculum" (Hertzog 2011). During the 1950s and 1960s linguists at the Foreign Service Institute (FSI) undertook continuous refinement of test factors, scoring procedures, scales, and tester training, resulting in the original structured oral interview format and the application of standardized rating factors. In the late 1960s, the Peace Corps "had become aware of the work of . . . FSI in the area of proficiency training. At the request of the Peace Corps, FSI agreed to test both trainees and volunteers at the beginning, at midpoint, and at the end of their training" (Thompson 1989, 228). This testing was subsequently delegated to the Educational Testing Service (ETS) after training by FSI, and "ETS undertook the first large-scale interview testing activity outside the U.S. government" (Thompson 1989, 229).

By 1985 the proficiency testing system had spread to other agencies besides the State Department "under the auspices of the Interagency Language Roundtable (ILR)" (Hertzog 2011), and is now known as the ILR scale or ILR skill definitions. Although originally designed for testing speaking and reading, the skill-level descriptions now cover writing, listening, translation performance, and interpretation performance. Newer additions to the skill-level descriptions include competence in intercultural communication and competence in "audio translation performance" ("the process of rendering live or recorded speech in the source language to a written text in the target language") (www.govtilr.org).

A typical language proficiency exam administered by a government agency involves two testers, one a native-speaker "tester" who interacts directly with the test-taker, and the other a certified "examiner" (native speaker or nonnative speaker), who supervises the exam, guides the tester, and takes notes on test-taker performance. In most cases in an oral exam, both tester and examiner are listening for particular co-occurring components of competence, such as comprehension, fluency, structural accuracy, discourse pragmatics, and range of lexicon. Scores on these elements are then entered on a rating scale and averaged to obtain a numerical score that is then converted into a 0–5 rating. It is important to note that the ILR skill-level descriptions are generic; they are not adapted to or revised according to language. This allows the system to verify that a "3" in Arabic, for example, is at the same performance level as a "3" in French.

The ILR scales for speaking and reading Without going into great detail, it may be useful to provide a summary of short skill-level descriptions used in the ILR scale to give a sense of how they are applied and what they indicate in terms of proficiency:

0	no proficiency
0+	memorized proficiency
1	elementary proficiency
1+	elementary proficiency, plus
2	limited working proficiency
2+	limited working proficiency, plus
3	general professional proficiency
3+	general professional proficiency, plus
4	advanced professional proficiency
4+	advanced professional proficiency, plus
5	functionally native proficiency

Thus there are six "base level" descriptions and five "plus" levels. The "plus" ratings on the scale indicate that the base level has been met and exceeded, but proficiency does not fully meet the requirements of the next base level. For example, an examinee may perform well above the "2" level in terms of extent of vocabulary, but this single factor is not enough to raise the score to a "3." Therefore the score may be given as "2+". Complete skill level descriptions for all modalities are available at the ILR website, www.govilr.org/skills/.

Factor analysis: Adams 1980 In an extensive study done in 1980 by the FSI testing unit, the five rating factors (at that time: accent, comprehension, fluency, grammar, and vocabulary) were compared for their power to "discriminate between contiguous S-ratings" (Adams 1980, 3).[4] That is, the study examined which factors most crucially affected scores at the various skill levels. Adams provides the following summary:

> The most consistent difference between S-0+ and S-1 is vocabulary. A person rated S-1 usually has more words at his/her disposal than a person rated S-0+. A person rated S-1+ is usually more fluent than a person rated S-1 but also exceeds in comprehension, grammar and vocabulary. A person rated S-2 comprehends better than a person rated S-1+, but also exceeds in grammar, accent and fluency. A person rated S-2+ exceeds a person rated S-2 primarily in fluency but also in comprehension, accent and vocabulary. *The major difference between a person rated S-3 and a person rated S-2+ is emphatically grammar.* Grammar at the 2+ to 3 interval is the best discriminator in the table [table provided in original]. Accent, vocabulary and comprehension also discriminate between these two levels. A person rated S-3+ is distinguished from a person rated S-3 primarily in comprehension but also in fluency and grammar. A person rated S-4 has a broader range of vocabulary than a person rated S-3+ but also has a better accent and better control of grammar. Nothing statistically significant distinguishes an S-4 from an S-4+. (1980, 3; emphasis added)[5]

This thumbnail sketch is over 30 years old but is still valuable and largely valid. In addition to this analysis, Adams concludes with an overview of skill level performances in oral interviews and depicts concise "models of average performance at each level," described here:

> An S-1 performance typically consists of words, understandable but badly pronounced, in an incomplete phrase environment; responses may be or may not be related to the questions asked. An S-1+ performance comes a little closer to conversation because there are enough words but communication falls short on the other factors. An S-2 performance is an actual conversation. It consists of appropriate sentences in response to linguistic stimuli at a rate comfortable for both participants in the conversation. Conversation is limited by lack of grammatical control and lack of words. An S-2+ is typically fluent but limited in linguistic structure. An S-3 performance is first of all grammatically accurate. At the S-3 level the individual controls the major features of the language and has the vocabulary necessary for general conversation and special interests. An S-3+ performance is typically close to bilingual with respect to comprehension and fluency but far from bilingual with respect to vocabulary, grammar, and accent. At the S-4 level persons demonstrate a broad range of precisely used words, not, of course, in a memorized speech but in unprepared dialogue. The S-4 is near-native in pronunciation and controls grammar almost down to the finest detail. (Adams 1980, 4)

Since the 1980s there has been substantial technical elaboration of scoring factors, procedures, and the skill-level descriptions, but Adams's pithy summary is still basically sound and useful as a starting point for thinking about Arabic speaking proficiency and how it is scored.

The ACTFL Proficiency Guidelines

The generic ACTFL language proficiency guidelines were inspired by the success and wide applicability of ILR standardized language testing, but were designed for measuring skill levels in academic contexts. Specifically, they were a response to "the need to evaluate language use, as opposed to knowledge of discrete surface linguistic features" (Savignon 1985, 129). The ACTFL materials were originally drafted and published in the early 1980s; Arabic-specific guidelines were originally drafted in 1985 and published in 1989 (see ACTFL 1989; Allen 1985, 1987; Alosh 1987; Stansfield and Harman 1987).[6] Recently, in 2012, revised ACTFL guidelines have been published online along with updated Arabic-specific "annotations and samples" for testing in Arabic (see http://actflproficiencyguidelines2012.org/arabic/).

ACTFL provides training and certification to proficiency testers in various languages. To take and pass the training course involves a substantial time commitment, but it is an important professional asset and ability. To see workshop and training offerings, consult the ACTFL professional training website at www.actfltraining.org. The basic ACTFL skill levels are:

Novice
   Low
   Mid
   High
Intermediate
   Low
   Mid
   High
Advanced
   Low
   Mid
   High
Superior
Distinguished

There are five base levels, but these skill levels are substantially more differentiated at the lower end of the proficiency spectrum than those in the ILR scale. This elaboration at the lower levels is designed to accommodate and accurately rate the wide range of proficiencies possible in the first years of foreign language learning in different academic environments. A rough equivalence between the ILR and ACTFL scales is as follows:

Novice = 0 to 0+
Intermediate = 1 to 1+
Advanced = 2 to 2+
Superior = 3 to 3+
Distinguished = 4 to 5[7]

A new, free online tutorial for Arabic students, available from the Center for Applied Linguistics (CAL), helps them understand and improve their performance on oral proficiency interviews (OPIs). See CAL's informative website at www.cal.org/aop/index.php.

S-3 Arabic Features: A Preliminary Model

In 1980, Arabic linguist Dr. Margaret Nydell, then director of the FSI Arabic Field School in Tunis, compiled an informal set of Arabic "grammatical features which should be mastered at each level of [spoken] proficiency" (I). At a later date, I compiled a collocation of grammatical features to be controlled at the S-3 level, based on Nydell's original list and her own testing and training experience. Although the list is by no means definitive, it provides a basic idea of the level of structural control necessary at the S-3 level in Arabic. Nydell's list is based on features of "Colloquial Eastern Arabic;" mine is geared more toward educated spoken Arabic. A combined version of this list is presented here as an example of one way to conceptualize the assessment of Arabic structural accuracy in oral proficiency interviews (OPIs).

- Morphological features:
  1. Nouns:
     number: singular, dual, plural forms, especially sound and broken plurals
     use of verbal noun and its derivation from the base verb
     nouns of place

continued

2. Adjectives:
   gender agreement structures
   number: singular, dual, plural
   comparative and superlative forms
   ān adjectives (*kaslān, taʕbān, kharbān*) and their inflections
3. Verbs:
   all persons and numbers (first, second, third; singular, dual, plural)
   tenses: past, present, future
   forms I-X
   regular and irregular morphology (e.g., hollow, defective, doubled roots)
   voice: passive and active
   mood: imperative, indicative, subjunctive
4. Pronouns:
   independent (subject pronouns)
   dependent (possessive and objective)
   indirect object pronoun (-*iyyāh*)
   demonstrative
   relative
5. Participles: active and passive
6. Numbers: cardinal and ordinal forms in context
- Syntactic features
   1. Noun-adjective phrases: agreement features, especially human and nonhuman
   2. *iđāfa;* genitive construct
      no definite article on first term
      pronounce *tāʔ marbūta* on first term if it is there
      use of *kull* and other quantifiers
   3. Prepositional phrases: correct uses of prepositions, especially *ʕind, and maʕ* as possessives
   4. Use of comparative and superlative adjectives with nouns
   5. Generic use of definite article
   6. Negation of equational sentences, adjectives of verb phrases
   7. Verbs:
      agreement of subject and verb
      use of compound tenses (e.g., habitual and progressive)
      verb-preposition idioms
      active participle as verb replacement
   8. Verb strings: use of modals + verbs (e.g., *lāzim, mumkin*)
   9. Compound/complex sentences:
      embedding: definite and indefinite relative clauses; resumptive pronoun
      subordinate clauses (e.g., *inna* and her "sisters")
      coordinate clauses (e.g., *wa-, fa-*, etc.)
      interrogative sentences
      conditional sentences

Interactive Testing: Learner Portfolios

One of the most creative and substantive developments in new foreign language assessment models has been the development of frameworks for the use of learner portfolios in both "milestone" and "culminating" tests (e.g., formative and final/summative assessments, respectively). Portfolio assessment has been described as "the systematic, longitudinal collection of student work created in response to specific, known instructional objectives and evaluated in relation to the same criteria" (NCLRC n.d., 3). This work can be in the form of a scrapbook, folder, website, or a multimedia presentation, or may include other forms of expression that are able to portray the learners' best work, their ideas, their self-assessments, and their reflections on their work.

As a stand-alone project or as a component of a final evaluation, a learner portfolio can document language proficiency and language use in ways that many students are likely to appreciate and to excel at. The components of a portfolio, called "portfolio artifacts," may be "creative or analytical, written or oral, visual or manipulable" (Liskin-Gasparro 1996, 177). Compiling Arabic language journals, diaries, pictures, artwork, realia, videos, social media interactions, and other language-related documentation, and integrating them into a complex learning narrative, can be a valuable learning exercise as well as an assessment tool, "involving students in actively reflecting on their learning" (Guard, Richter, and Waller 2003, 1). "Portfolios often have a reflective component, in which students write about each piece they select, explaining the reason for its inclusion in the portfolio, the circumstances surrounding its creation, and any changes in perceptions about the piece that the author may have experienced over time" (Liskin-Gasparro 1996, 176–177).

A successful portfolio project involves consultation with the teacher as well as independent choice of materials; it may also involve discussions with other learners or native speakers, or be a more private expression of a learner's intellectual and aesthetic judgments, performance, decisions, reflections, and selections. In this respect it is the kind of project that allows learner autonomy as well as one that may incorporate a great deal of interactive work.

Nationally Administered Standardized Examinations

There are, as of 2013, no nationally administered achievement tests to measure Arabic student performance on a large scale, nor are there advanced placement (AP) tests to assess secondary school students' ability in Arabic for accurate placement into university-level curricula. Researchers note that:

> Although the field of Arabic language teaching and learning is expanding greatly, there are still not many students available, especially at higher levels of proficiency, to norm or calibrate such exams, even if the norming takes place across several institutions. In addition, most Arabic programs are relatively small and teaching-focused; therefore, the programs often do not have enough resources available to develop their own in-house standardized tests. These concerns, along with the diglossic nature of Arabic, make developing standardized tests of Arabic particularly challenging. (Winke and Aquil 2006, 221)

The nearest equivalent to a nationally administered examination for Arabic continues to be the qualifying exam for the Center for Arabic Study Abroad (CASA) program, taken by advanced Arabic undergraduate or graduate students to earn fellowships for the prestigious CASA year of study abroad. For sample test questions see the CASA website at www.utexas.edu/cola/centers/casa/.

Professional Development and Certification

In addition to the training offered by government institutions for proficiency testing in the ILR framework and by ACTFL in an academic framework, there are international professional organizations and meetings dedicated to language testing, including the International Language Testing

Association (ILTA) (www.iltaonline.com) and the East Coast Organization of Language Testers (ECOLT) (www.cal.org/ecolt/index.html).[8]

 ## Study Questions

1. As a student or as a teacher, are you more comfortable with proficiency testing or achievement testing? What are the pros and cons of each, in your opinion?
2. For oral proficiency testing in Arabic, what do you believe are the most important factors in scoring?
3. For oral proficiency testing in Arabic, what are two of the most powerful complicating factors in judging performance?
4. Do you administer regular quizzes to your students? If so, what are the reasons and results of that quizzing?
5. Have you ever—as a student or teacher—compiled a portfolio of your skills? If so, what were the key elements in that experience? If you were to compile a portfolio again, would you do it differently or use the same process? If you have no experience with portfolios, would you be interested in finding out more?
6. In the Nydell-Ryding list of grammatical features required at the S-3 level, do you see all the elements that you would consider necessary? If not, what can you add or subtract?

 ## Further Reading

Alosh, Mahdi. 1987. "Testing Arabic as a Foreign Language." *Al-ʿArabiyya* 20, nos. 1 and 2:51–72. (An excellent overview of concepts, definitions, and procedures.)

Hadley, Alice Omaggio. 2001. *Teaching Language in Context*, 3rd edition. Boston: Heinle & Heinle. (Especially chapter 9, "Classroom Testing.")

Liskin-Gasparro, Judith. 1996. "Assessment: From Content Standards to Student Performance." In *National Standards, a Catalyst for Reform*, edited by R. C. Lafayette, 169–196. Lincolnwood, IL: National Textbook Company.

Malone, Margaret. 2010. "What Does It Take to Be Accepted as a Professional in the Language Testing Field?" http://nclrc.org/teaching_materials/assessment/testing_tips.html.

National Capital Language Resource Center (NCLRC). n.d. *Portfolio Assessment in the Foreign Language Classroom*. Washington, DC: National Capital Language Resource Center.

Norris, John M. 2006. "The Why (and How) of Assessing Student Learning Outcomes in College Foreign Language Programs." *Modern Language Journal* 90, no. 4:576–583.

Rammuny, Raji M. 1986. "A Model of Proficiency-Based Oral Achievement Testing for Elementary Arabic." *Foreign Language Annals* 19, no. 4:321–331. (Describes implementation of proficiency-based goals and oral proficiency-based testing at the University of Michigan.)

Shohamy, Elana. 2011. "Assessing Multilingual Competencies: Adopting Construct Valid Assessment Policies." *Modern Language Journal* 95, no. 3:418–429. (Points out some of the complexities involved in testing multilingual speakers or speakers who code-switch.)

Thompson, Richard. 1989. "Oral Proficiency in the Less Commonly Taught Languages: What Do We Know about It?" In *Georgetown University Round Table on Languages and Linguistics 1989*, edited by James E. Alatis, 228–234. Washington, DC: Georgetown University Press.

 ## Notes

1. For an overview of language testing research in the United States, see Spolsky 2000.
2. See chapter 11 in this book on mixed classes and heritage learners.
3. For more on language learning outcomes and definitions of assessment, measurement, and evaluation, see Norris 2006.

4. The research was based on a total of 834 oral interview tests in a wide range of languages (Adams 1980, 6).

5. "There was only one case of an S-5 in the entire sample and therefore analysis at that level could not be attempted" (Adams 1980, 3).

6. See also Thompson 1989, 230–232, on the relationship of ACTFL generic guidelines and the evolution of specific guidelines for less commonly taught languages.

7. See Hadley 2001, 12–19, on these equivalences, going up to the "superior" level. The level of "distinguished" performance was added to the scale at a later date.

8. See Malone 2009 for more details on these organizations.

Part IV

Planning and Managing the Elements of Teaching

Pedagogical Practice: Classroom Management

CHAPTER 9

Few outside the profession understand the courage it takes to step into a classroom.

Jay Parini

Generally speaking, both professors and students underestimate the need for practice.

Ambrose et al.

Learning to teach is learning to take risks. Although the teacher is ultimately managing the learning situation, she is also subject to the judgment of her students, their approval or disapproval, their respect or disrespect, their appreciation or disdain. Language teachers in particular find themselves faced with the challenging prospect of changing their students' behaviors, of teaching them sustained performance, and of bringing those students to levels of deliberate engagement with and in the target language and culture. Fortunately, most students are curious, tolerant, kind, generous, and enthusiastic about learning Arabic. They do, however, have high expectations of themselves and of their teachers. They will test you, just as you will test them. Just as you intend to teach skills and content to your students, you will also teach them by example. Students learn more from you than just language. That is why you must identify and draw upon elements of your own character and disposition in order to energize your teaching and to develop your own particular "voice," or persona, in the classroom. That voice should not be fake, although for classroom purposes it may seem artificial at first. Nonetheless, it will be a product of your own person, background, experiences, and influences.

✿ The Good Language Teacher

Here are some characteristics of good language teachers that students have reported:

The Good Language Teacher:

1. is explicit and encouraging about expectations;
2. gives students a sense of where the class is going and how they will progress;
3. provides a clear, informative syllabus;
4. sets realistic, appropriate goals and high standards;
5. establishes order and organization in the classroom;
6. is able to explain key concepts;
7. has in-depth knowledge of the subject;
8. is fully prepared for every class;
9. is professional and ethical in skills and conduct;
10. is a good listener;
11. maintains consistent positive regard and respect for students as individuals.

Taken together, these features constitute a nucleus of skills and attitudes that work in the Arabic classroom. This chapter presents several important classroom-based strategies and behaviors that facilitate good performance on the part of both teacher and student.

Teacher Language Awareness

Professional Arabic instructors, teachers, and professors are expected to develop and maintain **teacher language awareness (TLA).** This term refers to "the knowledge that teachers have of the underlying systems of the language that enables them to teach effectively" (Andrews 2007, ix). In particular, this concept refers to the explicit control of L2 grammar that teachers possess and use in the classroom, their "pedagogical content knowledge" (29). Note that "the language knowledge/awareness required by the teacher of a language is qualitatively different from that of the educated user of that language" (28). Teachers need the ability to provide explicit L2 information to their students and the ability to reflect about how to best manage the learning situation. Being an educated native speaker of a language is not on its own a sufficient qualification for teaching it.

For Arabic language teaching to speakers of western languages, TLA equates with an ability to provide level-appropriate instruction, to analyze learning difficulties, to generate key examples, to answer questions on pronunciation and grammar, to provide deliberate and extensive practice on key elements of Arabic, and to effectively explain particular points of language structure when they arise. TLA requires both declarative knowledge of linguistic structure and the procedural ability to apply this knowledge in the learning situation.

Dominance, Control, and Initiative

In my own training and teaching experience, I was fortunate to be made explicitly aware of the differences between dominance and control early in my career, and as a teacher trainer, I have found that explanation and illustration of the contrast between teacher dominance and teacher control in the classroom can be a significant help to new teachers.[1] In educational psychology, this issue is referred to as the stance or "autonomy orientation" of the teacher: whether she is "autonomy-supporting or controlling" (Ames 1992, 265). In other words, autonomy orientation refers to whether the teacher encourages learner autonomy and decision making or discourages it.[2] What is the psychological stance of the teacher and her relationship to learners? Does the teacher seek to keep students dependent on her (by constantly correcting them or slowing their progress), or does she seek to develop true L2 autonomy on their part? This is a key psychological factor in the development of pedagogical professionalism, metacognition, and self-awareness of teachers. Distinctions between leading and dominating, and between correcting and discouraging—for example—are of central importance in the classroom. A helpful distinction that has been used in methodology classes is to talk about the differences between dominance and control and the role of initiative. Dominance, or eminence, is where the teacher is at the center of all classroom activity. There is rarely interaction among the learners, and the teacher determines who will speak, when, and to whom.

Control, on the other hand, is the teacher's ability to orchestrate an effective learning situation in all its detail: to determine and plan learning goals, encourage interaction, monitor correctness, and give accurate diagnostic feedback. It includes efficient structuring of time, pacing, setting general tasks for students, and overall assiduous management of the learning situation.[3] Control does not need to result in dominance; in fact, a well-controlled class will be filled with learner activity and interaction. Sometimes this form of control is referred to as "authority." A teacher is an authority on her subject; she is also expected to exercise authority to establish an appropriate learning climate in the classroom.[4] Stevick deals with the concept of control in his book, *A Way and Ways* where he describes the difference between control and initiative (1980, 17–23). Control is something that you must understand, possess, and use wisely. Students may become anxious if some aspects of learning are left up to them (especially if they perceive that this is because you have run out of ideas). It is therefore essential that you exercise control in establishing and maintaining structure for all classroom activity. This kind of leadership creates a powerful learning framework in which you can then encourage initiative by the students, "the choice of who is going to say what to whom and when" (Stevick 1980, 19).[5]

 ## Classroom Management

Classroom management is an area of practical engagement between teachers and learners. In American classrooms learners have certain sociocultural expectations of teachers, and teachers of learners; much of the groundwork of any course is put in place during the first few days of class, so these are important for setting the tone for the rest of the semester or year. Knowing what these expectations are is essential, especially for instructors not educated in the American system or who are new to teaching in the United States.

Lesson Planning

Lesson planning refers to the day-by-day structuring of class time and activities. Lesson plans will help teachers—especially pre-service teachers, but also in-service teachers—map out the activities of particular class sessions and also to get used to the timing of certain activities. Lesson plans can be flexible, but like knowing one's part in a play, they can provide a scripted sequence of useful activities. Lesson planning is done to help teachers "feel more confident, to learn the subject matter better, to enable lessons to run more smoothly, and to anticipate problems before they happen" (Farrell 2002, 31).

Three factors are essential to Arabic language lesson planning:

1. Pacing: Pacing refers to the tempo of activities, which can be related to musical tempo. A symphony does not consist of a set of movements that are all at exactly the same tempo or speed. In fact, change in tempo is an important requirement for aesthetic balance and interest. Movements may be labeled, for example, as andante, allegro, largo, adagio, moderato, or vivace, according to the tempo, or speed, of the beat intended by the composer. In very much the same way, a language class needs to have a change in pace every so often in order to balance activity type and to retain student attention. As a teacher, you need to plan out this change of pace in advance for every class so that different tempos of activity are included.

2. Variation in activity type: Variation here refers to changes in the type or intensity of learning activities. As a general rule, learners will start to lose attention after about 15 minutes (or even less) on any one type of classroom work. If you have a 50-minute class period, then it needs to be divided up into at least three or four different kinds of activity segments varying as to intensity, modality (speaking, reading, writing, listening), interactiveness, and other factors.

3. Transitions: Smooth transitioning from one activity to another is a key professional skill. Being fully prepared with a handful of different activities and a sense of how the class session as a whole is to be calibrated will prepare you to make clear and logical shifts from one activity to another. Transitions should feel natural and logical, not abrupt and jarring; therefore, to maximize learning, transitions should be coherent and well-thought-out. They should fit smoothly into the course context. It is also important to inform students about switching from one activity to another. If change occurs too abruptly, students will

In a recent article on improving teaching, Whitney made the following observation:

During one of the sessions, a panelist, very new to the professoriate herself, mentioned that immediately after each class, before she does anything else or even touches her computer, she takes a large 5″ x 8″ sticky note and writes down what did or didn't work well in that class period. She sticks that to her papers from the class and then uses that note the next time she teaches the course to improve her teaching. This relatively simple tip has been a lifesaver to me. It's incredibly easy to forget such matters in the moments after leaving the classroom, but using the post-it note centers me enough to do some productive reflection, even if it is just for a fleeting moment. It also results in handy records that I can refer to the next time I teach the course. The result is better teaching and a mindset focused on continuous improvement. (2011)

Do you do something similar to this to remind yourself of successes, problems, or ideas for improvement?

be confused and anxious about what to do, but if it is announced briefly and distinctly, then students will relax and keep up. Your announcement does not have to be a complicated justification for change. It can be as simple as "well, now it's time to try something a little more lively," or "since you've been working so hard, sit back and let me tell you a story," or even, "and now, for something completely different."

As a general rule, it is wise to always have an extra learning activity prepared just in case you see that the class is dragging, or in case you have extra time. Sometimes it is important to be able to improvise, but even improvisation needs some previous thought, attention, and experience. **Be prepared**.

The First Days of Class

During the first few days of any Arabic class it is important for you to establish clear ground rules and guidelines for the rest of the semester. This is the most crucial time for organization of space, timing, assignments, and assessments because most students make judgments quickly about your competence and control. If you are a new teacher, take a few minutes to introduce yourself and establish your credentials and your expertise by talking about your professional background and relevant experience. This should not take long, but students like to know who their teachers are and be reassured that they will be in good, competent hands. Show that you are well organized by setting course parameters, goals, and expectations, and discussing the course content and syllabus. Also establish the rules of the road (in writing—you will be glad you did): be specific about comportment, attendance, class preparation, and timeliness of homework; establish rules about tardiness and missing preannounced tests. Let students know how their grades will be calculated, including factors such as class participation and homework assignments, as well as quizzes and tests. If students know that consistent tardiness or absences will affect their final grade, they are more likely to make efforts to be on time.

Classroom Shock

Classroom shock is akin to culture shock, but it refers explicitly to the disconnect between a teacher from one culture who is working with learners from another. The classroom is a culturally defined area of behavior where both teacher and learners have tacit expectations about each other's conduct. Richard Lutz, in his article "Classroom Shock: The Role of Expectations in an

Instructional Setting," describes the disconnect between him and a classroom of Japanese students who he later realized were "frantically trying to figure me out" (1990, 145). "Because the class is self-contained and under the direction of one individual there is the perception that everything is under control," he adds (152), but the ground rules of the host culture (for an Arab teacher in American culture, for example), cannot be ignored because they create the context for classroom instruction and strong expectations on the part of students. "There was constant strain to make the necessary adaptation, confusion in role and role expectations, surprise (on my part) upon learning of these problems, and a decided feeling of not being in control by both teacher and students" concludes Lutz (ibid.).

For Arabic teachers who may be new to American culture, it is worth examining expectations that may arise in US classrooms. Many of these expectations are similar to those in an Arab context, but some differ. The first expectation is that the teacher is qualified and knows not only the material, but how to teach. The second is that the teacher has a plan—for the semester, the week, the day—and that she will communicate this clearly. The third is that learning will take place in an organized manner. Fourth, students expect that regular and fair feedback will be given in the form of corrected homework, quizzes, and exams. Fifth, there is the expectation that there will be mutual respect between students and teacher.

Structuring Physical Space: Circles

Structuring the physical space is one of the most important and yet logistically challenging issues for language teachers, and "preparing a learning space requires at least as much competence as preparing a good lecture" (Palmer 1998, 133). Ideally, students sit in a circle, a semicircle, or in small groups for certain exercises.[6] This means that the classroom should have flexible seating and that you should direct the students on how to organize themselves.[7] With larger classes, sitting in two concentric semicircles often works. Sitting in a circle or semicircle means that everyone can see and make eye contact with everyone else. This is the first step in developing a sense of community in the classroom, and a crucial criterion for learning. Without clear control from you about classroom seating arrangements, students may drift into seats that distance them from you and/or from others, sit only with their friends, or hide out in the back row. Getting eye contact and initiating a sense of community among the class members is a major step in bringing them into an interactive relationship with each other and developing easy rapport. You may choose to sit with the students in a circle, may walk around outside the circle, or—with a semicircle—be at the front of the room or move about.

Research done by Little and Sanders reported on an ethnographic investigation of two foreign language classes. The research project resulted in the conclusion that "true communicative language learning requires something far more significant than a shift in classroom management techniques. In fact, communication does not actually take place in the classroom *unless the language learners are a community*" (1989, 277; emphasis added). The seating arrangement is a nontrivial component of your resources for establishing and stimulating a discourse community in the classroom.

Classroom Talk and Comprehensible Input

Although using the target language—in this case, Arabic—in the classroom might appear to be a noncontroversial feature of communicative language teaching, nonetheless, it remains an area of practice in need of clarification in terms of how much to use, what kind to use, and when to use it. Is there any role for the learners' L1 in Arabic language teaching? How can a teacher be optimally effective as a model of the target language? How can teacher-talk best be calibrated to language level? Many experienced Arabic teachers easily and automatically adjust to learner level, but this pedagogical skill has not yet received attention in terms of research and analysis as to the steps taken or the criteria involved in accommodating learner interlanguage. In order to provide comprehensible input from day one, it is evident that teachers need to attend to the nature of their speech and how it can be comprehended in terms of Krashen's i+1 criterion. Input cannot be random, as it may be in the real world. It must be adjusted and connected to the learner's capacity.

Choice of Variety: Standard, Regional, or Hybrid?

Arabic is not alone in having geographic and sociocultural diversity. In a recent article, John Lipski asks "which Spanish(es) to teach?", opening the door to analysis of variation in language classrooms (2009, 48). He notes that there are a number of "common denominators" in basic conversations among first-time acquaintances that enable Spanish speakers from different countries to communicate very well. "Many of the most regionalized terms," he states "are colloquial, and speakers can usually muster dictionary words when pressed for more decorous discourse" (2009, 51). This sounds very much like the leveling that takes place among native Arabic speakers from different countries when they speak with each other. If this core competence naturally evolves in native speakers, is there a formula, an algorithm, or guidelines for the most useful kind of Arabic to teach to nonnative speakers?

Lipski formulates the following questions (substituting "Arabic" for "Spanish"):

1. What sort(s) of Arabic should constitute the backbone of basic elementary and intermediate language programs?
2. What is (or should be) the effect of Arabic language variation on the choice of study-abroad programs?
3. How should matters of regional and social variation in Arabic be addressed throughout the Arabic curriculum? (2009)

These are program-wide questions that would be appropriate for discussion among faculty developing Arabic curriculum standards. Agreement on these topics may be elusive, but nonetheless the discussion is worth having in order to surface different approaches, ideologies, values, and practices among faculty.

Choosing a Medium of Instruction

Every program and every teacher needs to determine the nature of the teacher-talk modeled for students. You may consider that if you expect students to speak and listen in MSA as well as read and write, then you have to speak MSA. But what kind of MSA? Fully inflected for case and mood? Probably not, or at least not in all cases. *Fuṣḥā bidūn iʕrāb* (literary language without desinential inflection)? This is an option that represents a compromise between full-fledged literary language and spoken language, but it retains the vocabulary and grammatical structures of MSA. Should you speak educated spoken Arabic (*lughat al-muthaqqafīn*)? That is, literary Arabic with an admixture of common vernacular terms, sometimes termed "hybrid" Arabic.[8] It is also a compromise variant.

In other words, as an Arabic teacher, you need to consciously develop a range of registers for the classroom, and if you speak mostly or entirely in Arabic, you must make sure that what is communicated is understood by all. Some strategies for conveying meaning include repetition, simplification, illustration, acting out, rephrasing, and using the chalkboard to draw or write the message. Not all teachers, even native speakers, are comfortable conducting class in MSA because it is a variety of language not normally used for spontaneous speaking, even in educational situations. Sometimes the fallback language choice of the teacher in these cases is English or an admixture of Arabic and English. Teachers weak in oral *fuṣḥā* sometimes even use colloquial Arabic, but in my experience that is very rare.

Choice of Register: Modified Input

In line with "communication accommodation theory" (Giles and St. Clair 1979), which posits a number of elements involved when people from different backgrounds encounter each other, individuals tend to converge in language style and behavior with each other in order to show approval and solidarity, and in order to make sure that communication is clear. When one person has considerably more skill with language than another, the skilled person adjusts or adapts to the limited skills of the other, using slower speech, paraphrase, repetition, and other components of his or her linguistic repertoire in order to be understood. When you talk with students in a foreign language, constant calibration of speech with learner background needs to be maintained; you must be aware at all times of the general level of proficiency in a class, what they have previously studied, and how best to talk in a natural way that will be comprehensible and at the same time slightly beyond the exact knowledge of the learners (i + 1). At beginning or early intermediate stages of language study, teacher-talk may reflect some common principles of language directed to children—a universal kind of human adjustment that encourages both comprehension and language learning. There is a close relationship between the structural complexity of input provided to language learners (children or adults) and the learners' level of language proficiency or (in the case of foreign language learners) interlanguage. Self-calibrated language addressed to speakers who are less than fluent has been referred to by Krashen as "simple codes" (teacher-talk, interlanguage-talk, and foreigner-talk) (Krashen 1981, 128).

Caretaker Speech and Foreigner Speech

Two kinds of modified speech have been studied by linguists interested in language acquisition: caretaker speech (the speech of adults directed toward children) and foreigner speech (adjusted speech directed to limited-proficiency adults). Caretaker speech is what Krashen calls "roughly tuned" to the growing child's language ability (1981, 126). It is usually "not due to any conscious effort on the speech of the caretaker to teach language. Rather, caretakers modify their speech in order to communicate with children" (ibid.). This instinctive communicative effort leads to the usage of language that is within the child's realm of understanding, but also slightly beyond it, thus facilitating the child's progress in language acquisition.[9] Caretaker speech often has the following characteristics:

1. Many repetitions
2. Short, well-formed, intelligible sentences
3. Topics limited to the here-and-now and the immediate environment
4. Slower rate of delivery
5. Greater range of pitch and intonation
6. Adjusted lexicon
7. Well-formedness.

Such spontaneous but systematic adjustments are made by almost all human adults in order to guarantee connection and communication with children. Note that this kind of naturally adjusted, child-directed speech is not what is termed "baby talk," or simplified babble. It has an integrity of its own and is a genuine communicative register used to accommodate the child's limited capacity for comprehension.

Related to this is the phenomenon of foreigner-talk. However, **foreigner-talk** does not seem to be as easily calibrated or as instinctively systematic as caretaker speech; it can even be pidginized or ungrammatical in idiosyncratic ways, for example, when native speakers use inappropriately simplified forms (as, for example, in Egyptian *khawagati*, using *"anta kwayyis?"* when speaking to a foreign woman).[10] A well-known feature of attempted but unhelpful foreigner-talk in English is the tendency to speak louder; other problems in foreigner comprehension occur when native speakers use localisms or idioms, articulate poorly, or do not adjust speed of delivery—to name a few. Adjusting to limited-language interlocutors is apparently a procedure that certain people do intuitively well, and others seem to have difficulty doing. Given these types of spontaneous adjustments to speech that occur with certain types of interlocutors, it is possible to propose that certain characteristics of natural language registers do facilitate comprehension, and these can be touchstones for developing "teacher registers." These characteristics include:

1. Reduced "propositional complexity"[11]
2. Shorter sentences
3. Simple syntax
4. Repetition
5. Use of high-frequency lexical items
6. Slower rate of delivery
7. Careful articulation
8. Avoidance of idioms
9. Well-formedness.

These steps enable comprehension by making natural language more accessible through a reduction in complexity. Such reduction should not result in ungrammatical or inappropriate language, but simple language whose meaning is transparent to the learner.

Error Analysis and Error Correction

The nature of foreign language learner errors is diverse, and substantive research exists about instruction in many foreign languages, but very little research has been done to classify or analyze Arabic learner errors, their importance, the degree of interference they produce, or how best to correct them.[12] Language learners will make errors because they are involved in developing and testing their ability to comprehend input or to express themselves (via output). Errors made by learners are helpful in assessing their interlanguage and their progress toward communicative effectiveness. The role of error correction and/or intervention by the teacher in a classroom situation is a highly contested one, and one that lacks conceptual clarity. You want to avoid overcorrection, embarrassing learners, or making them hesitant and self-conscious, but if students do not realize that they are making errors, it is a disservice to let them continue for any amount of time because they may incorporate deviant forms into their interlanguage. In instructed Arabic, it is your responsibility to gently call attention to errors (in a range of possible ways), and for the most part, students expect corrective feedback as part of their learning experience.[13] Moreover, if some students in the class are producing correct forms and others are producing incorrect ones, then lack of corrective feedback undermines the assurance and performance of the students who are correct; they may even wonder if you are aware of the errors or if you are able to understand and explain the particular structures involved.

Error correction is thus an area that is fraught with affective issues as well as accuracy issues. With the current emphasis on fluency and interactive conversational skills, error correction has taken a back seat because it is often seen as discouraging and even disruptive if done during conversation, and because it is believed that learners who make errors will eventually perceive or notice that their interlanguage practice differs from authentic target language usage. That perception may, however, take a long time; moreover, learners may lose their motivation to self-correct if they believe they are managing well enough. What then, is the role of the teacher in providing an effective, encouraging, and efficient learning environment? Research increasingly shows that explicit corrective feedback is the most useful way of helping learners increase their accuracy. "Studies that have compared different types of feedback have produced varying results. In general, corrective feedback appears to be beneficial and it would seem that more explicit feedback options may be somewhat more effective" (Loewen and Reinders 2011, 45).

In many cases, what is called "negative feedback" simply fails to register, be noticed, or be processed by learners. The human psyche can be highly resilient and resistant to perceived threats to its integrity, to disappointment, or to unwelcome news. This is one reason why the act of correction is a delicate one that must take place in a context of mutual trust and confidence. Although this observation may seem rather too soft to many teachers, it is a professional responsibility to be equipped with a range of error correction strategies and a strong sense of when and where it is appropriate to use them in order not to discourage or embarrass learners, particularly when they are engaged in speaking. When a person is engaged in a spoken communicative activity, interrupting that activity to insert a corrective remark may make little impression on the speaker, who is focused on conveying meaning and preoccupied with that particular utilitarian task. Unless the learner's error interferes drastically with comprehension of the learner's language, immediate intervention is usually inappropriate. On the other hand, you are responsible for keeping track of learner errors and for providing feedback as soon as possible to guide learners to use of authentic target language conventions. Students do expect that they will be guided about errors; they will feel anxious and even shortchanged if they get neither confirmation nor correction of their attempts at the target language. Overly frequent or intrusive error correction, however, especially during speaking activities, "tends to be disruptive and can create feelings of frustration and inadequacy among students" (Hammoud 1996, 109).

◇ Error Types

As a teacher, you need to exercise judgment about when a learner is ready to hear, accept, and remember error correction. Developmental constraints may play a role here; if the learner is trying to say something that is too complex for his or her limited interlanguage, then correcting every bit of the output is not practical. If, on the other hand, the error is made in a context where the learner should be aware of the correct form, the correction may be useful as a reminder. The types of errors that require attention (focus) are normally (1) pervasive or high-frequency, (2) systematic, (3) stigmatizing, (4) salient, and/or (5) remediable. Learning to recognize and judge the quality of learner errors is a component of TLA, teacher language awareness.

As noted earlier, sources of error may include the learner's L1 and perhaps even a previously studied L2. This is referred to as language transfer (for example, English-speaking learners thinking of the Arabic "dual" category as "plural"—as it would be in English). In addition, many errors are in the form of logical overgeneralizations; a rule is learned and then applied, but the language context, particular item, or rules require another, perhaps less predictable form (such as generalizing the Arabic sound feminine plural for lexical items ending in *taāʔ marbūṭa*, resulting in errors such as "*madīnāt*" instead of "*mudun*"). As a strategy, assuring learners that their mistakes are logical is a useful way to ease the impact of corrective feedback. If interlanguage errors are retained and not corrected, this results in what has been termed **fossilization** or **stabilization,** a temporary state or an end-state that is substantially nonnative-like. Some readers may know individuals who have resided in a country for years but who still retain pronunciation and/or grammatical forms from their L1.[14]

If you point out an error to students but do not explain it, then students will need to identify the source of error themselves. This has been described as a procedure called "blame assignment"—a term from computing (and also social psychology) that refers to the identification of steps responsible for a failure or other ensuing negative consequences in the process of achieving a goal. In other words, students are asking themselves the question, "what went wrong?" in order to repair their performance. To help with this process, you can use a number of strategies:

• Corrective feedback strategies: Corrective feedback strategies can be used in nonjudgmental, constructive, and reflective ways (that is, reflecting the learners' statements back to them in correct form).

- Verbal corrective strategies allow for student reflection and self-repair:
  1. Confirmation checks ("I think you said that . . .")
  2. Clarification requests ("Did you mean . . .?" "Pardon me, but did you say . . .?")
  3. Repetition requests ("I didn't quite hear that . . . could you repeat it?")
  4. Recasts: As noted earlier, a recast is essentially a rephrasing of something that has been said by a student and that contains an error. The recast is a paraphrase similar to a confirmation check spoken by you, the teacher, but it contains the correct linguistic form rather than the erroneous one. You thus model the correct form for the learner by maintaining the meaning but putting it in your own words.[15] Research has shown, however, that a problem with recasts is that they are often not picked up on or noticed by students as corrections. Students may hear you repeat what they have just said in a slightly different way, but they attend primarily to meaning rather than to form.
  5. Explicit correction: noting the incorrect language and requesting or eliciting repair.
  6. Metalinguistic observation: commenting on the learner's utterance and perhaps asking a general question about it. ("Actually, in this context, the wording is usually different; can you think of saying it a different way?")
  7. As a general rule, you should avoid providing the correct answer and should instead provide prompts, clues, hints, or partial information that may elicit self-correction.
  8. As an option when a student fails to come up with a correct response, you may ask the class in general if anyone else can provide it. Most students do not want to embarrass or show up their peers by providing the right answer. It is important that your query be phrased in the form of asking for help or contributions: "Could anyone add to what Student A has said?" "Could anyone say this differently?" "Does anyone have another idea about how to do this?"

- Written corrective feedback: This strategy may be used in a number of ways and is usually appreciated by learners because it is both private and to the point. Therefore, new instructors should experiment with ways to provide explicit written feedback (both positive and negative) to learners. This can be done in a number of ways:
  1. Corrected homework: This is the most frequent and most important form of written feedback. Of key importance is the correction of grammatical, lexical, or spelling errors, but well-written homework deserves plus marks, too.
  2. Notes taken during oral work: It is a good idea to take notes during interactive oral work by students. This allows you to summarize and recall types of errors in general in order to organize further practice on specific points. It also allows for direct feedback to students in written form. One way of doing this is to be in touch with individual students by email, if they request it, for purposes of practice and error correction.
  3. Corrected quizzes and tests: Quizzes and tests handed back with corrections should also be places for feedback on errors; regularly scheduled weekly quizzes are a good source of information on student progress and also a way to provide consistent feedback to each one individually.

⬡ The Place of Practice

Practice sessions for musicians, dancers, or professional tennis players take up most of their working time. In fact, it has been estimated at least 10,000 hours of practice are needed in order to attain advanced proficiency in any skill.[16] To a considerable extent, such practice is also a component of language learning. Practice in language learning takes place in multiple ways. It can occur in the form of role-playing, rehearsal, task accomplishment, or specific language-based exercises, such as drills. As regards the latter, the issue of conscious and focused practice—whether in the form of written or spoken exercises—has been a conflicted as well as misunderstood topic in recent years of SLA research. However, the idea of deliberate practice as a component of skill acquisition is a lively topic of research, and preliminary findings indicate that deliberate practice makes a difference in rate of language acquisition as well as retention.

As noted later, in chapters 16 and 19 of this book, researchers in educational psychology have found that there are essentially three stages of knowledge development, called "cognitive, associative, and autonomous," or "declarative, procedural, and automatic," or "presentation, practice, and production" (DeKeyser 2007b, 98). Essentially, these stages describe the transition from knowing about something to being able to actually do that thing in a fluid, instinctive manner without having to consciously process every step in the activity.

> Research about practice has shown that learning and performance are best fostered when students engage in practice that (a) focuses on a specific goal or criterion for performance, (b) targets an appropriate level of challenge relative to students' current performance, and (c) is of sufficient quantity and frequency to meet the performance criteria. (Ambrose et al. 2010, 127)

> Goal-directed practice must be coordinated with targeted feedback in order to promote the greatest learning gains. The purpose of feedback is to help learners achieve a desired level of performance. Just as a map provides key information about a traveler's current position to help him or her find an efficient route to a destination, effective feedback provides information about a learner's current state of knowledge and performance that can guide him or her in working toward the learning goal. (137)

Deliberate practice or "concentrated controlled practice" (Andrews 2007, 52), in the form of structural drills, has been an unfashionable, contentious, and largely misunderstood area of recent pedagogical practice. DeKeyser notes:

> Clearly, form-meaning connections are the essence of language, and taking them apart more than necessary for practice activities would be unwise, but there are areas of language such as phonetics, phonology, and morphological paradigms where narrowly focused, repeated practice activities with forms can be useful . . . Such practice activities have traditionally been called drills. They have been alternately advocated, demonized, derided, and resuscitated, often without making the distinction between different kinds of drills. (2007a, 10)

The use of "drills" has been contentious for a number of reasons, among which are the following:

- Practice—especially drills on grammar, vocabulary, and pronunciation—has been interpreted by many researchers and instructors as completely mechanical and not at all meaningful or cognitively demanding.
- Some drills, if done in excess, can be boring and lead to learners tuning out rather than concentrating their attention. This is often due to an inappropriate level of challenge: Either the drills are too easy or too difficult.
- The issues of structural accuracy and error correction are central to the performance of drills and exercises, and error correction in particular has been an area where teachers from many different cultures feel hindered or discomfited in intervening.
- Error correction if done repeatedly and insensitively can be discouraging and even blocking to new learners.

On the other hand . . .

- Many learners want and enjoy drills, and even request them.

Adults often appreciate drills because the focus on accuracy in discrete chunks is useful in seeing how language as a system works, and also, one gets immediate feedback on accuracy.[17] Some even see periodic drills as relaxing because of the narrower framework of performance expected from them.

In short, appropriately challenging forms of practice, including drills, can lead to effective learning. It is the contention of this book that drills done as brief, regular learning exercises calibrated with the appropriate level of learning challenge can be effective components of the language learning experience. They should not be overdone, nor should they be lengthy, but they can be useful in providing focused practice for internalizing language structures.

"Work on the Hard Parts"

One reason that targeted exercises and drills are more acceptable in current language classroom practice is because of the concept of attention to "the hard parts" (Perkins 2009, 79). As educator David Perkins observes about activities such as athletics or musicianship, just practicing or playing through a whole piece of music (for example) many times does not guarantee that the difficult bits will improve. "Even as the rest of the piece improves in fluency and expressiveness, the hard parts remain a series of stumbles and fumbles" (ibid.). In order to see improvement in the hard parts, they need to be singled out, isolated, and deliberately practiced. "Good work on the hard parts is one of the fundamental structural challenges of teaching and learning," observes Perkins (2009, 83). By analogy it is quite clear that there are "hard parts" in language learning, too: bits of grammar, lexical usage, or pronunciation that present particular difficulties to learners. These hard parts do not always respond simply to target language exposure, task performance, or general learning activities. They are much more likely to improve if they are the subject of attention, focus, and deliberate practice. Facing up to these difficult bits rather than sliding over them will in the long run raise the level of overall performance and proficiency; it will improve, as Perkins calls it, the "whole game" (88).

A key point in focused attention on the hard parts is that once isolated, practiced, and improved, they need to be seamlessly reintegrated into learners' interlanguage and incorporated into smooth performance. As Perkins notes, "in general, trouble spots improved through advice and isolated exercise often relapse in the setting of the whole game. Incorporating the improved skill or understanding into the whole game needs to be a deliberate part of the process of deliberate practice. When we take learning the hard parts seriously, the rhythm of isolation and reintegration is fundamental" (2009, 88). Thus Perkins compares isolation and reintegration to a game of soccer, for example, wherein difficult moves may need to be drilled until they become second nature, and then reintegrated and put to use when playing a real game.

Interactive Support: Scaffolding

Within any class, opportunities arise for interaction, support, and progress. Experienced teachers usually know how to provide "scaffolding" for learners so that they can develop in their knowledge of the L2, beyond what they might achieve on their own. That is, the sociocultural context of the class itself is an important component of the structured learning experience. Learners and teacher can work together as a community to reach desired performance in the L2, but also to learn to strategize and support one another. The concept of pedagogical scaffolding on the part of the teacher has been defined as "strategic behavior determined by close and continuous scrutiny of what is easy and difficult for the learner, guided by 'a long-term sense of direction and continuity, a local plan of action, and a moment-to-moment interactional decision-making'" (DeGuerrero and Villamil 2000, 53).[18] This "scrutiny" is a key component in teacher awareness of learner performance, potential, and need. DeGuerrero and Villamil cite research that pinpoints six actions on the part of the "tutor" or teacher that characterize successful scaffolding:

> According to Wood, Bruner, and Ross (1976), tutorial interactions are crucial in fostering development in the human being. These authors hypothesized that successful scaffolding is characterized by six actions on the tutor's part: (a) recruiting the tutee's attention, (b) reducing degrees of freedom in the task in order to make it manageable, (c) keeping direction in terms of the goals, (d) marking critical features, (e) controlling frustration, and (f) modeling solutions. Although probably intuitive, these actions demonstrate a high degree of skill and fine-tuning on the tutor's part. (2000, 52)

The Zone of Proximal Development

In combination with the idea of scaffolding, a further concept developed by Lev Vygotsky in the context of his sociocultural theory is the **zone of proximal development** (ZPD). This "zone" refers to the context in which learning takes place (typically a classroom, but other venues are possible) and the potential level of educational development offered through the interactive assistance of others: teachers or peers. This kind of learning opportunity provides learners with a reliable source of engagement, encouragement, advice, and ideas. The ZPD has been defined as "the distance between what a learner can do by himself or herself and what he or she can do with guidance from a teacher or a more capable peer. The theory assumes that learners use the techniques used during collaborative efforts when encountering similar problems in the future" (Richards and Schmidt 2010, 644).

Small Group Work

In a communicative language learning setting, small group work is one of the key tools that teachers can use to increase learner participation and collaboration, increase scaffolding opportunities, and intensify the ZPD. Arrange for groups of students to undertake interactive projects together. It is not a good idea to allow students to group themselves because they will either flounder and not know who to work with, or the ones who know each other well will self-select to the same group. I have had success by going around the room and simply have students count off (in Arabic) by four or five (depending on class size), assigning the ones to one group, the twos to another, the threes to another, and so on. This allows people who do not usually sit together to mix with each other and it assures group diversity. Groups of three to five students usually work best.

Projects can be simple (e.g., each group has to translate three English sentences into Arabic, or vice versa; each group has to read and summarize a news article) or complex (each group member has to describe a particular airport to the others in Arabic); they can be short-term (ten minutes) or long-term (a multiweek project, such as writing and performing a skit). In most cases, each group shares its findings or results with the others, and this generates whole-group discussion.

 Conclusion

Good language teachers constantly balance, guide, and orchestrate the entire classroom experience, paying attention not only to content but also to classroom climate and tempo. Student interaction in the classroom community is fostered through a variety of strategies that encourage practice, participation, and performance, coordinated in both overt and subtle ways that lead to depth of understanding and effective learning outcomes.

One year I had great success with a class of 30 students by dividing them into six five-member teams and asking each to write and then act out a play about "Love at the University" based on their previous reading of Al-Tayyib Saleh's "*Sūzān wa-ʕAlī*" (lesson 26 in Abboud and McCarus's *Elementary Modern Standard Arabic* [EMSA]). I allowed the small groups to meet during class three times a week for 15 minutes for four weeks in order to draft, collaborate, and practice. Many rehearsed their skits together outside of class. During the last week of class, each group put on its own play, three during one class session and three during another. The results were both moving and hilarious. The groups' productions far exceeded what I expected in terms of linguistic and cultural sophistication, and the project gave rein to students' unexpected creative gifts.

⬡ Study Questions and Activities

1. What is the best language learning experience you have ever had, whether inside or outside of the classroom? What made it memorable?
2. As either a learner or a teacher, does the space and structure of classroom seating make a difference to you? How do you feel about asking students to regroup—either into one circle or into small groups? Do you see any problems with this procedure?
3. What has been your experience (as a learner or a teacher) with the use of Arabic in the classroom? How and to what extent do teachers use Arabic in the classroom? What are the advantages and disadvantages of using Arabic 100 percent of the time?
4. In your experience, does use of Arabic by the teacher vary with level of study? Does it vary with teaching method or pedagogical approach? Does it vary from individual to individual?
5. When you speak Arabic to students, to what degree do you consciously adjust your language? What are some of the strategies that you use to make it comprehensible?
6. What are some of the characteristics of Arabic learner interlanguage that you have noticed? Are there consistencies or systematic features that you can describe?
7. Discuss the concept of declarative and procedural knowledge and give examples from your own experience.
8. Bring a drill or exercise to class that you have selected out of an Arabic textbook and discuss why you chose it. What are its strengths and weaknesses? Would you improve upon it? Would you use it as a model for further exercises?
9. Crucial distinctions are made between pedagogical control and dominance, and between authority and authoritarianism. Think of examples of each, and discuss them with your classmates.

⬡ Further Reading

Andrews, Stephen. 2007. *Teacher Language Awareness*. Cambridge: Cambridge University Press.
Brown, H. Douglas. 2001. *Teaching by Principles: An Interactive Approach to Language Pedagogy*, 2nd ed. White Plains, NY: Addison Wesley Longman. (Especially chapter 13, "Classroom Management.")
Lightbown, Patsy M., and Nina Spada. 2006. *How Languages Are Learned*, 3rd ed. Oxford: Oxford University Press. (Especially pp. 125–130 on corrective feedback strategies.)
Perkins, David N. 2009. *Making Learning Whole: How Seven Principles of Teaching Can Transform Education*. San Francisco: Jossey-Bass. (Especially chapter 3, "Work on the Hard Parts.")
Stevick, Earl. 1980. *A Way and Ways*. Boston: Newbury House.
_____. 1996. *Memory, Meaning & Method*, 2nd ed. Boston: Heinle & Heinle.

⬡ Notes

1. Rardin et al. 1988, 27–28; Curran 1982a, 169–171. See also chapter 5 in this book.
2. "Learner autonomy is "a set of characteristics related to the ability and willingness to engage critically with the learning process. . . . The concept of autonomy in language learning . . . builds on a general shift of attention to the language and an increased recognition of the role of learners as active participants in the language learning process" (Loewen and Reinders 2011, 107).
3. Stevick declares: "Under 'control' I include two functions; first, the establishment and maintenance of rules for classroom behavior, including both deportment and learning procedures. With most classes, it will also include a certain amount of setting general tasks for the students to undertake. Second, 'control' in a language class means making it possible for the learner to find out readily how what he does compares with the language behavior of native speakers" (1976, 13).
4. Authority here is not to be confused with any form of authoritarian behavior or authoritarianism, which are restrictive, ego-centered, and rigid attitudes toward class conduct. Authority refers to the legitimate leadership that teachers exercise in the process of teaching.

5. "Mastery orientations are promoted in classrooms that afford students autonomy and decision making" (Blumenfeld 1992, 274).

6. Education authority Parker J. Palmer states that "what seems right to me after many years of searching, is to sit in a circle with my students" (Palmer 1998, 136). Palmer's subject is not foreign language teaching, but his discussion of learning space relates well to foreign language classrooms.

7. Rearranging classroom furniture is an unusual and unnatural procedure for students to grasp the first few times, and they are sometimes reluctant to move their chairs, but they do get used to doing it. Persevere gently.

8. Eid 2007, 2010.

9. Krashen also hypothesizes that the "net of structure cast by caretaker speech in an attempt to communicate with the child is of *optimal size*" (1981, 127; italics in original). That is, the speech net is not too dense or difficult (causing the child to tune out), nor is it too simple.

10. Reported on Arabic-L, July 27, 1994, by several subscribers. See also Tweissi 1990.

11. See Krashen 1981, 130.

12. This is, of course, quite apart from the substantial literature on *laḥn* developed in the classical and postclassical periods of the Arabic grammatical tradition. The classic work in English on error analysis is Pit Corder's *Error Analysis and Interlanguage* (1981), long out of print, but a pivotal text.

13. Immediate and detailed feedback on performance is one of the features of good teaching that students appreciate most (*Chronicle of Higher Education* 1990, A26).

14. Krashen has proposed that "the instrumental acquirer or learner 'fossilizes' (Selinker 1972) or ceases progress when he perceives that communicative needs are met. The integrative acquirer/learner fossilizes when he perceives that his social needs are met" (Krashen 1981, 39).

15. "The recast may be provided because the form is non-target-like yet the meaning is understood . . . or the recast may be provided as an attempt to clarify the meaning as well as the non-target-like form" (Mackey and Philp 1998, 342).

16. See Gladwell 2008, 39–42.

17. Stevick recounts the example of a good language learner he interviewed who "volunteered the information that he placed great value on drills, and that he rated teachers according to how 'limp and exhausted' they left him at the end of a drill session" (1996, 241).

18. Quoting van Lier 1996, 199.

Learning Styles, Strategies, and Affective Factors

CHAPTER 10

We must recognize that students are not only intellectual but also social and emotional beings, and that these dimensions interact within the classroom climate to influence learning and performance.

Ambrose et al.

This chapter is about ways that learners approach the task of acquiring a foreign language—Arabic in particular—and how teachers can foster the learning process. Language acquisition is a cognitive, affective, and social process, and multiple dimensions of personality, personal style, aptitude, experience, and intellect work across and within every learner to provide resources for tackling a new learning experience. It is important for teachers to keep in mind the difference between learning strategies and learning styles. Although they are often discussed together, they refer to two different aspects of learners' resources for language study. Learning styles and strategies play key roles in foreign language learning and can affect the learning outcomes of any class. A well-founded knowledge of the components of both styles and strategies should be part of Arabic instructors' professional preparation in educational psychology.

⬡ Learning Style

Learning style has been defined broadly as "an individual difference in how learners approach the learning process" (Loewen and Reinders 2011, 109). Learning style "is pervasive" and "is a mix of cognitive, affective, and behavioral elements" (Oxford 1990, 439). Learning styles reflect aspects of one's personality and may be altogether unconscious—some learners are outgoing and extroverted; others are more introverted and thoughtful; some learners prefer to process information in very clear sequential steps; others are more globally oriented and grasp the gestalt or wholeness of a new learning situation before they consciously analyze it. Learning style is basically built into one's personality and background. It is not unchangeable, but it is often unconscious and spontaneous. Leaver breaks learning style types down into four categories:

1. Environmental preferences (e.g., solitary/social, quiet/noisy, day/night, music/silence)
2. Sensory modalities and preferences: visual, auditory, motor (kinesthetic or mechanical)
3. Personality types (based on the Meyers-Briggs Type Indicator (MBTI)): introversion/extroversion, sensing/intuitive, thinking/feeling and judging/perceiving
4. Cognitive styles: global/particular, leveling/sharpening, synthetic/analytic, impulsive/reflective, inductive/deductive, concrete/abstract, sequential/random. (1998, 24–62)[1]

There are many other components to learners' preferred styles, and being able to identify particular style preferences in your students will help in advising, in designing particular lessons or exercises, and in tutoring for specific purposes. No one style is right or wrong; moreover, most people have access to a range of styles and fall somewhere on a continuum in their particular combination of preferences.

Style preferences can be an important source of added information for teachers. This does not mean that teachers should constantly shift their modes of instruction depending on whom they teach, but it does mean that teachers can be alert to learning preferences, especially if students are encountering difficulties with particular tasks or topics. As a teacher and advisor, I found it most instructive to take tests such as the MBTI and others to assess my own personality type and learning style because I learned something about my own preferences, and in subsequent discussion sessions I learned not to expect others to learn in exactly the same manner. It gave me more flexibility in recognizing learner problems and increased my repertoire of resources for the classroom.[2] A list of references and further readings about learning styles is provided at the end of this chapter.

Learning Strategies

Learning strategies are specific plans that learners make in order to acquire language. They may be unconscious, but are usually conscious ways of approaching the study of language with one's own resources—be it learning vocabulary with flashcards, or rehearsing a dialogue out loud, or studying in a group, or writing out exercises. In general, strategies refer to conscious actions taken by learners to improve their skills. These actions can be classified as follows:

- Cognitive strategies (including memorization and coping strategies) help learners form concepts, reason about, analyze, and apply L2 knowledge.
- Metacognitive strategies, or "how one thinks about one's own learning" (Leaver 1997, 136), help learners judge and select appropriate strategies for particular tasks.[3]
- Compensatory strategies help learners bridge gaps in their knowledge, get help, and guess intelligently.
- Affective strategies help learners stay motivated, upbeat, and positive even under stress.
- Sociocultural strategies help learners to:
  Cooperate with others, socialize with L2 speakers, seek L2 cultural experiences and contexts, and negotiate identity in the L2;
  Remember, recall, review, and use learned language effectively.[4]

Foreign language learning strategy research has dealt with many aspects of learner readiness, metacognition, and facility in acquiring language skills.

Strategies and Tactics

Strategy researcher Rebecca Oxford defines strategy as "a general plan of action used to meet a goal" (2011, 31). Strategies may have specific subgoals (such as learning how to conjugate a past-tense verb, memorizing vocabulary, or learning how to interact with a native speaker using specific politeness formulas) in addition to the overarching goal of language learning. In addition, strategies require the use of tactics, which Oxford defines as "specific, goal-directed actions that a given learner employs in a particular sociocultural setting for particular learning-related purposes and needs. Tactics are the way or ways the learner applies the strategy at a specific level in a given situation to meet immediate requirements" (ibid.).

Oxford further identifies a model for learners which she labels "the S2R Model." The S2R concept refers to "strategically self-regulated learners" (2011, 14), those who consciously manage their own learning through strategies and metastrategies (knowledge about strategies). A goal of language teaching is to make certain that learners become self-aware, objective, and effective managers of their own learning goals, styles, and strategies.

Previous success in learning a second or foreign language is often a significant factor in learner strategy and tactic choice, and the particular tactics that worked in one situation will most likely be called upon again, but sometimes alternative strategies and tactics need to be developed for specific language challenges.

Tactics for Arabic

Published research specifically addressing Arabic learning strategies is limited, but advice on learning strategies is often requested by Arabic students because some of the strategies that they have relied upon successfully with European languages do not produce the same impact or success level for Arabic learning.[5] Certainly the most frequent request I have from Arabic students is for advice on how to study vocabulary effectively. These students are often good language learners who find that Arabic vocabulary items do not yield to their ordinary studying tactics. One of the most useful things an Arabic teacher can do is to give concrete advice on vocabulary study tactics, and to model those tactics in the classroom.

Here are two areas of learning (vocabulary and pronunciation) with workable strategies and tactics that have been found effective in advising Arabic students.

Vocabulary

For vocabulary learning, advise learners as follows in order to enable deep lexical processing for retention of new words and phrases:

- Use all modalities: speaking, listening, reading, writing. Do not simply look at words in a list. Write each one out 5–10 times (handwriting provides motor memory that reinforces visual and auditory memory; write the entire word, including the short vowels); read the words out loud many times in different tones of voice (sing them if you like); listen to them repeatedly on a CD, online, or on a DVD.
- Put words in context: Listen to a text with new vocabulary items many times until you know it well; read it out loud to yourself. Make up sentences and variations on sentences with the new items. Try them out with your teacher and other students.
- Saturate your environment: Post sticky notes with Arabic vocabulary items all over so that you run into them again and again (on the bathroom mirror, the refrigerator, your pillow, your computer).
- Test yourself: Make (write out) a list of all the new Arabic vocabulary items you've accumulated and see if you can come up with the English equivalents. If there are any that you cannot remember, write them out as many times as you need to in order to remember. Then move on to the harder step: make a list of the English equivalents and see if you can come up with all the Arabic items. Write the Arabic items out and say them aloud. Do this at regular intervals (weekly, biweekly). When you write Arabic words, make sure you write correctly all the short vowels as well as the word skeleton. Writing the short vowels of an Arabic word is important for English-speaking learners because it has been shown that English speakers memorize words visually; if the short vowels do not appear it is significantly harder for learners to store them in memory.[6]

This topic is discussed in greater detail in chapter 18, on vocabulary learning, but for the time being, I offer this tip based both on experience and on current research: foreign learners at the beginning and intermediate stages cannot productively rely on the tactic that most native speakers of Arabic use to identify the meanings of new words—root and pattern identification. Foreign learners of Arabic need to build up *memorized core vocabulary* quickly; at later stages they will find the use of root/pattern information extremely useful, but much less so at the start.

Pronunciation

For pronunciation, discerning and pronouncing Arabic sounds can often be aided by the following techniques.

- Listen hard: Advise learners to listen attentively, acutely, and specifically for pronunciation (not just meaning). They should listen to native speakers carefully and intently. Listen to sequences of sound in CDs, movies, DVDs, television broadcasts, online videos, and broadcasts. Focus on sounds and sound sequences rather than trying to fully understand the content. If learners come across someone who speaks Arabic particularly clearly, with especially good articulation, they should go out of their way to listen to that person as often as possible, focusing on his or her way of speaking; trying to remember specifics of what that person does. Learners should imitate their teachers and other native speakers as closely as they can.
- Practice out loud: There is no substitute for practicing Arabic out loud. Learners must learn to use parts of their articulatory tract that they may never have used for speaking (pharyngeal muscles, for example). Correct and fluid pronunciation is a highly calibrated motor skill that is developed by means of hours and hours of deliberate practice. Advise learners to stand in front of a mirror and pronounce words, phrases, sentences. Tell them to exaggerate pronunciation at first; they may want to try different types of voices: soft, loud, singsong, scolding, loving. Have them (both on their own and in class) read passages out loud to get used to saying words grouped together in phrases. They may want to adopt one or two short words ("key words") that contain unfamiliar consonants (such as *ʕayn*) and work on being able to say those words perfectly.[7] Having a solid model as an anchor for pronunciation may be helpful.
- Write and pronounce: By handwriting and pronouncing at the same time the learner receives two memory inputs, manual and oral. In learning correct pronunciation learners will have to know the short vowels which are part of the spelling of most words, and it is a good idea to practice writing words out with vowels and repeating what they write as they write it, associating sound closely with script.

The above advice combines cognitive, social, and memory strategies. I have used many of these myself as a learner, but I have also learned some from my students (e.g., the one about sticky notes). It is useful to survey language learners at the end of a course or a semester to see what strategies have worked for them. This can be done as a debriefing type of conversation, or it can be done in writing. That information can be added to your teaching resource files as potential advice to future learners.

❖ Arabic Learning Strategy Research[8]

Four researchers have dealt specifically with Arabic learning strategies: Khalil, Elkhafaifi, VanPee, and Keatley et al. Khalil used Oxford's Strategy Inventory for Language Learning (SILL) to analyze strategies of 162 students of Arabic at the college level, looking at strategy use difference by level of proficiency and gender.[9] Results indicated that proficiency level was not a factor in strategy use, but that female students "used compensatory, metacognitive and social strategies significantly more often than males" (2003, 34).[10] Elkhafaifi's 2007–2008 analysis of listening strategies for 30 Arabic students also found that gender was a factor in strategy use, stating that "overall, females reported more strategy use than males" (2007–2008, 80). His results additionally showed that "cognitive strategy use predominates," and that "as the course level increased, so did reports of metacognitive strategy use" (81).

VanPee's 2010 study of vocabulary-learning strategies among 39 students at Georgetown University confirmed Elkhafaifi's finding about differences in strategies by gender but found that the concept of more diverse strategy use among successful students was not valid. The most successful students found a limited number of strategies that worked for them and stuck with them, rather than experimenting with others. Lower-performing students tried many different strategies, but had less success overall.

Keatley et al. (2004) studied a group of nine intermediate-level students and differences in learning strategies between heritage and nonheritage learners. For vocabulary, a range of memorization strategies (kinesthetic, auditory, visual) took first place over find/apply morphological patterning. In reading, direct vocabulary study took precedence over contextualized cues or root/pattern cues. Learners who had studied Latin or German found it easier to understand the system of desinential inflection. Interestingly, handwriting turned out to be a problem for many at the intermediate level because they had not been required to write clearly and quickly when they first learned the writing system, and a number of them had to strategize to improve their writing, mainly by painstaking practice and special attention to detail. For speaking MSA (the only option for these students), many reported needing to "find opportunities to practice" as a strategy, but heritage learners devised different strategies, needing to convert their vernacular skills into MSA through keeping separate language tracks in their minds and consciously monitoring their performance.

Teaching or talking about learning strategies and strategy awareness is sometimes useful, sometimes not. Students who feel that they already know how to study and learn may consider such work redundant. Other students may be ready for assistance in building and expanding their strategy repertoires. One useful idea may be to hold a study strategy session for students outside class time, or during your office hours, or one-on-one, so that those who seek help will be able to attend and benefit. It can also be useful to connect particular learning strategies and tactics with particular assignments or tasks; American learners in particular respond well to instruction that serves explicit pragmatic purposes.[11]

✧ Affect, Attitude, Motivation, Aptitude

In addition to understanding learning styles and strategies, it is essential that teachers understand psychological and cognitive factors in language acquisition. Foreign language learning has been shown to be an intense psychological encounter, not just an intellectual one. It is inherently stressful for many people because it entails a form of extreme adaptive behavior on the part of learners. In the language classroom, affective elements of learners come into play more than in other classroom situations, and language instructors in particular will find themselves dealing with elusive but important issues in the learning/teaching experience, including learner feelings, elements of risk, processes of retention, interpersonal relationships, attitudes, and anxieties. Because of recent political history, learners who enter upon Arabic study in the United States may carry with them negative attitudes and stereotypes about Arabic culture and society as well as sincere curiosity, interest in, and commitment to learning the language. They may therefore find themselves both anxious and intrigued by Arabic language and culture. It is important for Arabic instructors to be aware of possible mixed feelings of learners in order to be able to deal with anxiety that may arise or be acted out in the classroom, especially in terms of resistance.

Almost any foreign language learning situation demands a gradual adjustment of perspective; it also demands performance in the form of oral target language use and enactment; these factors can activate strong affective barriers in some learners.[12] This is why the relationship between teacher and learner must be one of trust and mutual respect. Perhaps more than any other language at the present moment, the teaching of Arabic involves humanistic concerns that arise naturally out of the context of place and time; there is a need for teacher awareness not just of language and techniques of teaching, but also of the psychological framework in which Arabic language learning has been placed. Fostering a sense of community in the classroom is a first step in situating

Arabic learning within a strong and supportive professional approach to developing transcultural and translingual confidence.[13]

In order to gear interaction with students to make the most of classroom time, it is helpful to know some basic concepts of educational psychology—about learner attitudes, motivations, and aptitudes. Having a basic understanding of the affective or feeling component of learner psychology helps instructors understand what is happening when they run into conscious or unconscious resistance on the part of language learners. Resistance takes many forms; it can cause serious tensions in the classroom, and can disrupt the learning experience for everyone unless the teacher knows how to identify it and to handle it gracefully and effectively. Moreover, teachers' understanding of affective factors can lead to a more solid and profound learning experience for the students. Some researchers associate this kind of understanding with a humanistic approach to teaching that reflects a conscious decision to take into account not just learners' intellects but also their feelings, values, and reasons for studying a foreign language.[14] These factors are especially relevant to foreign language study because learning to use and understand a new language entails a change in behavior, and for some this is more challenging than for others.

If a learner has doubts about his or her ability to learn, is anxious about performance or is ambivalent or even adversarial toward the target culture, these factors may interfere with or reduce the learners' ability to receive input and develop competence in the target language. One rough way of classifying learner attitudes is to describe them either as **receptive** or **defensive**. Receptive learners are interested, focused, tuned in, involved, and attentive to target language instruction and activities. They are often empathetic and approach the L2 with an open and flexible state of mind—showing curiosity and a lack of self-consciousness. Defensive learners, on the other hand, function differently. They are often learning only in order not to fail or to be embarrassed. The teacher may be seen as an adversary or at best a congenial sparring partner. Defensive learners may show their distance from the learning situation through body language: by yawning, daydreaming, sitting in the very back of the class, being unprepared, being chronically late or absent, or disrespectful toward the teacher. One way to deal with such resistance is for teachers to arrange for individual meetings with learners who show defensive or resisting behavior, and to counsel them. They are sending a very clear message that they are uncomfortable; so finding out why they are taking Arabic may be a first step in defusing a tense learning situation. Nonjudgmental listening, reflection, and counseling by the teacher can sometimes turn these situations around.

Learning a foreign language often entails involvement in communicative situations where the learner does not have full understanding of the meaning or form of language used. This is natural and to be expected, but some learners find it very stressful not to understand everything. **Ambiguity tolerance** refers to the level of anxiety the learners experience when they are faced with linguistic unknowns; some learners have automatic tolerance for a great deal of ambiguity; others feel a need for clarity at all stages and at all costs. Most learners fall somewhere in between. Oxford classifies this feature as "a potentially important dimension of language learning style" related to the concept of flexible thinking (as opposed to constricted thinking) (1990, 444). As Oxford reports, "learning a language and its corresponding culture is a difficult endeavor, often fraught with ambiguity and uncertainty on many levels: emotional, sociocultural, and linguistic. Therefore, it is not surprising that research indicates better language learning performance by students who can more readily tolerate ambiguity" (1990, 444).

Language learning **anxiety** has been a topic of interest and research for a number of years because of its importance in the overall achievement of learners, and its pervasiveness. At least two general types of anxiety are factors in classroom performance: facilitating anxiety and debilitating anxiety. These terms apply equally to the phenomenon of "stage fright," where one becomes nervous and anxious just before going on stage. The anxiety is normal; it is the type of anxiety that is crucial. Facilitating anxiety fosters alertness and readiness for a task and turns our energies up a notch, allowing us to perform our role well. Debilitating anxiety, on the other hand, interferes with our confidence and ability to perform by causing self-doubt, forgetfulness, and blocking.

Reducing, eliminating, or calming negative types of anxiety in the language classroom are skills that every teacher needs to cultivate.

Another important concept in language learning is the idea of **ego boundaries**. Guiora and Acton identified two basic constructs involved in personality and language learning: language ego boundaries and permeability of language ego boundaries. In their words, "both pronunciation ability and empathy are profoundly influenced by the same underlying processes, namely permeability of ego boundaries" (1979, 11). Learning a foreign language means learning to be different. All adults have developed their egos, characters, and personalities—but some have more rigid boundaries than others. A person with a healthy, well-defined sense of self will not normally be threatened by the requirement to behave in a different way—as when learning a foreign language. People with weaker egos who may be less sure of their identities may resist changing themselves in any way; in those cases, learning to speak a foreign language or behave according to different cultural norms may be interpreted as threatening, and their ego boundaries are stiffened.

 ## Motivation and Orientation

Closely related to affective issues are factors of motivation: Why have learners chosen to study Arabic? Two basic categories are usually cited; they are not at all incompatible but they are psychologically distinct from each other. Students may well incorporate both into their approach to language study.

- Instrumental/extrinsic motivation: Learners with instrumental or extrinsic motivation usually need knowledge of a foreign language in order to accomplish a specific task such as passing an exam, examining manuscripts, getting around as a tourist, for study abroad, or to undertake a professional position abroad such as a Foreign Service Officer. These needs are usually specific and straightforward.
- Integrative/intrinsic motivation: Learners with integrative, intrinsic, or (as it is sometimes referred to) "constitutive" motivation often have a desire to blend in with, identify with, or deeply understand the culture that they are studying. They may have an interest in a particular region or language because of family ties, or an attraction to a certain culture. For many of these learners, they derive a sense of satisfaction, reward, and self-esteem from the learning experience itself.[15]

In one of the few research projects done on Arabic learner motivation, Yasir Suleiman reveals that among the learners in his study, none exhibited either instrumental or integrative motivation. He reports that "the learners' primary motivation in studying Arabic is neither instrumental nor integrative, but rather intellectual and personal" (1991, 100). The "intellectual and personal" motivations highlighted in Suleiman's study signify potentially important distinctions that should be added to the traditional categories of instrumental and integrative in order to account for the greater range of interests of foreign language learners in today's globalized and internationalized context. Moreover, the concept of learning Arabic as an intellectual challenge for students who are already bilingual or multilingual is most certainly a valid feature that consistently attracts learners to Arabic classes. Many if not most American learners who study Arabic at the college level come to Arabic as an L3 or L4, bringing with them a curiosity about how languages work as well as a wealth of background knowledge and cognitive skills that may "play more of a central role [in L2 acquisition] than was previously assumed" (DeAngelis 2007, 130).

 ## Language Learning Aptitude

Language learning aptitude is a cognitive ability or potential that can be measured on standardized tests like the MLAT (Modern Language Aptitude Test) or the DLAB (Defense Language Aptitude Battery).[16] These tests measure factors such as ability to deal in an abstract way with elements of language (such as morphology or pronunciation), pattern recognition and sensitivity, working memory, and perceptual acuity (listening, seeing). The ability to perform certain language tasks; imitate sounds; think in terms of abstract categories such as agreement; and apply reasoning by analogy often correlates with ability in formal language learning situations and reflects a high degree of verbal intelligence. Aptitude, however, is not the sole determining factor in language learning success. Whereas a high score in language aptitude bodes well for a learner, other aspects of his or her personality may interfere with their ability; likewise, a lower score in language aptitude may be compensated for by strong motivation and good study skills.

Study Questions and Activities

1. How would you describe your own learning style (using Leaver's four categories)? Have you ever taken a learning style assessment?
2. Do you teach the way you like to be taught or do you teach differently? Discuss the reasons for your answer.
3. When you are teaching Arabic, do you give advice about study strategies? If so, how did you discover these strategies? Have you learned about strategies from your students, from your own learning experiences, or from others?
4. Do you think that strategies shift as students advance to higher levels of proficiency? If so, where do you perceive these shifts, and how do you as a teacher support these strategies?
5. When you read about ego boundaries and ambiguity tolerance, are these constructs meaningful to you either as a student or as a teacher?

Further Reading

Leaver, Betty Lou. 1997. *Teaching the Whole Class*. Dubuque: Kendall-Hunt.
O'Malley, Michael, and Anna Uhl Chamot. 1990. *Learning Strategies in Second Language Acquisition*. New York: Cambridge University Press.
Oxford, Rebecca. 1997. "Cooperative Learning, Collaborative Learning, and Interaction: Three Communicative Strands in the Language Classroom." *Modern Language Journal* 81:443–456.
_____. 2011. *Teaching and Researching Language Learning Strategies*. Harlow, UK: Longman/Pearson.
Suleiman, Yasir. 1991. "Affective and Personality Factors in Learning Arabic as a Foreign Language: A Case Study." *Al-ᶜArabiyya* 24:83–110.

Notes

1. See also Hadley 2001, 75–77.
2. "An instructor who attends a learning-styles seminar might start to offer a broader mixture of lectures, discussions, and laboratory work—and that variety of instruction might turn out to be better for all students" (Glenn 2009).
3. "Metacognition is a person's awareness of his or her own level of knowledge and thought processes" (Lang 2012).
4. After Oxford 1988, 7–8.
5. Elkhafaifi notes that "studies of Arabic learners in general are scarce" (2007–2008, 73).
6. In the literature on vocabulary learning, the "key word" technique (making a mnemonic association between the L2 word and an L1 word or concept) is often mentioned as a popular and efficient way to retain word meaning. However, most students I have worked with have found it of limited use in Arabic.
7. When I started studying Arabic in Beirut, the first word containing ᶜayn that I could pronounce accurately was *naᶜam*, 'yes,' which I heard around me on a daily basis, and which I kept repeating to myself until I got it. Having that one word as a touchstone was useful in developing correct pronunciation in longer words.
8. An earlier version of this summary was published in Ryding 2013.

9. See Oxford 1990.

10. Khalil references previous studies on strategies for Arabic learning including Aweiss 1993 and Alosh 1997.

11. Oxford reminds teachers to "avoid 'blind strategy training'—only explicit, overt strategy training really works for most students" (1994, 3).

12. As noted in chapter 2, Krashen described a particular phenomenon among language learners which he metaphorically termed the "affective filter." That is, if learners have negative or defensive feelings about the language, the culture, or the learning experience, those feelings can constitute a barrier to learning and prevent or weaken the intake of comprehensible input. When the affective filter is low, target language input is readily assimilated and learning can progress.

13. "The vision of education and classroom activity associated with culturally situated cognition is that of creating minicommunities and experiences that are simulations and extensions of productive and motivated communities of practice within larger society" (Derry 1992, 417).

14. See Stevick 1990 on humanism in language teaching.

15. See especially Brown 2001, 72–84, on extrinsic and intrinsic motivation; see also Krashen 1981, 21–23.

16. Information about the MLAT is available through the website of Second Language Testing, Inc. at www.2lti.com. DLAB information is more closely guarded.

Mixed Classes and Heritage Learners

CHAPTER 11

Heritage students are of all backgrounds, making language teaching far more complex than it ever was.

Haruo Shirane

At some point in almost every Arabic teacher's career, she will be faced with a mixed class. In fact, this is more often the case than not after the first-year level. These classes can be demanding in many ways: difficult to teach, difficult to plan for, difficult to control, difficult to grade. Many Arabic classes consist of students with different backgrounds and different strengths, including heritage students raised in Arabic-speaking homes.[1] This mixing of levels and experiences is of concern at all stages of Arabic education, from K-12 through university-level classes. Teaching such classes is one of the greatest challenges for instructors, especially new instructors, who often are in need of ideas and information about how to organize, control, and manage such diversity. This chapter examines interactional and educational issues involved in multilevel classes, from ethnic diversity to educational background diversity. One of the key issues for university-level instruction is accurate placement of entering students into appropriate levels of instruction. Although most placement decisions are estimates rather than exact determinations, there are a few general guidelines to follow.

⬡ Native Speakers of Arabic: "Fake" Beginners

Native speakers of Arabic raised and educated in the Arab world should not be allowed to enroll in beginning or intermediate Arabic classes. Although this statement may seem extraordinarily obvious, in my experience some university students who are Arabic native speakers and need humanities credits think that enrolling in Arabic (which they already know well) will increase their grade point average with little or no effort. Often they will try to justify this by saying that they do not really know "the grammar;" other times they may deliberately score poorly on placement tests, and sometimes they simply show up in class and have to be asked to leave. (This happens not just in Arabic classes, but other language classes as well.) As a result, native speakers who try to take lower-level foreign language courses in their own languages have been identified and labeled as "fake" beginners (as distinct from "false" beginners) (Sohn and Shin 2007, 415). These situations can be unpleasant, and some teachers find it difficult to tell any students that they are not suited for the class, but teachers and administrators who value the educational experience they provide for their students will not allow these "fake" beginners into low-level Arabic classes. This is not only because the class is inappropriate for their level, it is also because their native knowledge of Arabic can be starkly demoralizing for other students. Fake beginners can be distracting, they may hold erroneous but strongly expressed views about Arabic, they may act challenging or disrespectful toward the teacher because they are not usually there to learn but to display their own skills and prowess.

The best way to provide support for appropriate placement decisions along these lines is to have a written policy published on the department's web page and/or in the course catalog, stating that native speakers are welcome to sign up for advanced classes in Arabic literature or linguistics, but not for undergraduate language classes. Another check on fake beginners is to conduct a diagnostic oral interview in which students are questioned about their experience with the L2. Sohn and Shin state that "our experience shows that oral interviews . . . enable instructors to identify 'fake beginners' . . . who want to be placed into lower-level classes to boost their grade-point average" (2007, 415).

Please note that the above statements do not refer to heritage speakers who have been raised outside the Arab world, but only to those who speak and are literate in Arabic because they have been raised and educated in an Arab country.

False Beginners

False beginners are generally not "faking" their limited proficiency. They are students who have had some exposure to or instruction in a foreign language but who have limited use of it and do not fit into a higher level class. This expression contrasts with "true beginners" who have had no previous exposure to the L2.

Heritage Speakers

Placement for heritage speakers should involve a written test of their language skills as well as an oral interview. Arab Americans come from families with origins in many different countries, and with an entire range of attitudes toward spoken Arabic and Arabic literacy. Some families will speak a little Arabic, some will speak Arabic almost all the time; some students may visit their extended families in the Arab world and be comfortable with being bicultural as well as bilingual. Some may have been taught limited literacy skills, others may know almost nothing about reading and writing MSA. It is important to assess heritage strengths and weaknesses accurately in order not to waste the learners' time, and to encourage their interest in progressing at a rapid pace.

- Advantages that Arabic heritage speakers often bring to the beginning classroom include:
  1. Proficiency in a spoken regional vernacular
  2. Strong comprehension skills in vernacular
  3. Strong core of everyday vocabulary
  4. Familiarity with Arabic culture, values, and traditions
  5. High motivation to leverage their already considerable skills
- Disadvantages of heritage learners may include:
  1. Inability to read or write in Arabic
  2. Overconfidence in the ability of one variety of colloquial Arabic to serve in all situations
  3. Difficulty in raising their register of speech and in comprehension of professional, technical, or literary levels of language
  4. Impatience with those who are learning from scratch
  5. General lack of metacognitive awareness

Thus the central issue with heritage speakers is usually balance of skills. Their ability to communicate in everyday situations has often served them well until they reach the Arabic language classroom. When heritage speakers are placed with rank beginners in a first-year class, their combinations of strengths and weaknesses can put them at odds with their classmates because their skills are not being honed fast enough, their assets do not seem to be serving them efficiently, and they are frustrated. This can lead to disruptive behavior, an unwillingness to engage with the learning experience, and friction with the professor. In this situation, the asset combination that Arabic heritage speakers already have is being drained, diverted, or discouraged, when it should really serve as the cornerstone for building advanced proficiency skills and Arabic cultural literacy.

Whenever possible, heritage learners should receive individual attention and counseling about their language performance and the areas they need to improve, usually reading comprehension and writing. You may want to create a special accelerated study session for any heritage speakers in a mixed class, in addition to regular class work. But by far the most important step if your class has heritage students is to acknowledge and appreciate their language and culture skills, and to coopt their assets in order to assist the class as a whole to become an effective learning community. Heritage speakers usually want to share their knowledge, and can be valuable allies in drawing a class together for communicative purposes if they have your trust and confidence, and if they do not distance themselves from the other students. Achieving this balance of trust and faith in a mixed class is one of the most challenging situations you can face. Students must all feel they are making progress and that you are in full control of the learning situation.

An important consideration for all Arabic teachers is their professional understanding and awareness of variation, register, and vernacular language. Because a language variant is spoken rather than written, or because it does not conform with the written standard in many respects, does not make it substandard. Spoken Arabic serves its own discourse functions and is equal in linguistic and pragmatic value with the standard written variety. This understanding is especially important in dealing with heritage learners whose identities are anchored in their particular vernacular background, and who have not yet learned the spoken and written flexibility of native speakers. They should not be discouraged or penalized for their knowledge of a particular dialect. What is important is that Arabic heritage learners come to understand that context is the key to accurate choice of language register; that their awareness of situations and surroundings needs to be raised and nurtured, that their confidence in self-expression at any level can be enhanced.

Fast-Tracking Heritage Learners

If at all possible, heritage learners should be fast-tracked and mainstreamed as soon as possible into upper levels of course work to take advantage of their many linguistic and cultural assets. A separate, accelerated introductory course for heritage learners may be constructed.[2] At the university level, the ability to raise one's level of formality in speaking and the ability to use academic Arabic in both spoken and written contexts are key factors in designing a heritage course. In addition to surveying learners and developing a needs analysis for such a course, some goals and strategies for the course design could be:

1. For increasing literacy: rapid introduction of literacy skills through accelerated exposure to the script and orthography systems
2. For increasing reading skills and building MSA vocabulary: intensive reading of authentic Arabic texts starting with media and progressing to professional and literary topics
3. For increasing and expanding comprehension skills: repeated exposure to spoken MSA and/or classical Arabic texts, again starting with media Arabic and progressing to professional and literary topics[3]
4. For expression in writing: regular short writing assignments, group work, and assessment of self-expression skills
5. For building narrative skills in MSA: formal oral presentations of topics in Arabic in class, starting with concrete, informative exposées (brief, declarative presentations) and progressing to more abstract topics at a higher register
6. For vocabulary building: exposure to a range of texts, with study of Arabic derivational morphology (*ishtiqāq*) and dictionary work
7. For developing structural accuracy in MSA: substantial MSA grammatical exercises in class and as written homework assignments.

The classroom procedures for these activities and their sequencing require advance planning as well as a systematic needs analysis of particular heritage learner skills, because there are usually substantial variations as well as commonalities among heritage speakers. In addition, strong individual differences may emerge, especially in motivation and readiness for serious Arabic language study. In other words, even a class dedicated to heritage learners will be diverse in its composition.

Textbooks for Heritage Learners

As yet, there are no modern Arabic textbooks designed specifically to guide heritage learners in developing proficiency. One older book, prepared by the Middle East Center for Arab Studies (MECAS) in Lebanon in the 1960s, is titled *The Way Prepared* (*Al-Ṭarīq al-mumahhad*), and has often been used for working with heritage learners or foreign learners who have had some previous exposure to Arabic. It is based on a core vocabulary of 3,000 words developed by MECAS and, according to the first page of the preface, "it is practical. It is designed for students who are going to use Arabic in their work . . ." and is "written in the style which is used throughout the Arab world in newspapers." Passages are fully voweled at the start, but gradually the vowels are omitted and by the end of the book (82 pages), passages are unvoweled. Although designed originally for nonnative learners, this approach mirrors the way native speakers are gradually introduced to written Arabic, and this slim volume can be a useful resource for heritage speakers of Arabic who are learning the basics of Arabic script and are ready for short, practical texts.

Teaching Mixed-Level Courses

Although courses are often labeled with titles such as "first-year," "intermediate," or "advanced," it is actually rare that all students will be at precisely the same level of competence or proficiency. Especially in summer programs or study abroad programs that draw on a range of different schools, learners will bring different backgrounds, attitudes, and skills to their courses and may not fit precisely into a new framework. Even in a structured university program, not all students will fall into similar categories. Teachers need to have the confidence and resources to deal with this kind of disparity, especially because in foreign language learning, affect, motivation, and attitude can often be deeply affected by one's peers, and if one or two students do not fit in well with the rest, it can be disruptive and difficult for everyone, including the teacher.

The aim of most teachers is to work with students toward "a reasonable yet challenging goal" (Ambrose et al. 2010, 131). Discerning an appropriate level of challenge that suits a mixed class is a demanding task, but may be approached through giving structure and support to learners and also allowing them also to give structure and support to each other. In a mixed-level learning situation, developing a sense of community and shared responsibility for each other is a key to progress for all participants. This relates directly to Vygotsky's concept of the zone of proximal development (ZPD) (see also chapter 9), which refers to "the distance between what individuals can do on their own and what they can do with assistance from another individual" (Loewen and Reinders 2011, 181). Students working with you and with each other can create an optimal learning environment through providing what is usually termed "scaffolding" (structure and support). In the case of the students this scaffolding may be mutual in many ways. You, however, are the ultimate authority and guide for creating a strong and effective learning community in the Arabic classroom. Here are some general guidelines for instructing mixed-level classes.

Identify and Emphasize Strengths

As previously noted, in a mixed class it is particularly important to establish a sense of community among the learners. The primary strategy is to encourage the more advanced students to assume responsibility for the progress of others in the class as well as themselves. That is, rather than allowing them to show off their skills or act bored with topics they have already studied, it is up to you to bring them into a controlled, constructive relationship with the learning experience, with both you and the other students in the class. Many more emotionally mature students do this automatically; others need to be led into this role. Suggestions for bringing more advanced learners into harmony with the class include:

1. Assessing their strengths openly and allowing them to talk about their previous experiences with Arabic in front of the class (in Arabic, if possible)
2. Asking them what they have found most challenging about learning Arabic
3. In small group work, distribute the more advanced learners into each group; do not allow them to form a "superior" group together. Emphasize that you want them to share their strengths and take leadership roles.

Allow time for group reflection on the learning experience. At the end of class, perhaps once a week, devote five to ten minutes to feedback from all students in the class. This is not at all the same as letting them ask questions; it means allowing learners to express their reactions to the previous week's work—honestly giving their personal take on the class or specific activities. To get started, ask if anyone wants to volunteer to provide a reaction or let you know what they are thinking about the class (in Arabic or in English). This may be slow at first, but usually someone says something, and that then encourages others. Do not jump in and start talking yourself; this is a moment for learner reflection. Again, specifically ask for their reactions, not questions. Questions can be asked at any later time. By soliciting reactions and comments rather than questions, you allow learners to share observations—satisfaction as well as frustration—and this process can stabilize the class so that personal or academic differences have a chance to emerge and even out.

It is important to remember that when you listen to students expressing their reactions or feelings about the class, you should acknowledge their contributions by paraphrasing and putting into your own words what you have heard in order to check that you understand what they are saying, and not by asking them questions, defending yourself, or challenging their remarks. This may seem like a stilted process at first, but if practiced with integrity it can accelerate the creation of community and the quality of learning.[4]

Do Not Criticize a Student's Previous Teachers

This should go without saying, but I have witnessed situations where one teacher indicates dissatisfaction with a previous teacher's efforts. Even if you are disappointed in the quantity or quality of students' learning, it is *not* appropriate for any teacher to comment negatively on any previous teacher's methods, choices, or goals. This is a key ethical standard for professional academic conduct; no matter what you may judge personally to be the case, do not allow yourself to criticize another teacher in front of your students. This goes for your body language as well: no eye-rolling, no loud sighing, no frowning.

Use Small Group Work

Arrange for groups of students to undertake interactive projects together. As noted in chapter 9, it is not a good idea to allow students to group themselves. Either have students count off by fours or fives, and put all the ones together, the twos together, etc., or find another way to group them (alphabetically by last name or first name, for instance). The groupings should be random and diverse, and not consist of friends who will be distracted from the task by chatting with each other. It is important that more advanced learners be distributed among those who are less advanced.

Meet with Each Student Outside of Class

When classes are mixed in terms of levels and background, it is especially important to meet one-on-one with every student at least once for about 15 minutes during a semester; preferably more often. This can be a course requirement; about three weeks into a course, send around a sign-up sheet with 15- or 20-minute time slots on it and have them sign up to meet with you. If they ask why, just say you want to get to know them better individually. You will find that for the most part, they appreciate your making time to see them individually, and you will be better able to assess their motivations, backgrounds, and strengths. Some students may have questions or concerns that they would not automatically share with you, but this gives them the chance. This opportunity also opens the door to subsequent consultations during office hours. Once students have crossed your office threshold, they will be more likely to return.

Develop Goals and Review

If the class is very mixed and the students are new to each other, generate some shared goals and guidelines to get everyone on the same track. For example, devote the first week or the first part of every class to review grammar points or vocabulary that some may have covered and others not. This will allow everyone to calibrate his or her strengths with the rest of the class.

The topic of this chapter is one that arises constantly in teacher training; almost all teachers face it, and it requires tact and diplomacy, but also firmness and leadership. Finding out who your students really are as individuals is the first and most important step you can take to smoothing out the challenges of working with diverse and mixed classes.

Study Questions and Activities

1. In an article discussing the status and role of heritage languages, former MLA president Mary Louise Pratt refers to the United States as a "language cemetery," a place where foreign language skills are so discouraged that they eventually die (Pratt 2003, 111). How do you see this as it applies to Arabic as a heritage language? Do you think Pratt is right?
2. In mixed-level classes, tensions can arise among learners of different backgrounds. What are some of the ways that those tensions can be eased? Can they be avoided? Write a two-page paper presenting your own ideas on this topic and your own experiences as a teacher or as a student in such a class. What works? What doesn't?
3. Have you encountered "false" beginners in a first-year Arabic class? If you were the teacher, how did you handle this? If you were a student, how would you describe that person's relationship to the rest of the class?
4. What do you think of the concept of "zone of proximal development" (ZPD)? Do some research on this concept and write a two-page report on your interpretation of it and your experience with it. The article by DeGuerrero and Villamil is a good place to start.

Further Reading

Byrnes Heidi, ed. 2005. "Perspectives. The Position of Heritage Languages in Language Education Policy." *Modern Language Journal* 89, no. 4:582–616.

DeGuerrero, Maria C. M., and Olga S. Villamil. 2000. "Activating the ZPD: Mutual Scaffolding in L2 Peer Revision." *Modern Language Journal* 84, no. 1:51–68.

Ibrahim, Zeinab, and Jehan Allam. 2006. "Arabic Learners and Heritage Students Redefined: Present and Future." In *Handbook for Arabic Language Teaching Professionals in the 21st Century*, edited by Kassem Wahba, Zeinab Taha, and Liz England, 437–446. Mahwah, NJ: Lawrence Erlbaum Associates.

Kenny, Dallas. 1992. "Arab-Americans Learning Arabic: Motivation and Attitudes." In *The Arabic Language in America*, edited by Aleya Rouchdy, 119–161. Detroit: Wayne State University Press.

_____ 1959. *A Selected Word List of Modern Literary Arabic*. Beirut: Dar Al-Kutub. (This excellent word list was designed, as noted in the preface, in order "to comprise the intelligent layman's vocabulary." It consists of about 3,000 words, ten appendices, a gazetteer (geographical terms), and is both Arabic-English and English-Arabic. Out of print and difficult to find, it is nonetheless a classic of Arabic lexicography intended for foreign learners.)

Middle East Centre for Arab Studies (MECAS). 1967. *The Way Prepared* (*Al-Ṭarīq al-mumahhad*): *A Reading Book in Modern Arabic*. Beirut: Khayats. (Fifty carefully graded texts ranging from simple to complex. Initial texts are completely voweled but voweling is gradually reduced until it disappears at the end. This book is calibrated with the MECAS *Selected Word List of Modern Literary Arabic*).

Reynolds, Rachel R., Kathryn M. Howard, and Julia Deak. 2009. "Heritage Language Learners in First-Year Foreign Language Courses: A Report of General Data across Learner Subtypes." *Foreign Language Annals* 42, no. 2:250–269.

 Notes

1. A heritage language learner is "a person who is studying a language to which they have a family or cultural connection. In most instances, the target language is the language spoken by their parents, grandparents, or other ancestors. Often, heritage language learners have been exposed to the heritage language in the family environment; however, that exposure may vary from minimal to substantial" (Loewen and Reinders 2011, 80–81).

2. "The foreign language teaching profession should clearly understand that these students need an approach that builds on what they bring to the classroom rather than one that begins at ground zero" (Gutierrez 1997, 34). Along the same lines, Garrett declares that "heritage learners should have their own section or track, at least through the intermediate level, because their learning strategies and goals are quite different from those of nonheritage students; they need different materials as well" (2009, 727).

3. In one survey of suburban Detroit Arab American high school students studying Arabic, it was reported that "when asked to choose the MSA skill that was most important to them, [heritage] students reported that listening comprehension was the most important, followed by reading and writing" (Kenny 1992, 133).

4. See community language learning (CLL) sources for more description of this process, including works by Curran and Rardin.

Part V

The Pedagogy
of Comprehension

Comprehension and Arabic Input: Overview

CHAPTER 12

During comprehension two sources of information are used by readers and/or listeners. The first is explicit linguistic information found in the text (either written or spoken). The second is topic and world knowledge information held by the reader or listener.

Elizabeth Bernhardt

Understanding a sentence is much more akin to understanding a theme in music than one may think.

Ludwig Wittgenstein

The modalities or skills of language learning are usually identified as speaking, writing, listening, and reading. These four aspects of language are all essential, but they require different levels of effort, concentration, memory recall, motor skills (such as handwriting or speech articulation), and awareness. Reading and listening are comprehension-based and often described as "receptive" skills; speaking and writing are expression-based and described as "productive" skills. In general, spontaneous speaking is considered the most demanding skill because it calls for immediate production of accurate and context-appropriate language without time to prepare or carefully construct what one wants to say. Listening requires immediate recognition of target language vocabulary and structure under the pressure of time. Writing requires productive skills from the learner but often allows learners time to construct text thoughtfully. Reading has been considered the least demanding modality, allowing learners time to peruse text, think about meaning, and use dictionaries if necessary to access lexical unknowns.[1]

Foreign language learners face the substantial task of approaching all modalities at once, unlike first language learners who, as infants, first encounter listening comprehension, then make efforts at speaking and putting words together meaningfully, and later become literate. First language acquisition of Arabic starts out with listening and speaking vernacular Arabic in the particular colloquial variant that an infant is exposed to; most learners of Arabic as a foreign language have to start out listening to and trying to speak *fuṣḥā*, the literary language, as well as reading and learning how to write it—all at the same time.

⬡ Comprehension and Expression

The two-way street of language engages human beings in constant dyadic mental activity: comprehending language and expressing ourselves in language. To a great extent, SLA research has validated the idea that comprehension is fundamental; that is, it is the basis for building both understanding and self-expression. For this reason, comprehension studies in reading and listening are of vital importance to Arabic language teaching and learning. In particular, exposure to large quantities of **comprehensible input** can build learner confidence and competence at the same time. In this chapter and in the following two chapters, the two comprehension modalities of reading and listening are discussed. This chapter aims to provide an overview and introduction to theories of comprehension in both reading and listening, while the following two chapters focus on details of each one.

Comprehension: Schemata, or Background Knowledge

Much of the meaning of any text—read or heard—is not in the text, *per se*, but in the background or schematic knowledge of readers/listeners, allowing them to infer possible messages of a text. This type of preexisting knowledge is often referred to as a schema (plural: schemata). In general there are two types of schemata:

1. Formal schemata: background knowledge of the formal, rhetorical, organizational structures of different types of texts, genres, narratives, and speech acts (e.g., short stories, novels, news, fables, sports reports, conversation, formal speech, informal speech)
2. Content schemata: real-world knowledge about the content area of text or talk (e.g., mathematics, elections, soccer, bridge, gardening)

These components of cognitive awareness are crucial to comprehension. Readers' or listeners' failure to activate an appropriate schema results in various degrees of noncomprehension or misunderstanding. To these two types of schemata can be added a third: grammatical or structural schemata. That is, for example, in a language like Arabic which has grammatical morphemes such as case endings, mood markers, and other types of essential inflections, learners need background knowledge about grammatical structure in order to notice and pay attention to these features. If learners have little or no previous background knowledge or structure into which to fit these categories, they will not play an important role in comprehension. In fact, they will likely be ignored.[2]

 ## Bottom-Up and Top-Down Processing

These terms refer to the kind of orientation that a listener or reader takes to a text. Bottom-up processing begins with the text itself: using the words, structures, and organization to grasp the text's message. Top-down processing, much like schemata, begins with context and real-world knowledge: what the circumstances around the text are, what the general topic is, or what I as a reader/listener already know about this topic. Blending these two processes is what makes comprehension of any foreign language text—spoken or written—possible.[3]

Comprehension: Arabic Reading and Listening

Listening and reading can both "be characterized as problem-solving activities involving the formation of hypotheses, the drawing of inferences, and the resolution of ambiguities and uncertainties in the input in order to assign meaning" (Hadley 2001, 179). One topic that has increased in importance since the 1980s is the pivotal influence of comprehension in language learning, and the cognitive processes that make comprehension possible. Krashen's original "input hypothesis" and his focus on comprehensible input as essential to language acquisition placed comprehension at the forefront of research and of implementation in the classroom. Listeners and readers take in explicit language information and each processes that information according to their own experience and background knowledge. As Bernhardt puts it, "fundamentally, then, there is explicit language input and there is inferencing involved" (1990, 272). The inferencing process and the structure of individual schemata, or knowledge structures, are what Bernhardt refers to as the "nonvisible" facets of comprehension, "conceptually-driven, implicit, internal, reader/listener-based, and knowledge-based" (273). Particularly when it comes to cross-cultural inferencing, it becomes critical to consider what learners bring to the comprehension process, and to take advantage of what is already known in order to build new types and domains of knowledge pertinent to the target language and its culture. It is also crucial to prevent misunderstandings through attention to areas where meaning and cultural frameworks differ substantially in the target language from the learners' L1.

❖ Comprehensible Input and the Input Hypothesis

In the classroom situation, it is important for teachers to be able to provide comprehensible input, or **i + 1**, as Krashen described it. "The input hypothesis claims that humans acquire language in only one way—by understanding messages, or by receiving 'comprehensible input.' We progress along the natural order [of acquisition] . . . by understanding input that contains structures at our next 'stage'—structures that are a bit beyond our current level of competence. (We move from i, our current level, to i + 1, the next level)" (Krashen 1985, 2). Comprehension is fundamental to Krashen and he believes not only that "listening comprehension and reading comprehension are of primary importance in the language program" but also that the ability to express oneself in speech or writing is subsidiary, and founded on solid understanding of input (Krashen and Terrell 1983, 32). Since the 1980s and Krashen's first formulation of this principle, research has validated and elaborated upon the idea that input is key to language learning.

❖ Input Processing: Principles

One useful theory for discussing comprehension at early stages of language learning is that of input processing (IP), developed primarily by Bill VanPatten.[4] VanPatten proposes three principles that pertain to learner comprehension of a target language, focusing on what learners do in "initial data gathering" (2007, 127), that is, when they are first exposed to new input. First, learners tend to grasp words before structure; they "enter the task of SLA knowing that languages have words. They are thus first driven to make form-meaning connections that are lexical in nature" (117). Additionally, learners will seek out content lexical items (e.g., nouns, verbs, adjectives) before they deal with function words (e.g., particles, conjunctions) or inflections on nouns and verbs (e.g., genitive case, plural, past tense). VanPatten offers the following principle:

> "The Primacy of Content Words Principle: Learners process content words in the input before anything else" (ibid.).

Even more important for Arabic teaching is VanPatten's second observation that grammatical markers that provide redundant information (e.g., case-marking in Arabic, agreement inflections on adjectives) will only be processed by learners after they process lexical items for meaning:

> "The Lexical Preference Principle: Learners will process lexical items for meaning before grammatical forms when both encode the same semantic information" (2007, 118).

Related to this is VanPatten's observation that some learners may never process grammatical markers in the input if those markers provide information that they consider redundant to lexical content items. Thus his third principle, the Preference for Nonredundancy Principle, states:

> "Learners are more likely to process nonredundant meaningful grammatical markers before they process redundant meaningful markers" (2007, 119).

That is, if a grammatical marker provides key semantic information (such as the plural inflection on Arabic nouns), it will be processed before a grammatical marker that provides little or no additional semantic content (e.g., case marking on Arabic nouns). Van Patten comments: "one of the predictions of the IP model is that as long as comprehension remains effortful, learners will continue to focus on the processing of lexical items *to the detriment of grammatical markers*, given that lexical items maximize the extraction of meaning, at least from the learner's point of view" (119; emphasis added).

In addition to the three principles given above, VanPatten proposes six more:

1. "The First Noun Principle: Learners tend to process the first noun or pronoun they encounter in a sentence as the subject" (2007, 122).
2. "The L1 Transfer Principle: Learners begin acquisition with L1 parsing procedures" (122).

3. "The Event Probability Principle: Learners may rely on event probabilities, where possible, instead of the First Noun Principle to interpret sentences" (123).

4. "The Lexical Semantics Principle: Learners may rely on lexical semantics, where possible, instead of the First Noun Principle (or an L1 parsing procedure) to interpret sentences" (124).

5. "The Contextual Constraint Principle: Learners may rely less on the First Noun Principle (or L1 transfer) if preceding context constrains the possible interpretation of a clause or sentence" (124).

6. "The Sentence Location Principle: Learners tend to process items in sentence initial position before those in final position and those in medial position" (125).

All of these nine principles are focused on initial conditions, that is, on the learner's first encounter with a specific instance of target language input. VanPatten states that this "model attempts to describe what learners do on their own" that is, their instinctive attempts to deal with new information in the target language. He notes that the model is not about pedagogy or instructional intervention, although the model may assist teachers in sifting out patterns of misunderstanding, if they exist.

Implications for Arabic

Readers of this book who have had experience teaching Arabic will recognize in VanPatten's principles the preferences of many American learners to first seek out content words for comprehension before they begin to process items that indicate grammatical relations (e.g., gender agreement, case, and mood inflection). This is a major reason why vocabulary building is systematically prior to and fundamental for the development of grammatical competence in Arabic. What does this imply for teaching reading and listening comprehension in Arabic? Although this is a straightforward question, the answers are complex, especially for listening comprehension, where learners may experience great variation in input outside the classroom environment. Strategies and techniques that teachers can employ to facilitate learners' understanding of written or spoken text will advance learners' confidence as well as their competence.

⬡ Comprehension Facilitation: Advance Organizers

When devising an Arabic reading or listening task, it is important that the learners be prepared to read or listen in the most efficient and attentive way possible. To do this, many teachers have effectively used what are called "advance organizers," preparatory materials for introducing relevant information about the text to come. One definition of advance organizer states that it is "an activity which helps students organize their thoughts and ideas as a preparation for learning or studying something" (Richards and Schmidt 2010, 14). "Studies on student comprehension of relatively short reading and listening passages indicate that understanding is enhanced by prior presentation of an 'anchoring framework' such as pictures, key words, or scripts, linked to the context of the passage" (Herron et al. 1998, 238). In particular, declarative information or leading questions may be provided to learners to help direct their attention to key points of the comprehension exercise. In addition, "brainstorming, or idea gathering, is often suggested as a helpful advance organizer to textual materials," (240). You and your students together devise a list or a set of ideas that students think may surface in the reading. This kind of interactive and participatory preparation for reading or listening can be an effective alternative to specific pointers from you as to what to expect in a particular written or spoken text. Both declarative and brainstormed information, then, can lead learners to comprehend faster and more efficiently through providing a preview of what to expect.

One strategy for introducing a video suggests "that teachers write on the board several declarative sentences that outline, in chronological order, major scenes from [an] upcoming video, and then read the sentences aloud to the students prior to viewing the video" (Herron et al. 1998, 244–245). This kind of previewing is highly useful to students' cognitive processing of information because it orients them and directs their attention to preselected components of an upcoming text, allowing them a foothold of sorts, even though some of the text may be beyond their comprehension. This kind of pedagogical strategy can be used in a range of different approaches; it is not method-based, but method-neutral.

 ## Arabic Advance Organizers and Content-Based Instruction: A Case in Point

In 1997 Ryding and Stowasser published the results of an experiment in Arabic language and area studies integration implemented at the Foreign Service Institute (FSI). Authentic Arabic texts on various aspects of culture, history, economics, society, and international relations were selected for listening purposes as follow-ups to area studies lectures given in English on related topics. A key pedagogical challenge in using these texts about Arab culture and society was that they were in MSA, and that much of the content was still beyond the capabilities of the students. I provide an excerpt from the article here to describe how the idea of "advance organizers" was implemented for that project in Arabic listening comprehension.

A series of tasks was . . . designed for each text. The main point of these activities was *not* for students to be able to translate the texts, but for them to be able to

1. acquire some basic vocabulary
2. practice listening for specific bits of information
3. guess meaning from context

These have been identified as communicative skills that FSI students will need at post, and they are also skills that any learner can use in order to deal with language above his or her proficiency level.

Stages of activity

The text-based activities are divided into two stages. In the first stage, students are exposed to five sentences culled from the narrative matrix. These are "core" sentences that contain salient facts from the text. They are presented to the learners in writing, with translation. These sentences are then exploited by the teacher as a source for pronunciation and structure drills, and rehearsed extensively in class to prepare for eventual memorization. Students may ask questions on structure or vocabulary, but the aim of the class exercise is to get them used to comprehending sentence-length utterances as well as to have them grasp certain basic cultural facts. The assignment for the students is to copy all the sentences by hand and to memorize at least three out of the five for recitation a day or two later. Although the copying exercise may seem elementary, the issue here is that they are trying to handwrite in a completely new way, and the motor memory that results from writing in the new script reinforces their command of both the visual and the verbal input.

During the next class period, usually a day or two following the first, students are expected to recite their memorized sentences. While this obviously reflects audiolingual practice, it serves more purposes for Arabic learners in this phase, since in addition to

---

continued

giving them a toehold in the foreign language, it prepares them for listening to and at least partially comprehending a matrix narrative in which these concepts are embedded.

Students are [then] allowed to hear the entire narrative. . . . Since they are already familiar with the topic, getting the general idea is not beyond them. The second step is for them to listen specifically for their memorized sentences. This allows them to focus on familiar specifics and not to get distracted by what they *don't* know. The students are then provided with a list of approximately ten "listening items," key words or phrases from the text, and asked to listen specifically for them. These items are not glossed, and students are encouraged to guess their meaning from context, confirming or correcting their guesses with their teacher. The teacher winds up the exercise by reviewing the "listening list" and providing cultural and/or linguistic explanation of its items. The last thing the learners do at this stage is copy the tape for future reference. Usually they also want to see the written text at this point, and it is provided for them. The printed text itself, as well as the recording, can serve as a way of measuring their comprehension level in later months, when they can recycle it using different types of exercises and grasp considerably more of the content. One of the assets of using essential cultural texts is that whereas they can be used in the early phase of a course for training in partial skills, such as selective listening, they can also be recycled at later stages for different types of text-based tasks, incorporating more ambitious cultural and communicative goals.

The materials developed for the integration of area studies and language studies were highly successful components of the Arabic program. The students progressed through the taped and written area studies materials at the pace of two or three hours a week. It did not occupy much of their class time, but enough to give them a sense of having covered the material in the TL, and to get their feet wet in listening to narratives such as they might hear on radio or television, or in lectures and speeches.

The classroom activity traditionally associated with texts on the target culture—discussion and questions—has been explicitly avoided. This is for two reasons:

1. the students' level of spoken language skills is nowhere near high enough to do this, and
2. the language of discussion, spoken Arabic, would be different from the language of the text

Although they do not have total control of the text, the students have at least tackled a basic cultural topic in the TL and practiced several skills: listening comprehension, guessing meaning from context, reading, handwriting, and pronunciation. They have also acquired, at least in terms of recognition, some new and culturally significant vocabulary. This does not overtax their limited skill repertoire, and it lays the groundwork for building more advanced skills. Most importantly, what they have already covered in their area studies seminars in English has now been given a contextual linguistic reality. (Ryding and Stowasser 1997, 114–116)[5]

 ## Conclusion

Comprehension of texts can be facilitated in various ways that allow learners to grasp essential points, learn key vocabulary, raise their ambiguity tolerance, reduce anxiety, and practice listening for meaning. Advance organizers for comprehension tasks structure key pedagogical tactics for facilitating understanding in both reading and listening. The next two chapters of this book deal in detail with the skills of reading and listening in Arabic.

❀ Study Questions and Activities

1. In your experience, what kind of Arabic input is easiest to teach and/or understand: written or spoken?
2. Discuss advantages of top-down versus bottom-up processing for Arabic.
3. Discuss VanPatten's three basic principles of input processing. In your experience, are they all valid for Arabic? Is one of them more basic than the others?
4. Have you tried using advance organizers in your teaching? If so, discuss how you did it and its effectiveness.
5. Have you developed additional ideas about advance organizers for comprehension of written or spoken Arabic? How can you put these ideas to use in a classroom setting?

❀ Further Reading

Bernhardt, Elizabeth B. 1990. "Knowledge-Based Inferencing in Second Language Comprehension." *Georgetown University Round Table on Languages and Linguistics* 1990, edited by James E. Alatis, 271–284. Washington, DC: Georgetown University Press.

Hadley, Alice Omaggio. 2001. *Teaching Language in Context*, 3rd ed. Boston: Heinle & Heinle. (Especially chapter 4, "The Role of Context in Comprehension and Learning.")

Larson-Freeman, Diane, and Marti Anderson. 2011. *Techniques and Principles in Language Teaching*. Oxford: Oxford University Press. (Especially chapter 8, "The Comprehension Approach.")

❀ Notes

1. The reference here is to reading for information, not close reading or critical reading. See Krashen 1990 for a discussion of the importance of reading and writing.

2. See related issues in the section on input processing in this chapter.

3. "Comprehension is an associative process that entails making connections between explicit textual information and implicit conceptual information" (Bernhardt 1990, 272).

4. See chapter 2. Also, for an overview and bibliography, see VanPatten 2007.

5. A list of the area studies topics used for this project is included in appendix D.

Reading Comprehension in Arabic

CHAPTER 13

Unlike speech, which a child can acquire through normal interaction with others, reading is a skill that must be learned through instruction.

Michael Everson

But when we read [out loud] don't we feel the word-shapes somehow causing our utterance?

Ludwig Wittgenstein

Reading has traditionally been a privileged skill in the teaching of Arabic. It has been given primacy in academic programs from grammar-translation to audiolingual, communicative, and comprehension approaches, because it is the key to Arabic literacy. Even US government training programs focus extensively on learning to read modern standard Arabic for professional purposes. One could therefore say that reading remains the core skill in most professional and academic curricula.[1] One of the greatest advantages in learning to read Arabic is that the contemporary form of the language differs so little in grammatical structure from the classical form that progressing from one to the other is not as great a challenge as, say, reading contemporary Italian and then progressing to Latin. Naturally, there are substantive differences in style, rhetoric, topics, and vocabulary, but that said, the ability to read standard Arabic opens the door to centuries of Arabic culture and literature. Nonetheless, there has been precious little research on learning to read Arabic as a foreign language, and many teaching programs continue to use a grammar/translation approach when it comes to dealing with texts: students reading out loud and translating into English.[2]

Reading as Input

Krashen has advocated using extensive reading in the L2—especially at the post-beginner stages—as a primary form of L2 input. He advocates providing "a superrich environment in the first and second language that includes large libraries with compelling books, magazines, newspapers, and comic books, and classes that promote an interest in reading through literature and story telling" (1993, 19). That is, he encourages reading for pleasure in the L2. He further states, "comprehensible input in the form of reading is the source of our ability to read, our writing style, much of our vocabulary and spelling ability, and our more advanced grammatical development." He calls this the "reading hypothesis" (Krashen 1991, 413). In particular, he emphasizes that reading fosters the acquisition of "the written standard" (421) form of language necessary for academic literacy.

Extensive Independent Reading

Day and Bamford have provided a set of ten principles for extensive reading in the L2, in line with Krashen's comprehensible input hypothesis. At least part of the reason for assigning extensive reading is to help learners develop a taste and appreciation for L2 reading. The list is as follows:

1. The reading material should be easy. Learners should be able to grasp 98 percent of the words in a fiction text "for unassisted understanding."

2. A variety of reading material on a wide range of topics must be available.
3. Learners choose what they want to read.
4. Learners read as much as possible.
5. The purpose of reading is usually related to pleasure, information, and general understanding.
6. Reading is its own reward.
7. Reading speed is usually faster than slower.
8. Reading is individual and silent.
9. Teachers orient and guide their students.
10. The teacher is a role model of a reader (Day and Bamford 2002).

In their article, Day and Bamford provide detailed discussion of each principle and its application, noting that these principles are intended not as a rigid framework but as a tool for teachers "to examine their beliefs about reading in general and extensive reading in particular, and the ways they teach reading" (2002, 1).

Reading as Interaction

Readers, even L2 readers, interact with texts as they read by fitting the knowledge they are gaining into their own world-knowledge or schemata, and recalibrating their understanding as they progress though a reading passage. In literary theory, the "reader response" or "aesthetic response" to a text forms part of the interaction "on which a theory of literary communication may be built" (Iser 1978, ix). As Kramsch puts it, "Reading is the joint construction of a social reality between the reader and the text" (1985, 357). But as Kramsch points out, "foreign language learners, as non-intended readers, have the difficult task of understanding intentions and beliefs that are not necessarily part of their representation of the world" (ibid.). Therefore the interaction between an Arabic text and a nonnative Arabic reader may well require pedagogical intervention to help the learner construe, interpret, and appreciate the text. The complex cognitive resources needed in confronting an Arabic text require that "the reader . . . become capable of activating several cognitive processes simultaneously" (Koda 1992, 509).[3] The challenge of a different orthography combined with the cultural distance between English-speaking and Arabic-speaking communities means that the teacher has a key role to play not only in accelerating reading fluency but also in developing true transcultural competence.[4]

Complexities of Arabic Reading

The study and teaching of reading skills in Arabic is intertwined with the mechanics of learning Arabic script and phonology; it requires a considerable cognitive shift for learners because of its right-to-left directionality; it is more complex than reading in European languages and therefore slower to develop; it interrelates closely with the study of vocabulary;[5] and it often exhibits rhetorical organization that is difficult for learners to grasp without scaffolding provided by the instructor.[6]

Reading Comprehension in Arabic: First Stages

Because learning Arabic involves gaining control of a new form of script, initial stages of reading focus on learning how to process visual information that is challenging in four ways:

- The script and letters are totally new to the learners;
- The letters themselves change shape according to their position within words;
- The script is processed visually in the opposite direction from European languages; and
- The short vowels in ordinary (unadjusted) script are invisible.

Most of these challenges are readily overcome with intensive practice in learning orthography, handwriting, and reading in the new language; however, the fourth element, the absence of short vowel notation in ordinary script, remains a long-term salient issue for learners in processing new text. I am not here referring to the short vowels that act as inflectional markers (*iʕrāb*), but rather word-internal short vowels (*ḥarakāt*) that constitute meaningful components of words, which can only be learned through memorization and practice, and which constitute a consistent challenge of "recognition complexity" for learners of Arabic even at advanced levels of proficiency.[7] Past the introductory levels of learning script and pronunciation, subsequent reading instruction has the goals of both reinforcing comprehension and extending it in various ways, with the aim of helping students reach higher and higher levels of comfort with vocabulary and grammatical structure, as well as introducing more complex forms of narrative style. However, the perceptual challenges of Arabic orthography demand continuing pedagogical attention.

 # Print Perception

Bernhardt discusses three general stages in efficient print perception:

1. Features of letters (their shapes and diacritics)
2. Optimization of attention—the "rapid distinguishing between groups of letters" (such as *kabīr* and *khabīr*)
3. "Increasing economy"—ignoring context-predictable elements. (1986, 96)

As she also points out,

> Reading involves many more interacting factors than simply the perception of print," but "*perceptual questions are particularly relevant to research with readers who must switch orthographic or logographic systems in acquiring reading skills.* A credible hypothesis is that the apparent inherent difficulties in the learning of non-Western languages and of languages in non-Roman alphabets may be due partially to a set of developmental, perceptual stages through which readers must progress in order to reach a level of preparation for comprehension." (1985, 97; italics in original)

Taking this into account with Hansen's findings indicates that the pedagogy of Arabic reading may need to consider more profoundly the cognitive difficulties of word processing.[8]

 # Arabic Orthographic Depth

Arabic has what are termed both "shallow" and "deep" orthographies, that is, it differs in how it "portrays sound-to-symbol relationships" (Everson 2011, 260). For elementary school L1 speakers of Arabic, short vowels are marked in words for beginning learners ("shallow" script) to make word structure and pronunciation easily accessible. This practice of voweling continues but is gradually tapered off as children progress to more advanced reading levels. For most L2 learners, however, the "shallow" script is not available after the first few weeks of class (if at all). Most learners are actively discouraged from writing in or adding vowels to printed text and are encouraged to work independent of vowel marking. This is done because the L2 learners are expected to perform as adults; however, they are not often given the necessary time on task to develop a reliable and accurate core vocabulary based on shallow orthography. As one distinguished professor of Arabic observes,

> Arabic textbooks intended for foreign learners have traditionally followed the practice of not inserting the Arabic short vowels or other diacritical markers in the material. This tradition may derive from a parallel tradition of presenting Arabic writings for native learners just past the early stages of their schooling. However, the absence of vowels in books designed for foreign learners, as well as for native speakers, especially beginners, adds considerably to the difficulty of learning correct pronunciation of words and leads to serious errors. (Sawaie 2012, 142)

Everson reports on research that assessed "the voweling of the text and the presentation of words in context as critical components of L1 Arabic reading development" (2011, 260). The omission of short vowels in word presentation at early learning levels may be more important than previously considered. "Orthographic depth and morphosyntactic complexity may interact with L2 proficiency effects in determining L2 reading development, and . . . the steps associated with L1 reading efficiency (accuracy before speed) may apply to L2 word recognition development" (261).[9]

 ## Reading and Deciphering

Beginning learners need to be able to distinguish the various forms of letters within the context of a word, that is, the ability to read and "sound out" a word, and also to recognize it when it is heard. This ability should increase in speed as well as accuracy as learners develop more and more familiarity with a restricted number of texts. Rereading texts, reviewing them, and recycling them at a later date into course work has been shown to be an effective practice. The idea is to build a foundation of deep familiarity with the script, with words in context, and with key texts.

 ## Reading Aloud: Why?

The idea of reading a text aloud may sound like a first grade exercise that takes no or little brain power from students; however, there are certain skills in reading a non-Roman script that make reading aloud an important auxiliary exercise in developing fluency as well as recognition skills. Because of the invisibility of short vowels, every Arabic text read aloud is a test as well as an exercise. Larkin argues for "reserving a place for oral reading in the elementary Arabic classroom, provided it is oral reading that is specifically and attentively guided by the teacher" (1995, 157). She refers to this as "guided oral reading" (159). As she points out, "there is no way for the teacher to gain access to the decoding process that the student is employing without having him/her read aloud" (160). Reading Arabic aloud does four things for students:

1. It helps to improve accuracy and speed in pronunciation;
2. It helps in accurately identifying short vowels;
3. It helps in clarifying distinctions between long vowels and short vowels;
4. It provides input for developing a sense of morphological patterning in Arabic.[10]

This is a key step in learning Arabic. Studies have shown that what undermines learners' ability to read Arabic fluently and accurately is their inability to identify word structure efficiently because of the lack of short vowel marking, even at advanced levels.[11] Therefore, it is recommended that students be given extensive practice with the sound and shape of high-frequency words, and that these words be rehearsed and reviewed in systematic ways. Deliberate and repeated review of vocabulary and word structure improves greatly the ability to recognize words in different contexts as well as the confidence of learners when confronting new texts.

 ## Word Recognition in Arabic Text

The cognitive processes for reading comprehension are complex, but research findings are facilitating our understanding of comprehension. Georgetown University Medical Center neuroscientists have found that skilled readers of English "are able quickly to recognize words without sounding them out . . . because each word has been placed in a kind of visual dictionary." The report continues: "What we found is that once we've learned a word, it is placed in a purely visual dictionary in the brain . . . having a purely visual representation allows for the fast and efficient word recognition we see in skilled readers" (Georgetown University 2012, 1). "The brain first uses phonology to encode the word and match the sound with the written word. But after encountering a word a few more times, most people no longer need to employ the phonology," states postdoctoral research fellow Laurie Glezer in the article (Georgetown University 2012, 2).

This finding has far-reaching implications for English-speaking learners of languages with non-Roman scripts and may account for the difficulty "hump" that Arabic learners often encounter at the high-intermediate or advanced level, when extensive reading starts to be part of required assignments. It is one thing for beginners to learn how to decipher Arabic words; it is quite another to be able immediately to recognize words in context when time and extent of text coverage are determining factors of performance. English-speaking readers are unconsciously trying to form visual images of Arabic words, but those visual images are impoverished because they do not include short vowel markings, *ḥarakāt*. When it comes to homographs (words that appear identical in Arabic script when internal short vowel markings are invisible) in context, learners cannot rely on their "visual dictionary"—they must use other strategies to determine meaning.

Research done by Mughazy on native Arabic speaking readers has shown that "proficient readers of Arabic employ top-down strategies more frequently and efficiently than bottom-up strategies. In other words, they do not make significant use of vowel marking when made available. Rather, they rely on their knowledge of the content, morpho-phonemic patterns, and intuitions about the statistical probabilities of word order to disambiguate homographs" (Mughazy 2005–2006, 57).[12] The author notes that skilled Arabic readers use their experience with word frequency to decide on word meaning in context when it comes to deciphering homographs. Here is an area, then, where nonnative readers will need to develop specific reading strategies and coping mechanisms in order to build even a fraction of the knowledge that native Arabic readers use when processing a text. The invisibility of short vowels is usually downplayed as a factor in literacy development for Arabic learners, but from a visual perception point of view, and from a language acquisition point of view, the absence of short vowels is immediately and consistently problematic for developing word-knowledge and literacy.

✤ Research on Reading Comprehension in L2 Arabic

A recently published research article on Arabic as a second language by Gunna Hansen finds that Arabic script in and of itself is a significant obstacle to learner efforts at reading comprehension. When learners come from an L1 where words are spelled out in their entirety, they intuitively seek similar clarity in other languages; any significant differences in word representation and orthography conventions require complex cognitive computations—what Hansen refers to as a "heavily charged decoding system" (2010, 578). In a recent article I summarized Hansen's findings as follows:

> She calls the impact of the "unfamiliar graphemes" of Arabic "remarkable" in its effect on reading speed and decoding, and also notes that any improvement made during the first two years of study "seems to stagnate" thereafter. These are key findings with extensive implications for teaching materials and approaches. She closes with the observation that "a fundamental principle in reading instruction" for children is to expose learners "to a multitude of easily read text material without new vocabulary and unfamiliar grammatical structures." She advises building reading skills with adult foreign language learners in much the same way: "Texts should be understood so easily that learners' cognitive capacity can be directed toward word recognition alone—instead of an analytical process" (2010, 579). Certainly this contrasts with the usual practice of presenting new texts loaded with unfamiliar vocabulary and requiring students constantly to decipher words as well as grasp the text's meaning. (Ryding 2013)

The results of these published findings point to considerable differences between native English speakers and native Arabic speakers in cognitive processing at word level, indicating that for greater pedagogical effectiveness, attention must be paid to the way in which words are perceived and stored in memory, and to allowing for extensive reinforcement of vocabulary through recycling of familiar texts and themes. Arabic learners—even at the advanced stage—do not have access to the highly reliable frequency judgments used by native readers to analyze word meaning, nor do they have the extensive morphosyntactic background of native speakers that would enable them to accurately and rapidly predict derivational or inflectional forms of particular words. Teaching Arabic learners at least partial word-recognition strategies (such as the typical VSO sequence in written Arabic) may help them guess intelligently about word meaning and sentence structure, but in general, guessing the meaning of unfamiliar Arabic words remains a very high-level skill. Coady and Huckin point out that "guessing word meanings by use of contextual clues is far more difficult than is generally realized" (1997, 2).

Laufer, when discussing English as a foreign language, notes that there are a number of difficulty issues with context that disrupt or derail accurate guessing, including "deceptive transparency," deceptive morphology, idioms, "false friends," "synforms" (words that are similar or identical in form), "nonexistent textual clues," "unusable textual clues," "misleading and partial clues," and "suppressed clues" (1997, 25–32). If one adds to this the very different and subtle morphological variation in Arabic words, as well as the complexities of Arabic morphosyntax, English speakers learning Arabic as an L2 are faced with reading situations where they must develop very large "sight vocabularies"—automatic recognition of words—in order to penetrate ordinary Arabic text.

Repeated exposure to texts that recycle interrelated topics and vocabulary builds up learner ability to rapidly recognize words, collations, syntactic formulae, and genre types. Before moving on to more advanced or complex texts, then, a solid footing in easier, more accessible texts fosters the capacity for rapid retrieval of lexical and grammatical information.

Skimming, Scanning, and Gist

These three words are often used to describe activities that retrieve either general or particular information from a text. It is important to note, however, that accurate skimming is a very high-level skill requiring at least a 95 percent comprehension rate. It is a process wherein the reader quickly reviews a text in order to get the general idea of what is being discussed (gist). Scanning, on the other hand, is a process of searching a text for specific bits of information. Therefore, scanning is a more flexible type of task that can be done with authentic texts even at early stages of reading competence. With specific instructions from the teacher, learners can look over a text that they may not fully comprehend, but which offers them an opportunity to identify particular items such as: dates, names, particular phrases, or function words. Scanning accustoms learners to reading for particular items of information, but is not the same thing as getting the gist, or comprehending essentially the whole text.

Media Arabic

Media Arabic has become a widely studied genre for learners of Arabic. Student demand at the intermediate and advanced levels has made media Arabic a standard component of many undergraduate Arabic curricula. As a practical form of literacy accessible at second and third-year levels of study, it forms a language bridge to the more sophisticated genres of Arabic literature and commentary.[13] Moreover, it provides a key skill for students of international relations and Arabic area studies by opening up the world of contemporary journalism, opinion, and public life. As I have stated elsewhere, I see media Arabic

> as a kind of keystone in the Arabic language spectrum – a dominant primary producer of language in terms of abundance and influence. No other form of Arabic is so widely spread, so accessible to the inter-regional public. Arabic media is both constitutive and reflective of . . . Arab culture and world-view that contrasts in both sharp and subtle ways with what the West often attributes to Arab public opinion. This genre is therefore of central concern to those who study and teach Arabic language and culture in terms of its reach, its role, its structure, and its content. (Ryding 2010, 219)[14]

Because it is a genre that is always in process, media Arabic norms differ substantially from established and polished literary texts.[15] This makes it a viable bridge between intermediate and advanced Arabic language study. There is no escaping the vexed and difficult transition from language-focused to literature-focused instruction, but media Arabic in recent years has provided a path to higher-level competence and confidence in dealing with the more traditional forms of written Arabic as well as a wide range of new forms of literacy.

Reading and Translation

In the teaching of reading skills in Arabic, translation exercises serve effectively to increase learner awareness of grammatical structure and morphology. They can be used as an in-class activity, as homework, and for testing purposes. Although relegated to the sidelines for much of the past three decades, translation as a learning activity has resumed some of its stature and has been reinstated as an effective learning activity when incorporated into a communicatively-oriented classroom.[16] Writing in 2010, Guy Cook suggests that translation in language teaching (TILT) "has pedagogic advantages both for teachers and learners, that it is both a stimulus and an aid in the cognitively demanding task of acquiring a new language, and that for many language users it is a very practical and much-needed skill" (xvi). He points out that most language learners ultimately need to operate between languages rather than exclusively in the L2, and that this skill can be particularly effective in the real world. With regard to Arabic in particular, I agree with Cook's observation that "interlingual and intercultural contact and communication is a very delicate matter, especially in relations between Arabic and English speakers. . . . To avoid conflict and misunderstanding we need a knowledge of the two languages involved to be as accurate and explicit as possible" (Cook 2010, xii). Here it is useful to distinguish between translation as a learning process and translation as a product. Not all of us are teaching learners to be professional translators (although they are certainly needed). Translation exercises are used to focus on form, to raise learner awareness of morphology and syntax, and to accelerate familiarity with Arabic written expression. Given the complexities of written Arabic form in literature (and sometimes even in media sources), close reading and translation may be among the most effective strategies for developing Arabic learner reading proficiency.

Translation assignments also provide a clear window onto students' understanding of the target language, Arabic in particular. Previously unknown or undiagnosed misunderstandings or errors may appear in translation assignments and provide an occasion for written corrective feedback to learners. In general, translations going from English into Arabic are the most useful for evaluating learners' grasp of syntax and morphology; regular checking of Arabic to English equivalences is also useful for ascertaining control of written Arabic vocabulary and structure.

A few years ago I discovered an Arabic poem by Khalil Gibran, *la-kum lughat-u-kum wa-lī lughatī* ('You have your language and I have mine'). As far as I know, it has not been published in English translation. Because it is about the differences between literary and spoken Arabic, and what these differences mean to Gibran, I have used it as a translation exercise for classes in Arabic linguistics. The results have ranged from workman-like translations to truly gifted renderings, but the main objective of the exercise is to get inside the emotions of the author and to experience the Arabic language as he does through close, detailed analysis of his lines of poetry. Of course, such an exercise could be done in Arabic literature classes as well. (See Gibran 1966, 132–136)

From General Proficiency to Literature

The transition to studying literary works from a general, all-around competency in spoken and written Arabic requires a shift in competency that not all students are interested in or likely to make. For those who decide to pursue Arabic literary studies, it is important to distinguish this sort of knowledge from their previous achievements. One author offers "a definition of literary competency as something different from lexical, grammatical, or referential understanding: as an ability to recognize aberrant discourse. It presupposes, but is not limited to, the understanding of standard, literal, grammatical, serious discourse. Literary competency is a competency on top of competency; it's the supercompetency you need to deal with the superdiscourse that is literature" (Saussy 2005b, 19). By "aberrant" here, the author refers to discourse that departs from the norm: allusions, jokes, satire, figures of speech, parodies, and other forms of rhetoric that require a reader to recognize a particular verbal style, its implications, and its literary merit.

 Approaching Arabic Literature

The step from media language to Arabic literature can sometimes be facilitated through an approach to written Arabic texts that includes topics in popular culture as well as traditional, canonical texts. This is one aim and proposal of the MLA Ad Hoc Committee on Foreign Languages report of 2007, which called for "translingual and transcultural competence" (MLA 2007). Middlebury College Language Schools' Dean Michael E. Geisler, a coauthor of the report, states, "in addition to major works of literature, the curriculum covers film, the media, art and music, eminent thinkers in philosophy and the social sciences, a functional knowledge of the political and educational systems, a grasp of salient social and economic issues, a familiarity with popular and leisure culture, including sports and the role they play in the national narrative—all of these must be grounded in a thorough knowledge of the nation's (or nations') history" (2006–2007, 63). There is thus a growing interdisciplinary interest in the formation, negotiation, and development of identities as a result of increased globalization and resulting synergies and tensions. Discourse and identity as well as the social and linguistic construction of the self are central issues in literature, cultural studies, linguistics, and sociology; Arabic literature and cultural representation constitute a particularly rich and under-explored terrain for analyzing the dynamics of national, local, and international conceptions of self and identity.[17]

Noncanonical but compelling and relevant forms of Arabic literature remain to be discussed, studied, and defined in terms of their relation to Arabic cultural literacy. Other than *Alf layla wa-layla* ("The Thousand and One Nights"), the field does not yet have a consensus of what might constitute legitimate and critically formative noncanonical texts for Arabic L2 learners. Although this lack can be a drawback for academic program planning, it also allows for a certain flexibility and opportunity for experimentation in Arabic curricula, if departments are willing to negotiate new literary and cultural norms for learning Arabic as a foreign language. This is an area where research, application, and experimentation are greatly needed, along with professional communication on these topics.

 Classical Arabic Texts, Islamic Texts, and Modern Literature

Literature, according to Saussy, "is a realm where competency, in a particular and deep sense, happens" (2005, 18). The range of the written Arabic canonical literary corpus is both extensive and profound, stretching from the past to the present and from the west of the Arab world to the east. This vast expanse of literature created through the centuries both attracts and challenges us as scholars and as students; its content, styles, norms, and cultural references are not easy to teach; and many of them represent "benchmarks of ability" for learners who progress through the upper reaches of literary appreciation and analysis.[18] Most departments that teach Arabic organize the study of canonical literature into periods (pre-Islamic, classical, modern), and/or genres (poetry, belle-lettres, Islamic texts, historical narrative, drama, short stories, the novel). As an additional perspective, Allen suggests contextualizing the Arabic literary tradition under several other categories: the physical context (geography and environment), the linguistic context, the historical context, and the intellectual context.[19] The richness of Arabic literature may thus be approached from various angles, but most contemporary study still consists of traditional critical approaches: close reading, translation, and analysis of text.

A communicative and interactive approach to Arabic literature is not easy to imagine within traditional paradigms for dealing with classical texts. Kramsch, however, presents a framework for "an interactional methodology for discussion of literary narrative . . . It proposes to justify theoretically and to systemize within a discourse framework several pedagogical devices used intuitively by successful teachers" (1985, 358). Here is a summary of the interactive reading activities she suggests:[20]

A. Expressing and interpreting meanings:
1. Teacher defining topic, genre, period, and intended reader (for 5–10 minutes) as a prereading activity to provide background to the learner;
2. Collecting necessary vocabulary: done by allowing students (as a group) to read the first paragraph of a story (four minutes maximum), highlight the key words necessary for comprehension, and share them with the rest of the class (on the board);
3. Assembling the facts: from the vocabulary on the board, have students infer the content and possible structure of the paragraph;
4. Brainstorming conceptual associations: a group activity. In order to motivate and involve students, ask for their associations with some of the Arabic key words; these associations from their standpoint can be contrasted with those of a native speaker;
5. Predicting topic development: from the title of the text and the chosen vocabulary, infer possible developments;
6. Schema building: discovering key words, parallels and contrasts in meaning, illustrations of a given motif, regularities in content, sound, or form.

B. Negotiating meanings:
1. Exploring worlds of discourse: using perspectives and life experiences of learners to start to understand the possible realms of context for the narrative;
2. Brainstorming intentions and beliefs: "Brainstorming" is an activity that seeks quantity, not quality; "Students should be allowed (time limit four minutes) to say whatever comes to mind. The teacher should not select, comment, or judge in any way but merely record the students' suggestions on the blackboard." In response to a query from the teacher about the motives of a particular character, for example. "Such a reception dialogue, construed cooperatively by the group, forms a parallel text for later discussion in class;"
3. Putting the data in order, and ranking and voting. This activity deals with sequencing the previously elicited data and evaluating it.

Kramsch then describes six further activities: exploring alternatives and consequences, interpretive role-playing, exploring discourse forms, structural parallels, intratextual variations, and intertextual variations (1985, 359–364). These suggestions illustrate how students can be engaged in co-creating meaning within a literary framework and how they can gain confidence in their own ideas and opinions. Activities such as these contribute to developing what Byrnes refers to as "an explicit and encompassing second language reading pedagogy" (1998, 5).[21]

⬡ Study Questions and Activities

1. What are some pedagogical strategies that can be used to facilitate and/or accelerate word recognition by learners of Arabic as a foreign language?
2. Choose an Arabic text at the intermediate or advanced level that you might use in class. Looking through it: What sort of prereading activities could you use in class (or as an assignment) to provide learners with tips on organization and content that could give them insights about the text or the topic? Write an outline of what you have selected and why you have selected those particular items. (This may be done as a group in a brainstorming session, or as individual assignments where each teacher-in-training brings in a selected text along with prereading activities for group discussion.)
3. Is reading out loud a useful activity? Should teachers occasionally read short passages out loud to their students? Should students read out loud?
4. What are the pros and cons of always using authentic texts to teach reading?
5. Do you think that transliteration should ever be used in teaching Arabic? Why or why not?
6. Skimming, scanning, gist, and translation are key ways of dealing with Arabic texts. Evaluate each for its usefulness at different levels of proficiency. Write a two-page paper on the value of one of these activities.

⬡ Further Reading

Allen, Roger. 1998. *The Arabic Literary Heritage: The Development of Its Genres and Criticism.* Cambridge: Cambridge University Press.

___. 2000. *An Introduction to Arabic Literature.* Cambridge: Cambridge University Press. (This is a "revised and abridged" version of Allen 1998.)

Badawi, El-Said. 2002. "In the Quest for the Level 4+ in Arabic: Training Level 2-3 Learners in Independent Reading." In *Developing Professional-Level Language Proficiency*, edited by Betty Lou Leaver and Boris Shekhtman, 156–176. Cambridge: Cambridge University Press.

Brustad, Kristen. 2006. "Reading Fluently in Arabic." In *Handbook for Arabic Language Teaching Professionals in the 21st Century*, edited by Kassem Wahba, Zeinab Taha, and Liz England, 341–352. Mahwah, NJ: Lawrence Erlbaum Associates.

Byrnes, Heidi. 1998. "Reading in the Beginning and Intermediate College Foreign Language Class." Module for *Professional Preparation of Teaching Assistants in Foreign Languages*, edited by Grace Stovall Burkart. Washington, DC: Center for Applied Linguistics.

Frangieh, Bassam K. 2005. *Anthology of Arabic Literature, Culture, and Thought: From Pre-Islamic Times to the Present.* New Haven and London: Yale University Press. (A valuable anthology of selected Arabic readings from different eras and different genres for use with advanced learners.)

Fukkink, Rueben G., Jan Huylstijn, and Annegien Simis. 2005. "Does Training in Second-Language Word Recognition Skills Affect Reading Comprehension? An Experimental Study." *Modern Language Journal* 89, no. 1:54–75.

Hansen, Gunna Funder. 2010. "Word Recognition in Arabic as a Foreign Language." *Modern Language Journal* 94, no. 4:567–581.

Kramsch, Claire. 1985. "Literary Texts in the Classroom: A Discourse." *Modern Language Journal* 69, no. 4:356–366.

Mughazy, Mustafa. 2005–2006. "Reading Despite Ambiguity: The Role of Metacognitive Strategies in Reading Arabic Authentic Texts." *Al-Arabiyya* 38–39: 57–74.

Swaffar, Janet, Katherine Arens, and Heidi Byrnes. 1991. *Reading for Meaning: An Integrated Approach to Language Learning.* Englewood Cliffs, NJ: Prentice Hall. (This is an important, classic study of the pedagogy of reading in foreign languages.)

Ziadeh, Farhat J. 1964. *A Reader in Modern Literary Arabic.* Princeton: Princeton University Press. (A compilation of 34 Arabic readings, with detailed grammar and vocabulary notes and exercises on each selection, as well as an extensive Arabic-English glossary.)

✦ **Notes**

1. As Allen observed in 1995, "Development of the reading skill has remained the predominant goal of instruction. New textbooks and syllabi have focused on other skills too, but until relatively recently their organizing principles have been grammar-based and the primary pedagogical purpose of skill activities has been the internalization of the principles of the language" (1995, 105).

2. I believe that there may be many uses for well-conceived translation activities in reading classes, but that overdone, they may become stultifying.

3. Koda examines specifically "lower-level verbal processing skills—letter identification and word recognition in particular" (1992, 503).

4. See Koda 2010 for reading and transcultural competence.

5. "Vocabulary remains one of the greatest stumbling blocks to fluent reading" (Swaffar, Arens, and Byrnes 1991, 43).

6. "L2 teachers who want their classes to interact with texts have to be facilitators of the reading process rather than monitors of performance" (Swaffar, Arens, and Byrnes 1991, 70).

7. The term "recognition complexity" is borrowed from Pullum and Kornai 2012, 6, and from Ristad 2012. Although they deal with grammars in mathematical linguistics, the concept of recognition complexity is a very apt one for learners of Arabic facing unfamiliar unvoweled words. These words, even in context, must be identified and "solved" by cognitive processes that may use complex cognitive algorithms.

8. Bernhardt 1986 contains a description of a "recall protocol procedure" that could be very effective in Arabic reading instruction (108–112).

9. Some of the research on Arabic (and Hebrew) orthography and reading skills has been done in the framework of two hypotheses: the script-dependent hypothesis and the "orthographic depth hypothesis." See Everson 2011 for references and more in-depth discussion.

10. Larkin underscores the importance of "sensitivity to morphological patterns" of Arabic as an important element in reading aloud (1995, 165). She states that "the sound of the various patterns must . . . be internalized and indeed . . . they are more easily assimilated on the phonetic level" (ibid.).

11. See Hansen 2010.

12. An earlier study on Arabs learning English as a foreign language examined difficulties that Arabic speakers face in recognizing and remembering vowels within words, a significant problem that is labeled "vowel blindness" by the author (Ryan 1997, 189).

13. It also forms a bridge between written and spoken Arabic. "Media Arabic and educated spoken Arabic play key roles in bridging gaps between informal and formal varieties of Arabic, and in anchoring the development of communicative competence. Media language is a cornerstone of linguistic and cultural literacy in Arabic; a medium which can be a useful and pragmatic goal in itself, but also a partial goal or stepping stone for those whose eventual aim may be to study the Arabic literary tradition in all its depth, richness, and complexity" (Ryding 2010, 223).

14. See El-Essawy 2010 for a discussion of teaching vocabulary through media Arabic, and Abdalla 2010 for an analysis of media Arabic as a constituent of an Arabic curriculum. Ryding 2010 also discusses media Arabic textbooks.

15. "Media Arabic in particular, because of its status as a regional written standard and its contemporaneousness, represents a process at work rather than an achieved and uniform end point" (Ryding 2010, 220).

16. See, for example, Leonardi 2010.

17. For a concise overview of the Arabic literary canon and Arabic literary criticism see Cooke 1987. For a book-length introduction, see Allen 2000 and, for a more in-depth study, see Allen 1998. Suleiman 2011 is a book-length study of "Arabic, self and identity."

18. "A little-discussed role of literary works throughout history has been their adoption as benchmarks of ability: you know that you know Latin when you're able to read Virgil . . . ; you know that you know French when you can get through *Candide* or *Madame Bovary* on your own" (Saussy 2005, 17). Certainly this is the case for knowledge of key Arabic texts from the pre-Islamic to the modern period.

19. See Allen 2000, chapter two, "The contexts of the literary tradition."

20. For greater detail, see Kramsch 1985, 359–364.

21. In this paper, Byrnes provides highly useful charts and tables for devising reading tasks as well as a cogent and detailed discussion of L2 reading approaches.

Listening Comprehension in Arabic

The need for special attention to listening comprehension as an integral part of communication is now well-established.

Joan Morley

Listening is the first, most basic language activity, and listening comprehension occurs under many conditions—some straightforward and others much more complicated and difficult. Listening can be done for various reasons; sometimes one just happens to hear a conversation, other times, one participates; sometimes one needs to understand almost everything (as in listening to directions), other times a gist or general idea is enough. It is useful to discuss different categories of listening as well as goals of listening comprehension in order to analyze and design activities that will result in learners' ability to interact successfully with native speakers and to grasp important details of spoken language. At all levels of listening, a learner's background knowledge of a situation or topic is a key factor in framing accurate comprehension. Contrary to being a passive process, listening involves substantial mental activity and focus; some of this may be intuitive and unconscious in one's native language, but in a foreign language, it becomes an acutely conscious effort. Listening has been defined as "an active process in which listeners select and interpret information which comes from visual and auditory clues in order to define what is going on and what the speakers are trying to express" (Rubin 2006, 6, quoting Clark and Clark 1977). Morley states that "although listening traditionally has been the 'neglected' skill of language instruction, undeniably it is the single language skill used most in human communication" (1990, 317).

Participatory and Nonparticipatory Listening

Participatory, or interactive, listening occurs when one is engaged in a conversation or discussion and is making a contribution to the discussion. Careful listening to what others in the group have to say is necessary for forming one's own comments and questions. Understanding pragmatic discourse components such as turn-taking and emotional overtones as well as the variety of language being used are important parts of participatory listening. For Arabic listening comprehension in social situations, learners need to comprehend normal native speech style in Arabic so that they can participate successfully in group conversations. They also need to understand participation conventions (e.g., breaking in, overlapping, pauses, turn-taking, courtesy protocols).

Nonparticipatory listening, or one-way listening, describes a situation where one does not need to comment on the content (at least, not immediately), but where one is able to focus for a period of time on a talk, report, lecture, announcement, interview, or discussion as a nonparticipating observer. One may want to take notes and listen carefully for content or one may just want to grasp the general ideas being mentioned.

⬡ Factors in Listening

Many factors in listening are different from reading, although both are comprehension skills. In listening:

1. Word boundaries are not marked
2. There is no punctuation
3. There may be pauses, hesitations, or restarts
4. Language level may vary and code-mixing may occur
5. Speech sounds may shift slightly, depending on the speaker (for example, an Egyptian speaker will have different stress patterns than a Levantine Arabic speaker—even in MSA)
6. Grammatical structures may be simpler but also less complete than in reading
7. Speech may include omissions, mistakes, repairs, and corrections.

Certain factors make listening more demanding than reading:

1. Along with the lack of word boundaries, words cluster in phrases and may be hard to distinguish from each other
2. Rate of speech may be very fast
3. Words and phrases may be greatly reduced or contracted
4. In multisided discussion, turns may overlap
5. Processing requirements are heavy and listeners must process language immediately with no time for reflection
6. Listeners may lose concentration quickly because of heavy processing demands[1]
7. Casual speech may be highly colloquial (especially in Arabic)
8. Listening may occur with unfavorable conditions such as ambient noise (in a restaurant, for example).

If one adds to these factors the fact that listening in Arabic requires the listener's rapid calibration to the speech style, register, and language variant, then teaching listening in Arabic (both participatory and nonparticipatory) can be recognized as a skill that requires a vast range of competencies. Teaching Arabic for interactive skills will involve different strategies than teaching Arabic for listening and comprehension only. Students at the intermediate and advanced levels in particular will have listening anxieties when faced with new comprehension tasks. This is why many teachers have regular routines for introducing listening skills, including:

1. Prelistening activities such as advance organizers, orientations to topic, introducing key vocabulary, and activating learners' schemata (top-down processing)[2]
2. On-task strategies such as note-taking, clarification requests, and selective listening
3. Follow-up or postlistening tasks and tests to check comprehension, discuss problem areas, reinforce new knowledge, and aid retention.

⬡ Arabic Listening Comprehension Studies

Arabic listening comprehension research is an area where one author has contributed most of the field's research findings: Elkhafaifi (2001, 2005a, 2005b, 2007–2008), who has examined key aspects of listening in Arabic including strategies, anxieties, and prelistening. His 2001 article surveyed Arabic faculty as to their academic backgrounds, preferred methodologies, and their use of listening comprehension activities in the classroom. In his 2005a article Elkhafaifi studied over 400 students and the effects of learner anxiety on their ability to comprehend spoken Arabic, finding that second-year students showed the highest levels of anxiety for listening compared to both first-year and third-year students. He speculated that "second year Arabic is significantly more difficult than first-year because expectations increase, syntax and morphology become increasingly complex, more authentic material is introduced, and greater emphasis is placed on communicative practice, including listening comprehension" (2005a, 215).

In his 2005b article, Elkhafaifi evaluated two specific teaching strategies, "the effect of prelistening activities and repeated listening exposure on scores of Arabic students" (504). He determined that both of these activities, especially repeated exposure to a listening passage, significantly improve comprehension scores. Prelistening activities such as vocabulary preview and activation of learner background knowledge were also essential factors in improving scores.

As yet, however, there have been no equally researched studies of interactive Arabic listening comprehension or comprehension of "spontaneous free speech" (Byrnes 1983, 319). Almost all studies have been on nonparticipatory listening in MSA. For teaching Arabic in a communicative fashion, research is needed on participatory listening and on strategies for helping learners orient themselves in multispeaker situations where colloquial language will predominate or be mixed in. Because of the variable nature of spoken Arabic and its highly context-determined features, participatory listening in Arabic is especially complex and needs its own language-specific research.

⬭ Listening Checks: Dictation

One very useful procedure to check Arabic listening comprehension for detail is to give regular dictation (*imlāʔ*) exercises. As Hadley notes, dictation "resembles the real-world skill of note-taking" and "can be used to build comprehension skills at all levels of proficiency" (2001, 199). Dictation also has the advantage of combining "many discrete points of structure and vocabulary in natural language contexts" (ibid.). Dictations indicate for you exactly what the students hear, how they grasp orthography, and also how readily they are able to use Arabic script in handwriting. Often, students think they understand what they hear but they actually do not perceive sounds accurately; dictation exercises can be a constructive comprehension check that focuses on form. These exercises are also a useful way to break up other activities and change pace; most students appreciate the discipline as well as the narrowed focus on pronunciation and orthographic accuracy. I have found that involving learners in a joint effort to produce accurate dictations is the most effective way to proceed. Although dictation exercises may seem elementary or redundant to some teachers, the fact is that Arabic script needs considerable deliberate practice, as does listening comprehension. Dictation work includes both, and fits them together in the process. The cognitive load involved in Arabic dictation work is substantial, as are the psychomotor skills of developing rapid and legible handwriting. Dictation exercises can be designed to suit different levels of proficiency from beginning to advanced. Here are some tested procedures:

- Come to class ready with a set of words, phrases, sentences, or numbers that need to be practiced (usually not more than 10). At a midpoint in the class, tell students to take out paper for a dictation. I also ask for two or three volunteers who will write their dictation on the chalkboard at the same time. If none volunteer, I choose them, being careful not to choose individuals who seem to be struggling or anxious about their performance. Tell the students that you will say every dictation item three times; this primes them for their listening task. As they write down their perception of the dictation items, I move around the class and look over their shoulders to see how they are doing, to give hints and encouragement. I also look at the board and the work being done there. Those at the board are encouraged to collaborate on items that are unclear and to discuss them with each other. Still, they almost always wind up with slightly different versions of what was dictated. At the end of the dictation session, each student has a set of items to check and can also see what has been written on the board.
- To review the results, repeat the dictation items as you and the students all look at the words on the board. Ask the class if they agree with what is written on the board and if not, why not.

Any corrections almost always come from the students themselves as a group, and I give them a chance to discuss any differences in opinion. This allows them to draw conclusions about their own performance as well as to see what others are doing and compare. Most students are very gentle when making observations about their peers; they will usually direct their observations to the group at large or to you in the form of questions. Encourage this—it then gives them more opportunity for interactive work. Make sure that the students see the correct version by writing the items on the board yourself or simply by correcting what is on the board already. This works well with a group of 15–20 students or fewer. For larger classes, grouping students into teams also works well.

- At the end of the exercise, I sometimes collect the dictation papers, but since not everyone will have a paper (those at the board do not), I usually ask if anyone would like me to go over their dictation results by handing them in. They have revised their own papers, but some still want assurance that they have done so correctly. Often, students do. After class I can quickly review their work and write feedback on their papers. The reason students like this sort of activity is because it gives them immediate feedback on how well they perceive Arabic sounds and where they need to pay more attention. It is also a relaxed group activity that lowers any affective filters they may have. It is relaxed because this type of exercise is not graded; it is solely for the benefit of the learners. Finally, it provides a sense of accomplishment to learners.

Dictation benefits you as well because it allows you to see precisely how students as individuals are doing in terms of orthography, listening comprehension, and the psychomotor skill of handwriting. In addition to being useful classroom exercises, dictations may also be part of a preannounced quiz or test, especially during first-year classes. In that case, it is particularly important for learners to practice those skills before they are tested on them, and they will need to know that dictation will be included on an exam in order to prepare for it. If learners are not prepared for dictation and are graded for accuracy, most will become anxious. If prepared and practiced, learners will look forward to the challenges of dictation.

❀ **Dictation Items**

These vary depending on the level of the class and its interests. At the very beginning, dictation items may consist of letters plus long vowels (*hā, dhū, fī*) (try to choose meaningful sequences if at all possible), then short, one-syllable words (*min, dars, bāb*), then words with two syllables (*wāḥid, ʿamal, durūs*), and so forth. It is important when choosing such items to decide whether they are to be words or phrases that the students have already studied, in which case the exercise is for review, or whether the words or other items are to be completely new, thus testing the learners' ability to hear sounds that they have not yet associated with meaning, and that they have never seen. Either way is useful, and generally I mix these types of exercises. It is also beneficial to choose words or phrases for dictation that are going to be useful to the learners; they will be more motivated to master spelling and retention of vocabulary when they can see that the items will serve to enhance their performance. Again, the type of words or phrases depend on the level of the class and their interests. If it is a class in newspaper Arabic, then dictation of key vocabulary items or key phrases in the news will work well. If it is a beginning class, basic classroom items such as *bāb, kursī, lawḥ, qalam* may be given, at first, as well as names of countries such as *tūnis, lubnān, al-yaman*. Early on, and continuing through several levels, it is a good idea for learners to practice listening to numbers and writing them down. Dates, phone numbers, addresses, times, prices—all are essential comprehension components that need practice, starting out, of course, with simple numbers and progressing to the more complex. Hadley suggests the following dictation topics:

1. Questions in the target language: Students first write down the questions dictated by the teacher. Then they write the answers to those questions in the target language. Questions should either follow one another in a logical order or relate to a given theme.

2. Partial or spot dictations: Students fill in gaps on their written copy of a passage.
3. Dictation of sentences in random order: All sentences, when rearranged, form a logical paragraph or conversation. Students first write the dictated material and then rearrange it.
4. Dictation of directions for arriving at a destination: Students first write a set of directions dictated by the teacher. They then follow the directions on an accompanying map.
5. Dictation of a description: Students write the dictated material and then, from a set of alternatives, choose the picture that matches the description they have written down.
6. Full dictation of a passage: Students might be asked to answer comprehension questions on a passage after they have written it down. They might also be asked to circle items of a certain lexical or grammatical category (such as verbs in the future tense) to draw their attention to a topic that is being emphasized in a particular lesson. (2001, 199–200)

⬡ Listening Procedures

In his research, Elkhafaifi has focused on the effects of prelistening activities and on anxieties for Arabic learners in two recent articles.[3] His study on anxiety among Arabic learners found that there were "significant negative correlations among listening and foreign language learning anxiety, students' listening comprehension scores, and final grades as a measure of overall achievement" (2005a, 214). Elkhafaifi advises providing a great deal of comprehensible listening input, teaching listening strategies, alleviating stress, and being aware of learner anxieties at this level. According to Elkhafaifi 2005b, prelistening activities that presented and previewed vocabulary words, as well as prelistening activities that previewed.questions on the listening passage, "significantly improved students' overall scores" (509).

Aside from listening exercises provided in the textbook you are using, select some authentic texts for listening. Ideally they should be thematically related to course work or illustrate particular features of language that you want the learners to hear in context. At lower proficiency levels, "listening materials that present very familiar and/or predictable content and that are relevant to students' interests will be best" (Hadley 2001, 184). Plan to play or read the listening passage several times. As a general rule it should not be more than two or three minutes long, although you can build up to longer stretches of spoken Arabic for specific purposes, such as listening to a speech or to a news program. To prepare students for listening, give them some basic instructions on how to make the most of a listening exercise:

1. Make sure learners are aware of general listening strategies, such as not getting stuck wondering about one word and then missing the next stretch of speech.
2. Talk about purposes of listening: for gist, for detail, for tone, for key words, for topic.
3. Talk about listening first for gist, and then relistening for detail.
4. Just as one can scan a written text for specific bits of information, one can also scan in listening, paying attention or listening for particular items in a passage.
5. Talk about styles of Arabic rhetoric and provide examples for learners to hear.

Prelistening

Orient the learners to what they are going to hear. In particular, tell them what level or register of language they are hearing and whether it is authentic or acted. You may tell them the topic, unless it is part of their job to guess the topic. This is part of advance organizing material for use in class.[4] You may want to put selected vocabulary on the board or hand out a sheet listing key words or phrases to listen for. You can give the meaning of these items or ask students to guess them from context. You may also want to pose preview questions on the listening passage so that students can listen in particular for that information.

Classroom Listening and Discussion Activity

What are good examples of traditional Arabic oral histories, tales, proverbs, collective experiences, and other narratives that characterize local communities? How can these be blended into an Arabic course as cultural/listening activities? Think about the context of these narratives as well as their structure. Under what circumstances are stories told? Are they private (such as bedtime stories), morality tales, or public (entertainment or performances)? Who usually tells them—relatives, older people, teachers, colleagues, public storytellers? Are they very long, in many episodes, or short and pithy? Do they contain lessons on behavior or values, reassurances, humor, or a moral? Choose one or two of these stories for narration in the classroom and subsequent discussion.

During Listening

Give listeners a reason and a way to note down what they are hearing. For example, you might provide an outline where you ask them to fill in key words, or you might give them a list of topics to check off when they hear them. Encourage them to write notes in Arabic.

Postlistening and Follow-up

Multiple exposures to listening passages definitely increase listening comprehension. These multiple replayings can be done immediately after the first exposure or after the students have discussed their understanding of the passage. They may also be done on a following day as review. Elkhafaifi states that "the single most useful technique the instructor can employ is to provide multiple exposures to the listening passage" (2005b, 510). Comprehension check activities can range from classroom discussion and verification of understanding to homework assignments (e.g., brief commentary on what has been heard, or answers to specific questions). You may ask learners to hand in notes taken during the listening exercise (but alert them beforehand that you will be collecting them). If you have not had a great deal of experience in calibrating listening exercises with the level of the students, it is useful to check with them afterwards about their reactions to the exercise—was it too fast, too complex, hard to hear, or too easy? What percent did they understand? This is also a way to allow them to reflect on their anxieties and for you as their teacher to be aware of their concerns.

⬡ Study Questions and Activities

1. Assess the relationship between participatory and nonparticipatory listening in classrooms that you have been in. In your teaching or learning, have you focused more on one than the other? Which is more difficult?
2. Discuss the factors that make listening comprehension more complex than reading comprehension.
3. Have you used dictation exercises in the classroom? How often? If you have been a student of Arabic, did you look forward to dictations? Why or why not?
4. Design a listening exercise for a classroom of second-year Arabic students. Choose a 2-minute listening passage and compose a set of prelistening activities and a set of follow-up activities. Share this exercise with your classmates.

⬡ Further Reading

For listening practice and ideas, see Hadley 2001, 181–203, especially the chart on 189, and see also Brown 2001, 247–266.

Elkhafaifi, Hussein. 2005a. "Listening Comprehension and Anxiety in the Arabic Language Classroom." *The Modern Language Journal* 89, no. 2:206–220.

____. 2005b. "The Effect of Prelistening Activities on Listening Comprehension in Arabic Learners." *Foreign Language Annals* 38, no. 4:505–513.

____. 2007–2008. "An Exploration of Listening Strategies: A Descriptive Study of Arabic Learners." *Al-Arabiyya* 40-41: 71–86.

Philips, June K. 1991. "An Analysis of Text in Video Newscasts: A Tool for Schemata Building in Listeners." *Georgetown University Round Table on Languages and Linguistics 1991,* edited by James E. Alatis, 343–354. Washington, DC: Georgetown University Press.

Rubin, Joan. 1994. "A Review of Second Language Listening Comprehension Research." *Modern Language Journal* 78, no. 2:199–221.

✧ Notes

1. Adapted from Rubin 2006, 3–5 and Brown 1991, 252–253.

2. "Prelistening activities may be characterized as any kind of advance organizer that prepares students for the listening comprehension passage or exercise they are about to undertake" (El-Khafaifi 2001, 63).

3. Elkhafaifi 2005a and 2005b.

4. See chapter 12 on advance organizers for comprehension activities.

Part VI
Teaching Productive Skills

Teaching Arabic Pronunciation

CHAPTER

15

Real, high-quality practice depends on willingness to speak, and that in turn depends on ease in speaking.

Earl Stevick

Our goal as teachers of . . . pronunciation should . . . be more realistically focused on clear, comprehensible communication.

H. Douglas Brown

Pronunciation practice is a key component of learning to speak Arabic accurately. The ability to perceive and discriminate sounds in context is also an important factor in listening comprehension. Even in reading and writing, automaticity in associating Arabic sounds and script needs to be developed in the early stages of study and reinforced consistently. Research has indicated that explicit work on pronunciation may improve phonological accuracy as well as fluency, and pronunciation should be a part of regular review and attention by teachers and learners. Pronunciation has also been shown to be a central psychological factor in speakers' identity. Some language learners aim at approximating pronunciation as close as they can to native speakers, while other learners maintain their cultural distance by preserving their L1 accent. The main point in pronunciation instruction is to assure that learners are able to speak intelligibly and with comprehensibility in order to be understood and get meaning across. They should be able to make and recognize the phonemic distinctions of Arabic and develop smooth articulation and fluency. This chapter outlines issues and elements that are particularly important in the teaching of pronunciation and which can guide pronunciation practice in the classroom.

Explicit instruction in foreign language pronunciation was "a central component of language teaching during the audiolingual era" (Lightbown and Spada 2006, 104). With the shift to more communicative and acquisition-based instruction in the 1970s and early 1980s, teaching of pronunciation as a skill in itself was discouraged, if not ignored. There has therefore been less research in this area than in others, but more recent studies have indicated a reconsidered role for pronunciation instruction integrated into communicative curricula.[1] "By the mid-eighties, with greater attention to grammatical structures as important elements in discourse, to a balance between fluency and accuracy, and to the explicit specification of pedagogical tasks that a learner should accomplish, it became clear that pronunciation was a key to gaining full communicative competence" (Brown 2001, 283). Trofimovitch and Gatbonton discuss the effects of repetition and explicit focus on phonological features and properties, observing that repeated practice, or "practice involving repeated tasks or repeated sentences—leads to learning gains" and that in addition, "intensive form-focused training in perception and production of sounds" also yields learning gains (2006, 520–521). The authors conclude that repetition and focus on form (explicit attention to phonological features) need not be "rote, meaningless" instructional strategies, but that "*mindful* repetition in an engaging communicative context by motivated learners" has "measurable benefits for L2 speech processing" (532; emphasis in original).

⬡ Accuracy in Pronunciation and Fluency

There are two key factors in learning to pronounce Arabic (or any language) well. The first is accuracy in pronunciation and the other is fluency. The former focuses on precision in making phonemic distinctions and the latter on calibrating the articulation of strings of words into speech that flows without disruption, or, as Stevick puts it, "pronunciation as a continuum" (1996, 142).

Accuracy in pronunciation carries some psychological weight with most learners (Stevick refers to this as "the psychodynamic meanings of pronunciation" [1996, 142]). In order to be able to gain learners' attention to both correctness and fluency, it is necessary to understand what characteristics learners bring to the learning situation. Among these are the following:

- "Innate phonetic ability" (Brown 2001, 285): Some individuals have what has been called an "ear" for language; that is, they readily pick up the phonetics and phonological distinctions in the target language and are able to reproduce the target language sounds almost exactly. At the other extreme are individuals who are said to have a "tin ear," meaning that they have great difficulty reproducing what they hear or perceiving phonetic distinctions. Most students fall somewhere in the middle of this continuum. Many are good language learners who grasp pronunciation concepts quickly. Many are also good at approximating what they hear, and many have the basic study skills to improve with effort, focus, and intent.

- Ego and identity: Interestingly, studies have shown that psychological constructs such as ego strength and personal identity are directly related to and affected by phonetic features of spoken language, especially accent (see, for example, Guiora and Acton 1979). A healthy ego (i.e., neither weak nor overbearing) and permeable ego boundaries (related to attributes such as flexibility and empathy) can play important roles in language learners' ability and willingness to acquire a phonological system other than their own.[2] These studies were occasioned by what Guiora and Acton characterized as the notable "ease with which young children are able to assimilate authentic pronunciation in a foreign language in its native environment, and the equally apparent inability of almost all people, past the magic barrier of 10–12 years of age, to assimilate authentic pronunciation in a foreign language, under almost any circumstances" (1979, 10–11). Stevick writes, "in the view of Guiora and his colleagues, pronunciation is perhaps the most critical and the most valuable of the contributions that the language ego makes to total self-representations" (1996, 144). And further, that "people vary . . . both individually and culturally, with respect to the significance that pronunciation has as a medium for expressing their self-concept. They also vary with respect to their tolerance for the affective impact of hearing themselves or someone else sound foreign" (Stevick 1996, 145).

- L1 influence: L1 features of pronunciation may be transferred to the L2 (either appropriately or inappropriately).[3] While this is true for individual phonemes and distinctive sounds, it is especially true of stress and intonation, which tend to work below the level of conscious awareness and are transferred automatically. In teaching Arabic to Americans or other English speakers, it is not so much the difficult and unfamiliar sounds that cause learning difficulty as the sounds (such as Arabic *rā'* or Arabic *lām*) that seem to be similar to English but are actually very different. Arabic stress rules also need to be taught early on because they are so different from English and also because they are predictable (English stress is not predictable, but learned). Lightbown and Spada note that "it is widely believed that the degree of difference between the learner's native language and the target language can lead to greater difficulty" in acquiring L2 phonology (2006, 105). This often means that it takes longer for English-speaking learners to gain both accuracy and fluency in spoken Arabic.

⬡ Arabic Segmental Features

"Segmental features are minimal units of sound defined in phonetic terms. Traditionally, the fundamental components of pronunciation are phonemes, and acquisition of the target language phonological system is viewed as mastery of the phonemic distinctions embodied in its phonological inventory and of the phonetic variants of phonemes which occur in particular environments within syllables of words" (Pennington and Richards 1986, 209). Segmental features are often contrasted with suprasegmental features such as word stress and intonation.

Phonemes

The distinctive sounds of a language are called "phonemes." They are usually identified by a set of "distinctive features" that make each one unique and meaningful. A phonemic chart portrays the sounds of a language according to their point of articulation (in the vocal tract) and manner of articulation (e.g., fricative, stop), and for some sounds, whether they are voiced or not. In the English spelling system, not every letter of the alphabet represents a distinctive sound. For example, the letter "c" is usually pronounced as /s/ or /k/. Distinctive sounds such as /sh/, /th/, or /ch/ are not represented by single letters but by combinations of letters.[4] The Arabic alphabet, on the other hand, almost perfectly represents the phonemes of Arabic. For a more extensive discussion of Arabic phonology and a phonological chart, see Ryding 2005, 10–43.

Allophones

Allophones are accepted variants or realizations of phonemes. For example, the MSA Arabic phoneme /*jīm*/ may be pronounced /*jīm*/, /*gīm*/, or /*zhīm*/, depending on the speaker's native vernacular of spoken Arabic. None of these pronunciations is "wrong," they simply vary with the speaker. Another Arabic allophone would be with the vowel /*ā*/, which varies in pronunciation from a fronted vowel (*salām* 'peace') to a back vowel (*matār* 'airport'), somewhat like the difference in English between the "a" of "hand" and the "a" of "father."

Challenges for Learners

The sounds that Arabic learners may have difficulty with are those unrepresented in English. There are three sets of these: those that are semi-familiar, those which may be familiar but whose distribution patterns are different, and those that are completely unfamiliar.

The semi-familiar sounds

1. For sounds such as *khāʔ* (خ/خاء) learners may know it through having heard the Scottish pronunciation of "loch" for example, or the German pronunciation of "Bach," or the Yiddish expression "chutzpah." That is, it will probably not be completely unfamiliar to most learners.
2. The same goes for the phoneme *rāʔ* (ر/راء). It does not really sound anything like American /r/, but it is similar to Spanish or Italian /r/, which many Americans have heard. It is best to introduce *rāʔ* not as a regular American /r/ sound, but as a 'flap' as in the /t/ sound in the phrase "pot of gold" (usually pronounced 'potta gold' in American English); as the /t/ sound in 'gotta go,' or as the way the /r/ is sometimes pronounced in stiffly formal British English: "very good" ("veddy good").
3. *Ghayn* (غ/غين) is another sound that does not exist in English, but that may be familiar to students who have studied French, because it is a voiced velar fricative that resembles French /r/.
4. *Lām* (ل/لام): Americans have two pronunciations of /l/, only one of which is appropriate for most instances of Arabic *lām*, which is usually pronounced forward in the mouth, with the tip of the tongue. When Americans say the words 'leaf' or 'lady' they use the fronted pronunciation of /l/; when they say words where /l/ is preceded by a vowel, however, the quality of the consonant shifts to the back of the mouth, and the tongue is raised and pulled

back, as in 'well,' 'ball,' 'hole', 'hill.' It is important that this postvocalic pronunciation not be used in Arabic. Consider the difference between the Arabic word for 'elephant,' *fīl* (فيل), and the English word 'feel.' The /l's/ are very different.[5]

Different distribution

1. The Arabic phoneme *hā?* (هاء/ه) is not very different in pronunciation from English /h/. However, it differs in distribution within words. English /h/ is always followed by a vowel. In Arabic, *hā?* may be followed by another consonant, as in the name *Fahd* (فهد) or the name *Mahdi* (مهدي). It may also occur at the end of a word, which makes it hard for Americans to hear, as in the name *Nazīh* (نزيه).

2. The Arabic *hamza* phoneme is technically called a 'glottal stop'; the phonetic symbol for this is usually an apostrophe (') or a question mark without the dot (?). Although not part of the English alphabet, it is nonetheless a specific sound that English speakers use and can identify. It occurs clearly in the anxious expression, "oh-oh" (*?oh-?oh*) meaning 'something's not right here,' or 'look out,' or 'I think there's a problem.' It also occurs in the colloquial negative expression 'uh-uh,' (*?uh-?uh*) meaning 'no.' In each of these cases the glottal stop occurs both at the beginning and in the middle of the expression. It also occurs at the beginning of English words that start with vowels, such as 'ice' or 'under' when they begin an utterance; if they follow another word, the glottal stop is usually omitted. The glottal stop can be inserted for emphasis, however, as in "I said he was an ?ice skater, not a nice skater."[6]

Arabic words that begin with *hamza* sound to Americans as though they begin with a vowel, for example, *?islām* 'Islam', *?abadan* 'never' or *?ustādh* 'professor.'[7] Students will not normally "hear" the *hamza* or glottal onset unless their attention is called to it. In the middle of a word, the *hamza* is more clearly perceivable (as in the Arabic word *su?āl*, 'question'). At the end of a word, it is also difficult for most beginning learners to hear, so it needs practice (e.g., *masā?* 'evening' or *juz?* 'part,' or *qāri?* 'reader').

Unfamiliar Arabic sounds   The truly unfamiliar sounds in Arabic are only three: *qaaf* (ق), *ʕayn*, (ع) and *ħā?* (ح). Each of these sounds is pronounced using areas of the vocal tract that are not used in English: the uvula and the pharynx. In teaching the pronunciation and perception of these sounds, teachers can make use of a number of techniques to isolate, emphasize, and contextualize them:

1. Isolation: isolate a sound from a word in order to focus on it
2. Slowing and stretching: slow down and stretch out the sound
3. Diagrams of articulatory tract and technical explanation of articulation (McCarus and Rammuny 1979 have particularly good diagrams and explanations of pronunciation)
4. Repetition in various contexts, with different words
5. Assigned exercises for listening to phonology
6. Dictation exercises.

In teaching the pharyngeal consonants, it helps to explain to learners that the pharyngeal muscles are the ones used in swallowing. This helps learners identify where those muscles are and what they do. Ask students to touch their throats and swallow several times, then tell them that those muscles are used to make the sounds *ħā?* and *ʕayn*. Practice saying words with *ħā?* and *ʕayn* slowly and having students repeat them while touching their throats. In teaching the pronunciation of *qāf* (a voiceless uvular stop) it helps to explain that the uvula is the little piece of soft flesh that hangs down in the back of the mouth, and that the tongue needs to retract and touch this piece of flesh in order to make the correct *qāf* sound. Students usually are intrigued by this sound and enjoy practicing it.

Arabic Vowels as Music

The crucial length difference between long and short vowels is a challenge for American learners to hear, recognize, and imitate because it is not phonemic (meaningful) in English. English speakers differentiate vowels on the basis of quality (a, i, u), not quantity (or length: -ā, -ī, -ū). In this regard, it is often helpful to call learners' attention to musical notation in order to explain the difference between long and short Arabic vowels because duration is a distinctive feature of musical notes, and most students have at least some knowledge of musical notation. If a short vowel (such as *fatḥa*) is similar to a quarter note, then a long vowel (*alif*) would be like a half note or even a whole note; the half or whole note vowels represent durative sounds and are written as part of an Arabic word, whereas the quarter notes or short vowels are not. Having learners look at and practice vowel patterning as a form of music is useful in many ways and makes it easier to explain meaningful vowel contrasts in Arabic. Some linguists even refer to vowel distribution in Arabic as "melody."[8]

Doubling/Gemination

The process of germination, or doubling, a consonant sound (*tashdīd*, indicated by the *shadda* notation), is an important phonological process in Arabic but one that is unfamiliar to most learners of Arabic. It is important for learners to know that doubling, or *tashdīd*, may cause a difference in meaning, and that they need to give special attention to it (e.g., *darasa* 'he studied' vs. *darrasa* 'he taught'). "Not only is the difference between single and doubled or geminated consonants an important one in Arabic morphology but also, from a phonological and phonetic point of view, every Arabic syllable is clearly enunciated with its due quantitative weight" (Mitchell 1990, 3). Many English words are spelled with double consonants (e.g., occur, spell, correlate, embarrass), but the spelling does not reflect gemination, and English-speaking learners initially tend to ignore it as a pronunciation feature in Arabic.[9]

Minimal Pairs and Key Words

Minimal pairs are sets of two words that differ in only one distinctive feature of pronunciation but mean very different things, showing a contrast in meaning through contrast of one sound in a similar environment. For example, the Arabic words *sayf* 'sword' and *ṣayf* 'summer' differ only in one feature: the velarization of the fricative /s/ sound in the word for 'summer.' Ideally, minimal pairs differ only in one phonological feature; here it is the feature [+ velarization] that is added to the voiceless alveolar fricative, making *ṣayf* a completely different word from *sayf*.[10] Another pedagogical favorite and equally effective minimal pair contrasts the meaning of *kalb* 'dog' and *qalb* 'heart' in Arabic. These words are similar in form and different in only one respect—the point of articulation of the initial sound. In technical terms, the *kāf* is a voiceless velar stop; the *qāf* is a voiceless uvular stop, articulated slightly farther back in the vocal tract.

Although **contrastive analysis** was used widely in audiolingual approaches to teaching, it has been significantly less popular in contemporary language pedagogy because it focuses very explicitly on accuracy in phonological distinctions, which has been seen by some researchers as an "acquired" rather than as a "learned" skill, and in no need of explanation or attention. However, in recent years, some authors have revived this practice, referring to it as "the new contrastive pedagogy" (Pennington 2002, 93). In teaching Arabic, due to the nature of both script and phonology, it is often useful to draw students' attention to differences between the sounds and sound sequences of the L1 and the L2 in order to help them first discriminate phonemes and perceive differences, and subsequently be able to reproduce them when speaking. In the examples used above, the features of [+ velarization] and [+ uvular] are not typical speech sounds in English, and learners may have trouble hearing them at first. See Brown 2001, 288, for one way to teach pronunciation using minimal pairs.

Key words are high-frequency words that can easily and effectively be used to exemplify certain sounds and their contexts, such as the word *naʕam* ('yes') for medial *ʕayn*, or the word *khamsa* ('five') for initial *khāʔ*. These key words can be touchstones of pronunciation and eventual fluency, and teachers should be on the lookout for easy, frequent key words for learners to add to their vocabularies and for practice.

 # Word Stress

One of the most important but widely neglected topics in teaching Arabic phonology is word stress, the loudness or emphasis that is placed on a particular syllable.[11] Many Americans flounder or feel lost when pronouncing Arabic words because they do not know where the stress should be placed. Wrongly stressed words (such as **darast* instead of *darast*) can cause confusion for native Arabic speakers, as they may not easily recognize or be able to interpret Arabic words which are mispronounced. As one researcher states about the teaching of foreign languages, "if nonnative speakers fail to employ stress properly, their listeners will be lost in a sea of syllables" (Wong 1985). Erroneous stress patterns used by nonnative speakers can seriously disrupt comprehension and intelligibility. In English, word stress is for the most part unpredictable and phonemic (e.g., **com**bat (noun) and com**bat** (verb), or **sus**pect (noun) and sus**pect** (verb); that is, it can make a difference in the meaning of a word. Speakers of English learn stress by hearing it used or (if they have only seen the written word) by looking up the pronunciation of a word in a dictionary.[12] There are some general rules, but many exceptions.

In Arabic, stress is highly predictable according to a set of standard principles, and this should be explained to learners early on so that they have those rules to refer to when learning to pronounce new words. Linguistically untrained Arabic teachers are often uncertain about how to address Arabic stress rules and consequently often do not correct errors in stress. This issue is not unique to Arabic; many foreign language teachers lack professional confidence when dealing with this topic because of the technicalities involved.[13]

For native speakers of Arabic, stress is intuitive and unconscious; they may model word stress correctly, but not be able to explain why it is the way it is. Students will want to know why. Therefore, it is important for you to know the stress rules and be able to illustrate them and explain them. Introducing stress rules to students reduces student anxiety about pronunciation, even if the students may not master the rules immediately. If they know that rules exist and they can refer to them, that removes uncertainty and allows them to proceed.

Very briefly, MSA Arabic stress rules depend on syllable structure, and on whether a word is pronounced in full form or in pausal form. It is calculated from the end of a word. In full form, MSA stress falls either on the second syllable from the end of the word (*hunāka, katabtum*) if that syllable is strong (CVV or CVC), or it falls on the third syllable (*katabat*) from the end of the word if the second syllable from the end is weak (CV).[14] In pause form, stress falls on the final syllable if it is superstrong (CVVC or CVCC) (*mudarrisīin, katabt*).[15] Note that the stress rules that apply in most of the Eastern Arab world do not apply in Egypt.

 # Correcting Speech Errors

Many Arabic teachers hold back on correcting speech or pronunciation errors, especially—as previously noted—errors in word stress. This is for four reasons: First, correcting speech errors is a delicate and complex psychological skill. Learners will soon shut down if they are constantly corrected when speaking or lose their confidence in their ability to perform. Thus, speech error correction is a sensitive area of error analysis and feedback. The second reason is that teachers sometimes lack the technical training to provide explicit feedback to learners on what is wrong. The instructor simply repeats a correct version or recast of what the learner has said, but the learner may not "hear" or pick up on the correction. The third reason for refraining from correcting speech or pronunciation errors has to do with "face," the maintenance of personal dignity and respect. Cultural standards of politeness may interfere with the teacher's understanding of what, when, and how to correct speech errors because such correction may be seen as interference with the speaker or an attempt to point out a personal weakness. Fourth, pronunciation accuracy is an area where teacher expectations are sometimes not as high as they need to be; native Arabic speakers may not expect that their students are able to achieve a close approximation of good Arabic pronunciation and fluency and will be satisfied with only partial or limited performance.

❈ Options for Corrective Feedback on Pronunciation

When focusing on pronunciation accuracy, you as an Arabic instructor have a range of options open to you. These involve some general principles about correction in general and some strategies for pronunciation in particular.

- Timing: If a student is engaged in a speaking task, do not interrupt, but wait. You can wait until the student is finished and gently recast and/or explain his or her error, or you can wait until the entire exercise is done. In this case, at the end of an exercise or task, you may call attention to a general indication of problem areas without identifying the errors of individual students.
- Appropriateness: If learners are engaged in a pronunciation exercise, then immediate feedback is probably the best option so that learners are guided to optimal performance in a step-by-step manner.
- Technique: Language teachers must often make split-second decisions about how and when to correct. Experience is a wonderful guide, but if you are a novice teacher, then some basic principles apply: First and most important, don't overcorrect or undercorrect. Find a "middle way" that suits your teaching goals and style, and which is acceptable to most students. Second, let students know when and how you plan to provide corrective feedback. This will help prepare them for any interventions that you need to make. Third, it is okay to let an individual student know (after class) that you would like some time to work one-on-one with him or her on improving pronunciation.[16]

The teaching of Arabic pronunciation is a basic art that all teachers need to perfect. Importantly, this art covers not only the teaching of accuracy and fluency of articulation, but also the skills necessary for correcting pronunciation in encouraging, yet systematic ways. For students, it is the first step in learning Arabic; it is key to linking phonology and script. Achieving correct pronunciation is central to fluency, intelligibility, and comprehension, and above all, it is a rewarding personal achievement for learners. Nonnative speakers of Arabic may not reach 100 percent accuracy in pronunciation, but nonetheless can be effective and persuasive interlocutors as long as they are confident that they understand and can be easily understood.

❈ Study Questions and Activities

1. What do you think are the key elements in teaching Arabic pronunciation? What are the most important qualifications for the teacher?
2. In your experience, is pronunciation overemphasized or underemphasized in Arabic instruction?
3. Make a list of the five most challenging areas of Arabic pronunciation for foreign learners. Compare this list with others in your class.
4. Have you (as a learner or a teacher) discovered a particularly good technique for teaching pronunciation? If so, write a two-page paper that describes your approach and why it is successful.

5. Make a list of short, frequently used key words that each embody one Arabic consonant from the alphabet, and which you can recommend for new students to learn as pronunciation aids (e.g., *miftāḥ* for *ḥāʔ*; or *maʕlūm* for *ʕayn*). Compare your list with others in your class.

6. Read the section on stress rules in Ryding 2005, 25–31. Test the rules on five words that you come up with, and discuss them in class.

 # Further Readings

Brown, H. Douglas. 2001. *Teaching by Principles: An Interactive Approach to Language Pedagogy*, 2nd ed. White Plains, NY: Addison Wesley Longman. (Especially pp. 283–296 on teaching pronunciation.)

Lightbown, Patsy M., and Nina Spada. 2006. *How Languages Are Learned*, 3rd ed. Oxford: Oxford University Press. (Especially pp. 104–108 on teaching phonology.)

Ryding, Karin. 2005. *A Reference Grammar of Modern Standard Arabic*. Cambridge: Cambridge University Press. (Especially chapter 2 on phonology.)

Segalowitz, Norman. 2000. "Automaticity and Attentional Skill in Fluent Performance." In *Perspectives on Fluency*, edited by H. Riggenbach, 200–219. Ann Arbor: University of Michigan Press.

Stevick, Earl. 1996. *Memory, Meaning & Method*, 2nd ed. Boston: Heinle & Heinle. (Especially chapter 7, "The Meaning of Speaking.")

Notes

1. See Kissling 2012 and Trofimovitch and Gatbonton 2006.

2. Guiora and Acton also report that "hypnotizability," or the ease with which one enters into a trance state, also seemed to be a factor in improved prununication (1979, 18).

3. "Clearly, the native language is the most influential factor affecting a learner's pronunciation" (Brown 2001, 284).

4. See also chapter 12.

5. The Arabic word *allāh* may be pronounced with the 'heavy' or 'dark' /l/, depending on context (as in *wallah* or *wallāhu*). But this type of /l/ is highly restricted.

6. In certain forms of American English, the glottal stop is also a standard realization (or allophone) of /t/ in certain contexts. In my native Michigan dialect, I pronounce the word 'kitten' as [kiʔn], and 'mountain' as [mawʔn].

7. In the running transliteration text in this book, I do not indicate intial *hamza* unless I am focusing on it, as in this sentence.

8. For vowel melody in Arabic, see Moore 1990, 65–78.

9. English does not have phonemic gemination or doubling phoneme, but doubling of a consonant does sometimes occur across word boundaries when one word ends with the same consonant that the next word starts with, as in "hot tea," "good dog," or "big girl."

10. In Arabic the phonemes that include velarization (*ṣād, ḍād, ṭāʔ* and *ḍhāʔ*) are actually increased in complexity by the addition of a phonological feature (+ velarization). This is referred to as "secondary articulation" or "double articulation."

11. "Stress refers to the degree of effort involved in the production of individual syllables or combinations of syllables making up a word or longer utterance" (Pennington and Richards 1986, 210). Stress, like intonation, is referred to as a "suprasegmental" aspect of pronunciation.

12. Information about stress is always included in a good English dictionary. In an Arabic dictionary, stress is rarely mentioned because it is predictable and rule governed. It is accepted that even learners will know where word stress falls.

13. See Hardison 2010, 4.

14. Generally speaking there are only three permissible syllable types in MSA: CV (consonant + short vowel), CVV (consonant + long vowel) and CVC (consonant + short vowel + consonant). CV is considered "weak" and CVV and CVC are considered "strong."

15. Consult Ryding 2005, 25–31, for full explication and illustration of these rules.

16. See Brown 2001, 291, for a list of "basic options" for error treatment and "possible features" of those options.

Teaching Spoken Arabic

CHAPTER 16

lan tatakallama lughatī
"Thou shalt not speak my language."

Abdelfattah Kilito

Enthusiasm is more important to mastery than innate ability . . . because the single most important element in developing an expertise is your willingness to practice.

Gretchen Rubin

"In the United States, foreign language (FL) professionals have used the terms *communicative competence* and *proficiency* as synonyms for oral communication" (Larson 2006, 255; italics in original). The issues of communicative competence and proficiency have complicated as well as enriched Arabic instruction, learning strategies, goals, and achievement. With their emphasis on interaction and situated functional performance, they seem directed to and predicated on teaching flexible normative spoken language skills as the cornerstone for proficiency and achievement. However, in Arabic the question of which variety to be used in teaching spoken language is inordinately complex as well as crucial. Can Arabic be taught communicatively without engaging with vernacular language practice? And if so, how do teachers prepare learners for spoken interaction? Both writing and speaking demand a level of automatic performance which is largely built on previous exposure to language in context, but how does one arrive at the right combination of comprehensible input in MSA or in a vernacular variety? Teaching spoken Arabic remains a contested area of curriculum, as well as an important one. Different programs will take different approaches to this issue, making decisions based on institutional goals, curricular objectives, and student needs. To make informed decisions, faculty and administrators need to know the options open to them, the needs and goals of their students, the availability of materials, and what kind of spoken Arabic is authentic in which situations.

❖ Speaking in Arabic: Choices

In traditional communicative and audiolingual approaches to L2 teaching, speaking has been the privileged skill because it is considered the most cognitively demanding.[1] It was and is still thought that if learners can manage to speak correctly, control of the other modalities will ensue rapidly and with relative ease. To a great extent this is true for L2 learners whose L1 is reasonably close to the L2 etymologically, and where the natural variety of spoken L2 is normed and largely identical in structure and vocabulary with the standard written variety. It is possible to get a solid start in an L2 through enactment of situations and tasks, rapid oral rehearsal of key lines, and extensive oral practice with vocabulary and grammatical structures. Mutual reinforcement is found through listening, reading, and writing, which all practice essentially the same variety of language (e.g., standard French, standard Swedish).

Learners of Arabic face a different reality. Natural forms of spoken Arabic bear very different and sometimes inconsistent relations to written Arabic. Learners of standard Arabic cannot get reliable reinforcement from spoken interpersonal conversation to increase their competence, their fluency, their vocabularies, or their L2 intuition. Conversely, written Arabic, with its elegant grammatical processes, its extensive lexicon and plays on words, and its lengthy sentence structure, is not directly reinforced by natural, everyday spoken Arabic. Thus the link between the mutually reinforcing modalities of speaking, reading, and writing is much weaker in Arabic than in many other languages. A frequent practice has been to pass judgment on the worth and value of spoken vs. written language, and to separate the two, focusing primarily on the receptive skills of reading and writing in the literary variety of Arabic. Vernacular Arabic, since it is not used for writing (at least officially), has a disadvantage because of its long-term divergence from the classical idiom, the fact that it is unwritten, and its relatively mundane (although essential) uses in arranging and living one's life and work. In academic programs aiming primarily at developing literacy skills, the teaching of vernacular Arabic often has not fit.[2]

In order to approach the goal of functionality in all four modalities, most Arabic textbook writers in the 1960s and 1970s made the decision to apply standard structuralist and audiolingual approaches in speaking, listening, reading, and writing skills, using literary Arabic only, and avoiding the language of everyday life. This decision was driven and reinforced by the widely held notion in the Arabic speech community that spoken forms of Arabic are deviant, substandard, and lack "grammar." Thus when communicative learning goals and strategies came along, they, too, were applied to literary Arabic (MSA). As a result, however, learners "sound artificial and use a variety inappropriate to the occasion" when speaking with Arabs on everyday topics (Farghaly 2005, 45). In programs where MSA is taught as a spoken medium, "the teacher finds himself asking questions and talking to students . . . in a variety not appropriate to the topic of conversation" (ibid.). The vexing question of language variety choice faces all those who teach spoken Arabic skills.

❀ Vernacular Arabic

Perhaps the greatest difference between teaching Arabic and teaching most other living languages is the absence of attention to developing solid strategic skills based on actual conversational situations, that is, on what is called "primary discourse."[3] In particular, the absence from the classroom of the most basic everyday discourse constitutes a critical gap in the interlanguage of Arabic learners. *Without the ability to manage and communicate in real-life environments, and without grasping the discourse pragmatics that allow conversations to flow smoothly and effectively, even learners at advanced levels are on shaky ground.* They cannot confidently step outside the classroom; they cannot satisfy basic social and interpersonal requirements. This inability is a key psychological distractor that can undermine even the most skillful efforts to function at advanced levels within a normal range of experience. As long as Arabic learners are in sheltered classroom or academic environments, they can manage the tasks before them; in more realistically socially diversified and demanding contexts, however, they can be destabilized to the point of muteness. This is especially true if their efforts to communicate using *fuṣḥā* are ridiculed as inappropriate when in country.

Arabic learners in the United States and elsewhere are interested in visiting, living, and working in the Arab world, in engaging with Arabic as it is spoken, in understanding popular culture, and in making friends and acquaintances. It is increasingly important for learners of Arabic to be able to negotiate their study, social, and work relationships in a form of language accepted as normal by native speakers. It is also clear that speaking *fuṣḥā* in informal situations is problematic. One has to understand what people are saying as well as be able to express oneself. There is a need for vernacular-specific vocabulary, a need for appropriate grammatical structures, and a need for knowledge of intercultural pragmatics: for example, how to apologize, invite, refuse, ask questions, or use proper terms of address. Authentic discourse structures and processes are rarely taught in the AFL classroom.

Some conversational strategies useful for interactive activities include: starting a conversation, joining in, keeping it going, changing the subject, broadening the subject, coping with unexpected topics, finding common ground, requesting clarification, making a suggestion, extending an invitation, refusing an invitation, giving compliments, expressing gratitude. These and many other conversational functions are important skills for Arabic learners to know. One tactic for teaching them is to develop along with the students a set of conversational "routines" or key lines that they can rely on for tactfully handling everyday discourse.

A key question that often defies straightforward answers concerns which vernacular to teach. If a program decides to introduce a spoken language component, which of the several vernaculars is appropriate to include in the curriculum? The answer depends on several factors. Perhaps most importantly, it should be tied to study abroad options. If students are usually headed to Egypt, then Egyptian Arabic is the logical choice. If to Damascus, then Syrian Arabic—and so forth. If there is no one particular study abroad program, then a widely intelligible vernacular such as standard Jordanian or Egyptian might be an option. Staffing issues sometimes surface in this discussion. If a department has only a few native speakers and they are all Egyptian, for example, then it would seem logical that Egyptian be a choice for the curriculum, unless there is a strong tie to a different study abroad site. Faculty staffing may shift, however, as can study abroad opportunities, and such a decision may resurface for discussion and change. Flexibility is therefore a necessary feature of curricular decisions on this topic. One strategy for adjusting more readily to changes is to use a relatively dialect-neutral or cultivated hybrid form of spoken Arabic, such as educated spoken Arabic (ESA), as the primary form of instructed vernacular.

✿ Pedagogical Norms for Spoken Arabic

In the proceedings of a symposium on Arabic language teaching held at Leeds University (*Diglossic Tension: Teaching Arabic for Communication*), Dionysius Agius underscored the "pressing problem of what kind of Arabic should be taught to non-Arabic-speaking students" (1990, 3). He also alluded to the emergence of educated spoken Arabic (ESA) as a language variant which may be "taught for conversation" as an alternative to modern standard Arabic (MSA). Agius states that "there has emerged a language characterized by the aspirations of its speakers who, through a process of koineization have minimized local features peculiar to their dialects and have maximized borrowings from literary (formal) Arabic. . . . This is called Educated Spoken Arabic (=ESA)—a middle way between formal Arabic and dialects" (ibid.).

Here the role of "pedagogical norm," as mentioned in the introduction, would be a key issue to discuss and agree on for all Arabic language teaching programs. For Arabic, a pedagogical norm might be something like ESA incorporated into curricula parallel to modern standard Arabic, a balance that incorporates what Badawi regards "as the living language of culture and education in the Arab world" (2002, 159). Badawi is realistic about the complexities of Arabic sociolinguistics, both on the ground and in the minds of his fellow native Arabic speakers. As he notes about the idea of ESA as a linguistic reality, "it is not readily accepted, particularly by Arabs" (ibid.) as a legitimate or autonomous form of expression, despite the fact that it is widely and readily used by educated native speakers.

The primary drawback to using ESA as a pedagogical norm is that it is not itself "normed," but is highly variable along a continuum of situational formality mixed with personal educational background. And yet, Parkinson suggests that "it is simply a fact that people constantly mix *fusha* words, phrases, and other features in with their day-to-day speech for a variety of purposes. . . . In fact, I wonder if the mixed variety should not be considered the 'mother tongue' of many of these speakers" (2003, 39). In other words, the use of hybrid variants such as ESA is pervasive, accepted, and even expected in many situations.[4]

 ## Prestige Norms for Spoken Arabic

A further key concept in the establishment of pedagogical norms for spoken Arabic is the idea of the "prestige" variety of vernacular speech, or as Wahba puts it, "Educated Regional Arabic (ERA)," for example, Cairene Arabic in Egypt.[5] ERA, states Wahba, "is the medium of most oral communication. It provides spoken norms (with a relative variation from one Arab country to another) for all the Arab countries" (2006, 142). Prestige varieties may emerge from urban centers, centers of education, or upper social classes—the study of this phenomenon in the Arab world is only partially developed. However, it is important to know that MSA is not considered the only source of linguistic prestige in the Arab world or the only option for foreign language instruction. Cultivated hybrid variants such as ERA and ESA are linguistic facts in Arabic speech communities. In fact, Ibrahim states clearly that "there is a definite prestige norm in Arabic which is different from H" (1986, 119) and that "spoken Arabic (L) has its own local prestigious varieties which always comprise certain features that are not only different from but are often stigmatized by H norms" (124).[6] Badawi claims that "of all spoken varieties it is the most dynamic, versatile, and the one readily understood outside its particular geographical region" (1985, 15).

In noting that there is a "hierarchical order of prestige" among spoken Arabic vernaculars, Ibrahim also proposes that there is "a standard L," also called "an inter-regional standard L" (1986:120). He goes on to indicate that parallel to the established supra-dialectal H [MSA], "there exists a thriving supra-dialectal L based on the speech of such urban centers as Cairo, Damascus, and Jerusalem" (ibid.). Ibrahim does not call this variety "educated spoken Arabic," but states that it "is currently the prestige spoken variety in five countries and . . . seems to be spreading in active use and passive evaluative acceptance and comprehension within and without these countries" (1986, 125). Such a spoken standard, if subject to extensive study, analysis, and description, could be a widely applicable form of spoken Arabic for pedagogical purposes because of its broad intelligibility.[7] Thus Badawi, Ibrahim, and Wahba point to the existence of a regional prestige variety within each Arab country that is highly intelligible with other varieties of spoken Arabic. This is, I think, an important distinction: Teaching spoken or colloquial Arabic does not necessarily mean teaching the least prestigious variety of vernacular, but instead means teaching an "educated" or "prestige" variety that both serves learners in-country and travels well throughout the Arab world.

Meanwhile, however, most Arabic teachers are teaching strictly MSA and must calibrate their spoken language input to the requirements of learners at many different levels of proficiency. Selecting a form of MSA to speak in class necessitates a decision about whether or not to use *iʕrāb* at all times—a demanding choice. Most professors I have observed use *fuṣḥā bidūn iʕrāb* or a form of educated spoken Arabic as the preferred form of teacher talk with their students. If any standard spoken forms are used (such as *mish* instead of *laysa*, or *lēsh/lēh* instead of *limādhā* for 'why') these are explained to students as common colloquialisms that are not used in written language. In truth, every Arabic teacher must choose for himself or herself the level of formality that comes most naturally in the classroom situation, that meets the comprehension needs of the learners, that is highly intelligible, and that is compatible with departmental practice.[8]

 ## Practice

There are some fundamental principles that apply to teaching spoken Arabic, whether it is MSA, ESA, or vernacular, the most important of which is practice. By practice I mean listening as well as speaking, learning interactive skills, and engaging in a wide range of speaking exercises.

In developing oral skills, it is important for instructors to pay constant attention to learner inter-language in order to assess strengths and weaknesses and to determine where they need corrective feedback, additional vocabulary, practice in articulation, or other issues. Interim formative assess-ments in oral skills are useful if done regularly as part of standard classroom activities.

The rationale behind practice rests on some hypotheses of audiolingualism (habit formation) but also on more subtle shifts in cognitive control of L2 information. The idea is to proceed from declarative or explicit knowledge to implicit procedural knowledge through the mechanisms of practice, short-term retention, and rehearsal. This is related to Krashen's distinction between learn-ing and acquisition, as well as the key concept of transforming descriptive or declarative knowledge into instantly accessible resources for communication. This "proceduralization" or "automatiza-tion" requires a great deal of exposure to L2 input—ideally in an immersion environment—but in a classroom environment, it means plenty of time for practice. "Repeated behaviors of this kind allow the structuring . . . of declarative knowledge in ways that make it easier to proceduralize and allow the combination of co-occurring elements into larger chunks that reduce the working memory load. Once this crucial stage in skill acquisition has been reached, strengthening, fine-tuning, and automatization of the newly acquired procedural knowledge are then a function of the amount of practice, which increases speed and reduces the error rate and the demand on cognitive resources" (DeKeyser 1998, 49).

Interlanguage

It is clear that learners of foreign languages go through stages of competence, gradually develop-ing their ability to comprehend and express meaning. The term "interlanguage" (also referred to as "transitional competence") applies to learner language in its various stages as it more and more closely approximates the L2.[9] Coined as a technical term in 1972 by Selinker, "interlanguage" re-fers to the "separate linguistic system" of the learner "based on the observable output which results from a learner's attempted production of a TL norm" ([1972] 1983, 176). This concept is important as a tool for teachers so that they may recognize and analyze systematic deviations from target lan-guage norms and because it helps identify areas where intervention may be needed to assist learners in their development. The important thing to remember about interlanguage is that it is *systematic*. It is not just a chaotic combination of language bits; it stems instead from the students' attempts to apply organization to what they are learning. As learners of Arabic, students bring with them knowledge of their L1 or mother tongue, and they very likely also bring knowledge of a previously studied foreign language such as Spanish, French, or Latin. Any one of these language knowledge systems may influence learners through a process known as "language transfer," the attempt to apply rules from one language to another. Sometimes the rules from one language will conform to those of another, but many times, they do not, and are the source of interlanguage errors.[10]

Interaction in the Classroom

Interaction in the Arabic classroom has been a topic of extensive analysis and discussion, espe-cially regarding whether or not there is a useful construct for learners in the idea of "educated native speaker" (ENS) of Arabic.[11] The ENS model has been accepted for some time.[12] But for nonnative speakers learning Arabic, it is a distant and difficult goal because of the psycholinguistic complexity of native Arabic speakers' performance. For a model to be emulated, it needs to be approximated as closely as possible, but Wahba suggests a more "realistic" model for learners of Arabic as a foreign language: "the aim of Arabic language teaching/learning is not to achieve a mastery of Arabic . . . but to give the learners the opportunity to develop a diglossic competence and functional abilities that help the learner /user to perform tasks successfully when he or she deals with native speakers" (2006, 145). It is not always easy to choose the right variety of language for classroom interaction in Arabic as an L2; most teachers and programs opt for MSA, but as Elgibali and Taha note about the CASA program, "for the sake of fluency, we do not force learners to use case endings" (1995, 93).

Classroom interaction in the L2—between you and students and students among themselves—has been proposed as a way to both provide comprehensible input and facilitate L2 development. A key component of this interaction is "implicit negative feedback," which may occur when meaning has to be "negotiated" or clarified through trial and error. Interaction requires forced output by learners who may not have adequate interlanguage skills for a particular discourse task and who need to negotiate with their interlocutors about communicative intent. In order not to interrupt the flow or fluency of oral communication, you can record conversation for later playback and analysis, or you may choose to use another type of nonintrusive intervention such as recasts.

❖ Recasts as Spoken Interactive Corrective Feedback

Crucially, spoken interaction has been proposed as a point where the use of recasts for corrective feedback can be effective. Mackey and Philp quote Farrar's (1992) definition of recasts as "those utterances 'in which parents explicitly correct the child's sentence by adding syntactic or semantic information'" (Mackey and Philp 1998, 341). That is, parents or other caretakers normally rephrase a child's erroneous utterance in a way that focuses on content and provides an expanded or correct variant for the child. Recasts, as a form of clarifying feedback, "rephrase an incorrect or incomplete learner utterance by changing one or more sentence components . . . while still attending to its central meaning" (Richards and Schmidt 2010, 487). This kind of feedback is corrective but nonjudgmental, which allows for it to be used in negotiating meaning without disrupting a learner's focus, concentration, or effortful use of his or her interlanguage. Typical recasts, very much like the reflection that takes place in counseling-learning, are ways of reformulating what has been said by another in your own words. When used for corrective feedback, this reformulation retains the meaning of what was heard while at the same time providing a contexted correction of the previous utterance.[13]

Some researchers have found that learners do not perceive or notice corrections given in the context of recasts because this method of correction is so subtle and seems to confirm their intended meaning. This can be a problem if the learner does not notice the difference and does not register that a grammatical correction has been offered within the reformulation of the teacher. "Thus," explain Loewen and Philp, "in exploring the benefits of recasts, it is important to consider what aspects of recasts highlight the changes made to nontarget-like production. Certain elements may increase the salience of the recast, that is, help to draw the learner's attention to the recast form" (2006:538). These authors focus on the "uptake," or noticing, of corrections when delivered in a recast format. They found that intonation was a useful way of gaining the learners' attention, as was stress on the "changed element." Another strategy for using recasts was to engage the learner in more than just one exchange, called "extended episodes" (usually four or five turns); for example:

S: *daftarī kabīr min daftarihā*	دفتري كبير من دفترها.	My notebook is big than her notebook.
T: *ʕafwan, daftaruka kabīr. . . .?*	عفوا، دفترك كبير...؟	Sorry, your notebook is big . . .?
S: *kabīr min daftarihā.*	كبير من دفترها.	. . . big than her notebook.
T: *daftaruka AKBAR min daftarihā?*	دفترك اكبر من دفترها؟	Your notebook is BIGGER than her notebook?
S: *naʕam, daftarī akbar min daftarihā.*	نعم، دفتري اكبر من دفترها.	Yes, my notebook is bigger than her notebook.

Mackey and Philp report that a study by Lyster and Ranta (1997) "found that recasts were ineffective at eliciting student-generated repair when compared with other types of feedback:

clarification requests, repetition, metalinguistic feedback, and elicitation. However, they also point out that teachers have an overwhelming tendency to use recasts" (1998, 343). In Mackey and Philp's research project, they report that recasting was an effective measure, concluding that "these findings of a positive effect for recasts in the production of questions at higher stages suggest that recasts are a worthwhile issue for further research" (1998, 353). Loewen and Philp find that "recasts were widely used and that they were beneficial at least 50% of the time" (2006, 551). They conclude that recasts "represent a form of feedback that is pedagogically expeditious. A recast is time-saving, less threatening to student confidence, and less intrusive to the flow of interaction. . . . In addition, unlike explicit correction, recasts maintain the focus on meaning" (ibid.).

Recasts, then, are not unproblematic, but they are very useful if teachers acquire skills that help learners notice the differences between their own utterances and the recast done by the teacher, including intonation, stress, or other agreed-upon signals (such as hand signals).

❀ Chunks of Language

Much of any spoken language is routine, especially at ordinary everyday levels of communication. A number of researchers have come to see fixed expressions, prefabricated phrases ("prefabs"), and frequent collocations as chunks of language that can be taught at all levels to accelerate foreign language acquisition. That is, instead of approaching the skill of speaking on a word-by-word basis, students can learn chunks of discourse that more closely represent how native speakers store language for immediate use. "Such prefabricated patterns are easily encoded and permit the speaker to attend to the task of constructing the larger discourse. Equally, they lessen the decoding burden for listeners" (Miller and Weinert 1998, 385).

In fact, prefabs and chunking play key roles in construction grammar theory and cognitive linguistics. "Construction grammar and phraseological theories of language demonstrat[e] that much of communication makes use of fixed expressions memorized as formulaic chunks, that language is rich in collocational and colligation restrictions and semantic prosidies, and that the phrase is the basic level of language representation where form and meaning come together with greatest reliability" (Robinson and Ellis 2008, 5). Cognitive linguistics "holds that the basic units of language representation are constructions—form-meaning mappings, conventionalized in the child L1 learner and adult L2 learner speech communities, and gradually entrenched as language knowledge in the child L1 or adult L2 learner's mind" (4). That is, as I understand it, language competence is less governed by syntactic rules and algorithms and more dependent on chunked usage: phrases, collocations, and prefabricated units of frequently occurring language that are stored in memory as chunks.

There is a strong connection between the learning of L2 spoken discourse and the retention and use of chunks of language. This means that in teaching spoken Arabic, attention should be focused on memorizing and practicing units that occur as collocations and as formulaic routines (including idioms, but also other regularly occurring phrases and stock utterances) in order to facilitate

---

"There appears to be an important role for prefabricated speech in pragmatic development. As formulae and routines often consist of lexicalized sentence stems . . . with open slots, learners can decompose them and extend their use productively. . . . But the importance of formulaic speech is not limited to its role in the early stages as a stepping stone toward the higher realms of language use. Routine formulae constitute a substantial part of adult NS [native speaker] pragmatic competence, and learners need to acquire a sizable repertoire of routines in order to cope efficiently with recurrent and expanding social situations and discourse requirements" (Schmidt 1996, 163–164).

fluency and idiomaticity in self-expression. Arabic has a wealth of politeness formulas, idiomatic expressions, and standardized conversational routines that can ease learners into conversation and ultimately, as learners build their knowledge of these key phrases, lead to high levels of speaking proficiency.

Routines and Scripts

Much of spoken, everyday language is also characterized by predictable, routine discourse structures which can be learned as "scripts," or predictable sets of exchanges using largely formulaic language. Such scripts are normally based on situational needs and functions, such as greeting, requesting assistance, asking questions, negotiating meaning, or responding to particular situations. Scripts for studying, traveling, eating, going out, or meeting friends, for example, provide useful frameworks for acquiring spoken Arabic primary discourse skills. Most MSA textbooks are not designed around functional or situation-based needs, but some spoken Arabic textbooks reflect those needs. It is in this area where university language programs need to choose whether and/or how to teach basic primary discourse skills. Many programs do not, but this is also seen as a limiting weakness of Arabic instruction by students whose foremost interests lie in intercultural communication, study abroad, and interaction with Arabic speakers.

In this regard, Wahba gives a useful list of Arabic "tasks and their language variety" that identifies communicative functions and the type of Arabic needed to carry them out: ERA (Educated Regional Arabic), MSA, or both (Wahba 2006, 148–149). He refers to the observation by Roger Allen that "the organizing principle here is one that moves from function to form rather than the reverse" (ibid.). Within the range of daily communicative tasks that Wahba lists, most of the routine functions can be carried out in ERA with the help of particular "scripts" that suit each task, such as "identifying oneself," "order[ing] tea or coffee/food," bargain[ing] to buy something in the market." Although such language operations may not be seen as intellectually demanding, they provide essential frameworks for building more sophisticated communicative competence, and without them, learners may face paralysis in the most common everyday Arabic language situations.

To conclude this section, there is no single key to the issue of effective Arabic language programs, methods, and materials. But there is a central issue for resolution: the nature of instructed spoken Arabic. If a program aims at communicative competence, then the most important objective with regard to nonnative Arabic learners is to introduce interactive spoken skills early on in any curriculum and not to ignore them. Leaving crucial everyday communicative skills out of the curriculum unnecessarily handicaps and discourages students who are learning Arabic in order to live, study, and work in the Arab world and to be able to hold and understand sensible and creative conversations with Arab friends, acquaintances, and everyday contacts in a wide range of situations. When viewed from a sociolinguistic perspective, the interactional dynamics of Arabic vernaculars and the range of discourse norms, functions, formulae, options, strategies, and taboos is highly sophisticated and complex, even within a single speech community (say, Egyptian or Jordanian). I therefore think that the earlier exposure to spoken Arabic begins, the better. There is a great deal to learn, not so much in terms of traditional grammatical categories perhaps, but in terms of interactive strategies, creation of meaning, conversation protocols, and narrative skills. Our students are certainly up to the challenge, but are we prepared to venture into this discourse world?

Study Questions and Activities

1. How and to what degree have you used spoken Arabic in the classroom?
2. Do you feel comfortable using *fuṣḥā* for interactive activities or do you adjust your spoken language to some degree?

3. How do you feel about teaching oral *fuṣḥā* skills for everyday functional use?
4. Have you noticed different levels of Arabic learner interlanguage? What do you see as some of the salient characteristics of Arabic interlanguage at different levels of instruction?
5. To what extent do you assign pair work or group work to increase student interaction in Arabic? Do you think it is effective? If not, how could it work better?
6. Do you think that teaching spoken Arabic is different from teaching spoken French or English? If so, in what ways is it different?
7. Do the materials you have worked with provide adequate practice in speaking Arabic, or have you had to devise additional classroom work on these skills?

⬡ Further Reading

Al-Batal, Mahmoud. 1992. "Diglossia Proficiency: The Need for an Alternative Approach to Teaching." In *The Arabic Language in America*, edited Aleya Rouchdy, 284–304. Detroit: Wayne State University Press.

——. 1995. "Issues in the Teaching of the Productive Skills in Arabic." In *The Teaching of Arabic as a Foreign Language*, edited by Mahmoud Al-Batal. Provo, Utah: American Association of Teachers of Arabic.

Allen, Roger. 1990. "Proficiency and the Teacher of Arabic: Curriculum, Course, and Classroom." *Al-Arabiyya* 23:1–30.

Alosh, Mahdi. 2005. *Using Arabic: A Guide to Contemporary Usage*. Cambridge: Cambridge University Press.

Hamilton, Heidi, Cori Crane, and Abigail Bartoshesky. 2005. *Doing Foreign Language*. Upper Saddle River, NJ: Pearson/ Merrill-Prentice-Hall.

Leaver, Betty Lou, and Boris Shekhtman, eds. 2002. *Developing Professional-Level Language Proficiency*. Cambridge: Cambridge University Press.

Mora, Raimundo. 1995. "Silence, Interruptions, and Discourse Domains: The Opportunities to Speak." *Applied Language Learning* 6, no. 1&2:27–39.

Nattinger, J., and J. DeCarrico. 1989. "Lexical Phrases, Speech Acts, and Teaching Conversation." In *Vocabulary Acquisition. AILA Review* 6, edited by P. Nation and R. Carter, 118–39. Amsterdam: Free University Press.

Parkinson, Dilworth. 1985. "Proficiency to Do What? Developing Oral Proficiency in Students of Modern Standard Arabic." *Al-Arabiyya* 18, no. 1–2:11–43.

Ryding, Karin. 1991. "Proficiency Despite Diglossia: A New Approach for Arabic." *Modern Language Journal* 75, no. 2:212–218.

Wahba, Kassem. 2006. "Arabic Language Use and the Educated Language User." In *A Handbook for Arabic Language Teaching Professionals in the 21st Century,* edited by Kassem Wahba, Zeinab Taha, and Liz England, 139–156. Mahwah, NJ: Lawrence Erlbaum Associates.

Wilmsen, David. 2006. "What Is Communicative Arabic?" In *A Handbook for Arabic Language Teaching Professionals in the 21st Century*, edited by Kassem Wahba, Zeinab Taha, and Liz England, 125–138. Mahwah, NJ: Lawrence Erlbaum Associates.

⬡ Notes

1. It is also the most anxiety-producing experience for language learners. See Stevick 1996, 141.

2. From what I have seen and heard in professional fora, there is some sense that spoken Arabic vernaculars are simpler or less complex than *fuṣḥā* and therefore that teaching spoken Arabic is neither a challenging nor stimulating intellectual task because its structure and vocabulary are more rudimentary. In fact, the opposite may be true. Although the colloquials have fewer inflectional categories than *fuṣḥā*, they are by no means simple; they are, in fact, sometimes more highly complex in syntax—consider the complexities of the Egyptian Arabic negation system, for example. Also, when viewed from a sociolinguistic perspective, the interactional dynamics and the range of discourse norms, functions, formulae, options, strategies, and taboos are highly sophisticated and complex, even within a single speech community.

3. See Ryding 2006, 15–16.

4. In an earlier article, Parkinson reports on a study about the use of "modern *fusha*" wherein he shows that Cairene Arabic "speakers simply do not use it (at least in unmixed varieties) for 'daily life' kinds of communication" (1991, 40). Rather, they use an "educated urban variety" of speech.

5. Wahba 2006, 142. He states: "Based on their widely functional use in the Arab society, it seems that the MSA and the ERA represent the most integrated use of the four language skills, particularly in the speech of the educated speakers" (2006, 144).

6. The symbols "L" and "H" here are used to refer to the "low" and "high" varieties of Arabic, as discussed in Ferguson 1959a.

7. The US Department of State's Foreign Service Institute successfully pioneered in training American diplomats in "Formal Spoken Arabic" (educated spoken Arabic) for their assignments abroad, in recognition of the fact that their professional functions required a highly intelligible, regionally adjustable, cultivated, yet spontaneous form of spoken language.

8. See Hammoud 1996, 102–106, for a survey on "providing input" in Arabic classrooms.

9. See Corder 1981, 69 ff.

10. For more on interlanguage see Selinker 1972; Ortega 2007, 230–232; Corder 1981, 56–94; Richards and Schmidt 2010, 293–294.

11. See also chapter 2 in this book about the interaction hypothesis.

12. "We argue that, regardless of which geographical dialect is chosen, only the model of an educated native speaker should be presented to the foreign learner" (Elgibali and Taha 1995, 82).

13. In fact, the practice of using recasts may have been originated in the 1970s at the Foreign Service Institute, where training in Counseling-Learning/Community Language Learning provided foreign language instructors with a way to both show that they have understood the learner and at the same time, provide a corrected version of what was expressed incorrectly by the learner by rephrasing what they heard in their own words. A number of skilled teachers took this procedure up as an effective, nonintrusive way to introduce corrective feedback while at the same time reducing any affective resistance to corrections. See Stevick 1980, 100–226 (including a section by Irene Dutra 144–148) for an extensive discussion of CL/CLL, especially as it applies to the teaching of Swahili.

Writing in Arabic

CHAPTER 17

Insofar as we can distinguish between literary language and ordinary language, it is a learned literary competence that allows us to do so.

Haun Saussy

The Arabic writing system is one of grace and speed, of proportion and harmony among the letters themselves as they combine into words. It is also highly systematic, designed to perfectly accommodate the sounds of Arabic by providing complete grapheme-phoneme correspondence, or distinctive letter-forms for each Arabic phoneme (distinctive sound).[1] Not all languages have this efficient one-to-one matching. English, for example, has no single letter for the phonemes /sh/ or /ch/. On the other hand, English uses letters such as "c" to denote two sounds: /s/ and /k/ (*center* and *call*); it uses the letter "g" to represent the sounds /g/, /j/ and /zh/ (as in the words *gate, gentle*, and *beige*), and uses "x" to denote a sound combination: /ks/ or sometimes /z/ (both sounds occur in the word "Xerox"). English spelling is notorious for its irregularities. That is why spelling bees are such a popular form of competition in English-speaking countries, and why English speakers often have recourse to dictionaries, because even though they may know how a word sounds, they may not know how it is spelled—and vice versa. Arabic, on the other hand, has very close "fit" between the distinctive sounds of the language and the script system. One needs to remember, however, that the "letter" is not the sound, it is only a representation of the sound—and sound is primary. Arabic was a spoken language before it was a written language (as were all languages) and Arabic letters represent the system that was devised to best represent spoken language phonology. Where Arabic is most problematic to learners coming from other language traditions is in the invisibility of short vowels, the *ḥarakāt*. These short vowels are essential elements of pronunciation, but not ordinary orthography.

Writing ability as a fine-tuned motor skill and writing as a mode of expression are two very different topics. Primarily this book focuses on the former; but the teaching of composition and style, rhetoric, as well as expository, analytical, and creative writing at advanced levels of Arabic instruction is an under-researched topic that deserves greater professional attention.[2] This chapter approaches the pedagogy of writing from two perspectives: first, the introduction of script at beginning levels, and, second, the practices of writing at more advanced levels. The introduction of Arabic script is closely calibrated with the teaching of pronunciation as sound and script are learned together.

Sound and Script Together

Arabic writing is one of the most iconic visual symbols of Arabic culture, and learning sounds and script is one of the most rewarding early steps in learning Arabic. It could well be the most important step in the entire sequence of learning because it forms a foundation for learner confidence and provides a clear and significant accomplishment that serves as an initial benchmark for Arabic achievement. The knowledge of phonology and script can be learned, shown, exhibited, and demonstrated as evidence to friends and family that one is making progress. It opens the door to written language and therefore to the textual treasures of Arabic culture as well as to contemporary forms of written communication.

The development of literacy skills lies at the heart of most Arabic language instruction. It is the key to unlocking text and the first step in gaining a sense of the sound patterns of Arabic. The Arabic alphabet is wonderfully apt and consistent in its representation of the phonemes or distinctive sounds of the language. Each distinctive sound in Arabic is represented by a separate letter, and words tend to be spelled very much as they are pronounced (aside from the problem of invisible short vowels). Teaching the Arabic alphabet involves four main tasks:

- Learning how to pronounce Arabic sounds accurately;
- Learning how to write and recognize letters in context;
- Learning how to connect sound and script;
- Memorizing the alphabetic sequence of letters (a straightforward memory task).

The sequence of letters in the alphabet (*alif-bāʔ-tāʔ*) is essential for learners to know from the start of their study because it is a prerequisite for using an Arabic dictionary.[3] Learners will have to rely on this memorized sequence for the rest of their learning lives, and it needs to be mastered early on. Some teachers may be reluctant to use rote or memorized learning activities because they have been told that this is old-fashioned, but for a clearly defined task that consists of declarative knowledge and memorized ability, rote learning is not only efficient, it is necessary. This does not mean it has to be boring.

Steps in Teaching Sound and Script

One of the first steps to take is to make sure that your students know that each letter has a name (*alif, lām, mīm*) as well as the fact that each letter represents a distinctive sound /ā/, /l/, /m/. This may seem obvious but sometimes learners get confused about it, especially in the beginning, as they are picking out sounds and shapes. It is important to point out that in memorizing the alphabet sequence, learners are memorizing the names of the letters. A further point to remember is that the letter is not the sound; that is, it only represents the sound. Therefore, one does not pronounce "letters" (*ħurūf*); one pronounces what they stand for—a distinctive Arabic language sound. Here are some steps for teaching knowledge of the alphabet:

1. Let students know from day one that memorizing the alphabet sequence is one of the first goals of the class, and that it will be practiced every day. Explain why this is important: They need to know the sequence in order to use dictionaries efficiently. If you do not explain why this is important, some students may resist the memorization effort, thinking that it is too elementary or irrelevant for them.

2. Do not introduce the entire alphabet all at once and expect the students to memorize it. This overtaxes their memory and gives them nothing to connect with meaningfully. You may ask them to look at a chart that shows the entire alphabet and the shapes of the letters, but then explain that you will work with them systematically through each of the sounds/ letters, show how each is pronounced and written, and engage in plenty of practice associating sounds with letters and learning how to write connected script.

3. The alphabet order is best introduced and practiced in chunks of three to four letters at a time (*alif, bā' tā' thā'; jīm, ħā', khā'*, etc.), and rehearsed aloud by means of gradual buildup as the learning situation goes on through the semester and through the year. As lessons progressively introduce more letters, letters are added to what the learners need to produce and practice. By the end of the sequence of lessons on sound and script, students should feel comfortable reciting the entire alphabet.

4. Rehearsal of the alphabet order is easiest and most effective if done chorally at first, and then by calling on students either in groups or singly. During the first semester at least, the order of the alphabet should be a regular part of daily review routines. You can recite the sequence first, with students repeating chorally after you (this can be done at different speeds to vary the pace). Then ask the students as a group to reproduce the sequence two or three times, then go around the room asking students to produce one letter each in sequence. This can also be done backwards if you occasionally feel the need for variation.

Pacing is essential here. There is no time for deadly silence. This is a recall and recite task, a key component of learners' declarative and procedural knowledge about Arabic. The activities themselves should be organized ahead of time so that they are patterned and predictable. This activity needs to be done briskly and should not take up much class time. It can be done at the beginning of class, in the middle as a break from doing textbook work, or at the end—or a combination of these.

Bridging the Gap: Dictation Exercises

Spoken language and writing need to be taught together so that sound and script become automatically linked in the learner's mind. That is, the Arabic letters that represent particular sounds should be taught with a great deal of rehearsal, repetition, and mimicry as well as consistent practice in writing down of sounds heard—dictation. One of the most successful and popular forms of practice in listening and writing Arabic is the dictation exercise. It is popular with students because it allows them a specific period of time when they can focus on form. They can immediately check to see if they have heard an utterance correctly and also to see that they have written it down correctly. Dictations are useful at almost all stages of learning up to the advanced. Of course, the complexity and length of dictation items increases with length of time studied. Teachers should pronounce dictation items slowly and clearly at first, then follow that up with the items pronounced at a more natural speed; pronouncing something three times is usually enough for students to grasp what they hear and write it down. Make sure you let students know exactly how many times you will say the dictation items so that they are prepared to listen attentively. It is usual to start with one-word items first, then two, then three, and so on. Focus at first on familiar words; words you have been using in class. Then progress to less familiar or new words. Ask two or three students to volunteer to do the dictation exercise at the board. It is a good idea for you to move around the room, look over the students' shoulders at the items being written down, give gentle hints, and answer questions here and there. This is not a contest; it is a learning activity. Performance does not have to be perfect. For more explicit dictation procedures, see chapter 14 on listening.

Teaching Handwriting

Two things need to be remembered when one teaches handwriting: First, going from right to left is not easy—it is counterintuitive for English speakers and needs a great deal of practice. Second, learners should not simply copy printed Arabic from books. As is well known, handwriting conventions differ from printed Arabic in many ways, and need to be taught separately (such as the lack of "teeth" in the *sīn* or *shīn* in Eastern Arabic handwriting; the convention of connecting the diacritical dots on *tā'* or *thā'*, for example; or the particular handwritten form of the *lām-alif* ligature). By helping students learn how to write clearly and quickly, you are helping them reinforce their language skills. Arabic learners need to be able to develop clear and legible handwriting. This is necessary in order to do homework efficiently, in order to take notes on lectures, texts, and broadcasts, to take written tests, to create their own written texts, and to develop the ability to write quickly and accurately under various circumstances. This goal is not old-fashioned, esoteric, or useless. It is a key part of the mastery of written Arabic because it gives learners a skill that will last through all their studies and ultimate use of Arabic.

Handwriting is a physical motor skill that develops dexterity and reinforces what is learned. For example, the ability to write out a day's assignment in handwriting provides a digital memory connection with the sound and shape of words. In learning vocabulary, many students find that writing out vocabulary words in longhand assists them in retaining those words as well as in developing their control of the mechanics of the writing system. Attention to longhand writing tends to be one of the neglected or least-understood aspects of basic Arabic teaching, with some teachers bypassing the development of writing skills and emphasizing instead the ability to use an Arabic keyboard for purposes of composition and homework practice. I have even heard of teachers asking learners only to trace the forms of letters in the textbook, rather than to learn to write them in connected form as part of a new set of literacy skills. The key issue here is that of course keyboard skills and computer literacy can be essential for advanced learners, but they are not a substitute for being competent in the longhand writing system just as native speakers of Arabic are. The technology is centrally important, but it needs to be built on a sense of comfort with already mastered handwriting.

Writing practice goes along hand in glove with pronunciation practice so that sound and script become connected in learners' memories. Most Arabic textbooks are designed this way. The *Alif Baa* textbook, for instance, introduces sounds and script in chunks of 3–4 letters of the alphabet over ten lessons. Another popular but more traditional introductory text, McCarus and Rammuny's *Programmed Course in Modern Literary Arabic: Phonology and Script,* organizes the presentation of the alphabet and writing into 25 lessons, with one or two phonemes per lesson, including some extras such as a chapter on reading and writing numbers.

Learning each chunk of 3–4 letters (as well as the other symbols needed for writing and pronunciation, such as *shadda, hamza,* and *waşla*) can take up to 3–4 hours of classroom time as well as an equal (if not greater) amount of time in homework and self-study. The classroom time needs to be tightly planned, varied, and briskly paced; written homework needs to be assigned every day, corrected immediately, and handed back. The written homework does not need to be complicated or extensive, but should review points recently covered in class.

In addition to introducing new material, regular time for review needs to be built into every class. (This is a good general rule, but is particularly important during this initial stage of instruction.) Five or ten minutes of review at the beginning of every lesson will prove very useful for the learners, reinforce their progress, and give them a chance to ask about issues they may have been introduced to, but have not fully understood. A once-a-week quiz on lesson content keeps learners on their toes and provides them with graded feedback on their performance. As has been mentioned, regular quizzing is a good idea in general, but it is especially important during this phase because it helps to consolidate a great deal of new material.

Even while sticking to the task at hand, and making sure of progressive coverage of the subject matter, make time in every class to do at least some non-text-based activities and to rehearse interactive skills such as everyday greetings, basic question-and-answer topics, and essential vocabulary. If you spend three or four classroom hours per lesson (say, of *Alif Baa*), that is between thirty and forty hours for ten lessons to introduce script and phonology. If you cover two or three lessons of *A Programmed Course* in 3–4 hours, that equals forty to fifty hours for 25 lessons. Therefore, 30–50 classroom hours is about the right amount of time to spend on this first major task. The key to doing all of this is to be prepared, organized, and consistent in your presentations, your expectations, and your communication with the students. This may not happen the first time that you teach, but it will develop as you gain experience.

Students need regular handwritten homework assignments, especially during the first two years of study. This does not mean they cannot use computers for special projects or online work; it just means that the long-term development of confident handwriting skills is a priority in Arabic and should be practiced daily.

Arabic Notetaking: A Key Skill

Rapid and accurate longhand writing is especially important for the skill of notetaking. Whether one is listening to a lecture, a news broadcast, an interview, or another form of oral presentation, notetaking may well be a crucial skill for one's success—as a student, a researcher, a journalist, a diplomat, or a translator, for example. Some of the subskills required in notetaking include:

- Sustained attention and focus
- Rapid auditory processing and evaluation of new information, often delivered via new vocabulary items
- Organizational skills
- Critical thinking skills (gist versus detail, inference; synthesis, analysis)
- Spelling and grammar skills
- Ability to write comprehensibly under timed conditions
- Continual social decisions: Ask for clarification? Negotiate meaning? Wait? (Matson, Flynn, and Bia 2011)

For advanced learners of Arabic, the ability to write rapidly as one is listening is one that needs specific attention and training. As one researcher notes, "the facilitative effect of notetaking on lecture learning and recall is thought to derive from one or both of the two postulated functions of notetaking: (1) the encoding function and (2) the external storage function" (Dunkel 1985, 30). That is, the cognitive and mechanical process of writing down information as well as the result—a set of notes to refer to—reinforce each other. The same researcher states that in terms of training, "the instruction must be systematic, long-term, and must allow for continuous practice" (31). This is a skill that can be taught and practiced extensively in advanced Arabic classes.

 Literacy and Writing in Arabic

As Al-Batal has noted, "writing is perhaps the most neglected language skill in Arabic" (1995, 125). He observes that due to a lack of attention to writing in general, as well as to rhetorical processes and style, American learners' Arabic writing often seems like "an English composition written in Arabic words" (1995, 125). That is, it may be grammatically correct, but it does not conform to standards of Arabic style. He identifies *Adawāt al-rabt fī l-ʕarabiyya l-muʕāṣira* (Al-Warraki and Hassanein 1994) as one of the few textbooks that focus on developing correct written structure, especially the use of cohesive devices, or connectors. More recently, two textbooks have been published that can be used in developing writing skills in Arabic: Wahid Samy's *Arabic Writing for Style* (1999) and El-Mustapha Lahlali's *How to Write in Arabic* (2009).

 Writing and Close Reading

El-Essawy 2005 points out some of the challenges that still face the teacher of Arabic writing: shortage of materials, writing's "subservient" role in many programs, its subordinate status in the eyes of many learners, the difficulty of producing well-structured texts, and the "absence of

Rubin reports on findings that indicate that L2 "notetaking can affect the encoding process or the review/rehearsal process. For the encoding process, notetaking can increase meaningful chunking and thereby encoding of information, level of attention, effort, and assimilation of old and new information. For the review/rehearsal process, notetaking can provide mnemonics and information for reconstruction" (1994, 213).

research about characteristics of good writing style" in Arabic. To these she adds two more: first, the "over-emphasis on skimming and scanning in reading classes" that diverts attention from text structure, and, second, finding appropriate feedback strategies. As El-Essawy notes, intensive, close reading is one of the key processes for increasing accuracy in producing written texts. This procedure is often delayed or even avoided in undergraduate Arabic teaching because it is not considered an adequately "communicative" activity. Al-Batal also advises "intensive exposure to texts" and makes the observation that "native speakers of Arabic seem to become good writers in an almost unconscious way; they acquire the writing skill by extensive exposure to written texts through reading and by memorizing great numbers of essays and compositions written by their language instructors or printed in composition textbooks" (1995, 127). Therefore, despite a short- age of materials designed for teaching written Arabic, the strategy of exposing learners to texts that exhibit particular rhetorical and stylistic features and having them work intensively on them serves as a modeling process for raising awareness of text structure and discourse devices, and for activating vocabulary. Such texts do not have to be long; in fact, using short texts is probably better. But they should model specific aspects of written discourse. Thus, intensive reading can form a valuable part of a writing curriculum. In analytical writing, also, it is now theorized that careful and close reading precedes the writing process. "On the most basic level," writes one professor of composition, "it's reading comprehension: finding claims and finding evidence. Then you get to the much more interesting issues of analysis, which is how the writer is persuading the readers of claims" (Berrett 2012). In any learning situation where a writing project is assigned, there should be "instructor guidance throughout the course" (ibid.).

Process and Product

Writing (as well as translation) can be viewed as either a process or a product: a support skill that underpins performance in other modalities, or as an academic goal that results in a polished result. Sometimes, "making writing activities goal-oriented helps the students think of the content and structures of the language, the context within which the language is being communicated, the audi- ence to whom they are writing, and the appropriateness of the level of language used" (Al-Batal 1995, 129). A further observation on the teaching of writing is that the skill of composition is one of constant revision. Interaction and feedback from the teacher and from colleagues at various stages of the writing process are key elements in developing one's writing style and effectiveness, as are consideration and reconsideration of one's own work. It is not enough for an instructor to assign a substantial writing activity (such as an essay or a speech) and look at it only once. Such projects require repeated evaluation, reworking, and redrafting to produce the best, most eloquent results. Individual conferences with students on writing projects are very useful, as is peer feedback.

Analyzing Arabic Composition

One recent article (Husni and Watson 2006) details a long-term (ten-year) study and evaluation of Arabic learners' compositions. Most of these students were native speakers of English who had completed between one and two years of university study as well as a year of study abroad. This article focuses on error analysis, "identifying and analysing the kind of errors typically made by students in the written production of Arabic and, by extension, on producing teaching materials specifically designed to correct these errors" (2006, 208). The authors deal with a range of vari- ables in their analysis: syntax, morphology, orthography, vowel length, and lexicon. Some of the problem areas identified include: use of prepositions, inappropriate context for word use, greater attention to content than to structural accuracy, problems in using cardinal numbers, and incorrect selection of derived verbs (such as using a Form V verb when a Form VI is needed). This study is

Certain subprinciples can be recommended for writing assignments. Some of these may seem trivial, but I have found that having specific rules for written assignments helps to clarify expectations, to reassure students, and to prevent lax writing habits. Here are some general rules that have worked well for me in teaching first- and second-year Arabic. I do not present these as requirements that all teachers should adhere to, but as examples of specific practices that have been effective in managing written homework and its learning objectives.

- First, all short vowels should be indicated: both word-internal and inflectional. In a way, this is a very traditional approach, but it ultimately pays off in better vocabulary control for learners because of the attention required for this level of detail. It is an important requirement especially at the initial stages of study because it trains Arabic learners to focus on vowels as well as the consonant outline of words and builds accuracy of retained forms. Also, when students indicate inflectional vowel endings (*iʕrāb*) it indicates how well they understand syntactic relations. Very often, written homework surfaces unexpected problems in grammatical and orthographical accuracy and helps in diagnosing errors.
- Second, encourage learners to use pencil, not pen—especially in beginning courses. This makes it easier for them to make corrections and easier for the instructor to read.
- Third, have learners write on lined paper and skip one or two lines between lines of text. This allows the person correcting the material to see short vowels and diacritical marks clearly and to write comments or to illustrate better handwriting.
- Fourth, do not allow late written homework past a certain point in time. Announce at the beginning of a course (in writing) that homework that is more than a week late (or two days, or whatever you judge to be reasonable) will not be accepted, and that students will get an "incomplete" for that assignment. Otherwise, some chronically procrastinating students may hand you a stack of old assignments just before the final exam. Yes, it happens.

important because it is one of the very few classroom-based research articles on the pedagogy of Arabic composition. It points in some very clear directions: the connection between faulty phonology and spelling, inadequate attention to syntax and morphology, the interference of colloquial expressions, and lack of familiarity with the conventions of written Arabic discourse. Each one of these areas needs substantially more research, and, as the authors conclude, "given the practical orientation of this research, all present and future analytical work should be considered as a precursor to producing focused teaching materials designed to improve student performance in extended writing" (Husni and Watson 2006, 220).

✦ Conclusion

The topic of L2 Arabic writing—from learning the script to the act of composition—is a vast one, and certainly one that has attracted the least attention from language researchers. The pivotal role of writing in Arabic as a foreign language—both in terms of the complex mechanics of rapid handwriting and the place of written self-expression and composition as higher-level skills—has been greatly underestimated. These are fertile fields for study and for contributions to professional understanding of strengths and weaknesses in this important area of Arabic pedagogy.

Study Questions and Activities

1. If you were to design a course in Arabic composition, how would you do it? What would be your most important goals and how would you approach them?
2. Orthography and pronunciation are directly linked in Arabic; hearing, seeing, and pronouncing Arabic correctly are important to learning how to spell correctly. Do you think correct spelling in Arabic is more important than correct spelling in English? Argue your reasons.
3. In some programs, the skill of writing is of far less importance than the other three modalities (listening, reading, and speaking). Is there any place in such programs for writing skills? If so, how would they fit in and how would you justify their importance?
4. Discuss with your classmates a writing assignment that worked particularly well for you, either as a teacher or as a student of Arabic.
5. Discuss the relationship between dictation and writing and between dictation and notetaking.
6. Choose a short, exemplary passage (two or three pages) from an Arab author who is known for his or her rhetorical style. Discuss how you would have students read the passage and analyze it closely for grammatical structure, literary themes, cultural references, and rhetorical devices. Then, devise a writing assignment based on the reading. What objectives would you aim for in such an assignment? How would you prepare students for it and help them with it?

 ## Further Reading

Al-Batal, Mahmoud. 1989. *Nashāṭāt waḍhīfiyya li-tadrīs mahārat al-kitāba. Al-Arabiyya* 22:137–156.

_____. 1995. "Issues in the Teaching of the Productive Skills in Arabic." In *The Teaching of Arabic as a Foreign Language*, edited by Mahmoud Al-Batal. Provo, Utah: American Association of Teachers of Arabic.

Byrnes, Heidi. 1983. "Discourse Analysis and the Teaching of Writing." *ADFL Bulletin*, 15, no. 2:30–36.

Husni, Ronak, and Janet C. E. Watson. 2006. "Arabic as L2: Linguistic and Intercultural Issues in Composition." In *Grammar as a Window onto Arabic Humanism: A Collection of Articles in Honour of Michael G. Carter*, edited by Lutz Edzard and Janet Watson, 208–221. Wiesbaden: Harrassowitz.

Lahlali, El-Mustapha. 2009. *How to Write in Arabic*. Edinburgh: Edinburgh University Press.

Samy, Waheed. 1999. *Arabic Writing for Style (Al-Kitāba wa-l-uslūb)*. Cairo: American University in Cairo Press.

Notes

1. See Gordon 1970.
2. See Al-Batal 1989 for a comprehensive overview in Arabic on the pedagogy of Arabic writing.
3. Although Arabic dictionaries are organized according to lexical roots, the order of the roots themselves is alphabetical; that is, the root *j-r-b*, for example, will come before *j-r-d,* and so forth.

Part VII

Teaching Core Competencies

Teaching and Learning Vocabulary

CHAPTER
18

The ordinary vocabulary of our own language seems to be protected against forgetting within the limits of normal function, but it is quite different with words from a foreign language.

Sigmund Freud

Whether we are concerned with explicit or implicit grammatical knowledge, words inevitably come before structures.

David Little

Learning useful, frequent, and widely understood vocabulary should be the primary task of the beginning Arabic student, relying on the linguistic and cultural sophistication of the teacher to select the most pragmatic and practical items to work with. Vocabulary is the most essential tool that Arabic learners can use to construct meaning and it provides the context and anchor for grammatical structure. As with the teaching of other skills, the teaching and learning of vocabulary has different implications when used for active or receptive purposes. Active and receptive knowledge are, of course, two sides of the same coin. In conversational situations, learners need to know what to say, but equally importantly, they need to understand what is said. In reading Arabic, speed and depth of comprehension depend largely on solid vocabulary knowledge; in writing, accurate expression of meaning requires a sophisticated grasp of both denotational and connotational senses of words and expressions.

Al-Batal notes that (1) "there is strong agreement among researchers that vocabulary . . . has not received the attention it deserves" and (2) "the field still lacks consensus on processes of vocabulary acquisition, including its conceptualization, the role and definition of context, and the effectiveness of various vocabulary learning strategies" (2006, 331). He also refers to an "acute lack of research on vocabulary acquisition in Arabic" and states that in his opinion, "the acquisition of vocabulary is the most important challenge that learners of Arabic face" (332). This chapter introduces some essential concepts for teaching vocabulary as well as specific issues and strategies for Arabic instruction.

The Lexical Approach

Within the domain of second language acquisition research, there is a significant strand of theory that puts vocabulary and phraseology at the heart of learning (Willis 2003; Little 1994; Takač 2008).

> It is the ability to use conventionalized and predictable language sequences that brings an L2 learner closer to the native speaker. Namely, native speakers do not exercise the creative potential of syntactic rules of a generative grammar. . . . It is the use of idiomatic, frequent and familiar units that reflects a native-like competence. Therefore the task of the L2 learner is to acquire lexical sequences (collocations, phrases and idioms), as well as sequences within lexical units. (Takač 2008, 17)

With a solid and strategic knowledge of vocabulary, grammatical structures can often be figured out from context (in reading or listening). For this and a number of other reasons, "there may be good reasons for placing the mental lexicon rather than abstract syntactic rules at the centre of linguistic competence" (Little 1994, 107). Such an approach is highly useful for Arabic; vocabulary is an area where even good language learners face challenges, and where most learners seek to find solid footing in the language. I agree with Al-Batal that vocabulary acquisition constitutes the heart of the Arabic language learning challenge. In this respect it is interesting to note the findings of applied mathematician Andras Kornei, who "showed that 85 to 95 percent of the information content of any text must reside in word meanings rather than grammatical structure" (Pullum 2012).

⬡ Chunking, Prefabs, Collocations, and Formulaicity

Vocabulary learning is not just word-learning. It is learning predictable chunks of language that are meaningful, frequent, and useful for both self-expression and for reading and listening skills. As noted in chapter 11, these "chunks" have garnered a great deal of interest not only as a "collocation model," for teaching but also as a new foundation for understanding the cognitive structure of grammar. De Angelis cites studies about "how grammars are built: the lexical array and the structural template views" (2007, 59). The structural template view sees language as basically syntactic structures "into which lexical items are subsequently inserted" whereas in the lexical array view, "the lexicon selects arrays of lexical items directly from the lexicon and 'merges' them" into coherent syntactic structures (De Angelis 2007, 59). Thus it is possible that the lexicon is the primary factor in language structure as well as in word-meaning. Moon also makes a similar distinction: she distinguishes between the "collocationist view" of language that sees the "the strong patterning in the co-occurrence of words" as "underpinning grammatically well-formed utterances" (Moon 1998, 42, quoting Sinclair 1987, 319–325). She refers to the "idiom principle" of structural patterning, that is, "a language user has available to him or her a large number of semi-preconstructed phrases that constitute single choices, even though they might appear to be analyzable into segments" (ibid.).

These concepts thus underpin the emergence of "multi-word items" (Moon), "pre-fabs" (Bybee 2006), collocations, and "chunking" of lexical items as a central feature of L2 acquisition. That is, instead of seeing individual words as the primary components of meaning, separate from syntax, the idea is to see how words consistently and frequently co-occur in predictable units of expression. It is well known that both spoken and written discourse are characterized by the frequent and extensive use of conventionalized word sequences or formulas. These sequences carry a large percentage of the semantic and pragmatic message intended by the speaker/writer. This is true for all languages, and Arabic is no exception. In fact, conventionalized Arabic sequences are key components of communication and need to occupy a prominent place in any curriculum or any syllabus. Such sequences include idioms, formulaic language, and also conventionalized collocations known as "prefabs" (prefabricated sequences) (see Bybee 2006, 713).[1]

⬡ How Many Words? Which Words?

There are two numbers that surface regularly in vocabulary acquisition research (the great bulk of which is done for learning English as a foreign language): 700 and 2000. "The 700 most frequent words of English account for around 70% of all English text. That is to say around 70% of the English we speak and hear, read, and write, is made up of the 700 commonest words in the language" (Willis 2003, vi, as quoted in Little 1994, 116). Nation states that "usually, the 2,000 word level has been set as the most suitable limit for high-frequency words," and "counting the 2,000 most frequent words of English as the high-frequency words is still the best decision for learners going on to academic study" (2001, 14–15).[2] The key complicating factor for Arabic vocabulary acquisition and teaching is, of course, diglossia, the difference in spoken and written vocabularies, because of a lack of mutual reinforcement in spoken and written discourse. This is all the more important when one takes into account that one of the most important sources of L2 vocabulary building is a broad range of contexts and plentiful, diverse forms of comprehensible input. Nation emphasizes that the basic group of 2000 words, the high-frequency ones, is essential for learners and "in general, high-frequency words are so important that anything that teachers and learners can do to make sure they are learned is worth doing" (2001, 16).

As for Arabic word estimates, Al-Batal states that "we can estimate that for a learner of Arabic to reach the advanced level of proficiency, a vocabulary of 3,000–3,500 high-frequency words is needed" (2006, 333). He stresses additionally the need for "an estimate of the number of roots needed for each level. The integration of the root and pattern system into vocabulary acquisition becomes crucial at the intermediate-high level and beyond" (2006, 333). El-Essawy supports these estimates, with the notation that it is "easier in English to deal with issues like estimating vocabulary size and choosing vocabulary for active knowledge" (2010, 235). Whatever textbook is used and followed, vocabulary enrichment can be done systematically by the teacher to help bridge the gaps between the classroom and the real world. The key points here are not to overburden the learners and also to help them practice, review, and rehearse vocabulary in context.

For Arabic language teaching purposes the field is fortunate now to have the results of corpus-based lexical research in Buckwalter and Parkinson's *Frequency Dictionary of Arabic* (2011), which lists and defines in English the top 5,000 words of Arabic according to their frequency. The authors note that their corpus was 90 percent MSA, and that "much of the high-frequency vocabulary of spoken colloquial Arabic did not make the top 5,000 list" (Buckwalter and Parkinson 2011, 5). Nonetheless, this publication is an essential asset to further research, materials development, and Arabic pedagogy, and should be available to all those who engage in Arabic teaching. If one takes the first 2,000 words of Buckwalter and Parkinson's dictionary and supplements them judiciously with key words from spoken Arabic vernaculars, one might come up with an experimental core vocabulary for Arabic learners.

Vocabulary for Reading

Laufer refers to a "threshold vocabulary" that learners need in order to be able to transfer some of their L1 reading strategies to the L2. This is also called "sight vocabulary," i.e., "words whose forms and common meanings are recognized *automatically*" (Laufer 1997, 22; italics in original). Laufer goes on to say that "automatic recognition of a large vocabulary, or a large sight vocabulary . . . will free one's cognitive resources for (1) making sense of the unfamiliar or slightly familiar vocabulary and (2) interpreting the global meaning of the text" (1997, 23). She goes on to report that "the turning point of vocabulary size for reading comprehension is about 3,000 word families. If we represent the same number . . . in terms of [discrete] lexical items the level at which L1 readers can be expected to transfer their reading strategies to the L2 is 3,000 word families, or about 5,000 words" (1997, 23–24).

Other researchers agree: "L1 and L2 studies agree that about 5000 words in any language constitute ninety percent of the words needed to read a text for comprehension. [The] inference from such research is that the evidence argues for teaching high-frequency vocabulary to a point of automaticity . . . Similarly, ... a 1500–2000 word vocabulary (the goal of most elementary two-year L2 sequences) is inadequate for reading authentic texts" (Swaffar, Arens, and Byrnes 1991, 44).

Choosing Vocabulary Variants

From the outset, the Arabic teacher is confronted with choices:

- Should everyday vernacular vocabulary items be taught as well as the more literary or formal items presented in most MSA texts?
- Should learners be encouraged to engage in interactive tasks with each other and with the teacher using only text-based (MSA) vocabulary or should they be trained to interact more naturally?

These questions are normally not a problem for other languages, where the split between spoken and written functions is not as complex as in Arabic. In the majority of cases, living languages are taught first of all from a pragmatic, functional point of view, introducing the student to basic everyday situations, reciprocal interaction, and predictable conversation sequences in order to build a primary discourse base from which to grow. For Arabic this is usually not the case unless the course is in colloquial Arabic or educated spoken Arabic. The initial exposure to Arabic language in normal classroom situations is centered on learning formal language and literacy skills. Nonetheless, strategic vocabulary-building is a way to interconnect spoken and written Arabic, and to provide a foundation for both interactive skills and nonreciprocal skills such as reading and writing.[3]

Challenges for Arabic

Arabic vocabulary learning is both the most challenging and the most essential component of proficiency. For learners whose L1 is English, there are particular challenges in terms of the learning burden of Arabic vocabulary.

Nouns and Adjectives

For learners of Arabic as a foreign language, noun and adjective plurals constitute separate items that need to be stored in their mental lexicon, essentially doubling their cognitive load, or "learning burden."[4] That is why learning singular and plural together as a pair of items is one of the most effective ways of building up lexical resources (*dars/durūs; jarīda/jarā?id; madīna/mudun; kabīr/kibār; jadīd/judud*). There is no reason to delay the introduction of plural nouns and adjectives, even if the plural form is of the "broken" or "internal" type. First of all, learning plurals along with singulars from the outset removes the learning barriers and complexities of retrieving plurals as separate items, and speeds up acquisition. Second, by knowing the plurals of nouns, learners can begin to count items and to learn the number system—and one cannot start too early for that. Counting exercises and other essential quantifier use ('all,' 'some of,' several,' 'most') reinforce plural forms and solidify grasp of the number system. Third, once a core vocabulary matrix of singular and plural forms is available to the learner, patterns in plural morphology will begin to be perceptible, and the learner will be ready to grasp pluralization patterns more readily through either inductive or deductive procedures.

Basic Verbs

An important factor in slowing down Arabic acquisition and performance is that some of the most fundamental and frequent verbs in spoken Arabic are different from written Arabic (e.g., *shāf* 'to see, look' or *rāḥ* 'to go'). Verbs to a great extent determine the syntactic structures of sentences and one needs to control certain core verbs to be able to communicate at the most basic levels. Without any access to the key verbs of vernacular Arabic, most learners will be ill at ease in speaking situations. Verbs are certainly not the only items of difference between spoken and written Arabic, but they are perhaps some of the most salient. This does not mean that these verbs are not "Arabic;" it simply means that they are not usually accepted as standard literary lexical items. They are, however, part of the shared spoken matrix language that all Arabs know and use on a daily basis.

It may be possible to introduce them as "spoken but not written" lexical items and to use them on a regular basis in the classroom for speaking on informal topics.

On the other hand, introducing key vernacular verbs can be both subtly tricky and confusing if the teacher is not comfortable with code-mixing (shifting from MSA to colloquial and vice versa), and explaining code-mixing. In a formal instructional situation, clear lines of communication are essential, and teachers need to choose their avenues of approach according to the best interests of the students as well as their own beliefs about and comfort with a mixed approach.

In the Beginning: Emphasize the Frequent and Familiar

Although knowledge of derivational morphology (*ishtiqāq*, the root-and-pattern system; *awzān al-fiʕl*, how words are built) is a key resource for native speakers of Arabic working through a text, it is much less useful for beginning and intermediate foreign learners, because they need first to build up a solid core of frequently occurring lexical items in order to begin to perceive patterns automatically and to use componential analysis to determine meaning of unfamiliar items. This means that initial curricular focus should be on lexical items that will be both useful and easily learnable; on items that are of high frequency in both MSA and spoken Arabic (if possible), and on items that relate semantically and socially to frameworks that learners already know. Some successful strategies for building vocabulary include:

1. Learning **series** or sets of everyday words such as numbers, colors, positions and directions, days of the week, months, sizes, family relations, and other semantically related sets.
2. Learning **prefabs**. As mentioned earlier, prefabs (from 'prefabricated language') are "multiword composites" or phrasal lexical items that are commonly used as fixed phrases. "A prefab is a combination of at least two words favored by native speakers in preference to an alternative combination which could have been equivalent had there been no conventionalization" (Erman and Warren 2000, 31). It has been hypothesized that most speech and even much written text consist of these preset, prefabricated phrases. "Idioms, compounds . . . habitual collocations (provided they are noncompositional) and prepositional and phrasal verbs are all fairly easily identifiable and indisputable examples of prefabs" (33).[5]
3. Learning the most **frequently used items**. The key vocabulary items in any language will be based on frequency of use; for Arabic that naturally involves both spoken and written elements as well as teaching how to select appropriate sociolinguistic registers and contexts for various Arabic words and expressions.[6]
4. In the beginning, **fronting the familiar**. To accustom first-year learners to manipulating Arabic words and Arabic sounds, it is useful to provide them with lexical equivalents to concepts with which they are already familiar, such as names of people and places. The idea behind this is that by lightening the learning burden in the beginning, learners will be able more rapidly to string ideas together, to take in more grammatically complex concepts, and subsequently produce words accurately in context, with attention on the message rather than on the form. By using familiar terms in context, the grammatical structures that hold them together become both clearer and more salient. Building on learners' background knowledge of the general geography of the Middle East, for example, one can introduce names of places: cities, countries, seas, gulfs, rivers, deserts, mountains, and other landforms. By introducing a few key lexical items along with these such as cardinal directions (*sharq, gharb, janūb, shimāl*) and the words *madīna* ('city') and *ʕāṣima* ('capital'), a wide range of simple sentences can be constructed within informative contexts that can both present and reinforce geographical information. Likewise, names of famous people from the Arab world can readily be connected to various countries, such as leaders, authors, scholars, or historical figures. By building on meaning that is already known, learners can more readily focus on discrete linguistic challenges such as pronunciation and basic syntax.

Recycling and Repetition

As Al-Batal observes, "the frequency with which learners are exposed to vocabulary words appears to affect the learners' acquisition of words. . . . For a word to be acquired, it needs to be repeated 6 to 12 times" (2006, 336). At a minimum, most researchers cite 6–7 repetitions or recyclings of words as the lowest number of times words should be repeated for maximum learning (Nation 2001, 81). This does not mean repeating a word six times all at once; it means multiple, sequenced exposures: systematically recycling vocabulary in context through various means in the classroom over a period of time. The spacing and nature of repetition are key factors in fostering retention. Moreover, "retrieving rather than simply seeing the item again seems to strengthen the retrieval route (Nation 2001, 79). Also, "each retrieval of a word strengthens the path linking form and meaning and makes subsequent retrieval easier" (67).[7]

Nation particularly emphasizes the use of word cards or flash cards as retrieval practice for learners, and I agree with Al-Batal that student-generated word lists (i.e., vocabulary words copied down in list form in Arabic and English) are a key to retention and retrieval for learners of Arabic.[8] This traditional practice is successful despite the lexical items' being decontextualized. This is so for a number of reasons: it creates an easily portable review reference for students to carry around with them and consult; the writing of the Arabic words and their English equivalents creates a perceptual motor-memory trace in the learner's brain; and constant review of the harder-to-remember bits also reinforces the easier bits.

The Best Vocabulary Activity: Concentration

Educational games involve learning, focus, memory, competition, and interaction among people. It is sometimes useful to organize an educational game as a learning activity in the classroom, and as a break from routine classroom activities. Concentration (also known as "Memory") is a card game where the aim is for players to match pairs (two two's, two hearts, two queens, etc., depending on what is specified beforehand). All cards in a deck are turned facedown and laid out at random; each player gets a chance to flip over two cards at a time, to see if they match. If they match, they are called a trick, and the player gets to keep those two cards and to have another chance at flipping over two cards. If the cards flipped over do not match, they are turned facedown again, and remain in their original positions in the layout. This allows players to see the cards in place again and again, and to learn gradually where they are located within the layout. Players take turns at flipping over cards and taking tricks. The player with the most tricks at the end wins. Concentration can be played with any number of players, with teams, or even as a variant of solitaire.

In the Arabic language classroom, a variant of Concentration can be a highly effective tool for vocabulary acquisition. Using a set of flash cards or index cards cut in half, write Arabic vocabulary words on half of them, and their English equivalents on the other half. Shuffle them and mix them up thoroughly. Then spread them on a classroom table or big desk and have students take turns flipping over the cards two at a time, trying to match the Arabic and English words. The student with the most tricks or pairs at the end wins the game.

As a learning activity, it is important that a great deal of Arabic be spoken and used during the game; students must pronounce the Arabic words written on the cards that they turn over; if they turn over an English word, they should try to give the Arabic equivalent. The teacher should keep up a running commentary in Arabic, guiding the students in taking turns, asking who wants to start, cheering for a matched pair, encouraging for unmatched pairs, speculating on where the matching cards are, confirming pronunciation,

The Best Vocabulary Activity: Concentration—continued

asking questions, and so forth. You will find that students love this game. It is a break for them, it is interactive, and it is competitive; it helps build relationships, mutual support, and community. Most of all, it helps them learn. This game is effective because the students are focused on winning, not on vocabulary. In order to win, though, they have to remember what a word looks like and where it is located. If a word is pronounced every time it is turned over, the students hear it many times. The learning that takes place here is incidental, but powerful. Several variations on this game are possible:

1. Instead of pairing Arabic and English vocabulary words, pair singular and plural Arabic nouns (or adjectives), the singular written on one card and its plural on another.
2. Instead of writing just one word on a card, write a phrase and pair it with its English equivalent (such as *ahlan wa-sahlan* and "welcome" or *ṣabāḥ al-khayr* and "good morning").
3. Instead of pairing English and Arabic, put one part of a short Arabic sentence on one card, and the rest of it on another. Students have to match up the sentence parts.
4. I have two packs of cards made for teaching Arab children the names of animals. Each card has a picture of an animal and the letter that starts the name of the animal (e.g., the card for *tāʔ* is illustrated by a picture of *timsāḥ*, 'crocodile'). I use both decks and have students try to match them up.

It may take you some time to write out your own cards, but they can be used over and over again, once made. Sometimes students ask to borrow them. I also encourage students to make their own cards if they want to continue to play the game on their own time.

Dictionary Use and Dictionary Strategies

Dictionaries play a key role in most L2 learning situations and are a favorite resource for many language learners. The same can be said for the learning of Arabic vocabulary, but the role of dictionaries for Arabic learners is both more complex and more essential. Despite the intricacies of Arabic morphology necessary for dictionary use, the challenges and needs of vocabulary learning require that learners have access to a well-organized, well-researched, and reliable lexical reference work. Arabic dictionary use must be taught.[9] Without a solid knowledge of derivational morphology (both *ṣarf* and *ishtiqāq*), Arabic students will be unable to use a dictionary with any precision or reliability. Built and organized on the lexical root system, Arabic dictionaries provide a wealth of information clustered around each root, like a cloud of potential meanings. Finding a root morpheme, distinguishing the listings for different *awzān* or "forms" of the verb, then seeking the meanings of derived nouns, adjectives, and participles is a learning challenge in itself, requiring explicit declarative knowledge of Arabic morphological structure. In fact, dictionary use is a central issue faced by all learners of Arabic, and one that needs guidance, training, and consistent review by any Arabic teacher. El-Essawy states that it is "necessary to train learners to use dictionaries in order to find the proper entry required by checking [a] word's context and comparing it to [the] entry chosen" (2010, 237).

Certainly the most comprehensive and practical Arabic-English dictionary is the Hans Wehr *Dictionary of Modern Written Arabic*. Every serious Arabic student should have one, and strategies for its use should be explicitly taught. In fact, when dictionary use is introduced (as early as the first semester of Arabic, but at least in the second), students and teachers should read and discuss Wehr's introduction (vii–xv) as a foundation for understanding its structure, conventions, and optimal use. For an English-Arabic dictionary of optimal usage and practicality for students, I have long preferred the *Concise Oxford English-Arabic Dictionary*, edited by N. S. Doniach. It is learner-friendly, portable, accurate, and informative. Many colleagues, however, prefer Ba'albaki's excellent *Al-Mawrid* English-Arabic dictionary. As Arabic-Arabic dictionaries and reference guides for learners, *Al-Munjid fī l-lugha wa-l-aʕlām* is extremely useful, as is *al-Munjid al-abjadī*. These reference books include maps, cultural and historical information, tables, charts, and many other sources of data useful for teaching and learning Arabic language and culture.

⬡ Study Questions and Activities

1. The lexical approach puts vocabulary acquisition at the center of language learning. Do you agree with this? Why or why not?
2. There is substantially greater attention now to teaching vocabulary by "chunking" language items together, and to learning prefabs and standard collocations. Have you tried this as a learner? As a teacher, do you approach teaching prefabs differently from teaching individual words?
3. Do you use any word-learning games in the classroom? If so, which ones, and how do they work? Discuss this with your classmates.
4. Which dictionaries do you yourself use? Would you recommend these to learners?
5. The Hans Wehr *Dictionary of Modern Written Arabic* contains a valuable introduction (pp. vii–xv). Read the introduction and write a one-page summary of the most important points for students who are learning to use this dictionary.
6. The Buckwalter-Parkinson *Frequency Dictionary of Arabic* contains a number of word lists organized by semantic category, such as "food" or "sports." Take a look at these specialized lists and discuss which ones would be useful for teaching a beginning or intermediate class of Arabic. How might you teach them?

⬡ Further Reading

Al-Batal, Mahmoud. 2006. "Playing with Words: Teaching Vocabulary in the Arabic Curriculum." In *Handbook for Arabic Language Teaching Professionals in the 21st Century*, edited by Kassem Wahba, Zeinab Taha, and Liz England, 331–340. Mahwah, NJ: Lawrence Erlbaum Associates.

Buckwalter, Tim, and Dilworth Parkinson. 2011. *A Frequency Dictionary of Arabic: Core Vocabulary for Learners*. London: Routledge.

Erman, Britt, and Beatrice Warren. 2000. "The Idiom Principle and the Open Choice Principle." *Text* 20, no. 1:29–62. (Especially detailed on prefabs and idioms.)

Lancioni, Giuliano. 2009. "Formulaic Models and Formulaicity in Classical and Modern Standard Arabic." In *Formulaic Language: vol. 1: Distribution and Historical Change*, edited by Roberta Corrigan, Edith Moravcsik, Hamid Ouali, and Kathleen M. Wheatley, 219–238. Amsterdam: John Benjamins.

Little, David. 1994. "Words and Their Properties: Arguments for a Lexical Approach to Pedagogical Grammar." In *Perspectives on Pedagogical Grammar,* edited by Terence Odlin, 99–122. Cambridge: Cambridge University Press.

Nation, I. S. P. 2001. *Learning Vocabulary in Another Language*. Cambridge: Cambridge University Press.

Nation, Paul, and Robert Waring. 1997. "Vocabulary Size, Text Coverage, and Word Lists." In *Vocabulary: Description, Acquisition and Pedagogy*, edited by Norbert Schmitt and Michael McCarthy, 6–19. Cambridge: Cambridge University Press.

⟨⟩ Notes

1. On formulaicity in Arabic, see Lancioni 2009.

2. For the English *Academic Word List* see Nation 2001, 407–411.

3. It has been proposed that there is a kind of "lexical bar" (barrier) between spoken and written variants of most languages. This has been described by Nation (quoting Corson) as "a gulf between the everyday meaning systems and the high status meaning systems created by the introduction of an academic culture of literacy" (2001, 26).

4. "The 'learning burden' of a word is the amount of effort required to learn it" (Nation 2001, 23).

5. I recommend reading Erman and Warren, and note that they have a very useful glossary of terms for discussing prefabs as "Appendix 1" in their article.

6. The "Introduction" section of Buckwalter and Parkinson's *Frequency Dictionary of Arabic* (2011) contains a very useful discussion of frequency and its relevance to learning Arabic as a foreign language.

7. I strongly recommend Nation's chapter 3, titled "Teaching and Explaining Vocabulary," as a source of insight and classroom practice. Some Arabic flashcard programs online include Quizlet, Superflashcard, and Anki. I have found that some are easier to use than others.

8. Al-Batal states: "I have found that using paired lists at the lower levels of instruction can help students focus their attention on the new vocabulary, provided that these items are activated and contextualized further through class activities" (2006, 334).

9. Use of dictionary resources is one way to foster "noticing," or conscious awareness, of language structures on the part of learners. The use of a dictionary is "by definition a conscious act of focusing on a linguistic form" (Scholfield 1997, 295).

Pedagogical Grammar

CHAPTER 19

No matter what method of language teaching one employs, the teacher is best served by a clear, accurate understanding of how grammar and lexis are structured.

Andrea Tyler

To study grammar is to study culture–because, as Sapir reminds us, grammar is culture.

John Du Bois

The term "grammar" covers a wide range of phenomena. A broad definition would be: "Grammar is the cognitive organization of language."[1] One author points out that traditional grammar has "focused specifically on the rules that govern word formation (morphology) and sentence structure (syntax) in a particular language" (Andrews 2007, 61). Another author declares that "grammar in its widest sense includes all the ways in which words are put together to communicate meaning" (Garrett 1989, 31). A further definition of grammar is: "the explicit rules about language that are taught to learners" (Loewen and Reiders 2011, 76). In this sense of the term, these authors continue, "grammar consists of explicit knowledge that learners can be taught, similar to other subjects such as maths and science. In this definition of grammar one distinction that is made is whether a grammar is prescriptive or descriptive" (77). Yet another definition of grammar is as follows: the term "grammar" is "generally used to refer to the rules and formal features of language that learners must master as part of coursework . . . this kind of grammar is often called pedagogical grammar" (VanPatten and Benati 2010, 91). It is "pedagogical grammar," rather than theoretical grammar that is the primary concern of this chapter. Pedagogical grammar involves principles for teaching the rules and processes of language structure not for their own sake, but for the purpose of building a basic knowledge of how the language works and for proceduralizing that knowledge.[2] The study of grammar as "noncontextualized focus on form" (Byrnes 1998, 288) is of limited use and certainly not very interesting to most learners; but acquisition of grammatical structures learned through interaction and carefully planned activities creates a firm foundation for linguistic progress.[3]

Prescriptive and Descriptive Grammar

A prescriptive grammar is often portrayed as rules about how one *should* speak (according to language authorities) and is concerned with the correctness of practice. A descriptive grammar is not judgmental about particular forms of correctness; rather it describes "how people actually use language" (VanPatten and Benati 2010, 91). Thus for Arabic, there is a long tradition of prescriptive grammar applied to the written form of the language, but virtually no "prescriptive" grammar that applies to spoken variants. Many of the spoken variants or vernaculars have been studied and described by contemporary Arabic linguists, however, and these descriptions reflect the way that spoken Arabic is actually used in context.

The experience of traditional prescriptive *fuṣḥā* pedagogy in the Arab world has been difficult if not negative for many native speakers of Arabic. For example, Suleiman discusses the conflicted feelings that Edward Said had about *fuṣḥā* and his early antipathy toward it: "One reason relates to the mind-numbing experiences of being taught Arabic grammar in a rote-learning format that made the subject boring . . . very much as it does today for millions of students in the Arabic-speaking world" (2011, 89–90). As Suleiman points out, the didactic tone and dullness of *fuṣḥā* instruction combined with what Said refers to as "lamentably ungifted and repressive teachers and clergymen," were significant alienating factors in Said's personal educational experience (90–91). Edward Said eventually returned to *fuṣḥā* and "came to be a great admirer and champion of the language because of its eloquence and the elegance of its grammar," but his early learning experiences essentially caused him to disengage with it for many years. Such anxiety and dismay may not be everyone's experience, but it was not an uncommon one. It has the effect of making native speakers of Arabic doubt their own competence and avoid grammatical explanation. It is that kind of tedious and unimaginative approach to Arabic grammar that needs to be avoided in the modern Arabic classroom.[4] Arabic grammar can and should be fascinating (or at least interesting), not boring.

In general, in a classroom situation, it is helpful to use descriptive terms when discussing language structure, such as "this is the way Arabic works," rather than "you must do it this way or you are in error." This allows teachers to be objective specialists rather than placing them into a prescriptive role where they find themselves "enforcing" rules and overfocusing on correctness judgments. American students are more likely to respond positively to descriptions of structure than to prescriptive notions of right and wrong.

To evaluate the "perennially vexing" (Byrnes 2000, 491) role of grammar in contemporary communicative language teaching, one needs to objectively assess the pros and cons of elucidating grammatical structures in terms of both timing and amount of grammatical instruction. Too much time spent on extensive description and explanation of minor points of grammar is not useful, but grammar explained concisely, with a light touch, a few well-chosen examples, and consistently followed up on often works for adult language learners. In general, heavy doses of strictly grammatical information are frustrating for learners who need practice using the language and who need to make the most of classroom time. On the other hand, L2 input without any explanation of vocabulary or structure, and with little or no feedback to learners on their performance, is also not the best use of classroom time and can lead to equal levels of frustration. There is a middle ground: grammar instruction can play a key role in raising learners' levels of accuracy and in boosting their confidence within a communicative paradigm. It is really the delicacy and deftness of grammatical explanation that is the main point in Arabic language teaching. This delicacy is grounded in the teacher's solid understanding of Arabic grammatical structures combined with the ability to suit any explanation to the time and context where it will make a difference to the learners' grasp of correct language. This involves astute judgment on the part of the teacher as well as tact: judgment as to the timing and tact as to the process.

Much of the recent literature on SLA in instructed language settings discusses the role of "focus on form" as distinct from "focus on forms." As noted earlier, in chapter 2, this distinction was made by Long and Robinson in order to describe a type of grammatical intervention in the classroom that is "motivated by the so-called Interaction Hypothesis" (1998, 22) and based not in a grammatical syllabus, but usually within a content-based or task-based curriculum, exploiting "opportunities that arise naturally from the interaction of learners and tasks" (Long and Robinson 1998, 23). That is, focus on form is a way of noticing and discussing grammar points as they surface in the framework of a learning activity. "Focus on form is learner-initiated and it results in noticing" (Long and Robinson 1998, 40). Focus on forms (with an "s"), on the other hand, is considered a more traditional, grammar-based type of procedure where the teacher initiates or controls activities in which grammatical form is the central focus.

Focus on form (in other words, instruction on grammatical topics that surface during communicative activities) may be a useful way to attend to the need for accuracy when it arises. In most contemporary Arabic textbooks, minimal grammatical explanations are provided in order to help learners understand language structure. Often, however, the application of such explanations is difficult or complex, and although learners may think they understand, it is not until they have to use a particular structure that they and the teacher realize they have not quite grasped the point and all its ramifications. Paying attention to accuracy when language is in use—in an exercise, a task, or a presentation, for example—helps to contextualize rules and therefore helps to remember them. However, a general ordering of grammatical topics often proves to be a valuable pedagogical anchor for students. Maintaining a systematic "grammar thread" throughout a course, a syllabus, or a curriculum provides an organizing principle for linking and recycling key structural topics while at the same time not dominating or diverting attention from the development of fluency and general communicative competence.[5]

 ## The Role of Error Correction

At several points in this book, error analysis and correction have been discussed (see chapters 5, 9, and 16). A central concern for contemporary classroom methodology is the use or nonuse of corrective feedback during speaking activities; a tension exists between researchers who do not perceive "any significant effect of direct error correction on grammatical accuracy" (VanPatten 1985, 63–64), and those who state that "implicit learning is not sufficient for successful SLA and focus on form improves rate and ultimate L2 attainment" (Robinson and Ellis 2008, 7). Unfortunately, there are as yet few studies of the effects of instruction on acquisition of Arabic grammatical features. One exception is Alha::wary 2009a, who provides a review of "existing Arabic second language acquisition research" (21–48) as well as studies of the acquisition of gender, negation, mood, and case by Arabic learners (51–146), and a chapter on the pedagogical application of his research (173–181). Nielsen 1996, 1997a, and 1997b also provides in-depth study of Arabic L2 acquisition of morphological features.

 ## Arabic Grammar and the Limitations of Input

A primary acquisition strategy in communicative approaches is the comprehension of strategically varied and increasingly complex input, leading to the ability to convert that input into output or performance based on interactive experience. It is thought that exposure to the L2 will often be enough to provide a foundation for productive skills such as speaking. This concept was originated by Krashen and applied by Krashen and Terrell through monitor theory and the natural approach in the 1980s. In a subsequent article, however, Terrell began to question the absence of linguistic information and instruction for learning, reporting on his own experience with Moroccan Arabic:

> Consider my own attempts at learning Arabic during a five-week stay in Morocco. I knew no Arabic on arrival and soon found that even the simplest input was incomprehensible. I soon switched to an output strategy . . . [where] I would ask (in French) how you say X in Arabic and then repeat the response several times, trying to memorize it. Then I would try out the new word or phrase as often as I could. I learned to count, to purchase pastries, to order tea in the morning, and to use a few other routines. Clearly I acquired some words and phrases in Arabic, but what I acquired was my own version of these words and phrases based on my output, not on the input since I rarely heard these same phrases in the input directed to me. Indeed, I was rarely able to identify any individual words in the input and mostly determined the meaning of utterances directed at me through contextual guessing.
>
> In summary, some informal evidence exists that adults do not automatically use input to develop competence in the way Krashen has suggested. The question then naturally arises as to the role of grammar instruction in adult second language acquisition. If some adults do not process input as Krashen suggests then it may also be the case that a conscious knowledge of grammar may play a greater . . . role in language acquisition and processing than Krashen posits. (Terrell 1991, 53)

Thus Terrell discovered the opaque nature of a language that is noncognate with English and the need for active inquiry to sift out key vocabulary, phrases, and structures. It is interesting that as an acquisition strategy Terrell resorted to the standard audiolingual practice of eliciting items, repeating words and phrases, memorizing them, and rehearsing them in context. I cite this experience not only because it is a professional linguist who lived it and wrote about it, but also because it highlights a strategic difference between exposure to languages that are noncognate with English and those that are. In other words, learning some Spanish during a five-week stay in a Spanish-speaking country is a vastly different experience from trying to learn Moroccan Arabic, and much of the SLA research undertaken regarding input processing thus far has been based on the learning of European languages.

Therefore, Terrell's inquiry about "the role of grammar instruction in adult second language acquisition" is of direct interest to teachers of Arabic as a foreign language. The adjustment of language input directed to Arabic learners in order to make it comprehensible requires high levels of teacher awareness; but deciding on the timing, role, and nature of grammatical intervention requires equal if not greater sophistication and awareness. Alhawary advises "scheduling the learning objectives of [grammatical] forms (for example, what and when) and recycling forms in the input . . . As the data reveal, recycling such forms in the input is also necessary for acquisition (not just emergence) of such forms" (2009a, 178).

✧ Acquiring Arabic and Communicative Language Teaching

For Arabic learners, acquisition of structural accuracy as well as fluency depends on substantial amounts of target language input and practice. Controversy exists as to the need or usefulness of explicit instruction in target language grammar, and over the years of CLT's evolution into a popular approach for language teaching, a great deal of attention has been paid to justifying avoidance of grammatical explanation or circumventing it in the classroom.[6] Terrell notes that "in most communicative approaches direct and explicit grammar instruction has been accorded a somewhat peripheral position in the total course design" (1991, 53). Although CLT has in many respects downplayed or even excluded the importance of instruction in grammar, recent research has shown that adults do benefit from explicit attention to grammatical structures.[7] This is especially true in terms of developing readiness to reach advanced levels of proficiency. A principled integration of systematic grammar instruction, then, may play a key role in fostering proficiency.

It is my belief that the practice of avoiding explicit grammar instruction in Arabic has been inappropriately generalized based on overinterpretation of the role of comprehensible input and on misinterpretation of the roles of different modalities, of error correction, and of learner affect. A progressive deemphasis of grammar instruction coupled with expectancy of high levels of linguistic accuracy does not often work in the long run. At the more advanced proficiency levels, fluency without high levels of accuracy is recognized as a signal of inattention to or ignorance of discourse detail, and will hold foreign language learners back in terms of their proficiency ratings when tested. As a former certified proficiency examiner, I can attest to the very real and not uncommon phenomenon of the 2 (ACTFL "advanced") or 2+ speaker who despite fluency and even a reasonably large lexicon (in the case of a 2+), is unable to perform at a 3 (ACTFL "superior") level because of the absence or inconsistency of key elements of structural accuracy. That is, a 2 or 2+ can often get his or her ideas across, but in a nonstandard way and without acceptable command of grammatical structure.[8] Therefore, understanding the role of grammar instruction and applying it wisely in the classroom can be a key factor when teaching adults who have limited time to study the language and yet need to develop high levels of competence. This does not mean that explicit grammar instruction will fix all errors; it means that learners' understanding of rules can provide a foundation upon which to build structural competence.

The task of learning grammatical structures and rules can be accomplished through assimilation of spoken or written language and subsequent experimentation with using language for specific tasks. This is what is known from the study of first language acquisition by children. This kind of assimilation can and does also happen with foreign language learners, and much of the CLT movement is based on this concept. There are, however, important differences between first- and foreign-language teaching situations. In foreign-language teaching situations,

1. The learners are often adults
2. They do not have large amounts of time
3. They want to make the best use of their time
4. They often have specific communicative goals as well as time frames
5. They can understand explanations of rules.

These differences play into the fundamental difference hypothesis (FDH) (as noted in chapter 2), which "claims that first language acquisition and adult second language acquisition are fundamentally different in a number of ways" (VanPatten and Benati 2010, 89). That is, although adults may no longer have full access to the flexibility and absorptive capacity of a child's mind, they have learning experience, conscious motivation, and access to cognitive processes for solving problems which can aid them in figuring out language structure and in grasping grammatical principles.

With respect to the topic of grammar and grammar instruction, it is useful to review the distinction between declarative and procedural knowledge discussed earlier in this book (chapter 16). Declarative or descriptive knowledge is conscious awareness of and ability to explain what is known; it is "knowing that" something is the case. Procedural knowledge, on the other hand, is "knowing how." It may be conscious, but is often unconscious. It is knowledge that underlies the ability to perform. In language learning, it is important to proceed from declarative or descriptive knowledge (e.g., knowing that an Arabic adjective agrees with the noun it modifies in gender, number and definiteness) to procedural knowledge (using this structure correctly in speaking and writing). This is called "proceduralization" or sometimes "automatization"—that is, the learner becomes able to perform in the target language automatically, without paying too much attention to how he or she does it.[9] The processes and contexts of proceduralization and systematic skill development include rehearsal, memorization, and deliberate practice as well as substantial amounts of comprehended input.

 # Arabic Pedagogical Grammar

A key need for teaching Arabic language is a professional consensus on what the term "grammar" includes because many discussions of Arabic "grammar" and its role in the classroom seem to be at cross-purposes. Most native speakers of Arabic will equate the English term "grammar" with *naḥw* and *ṣarf*—roughly, syntax and morphology. There are key aspects to this equation, however, that do not correspond with each other, and which require clarification. Therefore, part of this chapter is devoted to definitions and to analysis of exactly which components of Arabic grammatical study are necessary or relevant to the needs of learners of Arabic as a foreign language. Grammatical structure has traditionally provided a base on which to build courses, syllabi, and materials, and therefore MSA materials were largely grammar-based until the 1980s. Since that time, both methodology and materials have evolved in less grammatically specific form in order to conform to contemporary concepts of communicative language teaching. While this is useful in many respects, in others, it makes it more complicated to identify what is central in terms of the teaching of Arabic grammar, versus what is peripheral. It is also more difficult to make choices in the classroom as to when and where to present and practice particular points of grammar.

The long tradition of Arabic grammatical analysis and theory dating back to over a millennium is a vast and important heritage for Arabic speakers and advanced students of the language.

But does it have any relevance to teaching basic or intermediate language skills? I would say that some familiarity with the foundational works of the tradition, at least, is useful (such as the works of Sibawayhi, Al-Khalil ibn Ahmad, Ibn Jinni and other seminal grammarians). From the early "explicatory descriptivism" of Sibawayhi (d. 793) to the "triumph of metatheoretical speculation" of Ibn Jinni (d. 1002), Arabic linguistic theory is a field that attracted the finest minds of classical Islam (Owens 2005, 115). The question of relevance to Arabic pedagogy has been addressed by Owens, who states that "students find it reassuring when learning the complicated morphology of weak verbs to know that what they are studying has been treated within a general Arabic theory of morphology (*ṣarf*), with complicated rules describing the behavior of semivowels (*qalb*)" (2005, 115). He goes on to state that "the tradition itself is testimony to the centrality of the Arabic language in appreciating Arabic-Islamic culture" (2005, 115). A qualified Arabic teacher should have at least broad acquaintance with the canonical texts of classical Arabic linguistic theory and the important movements within the theory, if only to point out, for example, that sometimes grammarians "agree to disagree" about certain topics and that sometimes there are two (or more) right answers to a question of grammar, such as the correct past tense form for 'I died': *mit-tu* or *mut-tu*. Knowledge of the heritage of Arabic grammatical theory—of the different schools (e.g., Basra and Kufa) and different authors—is a cornerstone of Arabic pedagogical training.

The classical Arabic terms referring to central categories of grammatical structures and relations are translated as 'syntax' (*naḥw*) and 'morphology' (*ṣarf*), but the English and Arabic terms, although close, do not cover identical semantic territory. In English, the word "syntax" refers to the relationships of words in the context of a sentence.[10] Morphology refers to the structure of words themselves and is divided into two areas: derivational or lexical (word-creation) morphology and inflectional (word-modification in context) morphology.[11] When sentential relations condition the form of words (for example, in assigning case-markers), the usual term in English is morphosyntax or morphosyntactic relations. In Arabic, key aspects of morphosyntax fall under the term *naḥw* (e.g., *iʕrāb*, desinential inflection). The Arabic term *ṣarf* refers to derivational morphology as well as some forms of inflectional morphology. That is, inflecting a verb for past or present tense would be *ṣarf*, but inflecting a verb for mood (e.g., subjunctive or indicative) would fall under the category of *naḥw*. In addition, *ṣarf* includes the Arabic system of derivational etymology or *ishtiqāq*—the many ways of creating word-stems or stem-classes from a triliteral or quadriliteral Arabic lexical root. The term *naḥw*, on the other hand, refers to intrasentential relations and also to the modification of words due to contextual constraints. The Arabic term *tarkīb al-jumla* also refers to syntax—literally, to the "construction" of sentences.

✧ Terminology for Desinential Inflection

A consistent source of confusion occurs when trying to find English equivalents for Arabic terms for desinential inflection (*iʕrāb*). In Arabic, both case and mood are reflections of syntactic operations or morphosyntax, and Arabic makes no distinction between the markers of desinence on nominals and on verbs, placing them into one category. In English and other European languages the traditional terminology for desinence is different. Markers on nominals are called "cases" (nominative, genitive, accusative), and case-marking paradigms are called "declensions." Nouns and adjectives fall into different, distinctive declensions (for example, "diptotes").[12] Verb-marking desinence, on the other hand, denotes what is termed "mode" or mood"—indicative, subjunctive, jussive, and verbs are inflected for these moods in verbal paradigms. Traditional Arabic terminology combines the concepts of "nominative" and "indicative" into one term: *ḥālat al-rafʕ*, or *marfūʕ*. Likewise, Arabic combines the notions of "accusative" and "subjunctive"—*ḥālat al-naṣb*, or *manṣūb*. Some learners may find this merging of terms confusing and it is useful for teachers to be able to explain the contrast between categories in the two languages.

Arabic Syntactic Relations: *ʕamal* and *muṭābaqa*, or 'Government' and 'Agreement'

These two terms refer to central components of Arabic syntax, *ʕamal* being the effect of certain words, structures, or concepts (*ʕawāmil*) on other words (transitive verbs, for example, taking a direct object in the accusative case), and *muṭābaqa* being the matching or congruence of categories within clauses and phrases (e.g., gender agreement, number agreement).[13] These are discussed more fully in Ryding 2005 (44–73).

The key feature of grammar instruction for teachers of Arabic for communicative competence is the category of *muṭābaqa* (agreement), which is far more salient and essential for students to learn than the category of *ʕamal* (which even many native speakers do not fully control). Agreement features are overtly marked in Arabic; for example, the feminine singular ending /-at/ (*tāʔ marbūṭa*) on Arabic adjectives modifying feminine nouns or nonhuman plural nouns, or the inflectional subject markers on verbs (e.g., *katab-ū*, 'they wrote'). Government (*ʕamal*) features are often in the form of short-vowel endings which may or may not be pronounced, and are normally not written.[14] Learner errors in agreement can seriously interfere with communication and distract native speakers (e.g., **anti daras* ['you (f.) he-studied]), whereas mistakes in *iʕrāb* are less egregious and in fact do not usually interfere with communicative intent (e.g., **lan yadrus-u* or **lan yadrus* rather than *lan yadrus-a* [he' will not study']). Moreover, agreement concepts apply to spoken Arabic vernaculars as well as MSA; the rules may not be exactly the same (for example, some vernaculars use plural agreement with dual nouns—e.g., *bintēn ḥilwīn* 'two pretty girls'), but many of the basic agreement principles still hold. In contrast, the use of case and mood endings—*iʕrāb*—applies to MSA and Classical Arabic, but not colloquial Arabic. Therefore the teaching of agreement (especially in gender and number, but also in definiteness) is far more broadly applicable to Arabic learner needs and experience.

It is essential for Americans and other English-speaking learners to develop attention to and awareness of gender and number agreement in Arabic. In noun-adjective phrases, for example, agreement features shift depending on number, gender, and even on humanness of the modified noun:

kitāb jadīd	a new book
kutub jadīda	new books
kātib jadīd	a new writer
kuttāb judud	new writers
kātiba jadīda	a new writer (f.)
kātibāt jadīdāt	new writers (f.)
kitābāni jadīdāni	two new books

In English, the word "new" does not change in any of these expressions. In Arabic, it changes a great deal, according to specific rules. Acquisition of the complex system of Arabic agreement as well as the morphology of plurals takes even native Arabic speakers a relatively long time. Anything that can be done to encapsulate and systematize such rules for learners of Arabic as a foreign language will help them acquire flexibility and ability to express themselves appropriately.

 Grammar and Vocabulary

Grammatical structures cannot be taught, illustrated, or learned without words. Vocabulary provides the initial wedge into language as well as a growing wedge into communicative performance, and in a very real sense, lexicon-building goes hand-in-hand with or even precedes the formal learning of grammatical structure. Therefore, in the beginning stages of language learning, focus should be on building a strong foundational lexicon (in accordance with the "lexical approach" mentioned in chapter 18). Once this is in place, the illustration and use of grammatical structures can take place and expand, even as learners' vocabulary expands. In particular, research attention is now being paid to teaching foreign language vocabulary in "chunks," or prefabricated phrases ("prefabs"), i.e., frequently occurring collocations that constitute much of language use. By teaching prefabs and chunks (such as noun-adjective phrases or *iḍāfas*), phrasal grammar is easily illustrated and becomes second nature to learners. Thus, rather than dealing always with rules of word order and word combination, much of basic Arabic syntax can be initially acquired through the development of a solid lexical foundation.

Morphology, or Word Structure

Morphology—the processes of word structure and inflection—is the central area of Arabic grammar. Arabic words form an interconnected web of relationships with their lexical roots, their derivational patterns, and with each other in syntax. The study of word structure and word stems (the bare forms that lack inflection) is usually referred to as "derivational morphology," and is distinct from the study of words as they interact with syntax in sentences—"inflectional morphology."

Derivational Morphology

Derivational or lexical morphology, which includes the creation of words or word stems, is an extensive area of language structure that is also very systematic in its processes and rules. It is the key resource for helping students learn to use Arabic dictionaries or Arabic-English dictionaries. Derivational morphology, however, is useful mainly for building vocabulary and for learning how to decode and understand stem classes (words) in context. In and of itself it is a field of substantial linguistic research interest. However, its relationship to communicative language teaching is indirect. It is an area where declarative knowledge (knowledge of "what") is the central skill component. That is, in order to grasp and apply the rules of Arabic derivation (*ishtiqāq* as well as aspects of *ṣarf*), learners use overt cognitive strategies and skills based on their understanding of the systematic semantic relationships between lexical roots and their possible elaborations (including *awzān al-fiʕl* and other types of derivation such as the *yāʔ* of *nisba*). One area where Arabic learners at all levels need to know and understand the components of derivational morphology is in using an Arabic dictionary, or an Arabic-English dictionary such as the Hans Wehr *Dictionary of Modern Written Arabic*. Because Arabic dictionaries are compiled according to lexical roots rather than according to orthography, and because dictionary use is a key skill for learners to possess, derivational morphology is a key component of teaching dictionary use.

Inflectional Morphology

Of great and even central importance for beginning and intermediate learners of Arabic is the area of inflectional morphology—how words change their form depending on context within sentences. The understanding and application of inflectional morphology is ultimately a form of procedural knowledge—use or comprehension of forms in context. Verbs inflect for many categories: tense, voice, person, number, gender and mood. Nouns inflect for number, gender, definiteness, and case. Humanness is a factor in some plurals. Adjectives inflect for the same categories as nouns, and in addition they inflect for comparative and superlative distinctions. All of these word variations must be acquired and proceduralized into a smoothly operating communication system. As mentioned earlier in this chapter, Arabic inflections for most categories are salient and key to conveying information. The exception to this is case and mood (desinential inflection), which are most often unmarked in spoken MSA as well as in vernacular Arabic.

    Two of the most pesky inflectional features of written Arabic are the dual inflection on verbs (*yadrusāni* 'they (two) study'), nouns (*qismāni/-ayni* 'two parts'), adjectives (*lubnāniyyāni/-ayni*

'Lebanese'), pronouns (e.g., *humā* 'they two'; *hādhāni/-ayni* 'these two'), and the category of non-human plural nouns that require agreement features in the feminine singular (e.g., *mudun kabīra* 'large cities'). These multiple morphological features require consistent review and reinforcement, and are able to trip up learners even at advanced levels.

The roles of derivational and inflectional morphology in learning Arabic are both important, but for different reasons. Derivation provides knowledge of word stems or stem classes that can then be incorporated into discourse, but inflectional morphology provides the "glue" that holds words together in meaningful form within sentence structures.

⬡ Syntax

The meaningful organization and order of words in sentences is usually referred to in English as syntax. The Arabic expressions *tarkīb al-jumal* and *naḥw* also refer to aspects of syntax. The construction of Arabic sentences involves dependency relations expressed through rules and conventions for agreement and government. When agreement and government affect individual words, those words inflect or change their form in order to conform to the requirements of Arabic grammar. Moreover, Arabic words may inflect in complex ways, and this is often an area where grammatical explanation and illustration can be helpful for adult learners.

Many is the time I have heard learners say, "I know all the words in the sentence, but I don't know what it means." I have even had this experience myself as a learner of Arabic. The length and complexity of Arabic sentences, their internal cross-referentiality, the subtle semantic distinctions between contexts of use for lexical items, and the challenges of multiply embedded clauses all work to complicate certain types of sentences, especially in literary texts (but also to some extent in media texts). Complex sentences may need to be carefully unwrapped, analyzed, and deconstructed not only in ways that allow learners access to the meaning and structure of that one example, but in ways that can be generalized and applied to other contexts.

This may appear as too tight a focus on grammatical structure in a communicative approach. However, I have noted that many learners think that they grasp the meanings of complex sentences when they actually do not. They know all the words (or they can look them up), and they make some contextualized guesses about the nature of the message, and then they move on. But they have not actually understood the entire sentence. If required to translate such a sentence accurately, they often cannot do it because of gaps in their understanding of syntax. This is one reason why translation exercises can be important at advanced levels of proficiency—not only to check comprehension but to develop an appreciation for meaningful syntactic and morphosyntactic detail.

Based on my experience in both academic and government programs, the most pervasive syntactic difficulties for English-speaking learners of Arabic tend to occur with *idāfa* structures, noun-adjective agreement structures, subject-verb agreement, and noun-pronoun alignment. Focus in the classroom needs to be on recognizing and using these key constructions in all sorts of exercises, including translation, transformation, presentation, and conversation in oral and written practice as well as reading and listening comprehension. Calling attention to these structures in reading assignments helps learners to notice and consciously be aware of their importance and the ways in which they are used. In the *idāfa*, the prohibition against using the definite article on the first term usually requires a great deal of practice. For noun-adjective agreement, the requirement for adjectives to match nouns in gender, number, definiteness, and case also needs substantial practice, as does noun-pronoun agreement in number, gender and (in some instances) case (e.g., the dual forms of relative and demonstrative pronouns such as *hādhāni* and *hādhayni, alladhāni* and *alladhayni*).

Another important syntactic structure to practice is Arabic verb-subject agreement. Because English verbs are not highly inflected, English-speaking learners need to learn to attend to this feature in Arabic clause structure, and to learn all (yes, all) the inflected forms of verbs in both voices (active and passive) and tenses (including past and present, and also compound tenses).

Again, using verbs in multiple contexts, in interactive exchanges, in speaking and writing, and in exercises is important. At more advanced levels of instruction, discourse analysis beyond the sentence level is a key topic of discussion and analysis, especially given the differences between English and Arabic stylistic, documentation, and argumentation conventions.

Pedagogical Priorities

What then, should Arabic teachers focus on in the classroom? How does one make choices about how and when to provide information on central points of grammar? A general rule for the first and second years of instruction would be to prioritize work on agreement structures (e.g., subject-verb agreement and noun-adjective agreement) over rules of syntactic government (e.g., the regimen of *inna* and "her sisters"), and to allot greater time to practicing inflectional morphology (e.g., learning verb conjugations and noun plurals) than to discussion of derivational morphology (how words are related to particular lexical roots). Obviously, all of these elements are important to learning Arabic grammar. For learners of Arabic as a foreign language, however, agreement and inflection play the most fundamental roles in learning to speak Arabic correctly. Whereas native speakers of Arabic come to the study of *fuṣḥā* with developed skills in Arabic agreement and in inflectional morphology (albeit in their own vernaculars), neophyte learners of Arabic need to grasp and extensively practice these two central components of grammar immediately and to have them reinforced at regular intervals.

The knowledge and correct use of desinential inflection or *iʕrāb* is a skill useful primarily for advanced Arabic students, for Arabic majors, for graduate students in Arabic language, literature, or linguistics, and for Arabic students focused on literacy and the study of classical texts. This does not mean that it should not be introduced or taught early in the study of the Arabic language; but it means that emphasis on control of the complex system of case and mood morphology should be emphasized more at advanced levels of study. Finally, at the advanced level of reading and beyond, accurate parsing of complex sentences needs to be practiced because of the extended length of many Arabic sentences and because of complex nesting rules and styles for embedding clauses.

A Principled Concept of Arabic Pedagogical Grammar

Garrett observed over twenty years ago that "almost everyone pays lip service to the claim that grammatical competence is an essential part of communicative ability, but there is no generally accepted theoretical or methodological stance on how it is to be achieved" (1989, 17). This chapter proposes that the place of grammar pedagogy—even in a communicative approach—is central for building Arabic learners' ability to progress rapidly and accurately in their interlanguage development. But different aspects of "grammar" may require different levels of attention at different times. Disconnected, extended lectures on prescriptive grammar or grammatical theory are seldom useful, but keenly attuned and systematic focus on key lexical, morphological, and syntactic issues in context can play a crucial role in building learners' confidence and competence, and in preparing them to progress to advanced levels of instruction and performance.

Study Questions and Activities

1. Define "pedagogical grammar" as it applies to Arabic language teaching. What are its key features? Write a two-page paper presenting your definition and opinions.
2. What is one element of Arabic grammar that you thoroughly understand? How did you come to understand it? How do you know you understand it?[15]
3. What can the Arabic grammatical tradition contribute to the contemporary practice of teaching Arabic as a foreign language?

4. Have you taught or been taught dictionary usage in Arabic? What are some of the key factors in Arabic dictionary use? How can these best be taught? When should they be taught?

5. Discuss the difference between declarative and procedural knowledge and its application to Arabic grammar.

❖ Further Reading

Alexander, Louis G. 1990. "Why Teach Grammar?" *Georgetown University Round Table on Languages and Linguistics 1990*, edited by James E. Alatis, 377–382. Washington, DC: Georgetown University Press.

Ellis, Rod. 2002. "The Place of Grammar Instruction in the Second/Foreign Language Curriculum." In *New Perspectives on Grammar Teaching in Second Language Classrooms*, edited by Eli Hinkel and Sandra Fotos, 17–34. Mahwah, NJ: Lawrence Erlbaum.

Hinkel, Eli, and Sandra Fotos, eds. 2002. *New Perspectives on Grammar Teaching in Second Language Classrooms*. Mahwah, NJ: Lawrence Erlbaum.

Larson-Freeman, Diane. 2003. *Teaching Language: From Grammar to Grammaring*. Boston: Thomson-Heinle.

Ryding, Karin C. 2006. "Teaching Arabic in the United States." In *Handbook for Arabic Language Teaching Professionals in the 21st Century*, edited by Kassem Wahba, Zeinab Taha, and Liz England, 13–20. Mahwah, NJ: Lawrence Erlbaum Associates.

_____. 2012. "Critical Languages and Critical Thinking: Reframing Academic Arabic Programs." In *Arabic Language and Linguistics*, edited by Reem Bassiouney and E. Graham Katz, 189–200. Washington, DC: Georgetown University Press.

Suleiman, Yasir. 2011. *Arabic, Self and Identity: A Study in Conflict and Displacement*. Oxford: Oxford University Press.

Terrell, Tracy D. 1991. "The Role of Grammar Instruction in a Communicative Approach." *Modern Language Journal* 75, no. 1:52–63.

Ur, Penny. 1988, 2007. *Grammar Practice Activities: A Practical Guide for Teachers*. Cambridge: Cambridge University Press.

❖ Notes

1. Bybee 2006, 711.

2. The term "pedagogical grammar" is "commonly used to denote (1) pedagogical process—the explicit treatment of elements of the target language system as (part of) language teaching methodology; (2) pedagogical content—reference sources of one kind or another that present information about the target language system; and (3) combinations of process and content" (Little 1994, 99).

3. One effect of privileging literary language and secondary discourse for Arabic teaching has been a skewed concept of grammatical accuracy and its role in instruction. Grammar rules are often considered by the Arabic-speaking public as applying only to written language and not to vernacular speech. Yet, all forms of spoken Arabic have structural integrity, conventions of use, and particular forms of rhetorical accuracy.

4. Suleiman comments: "What is needed is a real simplification of pedagogic grammar that attends to the meanings and functions of the language instead of the centuries-long obsession with the theory of regents, governance, and detailed grammatical parsing" (Suleiman 2011, 90).

5. "For LCTLs, especially for non-Indo-European languages, the need for explicit grammar teaching is obviously still much greater [than for non-LCTLs]" (Garrett 2009, 731).

6. "Sometimes SLA researchers have taken the unwarranted step of proscribing or prescribing pedagogical practices based upon their findings from natural SLA. To cite one example, because there is no focus on form in untutored SLA does not justify the absence of such a focus in the SL classroom. Focusing student attention on salient formal features of a SL presumably is more efficient than when learners are left to their own devices to become aware of such features" (Larson-Freeman 1990, 263).

7. See Ellis 2002, Hinkel and Fotos 2002, Larson-Freeman 2002, and Pennington 2002 on the role of explicit grammar teaching in the classroom. Terrell writes that although explicit grammar instruction (what he terms "EGI") may not be the most important factor in second language acquisition, ". . . it is . . . probable that instruction about forms or structures of the target language is beneficial to learners at a particular point in their acquisition of the target language" (1991, 55).

8. For discussion of the "terminal 2" phenomenon, where learners' skills tend to fossilize, see Higgs and Clifford 1982.

9. Note that this is just the opposite for studying one's native language: one already knows "how" to communicate, but one needs to learn the tools to help analyze the "that"—the conscious ability to explain what is tacitly known.

10. "Syntax concerns the ways in which words combine to form sentences and the rules which govern the formation of sentences" (Richards and Schmidt 2010, 579).

11. "Syntax, along with morphology, is a technical term for what people often refer to as grammar" (Loewen and Reinders 2011, 162).

12. For a description and examples of the eight Arabic nominal declensions, see Ryding 2005, 167–204.

13. Agreement is sometimes also referred to as "concord."

14. One exception is accusative nunation on adverbials, which is usually pronounced, even in spoken Arabic (e.g., *dāʔiman* 'always,' *abadan* 'never,' *aḥyānan* 'sometimes').

15. After Perkins 2009, 53.

Teaching Arabic Culture

CHAPTER 20

It becomes crucial to distinguish between the semblance and similitude of the symbols across diverse cultural experiences—literature, art, music, ritual, life, death—and the social specificity of each of these productions of meaning as they circulate as signs within specific contextual locations and social systems of value.

Homi K. Bhabha

What we have to understand is the almost numinous authority that [Islamic] art conveyed.

Peter Brown

The 2007 MLA report, "Foreign languages and higher education: New structures for a changed world," states that "language majors should be structured to produce a specific outcome: educated speakers who have deep translingual and transcultural competence" (MLA 2007, 237). Rather than aiming to duplicate exactly the competence and performance of a native speaker of a foreign language, language programs should aim at developing learners' ability to communicate effectively with native speakers and at developing their ability to make and grasp meaning from multiple perspectives. Transcultural competence, and connecting Arabic language and culture in thoughtful and stimulating ways, need not be considered yet another burden on an already-saturated scholarly agenda of teaching and research, but instead, viewed as an exploration of nontraditional territories, revised roadmaps, and expanded connections, where new tools and frameworks can be used to examine texts and other cultural artifacts from fresh viewpoints. Culture and identity can be studied as they are signified and created through the entire range of language within Arabic speech communities, including not only the standard literary variety, but also everyday language as it is co-created and realized in interaction.[1] The richness of these interactions, the depth and extent of the Arabic literary tradition, collective experience and memory, and the interplay of spoken and written language give Arabic culture a high degree of vibrancy and complexity.

The relationship between what we do as teachers and scholars of Arabic language and culture, however, and how this practice creates appreciation of and respect for Arabic culture, can be both vexing and demanding. The vexation results from issues of teaching for content and intercultural understanding in a world where Middle Eastern countries are often portrayed in terms of their opposition to Western interests and values.[2] The demanding part of this equation is balancing curricular choices between traditional and modern culture, between spoken and written texts, and among different definitions of the scope of culture, cultural studies, and regional studies.

The traditional division of language and literature departments founded on a hierarchical distinction between the teaching of language competence and the study of literature is now challenged because of an emerging recognition that the goals of many language learners reflect their interest in foreign cultures in a practical and professional way that requires advanced "translingual and transcultural competence . . . [placing] value on the ability to operate between languages" (MLA 2007, 237), rather than on strict monolingual literary training. It is still the case that in some institutions the only advanced courses available to language majors are in the realm of literary studies, but this is gradually changing. More departments are redesigning their undergraduate programs to reflect content-based approaches to language learning. Language courses designed

"We in ME studies are 'blessed' with a plethora of identities. Area studies confines us, like a geographical straightjacket, to one specific part of the world. However, we cannot navigate the cultural shoals of this particular part without in-depth linguistic knowledge, which in the US, has traditionally been the territory of NE or ME language departments. Many specialists in those departments have had, alas, too great a tendency to maintain linguistic knowledge as the end-all and be-all of the discipline and to insist that serious scholarship must revolve around the decipherment of texts." (Malti-Douglas 1996, 311)

to foster competence in professional fields such as international relations or in the pragmatics of intercultural discourse are often in tension, however, with those designed to develop critical skills in literary analysis. This tension need not be negative, but it does require explicit discussion of departmental structure and goals that include interdisciplinary work. Interdisciplinary programs for regional studies often operate in tandem with foreign language study.

What has been missing from many curricula in Arabic language and culture is a sense of the value of everyday sociopragmatics, creativity, and aesthetics, and how understanding these helps a learner to integrate language, behavior, and appreciation of difference. I am not talking here about visiting a Lebanese grocery store, an Arabic bookstore, or a Moroccan restaurant (the four-F approach).[3] These can be interesting and useful activities, but they do not provide the intellectual scope of experience needed to begin comparing cultural values. They do not touch upon the humanities framework that should inform Arabic teaching. The world of Arab cultural practices and products, institutions, aesthetics, and values is best communicated if it is taught within and around a network of human creations: things that are spoken, written, woven, drawn, built, chanted, broadcast, carved, designed, or sung. Or those things that are connected to judgment and feeling: what is laughed about, cherished, worshiped, admired, disliked, feared, popular, taboo, desired, or awe-inspiring.

Three main interdisciplinary options for the study of language and culture have evolved in US higher education over the past 50 years: area studies, cultural studies, and (more recently) cultural area studies. These options do not cover all aspects of individual cultures, but they give a sense of how the interdisciplinary study of regional cultures has been organized, and the role of language learning within each paradigm.

Area Studies

University programs in Middle Eastern Studies or Near Eastern Studies are often home to languages of the Middle East, especially Arabic, but also Hebrew, Persian, Turkish, and others (e.g., Kurdish, Armenian, Dari). If these programs are not the home department, then they are nonetheless often involved with language, literature, and culture departments as constant suppliers of students who need advanced foreign language proficiency in order to meet degree requirements. As a result, some programs have developed Arabic language courses to engage and sustain the needs of area-studies students, such as courses on geography, history, media, and diplomacy.[4]

Academic language and area studies programs were developed initially during the 1950s to bring a higher level of sophistication and awareness of foreign areas and their languages to university course work and to broaden the horizons of undergraduate and graduate education. The particular strength of area studies is the combination of regional expertise in a variety of disciplines with advanced levels of language proficiency, clustering courses around a geographic area, and focusing on regional and intraregional issues. Originators of the area studies paradigm theorized that depth of regional knowledge was necessary in order to grasp fully the emerging strategic, diplomatic, and economic issues of the post-World War II and Cold War eras, grounded in in-depth study of specific languages, cultures, and histories. Both humanities and social science course work were considered essential for a well-rounded program, but intensive study and use of the regional language or languages was originally at the heart of the area studies curriculum.[5]

The essential characteristics of a successful language and area program were summarized in a 1959 Department of Education document, as follows:

1. A clearly defined geographical area.
2. For this area, attention to both language and related area study.
3. In the area study, inclusion of both humanities and social sciences.
4. Interrelated programs of research and instruction.
5. An adequate library in the languages and materials relevant to the area of study.
6. Long-term institutional backing for the program. (Mildenberger 1959, 2)

Although area studies programs were successful in attracting students and in developing academic centers focused on integrated regional studies, there arose a sense among certain departments, faculty, and disciplines that academic regional expertise could only be acquired at the expense of intellectual depth; that the array of courses organized by regional themes was too superficial in nature to guarantee full understanding in any one field. Area studies as seen by some political scientists has been portrayed as "journalistic, 'atheoretical,' and generally mushy" (Shea 1997, A13). Tension between interdisciplinary work and strict disciplinary study pervades many campuses, and has caused reexamination of area studies programs during the past two decades.

More recent approaches to international studies aim to transcend rather than integrate disciplines and geographical areas, centering on key global issues as ways to internationalize the curriculum, such as environmental change, migration, human rights, science and technology, and conflict resolution. This new approach for global studies does not necessarily leave foreign language study behind, but foreign language competence tends to be less of a central concern. Unless each of these global themes or topics is grounded in actual practice in a particular region of the world, however, the theoretical knowledge gained from such a curriculum remains distant and divorced from real-world applications. Knowledge of key foreign languages remains the fundamental and essential skill for understanding the local issues underlying global concerns at the international level. "The study of global processes and a grounded understanding of world regions constitute the yin and yang of a solid internationalist curriculum," states one scholar, emphasizing the need to "teach about regions in their global context" (Moseley 2009, 2).

Area studies and global studies are thus the two major components of higher education in international relations. An ideal curriculum combines foreign language study, regional understanding, and a grasp of the global interfaces of transnational issues.[6] As Edward Said has noted in this regard, there is a deep "importance not of synthesis and the transcendence of opposites but of the role of geographic knowledge in keeping one grounded, literally in the . . . structure of social, historical, and epistemological contests over territory—this includes nationalism, identity, narrative, and ethnicity—so much of which informs the literature, thought, and culture of our time" (Said 2001, 68).

⬡ Cultural Studies

Another approach to the study of culture is through the prism of cultural studies, a broad-based approach to social and cultural phenomena that has come to include many nontraditional components of cultural production. More humanities-based than area studies, and more focused on literary and aesthetic concerns, cultural studies covers a great deal of ground and means slightly different things to different scholars. In order to provide a sense of the boundaries of the field, some definitions are provided here:

1. "Cultural studies is perceived, correctly, as an expansion of the range of objects of study beyond traditionally appreciated literature—first in order to include works by authors deemed to have been marginalized unfairly, second to approach non-traditional aesthetic material from popular culture (such as film), and third to move beyond the aesthetic altogether to a study of the artifacts of everyday life" (Berman 1999, 168).

2. "Cultural studies is . . . committed to the study of the entire range of a society's arts, be-
    liefs, institutions, and communicative practices. . . . In cultural studies traditions, . . . cul-
    ture is understood both as a way of life—encompassing ideas, attitudes, languages,
    practices, institutions, and structures of power—and a whole range of cultural practices:
    artistic forms, texts, canons, architecture, mass-produced commodities, and so forth"
    (Grossman, Nelson, and Treichler 1992, 4). "A common misconception is that cultural
    studies is mainly concerned with popular culture," but it "is not simply about popular
    culture—though it is perhaps always in part about the rules of inclusion and exclusion that
    guide intellectual evaluations" (Grossman, Nelson, and Treichler 1992, 11).
3. According to various sources in a lively 1997 *Forum* discussion in *PMLA*, the journal of
    the Modern Language Association, cultural studies are said to cover the following areas:

    -   It includes "all canonical and uncanonical writers."
    -   It examines the "complexity of symbolic production within a culture." It focuses
        on marginalized cultures and neglected discourses, including the entire "network
        of signifying practices and representational strategies of a culture."
    -   Cultural studies examines "the symbolic inventory of a specific society."
    -   "Cultural studies represents less a turning away from the literary, defined as a
        distinct discourse with particular uses of language and models of reading, than a
        broadening of the scope of study beyond a static site of privileged cultural experi-
        ence both to a wider array of texts and to the historical circumstances contributing
        to specific writing and reading practices."
    -   "Cultural studies describes and mediates the discourses that relate everyday lives
        to the social structure."
    -   "By culture, cultural studies refers to the social, economic, political, and institu-
        tional conditions under which meaning is produced, transmitted, and interpreted.
        In its analysis of how individuals make sense of the world by constituting culture,
        Cultural Studies is centrally concerned with identities, institutions, power, and
        change" (*PMLA* 112 (1997): 2:257–286).

The role of foreign language study in cultural studies programs depends on where they are
housed. If such a program is part of an Arabic department curriculum, for example, Arabic
language competence would be a key requirement for the program. Although foreign language
competence at the advanced level is important for many topics within cultural studies, it is
sometimes considered optional, or as a requirement that can be readily waived, especially if
the courses are primarily in English. Some cultural studies programs and courses are housed in
English departments even though they may deal extensively with cross-cultural concepts, texts,
and artifacts.[7]

One of the best books in English for dealing with issues that westerners face in the context
of Arab culture is Margaret Nydell's *Understanding Arabs: A Guide for Modern Times*. Written
for the general public, it is a candid and lucid guide to the values and cultures of the Arab
world written from the author's perspective of having lived and worked there for many
years as a professional linguist. Chapters such as "The Social Structure," "The Role of the
Family," "Religion and Society, "Friends and Strangers," "Communicating with Arabs,"
and "Patterns of Change" are well worth assigning and discussing in class, especially at the
beginning and intermediate levels. The appendix on Arabic language provides a concise
overview of Arabic linguistic topics such as dialects, grammatical structure, and calligraphy.
Although this book is written in English, many language-centered and language-related
topics arise in it which can be illustrated, discussed, and critiqued in Arabic.

Cultural Area Studies

In a variation of cultural studies and area studies that takes into account both the centrality of foreign language competence and a broader range of cultural phenomena, Michael Geisler has characterized culture as "the reference knowledge of a native speaker" or "the background noise" that is taken for granted by anyone reading a major newspaper. For example, "students need to know the central cultural metaphors or 'key words' . . . that are generated by various historical traditions and discourses" (Geisler 2008, 234).[8] This is not limited to what is often referred to as "high" culture, but also includes elements of national cultural narrative such as:

- Foundational myths and stories
- Popular culture
- Dominant national sports, the cultural metaphors these have created, and their relationship to the "national imaginary"
- Media culture (popular heroes/heroines, major political developments), local and regional personalities, celebrities
- "Lieux de mémoire"—sites of memory—shared experiences that make a nation, including national symbols
- Major social issues
- Patterns of leisure activity (e.g., picnicking, sports, tourist travel, photography, backgammon)
- Patterns of everyday social interactions
- Noteworthy accomplishments in art, music, architecture, and design
- Social and historical narratives inscribed in legal systems, educational systems, economic and social welfare systems
- Major hegemonic and counterhegemonic traditions (counternational narratives)
- Geographic constraints on the national narrative (how are boundaries defined, and under what conditions?)
- Local historiography (e.g., the telling and retelling of history, the examination and study of local historical narratives)[9]

This list is useful because it is both general and specific, and because one can relate its components to different cultures. It gives rise to thoughts of how it could apply to the cultures of various Arab countries and cities, countrysides and regions. As a variation on typical area studies interests and themes, it engages learners at a deeper cultural level, not exclusively with canonical literary works, but within a range of cultural accomplishments, histories, narratives, and activities that characterize the social and cultural environments of particular speech communities.

 ## Interweaving Cultural Area Studies in the Arabic Classroom

All three of the above approaches to culture—area studies, cultural studies, and cultural area studies—are interdisciplinary. For the language classroom, this means introducing topics that are related to language but that are integral to other fields of study, as well. Individual programs can

---

Cultural Activity 1:

Where could you find pictures, videos, or examples of (for example) Arab landscape design? Of formal gardens and exterior spaces? How would you present these to a class? What kind of research would you need to do? How would you structure a discussion? Topics such as perspective, balance, color, aesthetics may arise. If you are a native speaker of Arabic, what resonates for you in such designs, what makes them pleasing, stimulating, or moving?

work out the logistics, choices, and rationales that tie course work together with program goals and standards. It is important to note that bringing such topics into the Arabic language classroom does not necessarily require that the language teacher have expert knowledge on them, but that the teacher provide a framework for discussion of cultural practices and products, especially as they compare with L1 culture. Knowledge of key practices and values will help prevent culture shock when learners visit the Arab world, and having students reflect on their own cultural values will lead them to be more open and objective in their assessment of others.[10] Some examples of classroom activities might be:

1. Studies of "visual culture," as a component of the curriculum, examining a range of created visual images that embody particular cultural values and aesthetics, such as architecture, landscaping, weaving, painting, photography, or film.[11]
2. Studies of "designed spaces"—examination of both exterior and interior design and how these are reflected in Arabic poetry, literature, and aesthetic values. Gardens, parks, zoos, public buildings, sculpture, homes, sacred sites, and other places in both public and private space can offer a thematic link between courses or within a particular course.
3. Studies of environmental issues and their impact on literary expression, on popular culture, on political movements, on contemporary art, for example.
4. Study of "decorative arts" in general and their interpretation in the various periods and places of Arabic culture.
5. Studies of the associations and symbolic meanings of animals, which is often very different from one culture to another. For example, dogs are symbols of devotion, protection, and companionship to Americans and other westerners, whereas the attitude toward them is profoundly different in the Arab world. Think of three or four animals that are positive symbols of aspects of Arab culture (e.g., horses, falcons, lions) and develop a 20-minute module around them, what they imply about Arabic culture, and how this may contrast with American culture. Similarly, you may want to discuss the most feared animals (e.g., snakes, spiders, crocodiles, scorpions) and what they can symbolize. As a discussion and presentation topic, you may also want to ask students to make their own lists of three or four animals and what they symbolize to Americans. For example, a mule often symbolizes stubbornness, an owl wisdom, a swan beauty. Are these meanings shared across American and Arab cultures? This is also an excellent exercise for learning animal names—a topic that does not often arise in contemporary textbooks.

Before the discussion of any cultural topic, it is essential to introduce and develop a set of key vocabulary items required for understanding core concepts, and to interweave language exercises, such as assigning a written presentation on a particular topic that students develop with the teacher. In addition, select aspects of Arab culture that students can compare with their own culture, and discuss the similarities and differences. Bring out the ability of students to talk about their own perspectives and traditions, as well as their ability to appreciate the differences between their culture and Arab culture. This kind of exercise helps them develop the kind of "translingual and transcultural competence" that will serve them well as interlocutors with Arabic speakers. "By attending both to their own agenda and to that of their interlocutors, language learners can start using the foreign language not merely as imperfect native speakers, but as speakers in their own right" (Kramsch 1993, 28).

⬡ The Standards and Culture

The Standards for Foreign Language Learning include the study of culture (as one of the five C's,) and recommend that learners gain explicit knowledge and understanding of other cultures.[12] The Arabic culture standards state:

> Standard 2.1: Students demonstrate an understanding of the relationship between the practices and perspectives of the various cultures of the Arab world.

Standard 2.2: Students demonstrate an understanding of the relationship between the products and perspectives of the various cultures of the Arab world. (National Standards 2006, 128–130)

The key word in this context is "perspectives," indicating the viewpoint or standpoint of the peoples and cultures of the Arab world.[13] The aim is to understand both practices and products of Arab culture. Standard 2.1, practices, focuses on social interactions, including values, norms, traditions, behaviors, and expectations that characterize interactions among Arabic speakers. Standard 2.2, products, focuses on cultural products and artifacts created and valued in the Arab world, such as poetry, textiles, gardens, ceramics, and architecture.

Both formal and informal approaches to each of these types of culture can be used. For Standard 2.1, there is the world of everyday intercultural pragmatics and traditional narratives that characterize informal discourse, and there is the world of more formalized discourse and its expected patterns (such as recitation or lecturing). For Standard 2.2, there is a world of everyday culture that incorporates (for example) the values of home design, food preparation, folk art, and recreational activities, and there is another world of more formal cultural appreciation and activity as seen (for example) in museums, palaces, art galleries, landscape design, archaeological sites, and performance art. The two aspects of culture—practices and products—are not separate; they are interwoven with each other through language, and can be a vital part of the Arabic language classroom.

Instead of incorporating the study of culture solely by means of the traditional "four F's" (folk dances, festivals, fairs, and food) mentioned earlier, the Standards encourage exploration of a wide network of cultural models, traditions, behaviors, values, and achievements.[14] By foregrounding new approaches to cross-cultural understanding, the multiple paths of symbolic production, the cultures of different periods in the Arab world, and the role of marginalized oral discourses, language programs can be enriched through a kind of multilayered but coherent interdisciplinarity.

Intercultural Communication

The role of discourse in constituting and creating culture connects what is said to what is constructed through language. "Our culture is now subjectivity and historicity; and is constructed and upheld by the stories we tell and the various discourses that give meaning to our lives. . . . By defining culture as discourse, we are looking at the interculturally competent individual as a symbolic self that is constituted by symbolic systems like language, as well as by systems of thought and their symbolic power" (Kramsch 2010, 356). This statement about the role of discourse in forming our lives relates directly to issues of cross-cultural competence and the depth of meaning contained in our daily practices of communication.

Within the spheres of discourse practice, culture, and cross-cultural competence falls the area of interpersonal communication that is also intercultural communication, and which requires both declarative and proceduralized knowledge of discourse norms, customs, and behaviors. When interacting with Arabs, Americans naturally need to incorporate knowledge of intercultural

---

Cultural Activity 2:

Have students identify and explain in Arabic three aspects of American culture that might be unfamiliar or strange to people of other cultures. Some examples might include:

1. Foods: corn-on-the-cob, popcorn, peanut butter, pumpkin pie, cotton candy
2. Social and health problems: clutter, hoarding, anorexia
3. Cultural practices: garage sales, tailgating, state fairs
4. Sports: baseball, football (not soccer), ice hockey.

sociopragmatics. "Values, beliefs, traditions, customs, norms, rituals, symbols, taboos, deportment, etiquette, attire, and time concepts are some of the extralinguistic elements that typically shape the form and content of interactions. These elements are often the source of expectations regarding behavior, such as gestures, body language, physical distance between speakers, and deference due to status, age, and gender (ILR website draft of intercultural skill levels: 1). Not meeting those expectations may result in what has been called "cross-cultural pragmatic failure."[15] Tannen lists eight "levels of communication differences" that may occur when talking cross-culturally: when to talk, what to say, pacing and pausing, listenership, intonation, formulaicity, indirectness, cohesion and coherence (1984, 2–8). Scollon and Scollon point out that "confusion in goals or in interpreting the main point of another's speech is caused by the fact that each side is using different principles of discourse to organize its presentations" (1995, 2001, 1). They also list seven "main components for a grammar of context" that include scene, key (mood or tone), participants, message form, sequence, co-occurrence patterns (how these components interact), and manifestation (2001, 32–33).

Taking a perspective that focuses on "the symbolic dimension of intercultural competence," Kramsch states that the "interculturally competent speaker" asks and reflects upon the following questions:

- Not which words, but whose words are those? Whose discourse? Whose interests are being served by this text?
- What made these words possible, and others impossible?
- How does the speaker position himself or herself?
- How does he or she frame the events talked about?
- What prior discourses does he or she draw on? (Kramsch 2010, 360)

The study of cross-cultural discourse and intercultural competence is a field rich in itself; when studied in relationship to a particular culture and language (e.g., Arabic), important discourse factors surface for discussion, analysis, and practice. This area of linguistic and cultural understanding and behavior is complex in many ways for learners of Arabic, especially because it covers conduct of conversation in spoken or vernacular Arabic as well as texts in MSA or in classical Arabic. It is a significant area of Arabic cultural practices and procedures that has not been well defined in teaching Arabic as a foreign language; it has traditionally been taught informally if at all. Delineating this area as a distinct framework for language work, and for raising awareness of intercultural implications of spoken and written texts, brings language into the repertoire of symbolic systems (like music and art) that demand our attention as scholars and teachers of Arabic as a foreign language.

One discourse challenge that Americans may encounter in the Arab world is the difference in value of paying compliments to someone—about their home, their children, their possessions. Whereas Americans are taught to express their admiration and approval openly and spontaneously as a sign of politeness and courtesy, such admiration may not be welcome to a traditional Arab because of what is known as "the evil eye," *al-ḥasad.* This can therefore easily be an area where values clash and misunderstandings arise. Sometimes an ordinary expression of admiration is misunderstood as an expression of envy, a destructive power that needs to be warded off; even if it is understood as a compliment, it may cause the listener to be uneasy rather than pleased. This does not mean that admiration cannot be expressed. It means that learners need to understand the discourse pragmatics of admiration; specifically, what to say in which contexts.

Leading a classroom discussion on this topic will be enlightening for learners and should also lead to other areas of discourse where knowledge of Arabic sociocultural context—of what to say when—is crucial. A good discussion of this topic is found in Mughazy 2000.

Assessing Cultural and Intercultural Understanding

Testing knowledge of particular cultural phenomena (such as classical poetry or Islamic art) is different from testing performance knowledge of "intercultural communication" and the sociocultural appropriateness of language skills. As one way of approaching assessment of intercultural understanding, new skill level descriptions have been developed for "competence in intercultural communication" by the ILR, designed to rate test takers on their ability "to take part effectively in a given social context by understanding what is being communicated and by employing appropriate language and behavior to convey an intended message" (ILR website revised draft: 1).[16] Arabic-specific cultural assessment guidelines have been developed by Lampe for the National Foreign Language Center.[17] These guidelines are an attempt to capture and evaluate the "practices and perspectives" component of the Standards. Although these guidelines are still in draft form, they may provide material for discussion of the teaching, learning, and assessment of intercultural skills in an academic department.

For assessing learner understanding of specific aspects of the target culture, in addition to traditional testing procedures and research assignments, "portfolios may be one of the few appropriate alternatives to traditional classroom achievement assessment that lend themselves to both formative and summative assessment and are able to evaluate process as well as product" (Schultz 2007, 18). A semester-long thematic portfolio project that counts for a certain portion of a student's grade (for example, 25 percent) would be one way to develop learners' ability to engage in research, to discover, and to analyze particular aspects of Arab culture.[18]

Study Questions and Activities

Cultural topics require some research and preparation but are well worth it. In all cases, consider what kind of core vocabulary will be needed to discuss a particular topic at beginning, intermediate, or advanced levels.

1. What are the most important historical sites within a particular Arab country? What is their significance to the country as a whole, as a nation? To the Arab world? How would you introduce these to a class, and what would be some tasks that students could undertake to find out more about such sites?[19]
2. Peter Brown comments that "the greatest barrier between ourselves and the culture of this great civilization [i.e., Islamic civilization is] . . . the overwhelming predominance of ornament in its art" (2011, 28). Discuss the idea of "ornament" and "ornamentation" as themes predominant in the art of the Arab world and contrast this idea with the idea of "ornament" in American culture.[20] Would you describe the differences in the meaning of "ornament" as a cultural gap or (as Brown does) a cultural barrier?
3. The sociopragmatics of intercultural communication are rarely discussed in MSA textbooks. Make a list of five key conversation skills that every Arabic learner should know; for example: how to apologize, how to address an older person, how to politely accept an invitation, how to change the subject, and so forth. Compare your list with others in your class and discuss how these discourse skills can be taught.
4. Several cultural activities have been suggested in the text of this lesson. Pick one and develop an outline of how you would present the activity in class. What would be the goals of the activity, the procedures, the content, the linguistic needs?
5. The books of linguist/anthropologist Edward Hall are clearly written and fascinating studies of contrasting cultural behaviors. Choose one of these books and write a three-page review of it as a semester project.

⬡ Further Reading

Allen, Roger. 2000. *An Introduction to Arabic Literature*. Cambridge: Cambridge University.

Brown, H. Douglas. 1986. "Learning a Second Culture." In *Culture Bound: Bridging the Cultural Gap in Language Teaching,* edited by Joyce Merrill Valdes, 33–48. Cambridge: Cambridge University Press.

Geertz, Clifford. 1973. *The Interpretation of Cultures*. New York: Basic Books. (Especially Part I, on "thick description.")

Geisler, Michael E. 2008. "The MLA Report on Foreign Languages: One Year into the Future." *Profession 2008*: 229–239.

Grabar, Oleg. 1987. *The Formation of Islamic Art*. New Haven: Yale University Press.

_____. 1992. *The Mediation of Ornament*. Princeton: Princeton University Press.

_____. 2006. *Islamic Visual Culture, 1100–1800*. Aldershot, UK: Ashgate.

Hadley, Alice Omaggio. 2001. *Teaching Language in Context*, 3rd edition. Boston: Heinle & Heinle. (Especially chapter 8, "Teaching for Cultural Understanding.")

Hall, Edward T. 1959. *The Silent Language*. Greenwich, CN: Fawcett.

_____. 1976. 1981. *Beyond Culture*. New York: Anchor Books.

_____. 1983. *The Dance of Life*. New York: Anchor Books.

Kramsch, Claire. 1998. *Language and Culture*. Oxford: Oxford University Press.

_____. 2010. "The Symbolic Dimensions of the Intercultural." *Language Teaching* 44, no. 3:354–367.

Nydell, Margaret. 2006. *Understanding Arabs: A Guide for Modern Times*, 4th edition. Yarmouth, ME: Intercultural Press. (The clearest and most practical handbook for westerners encountering Arab culture.)

Scollon, Ron, and Suzanne Wong Scollon. 1995, 2001. *Intercultural Communication*, 2nd ed. Malden, MA: Blackwell. (This is an excellent introduction to intercultural discourse and its components.)

⬡ Notes

1. Kramsch sees language as a central binding force within a culture, defining "culture" as follows: "Membership in a discourse community that shares a common social space and history, and a common system of standards for perceiving, believing, evaluating, and acting" (1998, 127).

2. In his article reviewing exhibits at the new and expanded Islamic galleries of the Metropolitan Museum in New York, Peter Brown remarks that "the world of Islam suffers from having been a charged opposite to the West . . . [and] as a result this civilization has been regarded by many 'as more than usually inaccessible'" (2011, 26).

3. Hadley has an excellent chapter on "Teaching for cultural understanding." In it she describes a number of ways to integrate culture in the language classroom, among them the standard "four-F approach to teaching culture: folk dances, festivals, fairs, and food" (2001, 348).

4. For example, an advanced Arabic course developed at Georgetown University titled "Map of the Arab World" is one that serves as a thematic pivot to introduce the cultures, societies, geography, and history of the countries of the Arab world.

5. "Insofar as possible the medium of presenting these [area studies courses] will be the target language of the learner" (Mildenberger 1959, 2).

6. "Some argue that globalization reduces the importance of regional and local differences and that the English language has gained unchallengeable ascendancy. But there is no evidence that globalization is having such effects. The world remains fractionalized, even polarized. Ethnic, racial, national, and religious divisions may be growing even more important, not less" (Yankelovich 2005).

7. For readers who may want to investigate postcolonial theory as it relates to Arabic literature, history and cultural studies, consult the writings of Edward Said on orientalism, on culture and imperialism, and Homi Bhabha's *The Location of Culture* as starting points.

8. Here Geisler uses the term "key words" to mean "key concepts" in the study of language and culture. See Duranti 2001 for more on "key terms in language and culture."

9. This list was transmitted to me and others in an email dated May 5, 2006.

10. "Culture shock refers to phenomena ranging from mild irritability to deep psychological panic and crisis" (Brown 1986, 35). For Americans visiting the Arab world, culture shock can be a very real problem that can alienate students and disrupt their learning experience. Dealing with key aspects of Arab values and

behavior beforehand is an essential responsibility of any language teaching program that intends to send its students abroad.

11. See Grabar 2006. In this respect, the study of calligraphy—for example—combines the values of both language and visual aesthetics and how they have been interwoven in Arabic culture since the earliest days of written text.

12. See appendix E for a brief summary of the Standards.

13. "Perspectives can be defined as the underlying—often subconscious—beliefs, attitudes, and values that influence people's behavior and determine what they do, how they do it, and why" (Schultz 2007, 10).

14. See note 6 in this chapter and Hadley 2001, 348.

15. "Cross-cultural pragmatic failure, as it has been called, occurs because of insufficient knowledge, either of the formal rules of the language in which an interaction takes place (rules that relate to its lexicon, its phonetics, its syntax), or of more elusive aspects related to implicit cultural norms and values, often not adequately taught in foreign language classrooms" (Peeters 2008).

16. Available at www.govtilr.org/skills/intercultural_postingdraft.pdf.

17. See Lampe 2007.

18. For a detailed example of such a portfolio, see Schultz 2007, 23–26.

19. To list some examples: Carthage in Tunisia, Tyre and Sidon in Lebanon, Mecca and Medina in Saudi Arabia, the Dead Sea in Jordan, the pyramids in Egypt. The Middle East and North Africa provide rich and extensive multicultural sites of memory that are useful and, indeed, crucial for discussion of the cultural heritage of the Arab world.

20. See Grabar 1992 for discussion of this topic.

Appendix A

Arabic Resource Organizations and Websites

AATA, the American Association of Teachers of Arabic

This professional organization publishes an annual journal, *Al-'Arabiyya*, and has its annual meeting alongside that of the Middle East Studies Association (MESA).
Website: www.aataweb.org

ACTFL, American Council for the Teaching of Foreign Languages

ACTFL provides proficiency tester training and certification in Arabic and has established an Arabic SIG (special interest group) that specializes in Arabic instruction, assessment, and curriculum issues. Website: www.actfl.org

Arabic-L

This is a very active, moderated discussion list based at Brigham Young University. It covers everything from pedagogy, to literature, to publications, to linguistics, to study abroad questions. To subscribe to the list, contact arabic-l-subscribe-request@listserv.byu.edu.

CARLA, the Center for Advanced Research on Language Acquisition

This well-established language resource center provides many resources for less commonly taught languages (LCTLs), including summer training institutes and workshops. Website: www.carla.umn.edu

The Center for Applied Linguistics in Washington, DC

This resource center for applied linguistics can provide consultation and information on a wide range of topics for Arabic and other LCTLs. Website: www.cal.org

LRCs: Language Resource Centers

There are 15 federally funded LRCs that provide foreign language consultation, teacher training, research, materials, assessment activities, and other resources to developing programs. See the website for a list of current grantees. Website: www.ed.gov/programs/iegpslrc/awards.html

NCLRC, the National Capital Language Resource Center, based in Washington, DC

This particular LRC has taken a special interest in K-12 Arabic programs, publishes an informative monthly newsletter, will publish job opportunities, and provides individual advice to programs. Website: www.nclrc.org

NCOLCTL, the National Council of Less Commonly Taught Languages

This active organization holds an annual conference in April that brings together scholars and administrators from all LCTLs. In addition, its website and their publications are key connections among LCTLs. Since many of these languages face similar issues and problems, the existence of NCOLCTL helps strategize support and development for the entire field. Website: www.ncolctl.org

NFLC, the National Foreign Language Center

Based at the University of Maryland, the NFLC is dedicated to improving the nation's capacity in terms of foreign language needs. It provides consultation, research, collaboration, and materials for LCTLs in particular. Website: www.nflc.org

NMELRC, the National Middle East Language Resource Center

This richly developed and well-organized center provides a great deal of information on its website: curriculum development, materials, and teacher training resources for Arabic, Hebrew, Persian, and Turkish. Website: www.nmelrc.org.

Startalk

This federally funded effort has introduced a wide range of summer programs in Arabic and Chinese over the past two years. A key feature of the Startalk approach is that in addition to providing funding for teaching these languages, they also provide an equal amount of support for teacher training programs in these languages. Website: www.startalk.umd.edu, or www.nflc.org/projects/current_projects/startalk/

Title VI Middle East National Resource Centers (NRCs)

These federally funded centers offer many academic activities, programs, and seminars dealing with the Middle East, as well as substantial outreach programs to communities and K-12 schools. A list of funded centers is available at the website. Website: www.ed.gov/programs

University Departments and Centers

Sometimes university departments of Arabic or Middle Eastern languages have websites that offer program development information and links to useful resource materials. See, for example, the Arabic and Islamic Studies Department at Georgetown University: arabic.georgetown.edu. See also the Center for Contemporary Arab Studies at Georgetown University (www.ccas.georgetown .edu) and the Department of Middle East Studies at the University of Texas at Austin (www.utexas .edu/cola/depts/mes/).

Appendix B

Terminology for Discussing Arabic as a Foreign Language

Forms of Arabic

Many English terms are used to refer to standard Arabic (*fuṣḥā*) and to vernacular Arabic (*ʕāmmiyya*). Here is a list of some common expressions used to refer to various forms of Arabic.

Contemporary Arabic (*fuṣḥā*):

Literary Arabic; Modern Literary Arabic

Modern Standard Arabic (MSA)

Standard Arabic (SA)

Written Arabic; Modern Written Arabic

For all intents and purposes, the above terms refer to written Arabic of the 19th to 21st centuries. Sometimes, more specific terms, such as "media Arabic" or "broadcast Arabic," are also used to identify the language of particular genres.

Earlier Written Forms of Arabic

The term "Classical Arabic" usually refers to the language of pre-Islamic Arabic poetry composed in the 5th and 6th centuries as well as Qur'anic Arabic, and extends through the early Islamic, Ummayyad, and early Abbasid periods of literature. It "designates that form of Arabic which was described by the Arab grammarians of the 8th century and called by them *al-ʕarabiyya*" (Fischer 2006, 397). For excellent concise descriptions of the "history of Arabic" and "Classical Arabic," in English, see Fischer 2006 and Ferrando 2007.

The term "Middle Arabic" refers to Arabic texts written in varieties that deviate in some ways from the classical norm and are classified not in terms of a chronological era, but in terms of the "mixed" form of Arabic used. Owens states that these texts "begin to be relatively numerous in the tenth century" (2006, 7). There is a substantial research tradition that examines the nature of Middle Arabic. For more on this topic see Lentin 2008, Owens 2006, 46–47, and Larcher 2001.

For Everyday Spoken Arabic: *ʕāmmiyya*

Colloquial Arabic

Arabic dialect

Popular language

Spoken language

Vernacular Arabic

Among these, the English term "dialect" seems to be stigmatized by some native speakers of Arabic, stemming apparently from issues of postcolonial sensitivity to inter-Arabic distinctions. All of these terms, however, refer to basically the same range of variation in Arabic: the spoken, everyday, common language that is learned as a first language or mother tongue by native Arabic speakers.

For Hybrid or Mixed Forms of Spoken Arabic: *lughat al-muthaqqafīn*

Educated spoken Arabic

Formal spoken Arabic

Prestige spoken Arabic

Inter-Arabic

Arabic koine

fuṣḥāmiyya

The terms in this category refer to mixed or hybrid forms of Arabic that have either a colloquial base (matrix language), or a standard Arabic matrix. In general, they are spoken forms of language, although in some cases (such as in plays or in written dialogs in novels) they are used in written form, referred to by Rosenbaum as *fuṣḥāmiyya* (2000). Most urban colloquial forms of Arabic share core features of morphology and syntax, despite differences in everyday lexical choices. This makes the existence of a spoken interdialectal norm possible and generally used in cases where regiolects differ. Charles Ferguson identified these features as components of what he called the "Arabic koine" (1959a). These features and, more importantly, the strategies for using them in interactive discourse are part of the language spectrum that is now referred to most often in English as "educated spoken Arabic."

Particularly well-known are the distinctions drawn by El-Said Badawi in his 1973 Arabic work, *Mustawayāt al-ʕarabiyya al-muʕāṣira* ('Levels of Contemporary Arabic'), and his 1985 article in English, characterizing a continuum of sociolinguistic variants and labeling the major distinctions, ranging from the most literary to the most colloquial. His categories are as follows (1985, 17):

Level one	*fuṣḥā al-turāth*	Classical Arabic
Level two	*fuṣḥā al-ʕaṣr*	Modern Standard Arabic
Level three	*ʕāmiyyat al-muthaqqafīn*	Educated Spoken Arabic
Level four	*ʕāmiyyat al-mutanawwirīn*	Semiliterate Spoken Arabic
Level five	*ʕāmiyyat al-ʔummiyyīn*	Illiterate Spoken Arabic

As Badawi notes, these distinctions are not fine-grained; the levels bleed into one another and their boundaries are fuzzy and penetrable. Choice of language variants among Arabic speakers on any occasion is dependent on situational factors and on educational background.

Academic Arabic

Academic Arabic (AA) is MSA or Classical Arabic used primarily for reading and analyzing texts of various genres and periods, and may also be used for listening to formal lectures. In terms of Arabic as a foreign language, it is a skill that requires learner comprehension and interpretation. Learners may also be required to make formal oral presentations or to write formal essays, but by and large, AA is a comprehension skill.

Appendix C

Some Essential Applied Linguistics Terminology

Here are some basic terms that are widely used in the field of applied linguistics as applied to foreign language teaching.

Affective Filter

Potential feelings of resistance, defensiveness, or other negative emotions that can interfere with foreign language learning.

Communicative Competence

"The ability to use language in a variety of settings, taking into account relationships between speakers and differences in situations" (Lightbown and Spada 2006, 196).

Communicative Language Teaching (CLT)

"Communicative language teaching is based on the premise that successful language learning involves not only a knowledge of the structures and forms of a language, but also the functions and purposes that a language serves in different communicative settings. This approach to teaching emphasizes the communication of meaning in interaction rather than the practice and manipulation of grammatical forms in isolation" (Lightbown and Spada 2006, 196).

Comprehensible Input

Spoken or written language that is understandable by learners even though they might not grasp every word.

Curriculum

"The course of study that is employed by a school or in a class" (Loewen and Reinders 2011, 47).

Educated Native Speaker

Someone who has been raised and educated at least through the secondary level in a particular country or culture.

Foreign Language

A language learned in an instructional setting "where that language is not the dominant language of society and the learners do not have any familial or social ties to the language" (Loewen and Reinders 2011, 68)—for example, learning Arabic in the United States. Sometimes referred to as "second language."

Fossilization

"Refers to the end-state of SLA, specifically to an end-state that is not native-like" (VanPatten and Benati 2010, 87). The end-state may be a temporary or transitory one, or it may be permanent, as when a person retains a foreign accent despite years of residence in a country. Some researchers dispute this term and prefer the term "stabilization" instead.

Fundamental Difference Hypothesis

States that there are essential differences between children learning their L1 and adults learning an L2.

Heritage Language

"A second language that is being studied by someone who has some type of family relationship with the language" (Loewen and Reinders 2011, 80).

i + I

Refers to comprehensible input (i) that is just slightly beyond the learners' capacity to fully understand.

Interlanguage

"The language system that is created by L2 learners as they develop their L2 knowledge towards target language norms" (Loewen and Reinders 2011, 98).

Metalanguage

"The language used to analyze or describe a language" (Richards and Schmidt 2010, 361).

Monitor

A faculty of mind that allows foreign language learners to observe their L2 production (or inter-language), evaluate it for inaccuracies, and make corrections.

Norm

"That which is considered appropriate in speech or writing for a particular situation or purpose within a particular group or community" (Richards and Schmidt 2010, 398). A pedagogical norm "consists of a neutralized variety of the language conceived for pedagogical purposes" (Etienne and Sax 2009, 598).

Pace

The speed, rhythm, or tempo at which one proceeds in a classroom; it may be quick and lively, slow and stately, careful and quiet, loud and spirited, and so forth.

Proficiency

"A term used to refer to learners' knowledge of and ability to use the target language" (Loewen and Reinders 2011, 142).

Reverse Privileging

In the teaching of Arabic, privileging the teaching of secondary discourse (formal, public, literary) over the teaching of primary discourse (everyday, familiar, vernacular).

Second Language

"A second language is one that is learned where the language is spoken, such as English in the United States" (VanPatten and Benati 2010, 145). Note that the terms "foreign language learning" and "second language learning/acquisition" are not always considered distinctive and may be used to refer to the same situation.

Second Language Acquisition (SLA)

The investigation of how languages "other than one's first language are learned" (VanPatten and Benati 2010, 153).

Standards/Standards

Refers to the National Standards in Foreign Language Learning project and to the published *Standards for Foreign Language Learning in the 21st Century*, which covers language-specific as well as general standards, including Arabic.

Target Language

The language being studied.

Teacher Language Awareness (TLA)

"The knowledge that teachers have of the underlying systems of the language that enables them to teach effectively" (Andrews 2007, ix).

Ultimate Attainment

"The point at which learners seem to stop progressing" (VanPatten and Benati 2010, 162).

Additional References

Ferguson, Charles A. 1962. *Glossary of Terms Related to Languages of the Middle East*. Washington, DC: Center for Applied Linguistics.

Lightbown, Patsy M., and Nina Spada. 2006. *How Languages Are Learned*, 3rd ed. Oxford: Oxford University Press. (See the comprehensive glossary, pp. 194–206.)

Loewen, Shawn, and Hayo Reinders. 2011. *Key Concepts in Second Language Acquistion*. Houndsmills, Basingstoke, Hampshire: Palgrave McMillan.

Richards, Jack C., and Richard Schmidt. [1985] 2010. *Longman Dictionary of Language Teaching and Applied Linguistics*. Harlow, England: Longman.

VanPatten, Bill, and Alessandro G. Benati. 2010. *Key Terms in Second Language Acquisition*. London: Continuum.

Appendix D

Area Studies Topics for Integration into Arabic Classes

The following is a list of area study topics covered during the academic FSI year in Arabic as an integral part of the language training program in the 1980s and 1990s, and as drafted by Ryding and Stowasser (1997). This list pertains specifically to the Middle East during that period of time and was geared to the interests of Foreign Service Officers. It provides a sense of the overall approach and organization of area studies topics, but would need substantial updating for areas of current interest.

Segment I: Introduction to the Region (four weeks)

> This is covered in the first seven lessons of the textbook, *Formal Spoken Arabic: Basic Course* (see Ryding 1990), specifically, regional geography and identity of key political figures.

Segment II: The Cultural System (four weeks)

1. The Prophet Muhammad and the Rise and Spread of Islam
2. a. The First *sūra* (verse) of the Holy *Qur'ān*
   b. The Five Pillars of Islam
3. The Orthodox Caliphs and the Rise of the Shī'a
4. Religious Traditions and Social Customs

Segment III. Current Social Issues (five weeks)

1. Women's Issues in the Arab World
2. Urbanization and Labor Migration in the Arab World
3. Education in the Arab World
4. The Media in the Arab World

Segment IV: Domestic Economic Development (five weeks)

1. Agriculture and Industry in Egypt
2. Industrial Development in Saudi Arabia
3. The Gulf Cooperation Council
4. International Economic Relations: OPEC and OAPEC

Special Session: A Poem by Nizar Qabbani, as sung by Abd al-Halim Hafez

Segment V: Current International Issues (five weeks)

1. Arab American Relations
2. a. Arabism and Arab Unity
   b. A Short Selection from Al-Husri's *Arabism First*

3. The Arab-Israeli Problem
4. The War between Iraq and Iran
5. The Lebanese Civil War

Segment VI: Historical Legacies (five weeks)

1. Introduction to Arab History
2. The History of Egypt (Case Study)
3. The History of Iraq (Case Study)
4. Arab Nationalism: A Statement by Sati' Al-Husri
5. From the Islamic Renaissance to Twentieth-Century Western Technology

Segment VII: Political Systems (four weeks)

1. Fact Sheet on Egypt
2. Fact Sheet on Iraq
3. The Military in Politics
   a. A General Overview
   b. Case Study: The Sudan
4. A Biographical Study of the Life of King Hussein of Jordan

Segment VIII: Regional and International Political Economics (two weeks)

1. The Organization of Arab Petroleum Exporting Countries (OAPEC): Conference on Cooperation between OAPEC and Japan (case study)
2. Historical Dimensions of US-Arab Economic Relations

Segment IX: Inter-Arab and International Issues, Foreign Policy Issues (six weeks)

1. The Iran-Iraq War (extended text)
2. The Gulf Cooperation Council (extended text)
3. Basics of US Policy in the Middle East
4. Saudi-US Relations
5. US Policy toward Terrorism
6. Atomic Energy: Hopes and Fears

Appendix E

Standards for Foreign Language Learning: Generic Summary

From *Standards for Foreign Language Learning in the 21st Century*, compiled by the National Standards in Foreign Language Education, 2006, 9. The Arabic-specific standards, descriptions, and examples can be found on pages 111–155 of that publication.

1. Communication: Communicate in languages other than English.

   Standard 1.1. Students engage in conversation, provide and obtain information, express feelings and emotions, and exchange opinions.

   Standard 1.2. Students understand and interpret written and spoken language on a variety of topics.

   Standard 1.3. Students present information, concepts, and ideas to an audience of listeners or readers on a variety of topics.

2. Cultures: Gain knowledge and understanding of other cultures.

   Standard 2.1. Students demonstrate an understanding of the relationship between the practices and perspectives of the culture studied.

   Standard 2.2. Students demonstrate an understanding of the relationship between the products and perspectives of the culture studied.

3. Connections: Connect with other disciplines and acquire information.

   Standard 3.1. Students reinforce and further their knowledge of other disciplines through the foreign language.

   Standard 3.2. Students acquire information and recognize the distinctive viewpoints that are only available through the foreign language and its cultures.

4. Comparisons: Develop insight into the nature of language and culture.

   Standard 4.1. Students demonstrate understanding of the nature of language through comparisons of the language studied and their own.

   Standard 4.2. Students demonstrate understanding of the concept of culture through comparisons of the cultures studied and their own.

5. Communities: Participate in multilingual communities at home and around the world.

   Standard 5.1. Students use the language both within and beyond the school setting.

   Standard 5.2. Students show evidence of becoming life-long learners by using the language for personal enjoyment and enrichment.

Appendix F

Some MSA Arabic Textbooks

These are by no means the only textbooks available for teaching Arabic, but they represent some of the most widely used and reliable ones. I include some materials from the 1960s and 1970s because of their quality, their attention to grammatical structure, and especially because of their detailed texts and exercises.

Abboud, Peter, et al. 1971. *Intermediate Modern Standard Arabic*. 3 vols. Ann Arbor: University of Michigan, Department of Near Eastern Studies.

Abboud, Peter F., Ernest N. McCarus, et al. (1968), 1983. *Elementary Modern Standard Arabic*. Parts one and two. Cambridge: Cambridge University Press.

Abboud, Peter F., Aman Attieh, Ernest McCarus, and Raji M. Rammuny. 1997. *Intermediate Modern Standard Arabic*. rev. ed. Ann Arbor: Center for Middle Eastern and North African Studies.

Alosh, Mahdi. 2000. *Ahlan wa-sahlan: Functional Modern Standard Arabic for Beginners. Instructor's Handbook: Interactive Teaching of Arabic*. New Haven: Yale University Press.

Attar, Samar. 1998. *Modern Arabic: An Advanced Course for Foreign Students: The Arab–European Encounter*. Beirut: Librairie du Liban.

Al-Warraki, Nariman Naili, and Ahmed Taher Hassanein. 1994. *Adawāt al-rabt fī l-ʕarabiyya l-muʕāṣira (The Connectors in Modern Standard Arabic)*. Cairo: American University in Cairo Press.

Ashtiany, Julia. 1993. *Media Arabic*. Edinburgh: Edinburgh University Press.

Badawi, El-Said M. 2006–2008 [© 1987]. *Al-kitāb al-asāsi fī taʕlīm al-lugha l-ʕarabiyya li-ghayr al-nāṭiqīn bi-hā*. 3 vols. Cairo: American University in Cairo Press.

Bellamy, James A., Ernest McCarus, and Adil I. Yacoub. 1963a. *Contemporary Arabic Readers IV: Short Stories. Part One: Texts*. Ann Arbor: University of Michigan Press.

____. 1963b. *Contemporary Arabic Readers IV: Short Stories. Part Two: Notes and Glossaries*. Ann Arbor: University of Michigan Press.

____. 1966a. *Contemporary Arabic Readers V: Modern Arabic Poetry. Part One: Texts*. Ann Arbor: University of Michigan Press.

____. 1966b. *Contemporary Arabic Readers V: Modern Arabic Poetry. Part Two: Notes and Glossaries*. Ann Arbor: University of Michigan Press.

Brustad, Kristen, Mahmoud Al-Batal, and Abbas Al-Tonsi. 2010. *Alif Baa: Introduction to Arabic Letters and Sounds*. 3rd ed. Washington, DC: Georgetown University Press.

____. 2011. *Al-Kitaab fii taʕallum al-ʕarabiyya, Part One*. 3rd ed. Washington, DC: Georgetown University Press.

____. 2006. *Al-Kitaab fii taʕallum al-ʕarabiyya, Part Two*. 2nd ed. Washington, DC: Georgetown University Press.

____. 2007. *Al-Kitaab fii taʿallum al-ʿarabiyya, Part Three*. Washington, DC: Georgetown University Press.

Cowan, David. 1964. *An Introduction to Modern Literary Arabic*. Cambridge: Cambridge University Press.

Dickins, James, and Janet C. E. Watson. 1999. *Standard Arabic: An Advanced Course*. Cambridge: Cambridge University Press.

Frangieh, Bassam K. 2005. *Anthology of Arabic Literature, Culture, and Thought: From Pre-Islamic Times to the Present*. New Haven and London: Yale University Press.

Lahlali, El-Mustapha. 2008. *Advanced Media Arabic*. Washington, DC: Georgetown University Press.

____. 2009. *How to Write in Arabic*. Edinburgh: Edinburgh University Press.

McCarus, Ernest N., and Raji Rammuny. (1979) 2003. *A Programmed Course in Modern Literary Arabic: Phonology and Script*. Originally published Ann Arbor: University of Michigan Press; Troy, MI: International Book Centre.

McCarus, Ernest N., and Adil I. Yacoub. 1962. *Contemporary Arabic Readers I: Newspaper Arabic*. Ann Arbor: University of Michigan Press.

McCarus, Ernest N., Adil Yacoub, and Frederic J. Cadora. 1964a. *Contemporary Arabic Readers III: Formal Arabic. Part One: Texts*. Ann Arbor: University of Michigan Press.

——. 1964b. *Contemporary Arabic Readers III: Formal Arabic. Part Two: Notes and Glossaries*. Ann Arbor: University of Michigan Press.

Middle East Centre for Arab Studies (MECAS). 1950. *The First Thousand Words: A Basic Vocabulary for Foreigners (Awwal alf kalima fī l-lugha l-ʿarabiyya li-l-ṭullāb al-ajānib)*. Beirut: American Press.

____. 1959. *A Selected Word List of Modern Literary Arabic*. Beirut: Dar Al-Kutub.

____. 1965. *The M.E.C.A.S. Grammar of Modern Literary Arabic*. Beirut: Khayats.

____. 1967. *The Way Prepared (Al-Ṭarīq al-mumahhad): A Reading Book in Modern Arabic*. Beirut: Khayats.

Pragnell, Fred. 1984, 2003. *A Week in the Middle East: An Arabic Language Reader*. London: Lund Humphries. Revised edition, Kingston upon Thames, Surrey: Pragnell Books.

____. 2003. *The Arab News: An Arabic-English Reader for Intermediate Students*. Kingston upon Thames, Surrey: Pragnell Books.

Rammuny, Raji. 1980. *Advanced Arabic Composition Based on Literary Texts and Audio-Visual Materials (al-inshāʔ al-ʿarabiyy li-l-marHala l-mutaqaddima min khilāl nuṣūṣ adabiyya wa-mawādd samʿiyya - baṣariyya)*. Ann Arbor: Department of Near Eastern Studies, University of Michigan.

____. (1987) 1993. *Advanced Business Arabic (Al-lugha l-ʿarabiyya li-l-aʿmaal wa-l-shuʔūn l-tijāriyya)*. Troy, MI: International Book Centre.

____. 1994a. *Advanced Standard Arabic through Authentic Texts and Audiovisual Materials. Part One, Textual Materials (Al-lugha l-ʿarabiyya li-l-marāḥil al-mutaqaddima min khilāl nuṣūṣ wa-mawādd samʿiyya baṣariyya aṣīla. Al-juzʔ al-awwal)*. Ann Arbor: University of Michigan Press.

____. 1994b. *Advanced Standard Arabic through Authentic Texts and Audiovisual Materials. Part Two, Audiovisual Materials. (Al-lugha l-ʿarabiyya li-l-marāḥil al-mutaqaddima min khilāl nuṣūṣ wa-mawādd samʿiyya baṣariyya aṣīla. Al-juzʔ al-thānī)*. Ann Arbor: University of Michigan Press.

Ryding, Karin C. 1990. *Formal Spoken Arabic: Basic Course*. Washington, DC: Georgetown University Press.

Ryding, Karin C., and David J. Mehall. 2005. *Formal Spoken Arabic: Basic Course*. 2nd ed. Washington, DC: Georgetown University Press.

Ryding, Karin, and Abdelnour Zaiback. (1993) 2005. *Formal Spoken Arabic: FAST Course*. Washington, DC: Georgetown University Press.

Samy, Waheed. 1999. *Arabic Writing for Style (Al-Kitāba wa-l-uslūb)*. Cairo: American University in Cairo Press.

Schultz, Ekehard, Günther Krahl, and Wolfgang Reuschel. 2000. *Standard Arabic: An Elementary-Intermediate Course*. Cambridge: Cambridge University Press.

Younes, Munther A. 2001. *Hikāyāt kalīla wa-dimna (Kalila wa Dimna: For Students of Arabic)*. Ithaca, NY: Spoken Language Services.

Ziadeh, Farhat J. 1964. *A Reader in Modern Literary Arabic*. Princeton: Princeton University Press.

Ziadeh, Farhat J., and R. Bayly Winder. 1957. *An Introduction to Modern Arabic*. Princeton, NJ: Princeton University Press.

References

Abboud, Peter F., and Ernest N. McCarus, eds. 1983. *Elementary Modern Standard Arabic (EMSA)*. Two parts. Cambridge: Cambridge University Press.

Abdalla, Mahmoud. 2010. "The Place of Media in the Arabic Curriculum." In *Arabic and the Media: Linguistic Analyses and Applications*, edited by Reem Bassiouney, 253–290. Leiden: Brill.

Abd-el-Jawad, Hassan R. S. 1992. "Is Arabic a Pluricentric Language?" In *Pluricentric Languages: Differing Norms in Differing Nations*, edited by Michael Clyne. Berlin: Mouton de Gruyter.

ACTFL (American Council on the Teaching of Foreign Languages). 1989. "ACTFL Arabic Proficiency Guidelines." *Foreign Language Annals* 22, no. 4:373–392.

____. 2012. *ACTFL Proficiency Guidelines: Speaking, Writing, Listening, and Reading*. Arabic annotations and samples. Available at http://actflproficiencyguidelines2012.org/arabic/.

Adams, Mary Ann. 1980. "Five Co-Occurring Factors in Speaking Proficiency." Unpublished paper. Washington, DC: Department of State/Foreign Service Institute/School of Language Studies.

Adams, Thomas M. 2007. "Beyond Language and Literature Departments: History, Culture, and International Study." *ADFL Bulletin* 38:1–2:13–21.

Adamson, Bob. 2006. "Fashions in Language Teaching Methodology." In *The Handbook of Applied Linguistics*, edited by Alan Davies and Catherine Elder, 604–622. Malden, MA: Blackwell.

Agius, Dionisius, ed. 1990. *Diglossic Tension: Teaching Arabic for Communication*. Leeds: Folia Scholastica.

Alatis, James, ed. 1990. *Georgetown University Round Table on Languages and Linguistics 1990*. Washington, DC: Georgetown University Press.

Al-Batal, Mahmoud. 1989. *Nashāṭāt waḍhīfiyya li-tadrīs mahārat al-kitāba*. *Al-Arabiyya* 22:137–156.

____. 1992. "Diglossia Proficiency: The Need for an Alternative Approach to Teaching." In *The Arabic Language in America*, edited by Aleya Rouchdy, 284–304. Detroit: Wayne State University Press.

____, ed. 1995a. *The Teaching of Arabic as a Foreign Language*. Provo, UT: American Association of Teachers of Arabic.

____. 1995b. "Issues in the Teaching of the Productive Skills in Arabic." In *The Teaching of Arabic as a Foreign Language*, edited by Mahmoud Al-Batal. Provo, Utah: American Association of Teachers of Arabic.

Alexander, Louis G. 1990. "Why Teach Grammar?" *Georgetown University Round Table on Languages and Linguistics 1990*, edited by James E. Alatis, 377–382. Washington, DC: Georgetown University Press.

Alhawary, Mohammad T. 2009a. *Arabic Second Language Acquisition of Morphosyntax*. New Haven: Yale University Press.

____. 2009b. "Second Language Acquisition." In *Encyclopedia of Arabic Language and Linguistics*, edited by Kees Versteegh, Volume 4, 138–146. Leiden: Brill.

____. 2009c. "Speech Processing Prerequisites or L1 Transfer? Evidence from English and French L2 Learners of Arabic." In *Foreign Language Annals* 42:2:367–390.

Allen, Heather Willis. 2009. "In Search of Relevance: The *Standards* and the Undergraduate Foreign Language Curriculum." In *Principles and Practices of the Standards in College Foreign Language Education*, edited by Virginia M. Scott, 38–52. Boston: Heinle.

Allen, Roger. 1985. "Arabic Proficiency Guidelines." *Al-Arabiyya* 18:1&2:45–70.

____. 1987. "The ACTFL Guidelines and Arabic." *Al-Arabiyya* 20:1&2:43–49.

____. 1989. "The ACTFL Arabic Proficiency Guidelines." *Foreign Language Annals* 22:4:373–392.

____. 1990. "Proficiency and the Teacher of Arabic: Curriculum, Course, and Classroom." *Al-Arabiyya* 23:1–30.

____. 1998. *The Arabic Literary Heritage: The Development of Its Genres and Criticism.* Cambridge: Cambridge University Press.

____. 2000. *An Introduction to Arabic Literature.* Cambridge: Cambridge University Press.

Alosh, Mahdi. 1987. "Testing Arabic as a Foreign Language." *Al-Arabiyya* 20:1&2:51–72.

____. 1991. "Arabic Diglossia and Its Impact on Teaching Arabic as a Foreign Language." In *International Perspectives on Foreign Language Teaching*, edited by G. L. Ervin, 121–137. Lincoln, IL: National Textbook Co.

____. 1997. *Learner, Text and Context in Foreign Language Acquisition: An Arabic Perspective.* Columbus, OH: Ohio State University National Foreign Language Resource Center.

____. 2005. *Using Arabic: A Guide to Contemporary Usage.* Cambridge: Cambridge University Press.

Alosh, Mahdi, Hussein M. Elkhafaifi, and Salah-Dine Hammoud. 2006. "Professional Standards for Teachers of Arabic." In *Handbook for Arabic Language Teaching Professionals in the 21st Century*, edited by Kassem Wahba, Zeinab Taha, and Liz England, 409–417. Mahwah, NJ: Lawrence Erlbaum Associates.

Ambrose, Susan A., Michael Bridges, Michele DiPietro, Marsha C. Lovett, and Marie K. Norman. 2010. *How Learning Works: Seven Research-Based Principles for Smart Teaching.* San Francisco: Jossey-Bass.

Ames, Carole. 1992. "Classrooms: Goals, Structures, and Student Motivation." *Journal of Educational Psychology* 84:3:261–271.

Andrews, Stephen. 2007. *Teacher Language Awareness.* Cambridge: Cambridge University Press.

Antonek, Janice L., Dawn E. McCormick, and Richard Donato. 1997. "The Student Teacher Portfolio as Autobiography: Developing a Professional Identity." *Modern Language Journal* 81:1:15–27.

Association of Departments of Foreign Languages (ADFL). 2008. "Best Practices in Study Abroad: A Primer for Chairs of Departments of Foreign Languages." *ADFL Bulletin* 39:2&3:89–94.

Aweiss, S. 1993. "Cognitive Processes in Foreign Language Reading: Reasoning Operations, Comprehension Monitoring, Strategy Use, and Knowledge Sources." *Al-Arabiyya* 26:1–17.

Baʿalbaki, Munir. 1981. *Al-Mawrid: Qāmūs inklīzī -ʕarabī.* Beirut: Dār al-ʕilm li-l-malāyīn.

Bäbler, Adriana. 2006. "Creating Interactive Web-Based Arabic Teaching Material with Authoring Systems." In *Handbook for Arabic Language Teaching Professionals in the 21st Century*, edited by Kassem Wahba, Zeinab Taha, and Liz England, 275–293. Mahwah, NJ: Lawrence Erlbaum Associates.

Badawi, El-Said M. 1973. *Mustawayāt al-lugha al-ʕarabiyya al-muʕāṣira fī miṣr.* Cairo: Dār al-maʕārif.

____. 1985. "Educated Spoken Arabic: A Problem in Teaching Arabic as a Foreign Language." In *Scientific and Humanistic Dimensions of Language*, edited by Kurt R. Jankowsky, 15–22. Washington, DC: Georgetown University Press.

____. (1987), 2006–2008. *Al-kitāb al-asāsi fī taʕlīm al-lugha l-ʕarabiyya li-ghayr al-nāṭiqīn bi-hā.* 3 vols. Cairo: American University in Cairo Press.

____. 2002. "In the Quest for the Level 4+ in Arabic: Training Level 2–3 Learners in Independent Reading." In *Developing Professional-Level Language Proficiency*, edited by Betty Lou Leaver and Boris Shekhtman, 156–176. Cambridge: Cambridge University Press.

Bain, Ken. 2004. "What Makes Great Teachers Great?" *Chronicle of Higher Education*, April 9, 2004, B7–B9.

Bartlett, Thomas. 2003. "What Makes a Teacher Great?" *Chronicle of Higher Education*, December 12, 2003, A8–A9.

Bellamy, James A., Ernest McCarus, and Adil I. Yacoub. 1963a. *Contemporary Arabic Readers IV: Short Stories. Part One: Texts*. Ann Arbor: University of Michigan Press.

____. 1963b. *Contemporary Arabic Readers IV: Short Stories. Part Two: Notes and Glossaries*. Ann Arbor: University of Michigan Press.

____. 1966a. *Contemporary Arabic Readers V: Modern Arabic Poetry. Part One: Texts*. Ann Arbor: University of Michigan Press.

____. 1966b. *Contemporary Arabic Readers V: Modern Arabic Poetry. Part Two: Notes and Glossaries*. Ann Arbor: University of Michigan Press.

Berman, Russell. 1999. "Cultural Studies and the Canon: Some Thoughts on Stefan George." *Profession 1999*, 168–179. New York: Modern Language Association.

Bernhardt, Elizabeth B. 1986. "Reading in the Foreign Language." In *Listening, Reading and Writing: Analyses and Applications*, edited by Barbara Wing. Middlebury, VT: Northeast Conference on Teaching Foreign Languages.

____. 1990. "Knowledge-Based Inferencing in Second Language Comprehension." *Georgetown University Round Table on Languages and Linguistics 1990*, edited by James E. Alatis, 271–284. Washington, DC: Georgetown University Press.

____. 2006. "Student Learning Outcomes as Professional Development and Public Relations." *Modern Language Journal* 90:4:588–590.

Berrett, Dan. 2012. "Freshman Composition Is Not Teaching Key Skills in Analysis, Researchers Argue." *The Chronicle of Higher Education*, March 12, 2012. http://chronicle.com/article/Freshman-Composition-Is-Not-/131278/.

Bhabha, Homi K. 1994, 2012. *The Location of Culture*. London: Routledge.

Bishai, Wilson B. 1966. "Modern Inter-Arabic." *Journal of the American Oriental Society* 86:319–323.

Blair, Robert W., ed. *Innovative Approaches to Language Teaching*. 1982. Boston: Newbury House.

Blake, Robert J. 2008. *Brave New Digital Classroom: Technology and Foreign Language Learning*. Washington, DC: Georgetown University Press.

____. 2009. "The Use of Technology for Second Language Distance Learning." In *Technology in the Service of Language Learning: Update on Garrett (1991) Trends and Issues*, edited by Barbara A. Lafford, 822–835. *Modern Language Journal* 93: Focus Issue.

Blumenfeld, Phyllis C. 1992. "Classroom Learning and Motivation: Clarifying and Expanding Goal Theory." *Journal of Educational Psychology* 84:3:272–281.

Boussofara-Omar, Naima. 2006. "Diglossia." In *Encyclopedia of Arabic Language and Linguistics*, edited by Kees Versteegh, vol. I: 629–637. Leiden: Brill.

Brosh, Hezi, and Elite Olshtain. 1995. "Language Skills and the Curriculum of a Diglossic Language." *Foreign Language Annals* 28:2:247–260.

Brown, H. Douglas. 1986. "Learning a Second Culture." In *Culture Bound: Bridging the Cultural Gap in Language Teaching*, edited by Joyce Merrill Valdes, 33–48. Cambridge: Cambridge University Press.

____. 2001. *Teaching by Principles: An Interactive Approach to Language Pedagogy*. 2nd ed. White Plains, NY: Addison Wesley Longman.

Brown, Peter. 2011. "On the Magic Carpet of the Met." *The New York Review of Books,* December 8, 2011: 26–28.

Brustad, Kristen. 2006. "Reading Fluently in Arabic." In *Handbook for Arabic Language Teaching Professionals in the 21st Century*, edited by Kassem Wahba, Zeinab Taha, and Liz England, 341–352. Mahwah, NJ: Lawrence Erlbaum Associates.

Buell, Lawrence. 2005. *The Future of Environmental Criticism: Environmental Crisis and Literary Imagination*. Malden, MA: Blackwell.

Bybee, Joan. 2006. "From Usage to Grammar: The Mind's Response to Repetition." *Language* 82:4:711–733.

Byrnes, Heidi. 1983. "Discourse Analysis and the Teaching of Writing." *ADFL Bulletin*, 15:2:30–36.

____. 1998. "Reading in the Beginning and Intermediate College Foreign Language Class." Module for *Professional Preparation of Teaching Assistants in Foreign Languages*, edited by Grace Stovall Burkart. Washington, DC: Center for Applied Linguistics.

____. 2000. "Shaping the Discourse of a Practice: The Role of Linguistics and Psychology in Language Teaching and Learning." *Modern Language Journal* 84:4:472–494.

____. 2002a. "Toward Academic-Level Foreign Language Abilities: Reconsidering Foundational Assumptions, Expanding Pedagogical Options," In *Developing Professional-Level Language Proficiency*, edited by Betty Lou Leaver and Boris Shekhtman, 34–58. Cambridge: Cambridge University Press.

____. 2002b. "The Role of Task and Task-Based Assessment in a Content-Oriented Collegiate Foreign Language Curriculum." *Language Testing* 19:419–437.

____, ed. 2005. "Perspectives: The Position of Heritage Languages in Language Education Policy." *Modern Language Journal* 89:4:582–616.

Canale, M., and Swain, M. 1980. "Theoretical Bases of Communicative Approaches to Second Language Teaching and Testing." *Applied Linguistics* 1:1–47.

Carey, Benedict. 2010. "Forget What You Know about Good Study Habits." *New York Times*, September 7, 2010. Retrieved from www.nytimes.com/2010/09/07/health/views/07mind.html.

Chomsky, Noam. 1957, 2002. *Syntactic Structures*. Berlin: Mouton de Gruyter.

____. 1959. "A Review of B.F. Skinner's *Verbal Behavior*." *Language* 35:1:26–58.

____. 1965. *Aspects of the Theory of Syntax*. Cambridge, MA: MIT Press.

____. 1981. *Lectures on Government and Binding*. Dordrecht: Foris.

Clark, H. H., and E. V. Clark. 1977. *Psychology and Language*. New York: Harcourt Brace.

Coady, James, and Thomas Huckin, eds. 1997. *Second Language Vocabulary Acquisition*. Cambridge: Cambridge University Press.

Cook, Guy. 2010. *Translation in Language Teaching*. Oxford: Oxford University Press.

Cook, Vivian. 1994. "Universal Grammar and the Learning and Teaching of Second Languages." In *Perspectives on Pedagogical Grammar*, edited by Terence Odlin, 24–48. Cambridge: Cambridge University Press.

Cooke, Miriam. 1987. "Literary Criticism: The State of the Art in Arabic." *Al-Arabiyya* 20:227–296.

Corder, S. Pit. 1981. *Error Analysis and Interlanguage*. London: Oxford University Press.

Crane, Cori. 2002. "Genre Analysis: A Step toward Understanding the Different Stages of Advanced Language Instruction." Presentation at ACTFL-AATG 2002 meeting, Salt Lake City, November 23, 2002. Accessed 5/24/2006 at www3.georgetown.edu/departments/german/programs/curriculum/manuscripts/crane.

Crawford, Jane. 2002. "The Role of Materials in the Language Classroom: Finding the Balance." In *Methodology in Language Teaching: An Anthology of Current Practice*, edited by Jack C. Richards and Willy A. Renandya, 80–91. Cambridge: Cambridge University Press.

Curran, Charles A. 1968. *Counseling and Psychotherapy: The Pursuit of Values*. Apple River, IL: Apple River Press.

____. 1972. *Counseling-Learning: A Whole-Person Model for Education*. New York: Grune and Stratton.

____. 1976. *Counseling-Learning in Second Languages*. Apple River, IL: Apple River Press.

____. 1978. *Understanding: An Essential Ingredient in Human Belonging*. Apple River, IL: Apple River Press.

____. 1982a. "Community Language Learning." In *Innovative Approaches to Language Teaching*, edited by Robert W. Blair, 118–133. Boston: Newbury House.

____. 1982b. "A Linguistic Model for Learning and Living in the New Age of the Person." In *Innovative Approaches to Language Teaching*, edited by Robert W. Blair, 134–145. Boston: Newbury House.

Darder, Antonia, Marta P. Baltodano, and Rodolfo D. Torres, eds. 2009. *The Critical Pedagogy Reader*. 2nd ed. New York: Routledge.

Day, Richard, and Julian Bamford. 2002. "Top Ten Principles for Teaching Extensive Reading." http://www.nflrc.hawaii.edu/RFL/October2002/day/day.html.

De Angelis, Gessica. 2007. *Third or Additional Language Acquisition*. Clevedon: Multilingual Matters.

DeGuerrero, Maria C. M., and Olga S. Villamil. 2000. "Activating the ZPD: Mutual Scaffolding in L2 Peer Revision." *Modern Language Journal* 84:1:51–68.

DeKeyser, Robert M. 1998. "Beyond Focus on Form: Cognitive Perspectives on Learning and Practicing Second Language Grammar." In *Focus on Form in Classroom Second Language Acquisition*, edited by Catherine Doughty and Jessica Williams, 42–63. Cambridge: Cambridge University Press.

____, ed. 2007a. *Practice in a Second Language*. Cambridge: Cambridge University Press.

____. 2007b. "Skill Acquisition Theory." In *Theories in Second Language Acquisition*, edited by Bill VanPatten and Jessica Williams, 97–114. New York: Routledge/Taylor & Francis.

Derry, Sharon J. 1992. "Beyond Symbolic Processing: Expanding Horizons for Educational Psychology." *Journal of Educational Psychology* 84:4:413–418.

Dickins, James, and Janet C.E. Watson. 1999. *Standard Arabic: An Advanced Course*. Cambridge: Cambridge University Press.

Doniach, N. S. 1982, 1990. *The Concise Oxford English-Arabic Dictionary of Current Usage*. Oxford: Oxford University Press.

Dunkel, Patricia. 1985. "Listening and Notetaking: What Is the Effect of Pretraining in Notetaking?" *TESOL Newsletter* 19:6:30–31.

Duranti, Alessandro, ed. 2001. *Key Terms in Language and Culture*. Malden, MA: Blackwell.

Edgerton, Russell, Patricia Hutchings, and Kathleen Quinlan, eds. 1991. *The Teaching Portfolio: Capturing the Scholarship in Teaching*. Washington, DC: American Association for Higher Education (AAHE).

Eid, Mushira. 2007. "Arabic on the Media: Hybridity and Styles." In *Approaches to Arabic Linguistics*, edited by Everhard Ditters and Harald Motzki, 403–434. Leiden: Brill.

El-Essawy, Raghda. 2005. "Facing Challenges in the Writing Classroom." Presentation at Middle East Studies Association conference, November, 2005.

____. 2010. "A Framework for Teaching Vocabulary through Printed Media." In *Arabic and the Media: Linguistic Analyses and Applications*, edited by Reem Bassiouney, 229–251. Leiden: Brill.

Elgibali, Alaa, and Nevenka Korica. 2007. *Media Arabic (lughat wasāʔil al-ʔiʕlām al-ʕarabiyya): A Coursebook for Reading and Arabic News*. Cairo and New York: American University in Cairo Press.

Elgibali, Alaa, and Zeinab Taha. 1995. "Teaching Arabic as a Foreign Language: Challenges of the Nineties." In *The Teaching of Arabic as a Foreign Language*, edited by Mahmoud Al-Batal, 79–102. Provo, UT: American Association of Teachers of Arabic.

Elkhafaifi, Hussein. 2001. "Teaching Listening in the Arabic Classroom: A Survey of Current Practice." *Al-Arabiyya* 34:55–90.

____. 2005a. "Listening Comprehension and Anxiety in the Arabic Language Classroom." *The Modern Language Journal* 89:2:206–220.

____. 2005b. "The Effect of Prelistening Activities on Listening Comprehension in Arabic Learners." *Foreign Language Annals* 38:4:505–513.

____. 2007–2008. "An Exploration of Listening Strategies: A Descriptive Study of Arabic Learners." *Al-Arabiyya* 40–41:71–86.

Ellis, Rod. 2002. "The Place of Grammar Instruction in the Second/Foreign Language Curriculum." In *New Perspectives on Grammar Teaching in Second Language Classrooms*, edited by Eli Hinkel and Sandra Fotos, 17–34. Mahwah, NJ: Lawrence Erlbaum.

____. 2003. *Task-Based Language Learning and Teaching*. Oxford: Oxford University Press.

____. 2010. "Second Language Acquisition, Teacher Education and Language Pedagogy." *Language Teaching* 43:2:182–201.

Erman, Britt, and Beatrice Warren. 2000. "The Idiom Principle and the Open Choice Principle." *Text* 20:1:29–62.

Etienne, Corinne, and Kelly Sax. 2009. "Stylistic Variation in French: Bridging the Gap between Research and Textbooks." *Modern Language Journal* 93:4:584–606.

____. 2011. "Best Practices in Teaching Logographic and Non-Roman Writing Systems to L2 Learners." *Annual Review of Applied Linguistics, 31: Topics in Second Language Pedagogy*, 249–274. Cambridge: Cambridge University Press.

Farghaly, Ali. 2005. "A Case for an Inter-Arabic Grammar." In *Investigating Arabic: Current Parameters in Analysis and Learning*, edited by Alaa Elgibali, 29–49. Leiden: Brill.

Farrar, M. J. 1992. "Negative Evidence and Grammatical Morpheme Acquisition." *Developmental Psychology* 28: 90–98.

Farrell, Thomas S. C. 2002. "Lesson Planning." In *Methodology in Language Teaching: An Anthology of Current Practice*, edited by Jack C. Richards and Willy A. Renandya, 30–39. Cambridge: Cambridge University Press.

Fasold, Ralph. 1984. *The Sociolinguistics of Society*. London: Blackwell.

Ferguson, Charles A. 1959. "Diglossia." *Word* 15: 325–340.

Ferrando, Ignacio. 2007. "History of Arabic." In *Encyclopedia of Arabic Language and Linguistics,* edited by Kees Versteegh, vol. 2, 261–268.

Fischer, Wolfdietrich. 2006. "Classical Arabic." In *Encyclopedia of Arabic Language and Linguistics,* edited by Kees Versteegh, vol. 1, 397–405.

Frangieh, Bassam K. 2005. *Anthology of Arabic Literature, Culture, and Thought: From Pre-Islamic Times to the Present*. New Haven and London: Yale University Press.

Fukkink, Rueben G., Jan Hulstijn, and Annegien Simis. 2005. "Does Training in Second-Language Word Recognition Skills Affect Reading Comprehension? An Experimental Study." *Modern Language Journal* 89:1:54–75.

Garrett, Nina. 1989. "The Role of Grammar in the Development of Communicative Ability." *Applied Language Learning* 1:1:15–32.

____. 2009. "Computer-Assisted Language Learning Trends and Issues Revisited: Integrating Innovation." *Modern Language Journal* 93, Focus Issue: Technology in the Service of Language Learning: Update on Garrett (1991) "Trends and Issues," edited by Barbara A. Lafford, 719–740.

Gass, Susan. 2003. "Input and Interaction." In *The Handbook of Second Language Acquisition*, edited by Catherine J. Doughty and Michael H. Long, 224–255. Malden, MA: Blackwell.

____. 2006. "Models of Second Language Acquisition." In *A Handbook for Arabic Language Teaching Professionals in the 21st Century,* ed. Kassem Wahba, Zeinab Taha, and Elizabeth England, 21–33. Mahwah, NJ: Lawrence Erlbaum Associates.

Gass, Susan, and Alison Mackey. 2007. "Input, Interaction, and Output in Second Language Acquisition." In *Theories in Second Language Acquisition*, edited by Bill VanPatten and Jessica Williams, 175–199. New York: Routledge.

Gass, Susan, and Larry Selinker. 2001. *Second Language Acquisition: An Introductory Course*. 2nd ed. Mahwah, NJ: Lawrence Erlbaum.

Geertz, Clifford. 1973. *The Interpretation of Cultures*. New York: Basic Books.

Geisler, Michael E. 2006–2007. In "Forum on Language Policy and the Politics of Language." *ADFL Bulletin* 38:62–64.

____. 2008. "The MLA Report on Foreign Languages: One Year into the Future." *Profession 2008*: 229–239.

Georgetown University website. 2012. "'Visual dictionary' Supersedes Phonology for Skilled Readers." Available at www.georgetown.edu/story/brain-words-perception-discovery.html. Accessed on January 14, 2012.

Gibran, Gibran Khalil. (1932) 1966. *Jubrān ḥayyan wa-mayyitan* (Gibran, Living and Dead), edited by Habīb Masʕūd. Beirut: Dār al-Riḥāni li-l-ṭabāʕa wa-l-nashr.

Giles, Howard, and Robert N. St. Clair. 1979. *Language and Social Psychology.* London: Blackwell.

Gladwell, Malcolm. 2008. *Outliers: The Story of Success.* New York: Little, Brown.

Glenn, David. 2009. "Matching Teaching Style to Learning Style May Not Help Students." *The Chronicle of Higher Education* December 15, 2009. Retrieved from http://chronicle.com/article/Matching-Teaching-Style-to/49497 on December 16, 2009.

Gordon, Cyrus. 1970. "The Accidental Invention of the Phonemic Alphabet." *Journal of Near Eastern Studies* 29:3:193–197.

Grabar, Oleg. 1987. *The Formation of Islamic Art.* New Haven: Yale University Press.

____. 1992. *The Mediation of Ornament.* Princeton: Princeton University Press.

____. 2006. *Islamic Visual Culture, 1100–1800.* Aldershot, UK: Ashgate.

Grossman, Lawrence, Cary Nelson, and Paula Treichler, eds. 1992. *Cultural Studies.* New York: Routledge.

Guard, Nicky, Uwe Richter, and Sharon Waller. 2003. Portfolio assessments. Accessed 5/30/2006 from www.llas.ac.uk/resources/good practice.aspx?resourceid=1441.

Gutierrez, John R. 1997. "Teaching Spanish as a Heritage Language: A Case for Language Awareness." *ADFL Bulletin* 29:1:33–36.

Hadley, Alice Omaggio. 2001. *Teaching Language in Context*, 3rd ed. Boston: Heinle & Heinle.

Hall, Edward T. 1959. *The Silent Language.* Greenwich, CN: Fawcett.

____. 1976, 1981. *Beyond Culture.* New York: Anchor Books.

____. 1983. *The Dance of Life.* New York: Anchor Books.

Halliday, M. A. K. 1985. *An Introduction to Functional Grammar.* London: Edward Arnold.

Hamilton, Heidi, Cori Crane, and Abigail Bartoshesky. 2005. *Doing Foreign Language.* Upper Saddle River, NJ: Pearson/ Merrill-Prentice Hall.

Hammoud, Salah-Dine. 1996. "A Survey of Current Classroom Practices among Teachers of Arabic." *Al-Arabiyya* 29:95–128.

Hansen, Gunna Funder. 2010. "Word Recognition in Arabic as a Foreign Language." *Modern Language Journal* 94:4:567–581.

Hardison, Debra M. 2010. "Trends in Teaching Pronunciation." *CLEAR News* 14:2:1–5. (Center for Language Education and Research.)

Herron, Carol, Steven P. Cole, Holly York, and Paul Linden. 1998. "A Comparison Study of Student Retention of Foreign Language Video: Declarative Versus Interrogative Advance Organizer." *Modern Language Journal* 82:2:237–247.

Higgs, Theodore V. 1985. "Language Teaching and the Quest for the Holy Grail." In *Teaching for Proficiency, the Organizing Principle*, edited by Theodore V. Higgs, 1–9. Lincolnwood IL: National Textbook Company.

Higgs, Theodore V., and Ray Clifford. 1982. "The Push toward Communication." In *Curriculum, Competence, and the Foreign Language Teacher*, edited by Theodore V. Higgs, 57–79. Lincolnwood, IL: National Textbook Company.

Hinkel, Eli, and Sandra Fotos, eds. 2002. *New Perspectives on Grammar Teaching in Second Language Classrooms.* Mahwah, NJ: Lawrence Erlbaum.

Husni, Ronak, and Janet C. E. Watson. 2006. "Arabic as L2: Linguistic and Intercultural Issues in Composition." In *Grammar as a Window onto Arabic Humanism,* edited by Lutz Edzard and Janet Watson. Wiesbaden: Harrassowitz.

Hutchings, Patricia. 1994. "The Teaching Portfolio." Presentation at portfolio workshop, Georgetown University, Washington, DC, April 1994.

Hutchings, Patricia, and Lee Shulman. 1994. "Teaching as Scholarship: Reflections on a Syllabus." Project: From Idea to Prototype: The Peer Review of Education. Washington, DC: American Association for Higher Education.

Ibrahim, Muhammad H. 1986. "Standard and Prestige Language: A Problem in Arabic Sociolin-
    guistics." *Anthropological Linguistics* 28, no. 1:115–126.
Ibrahim, Zeinab, and Jehan Allam. 2006. "Arabic Learners and Heritage Students Redefined: Pres-
    ent and Future." In *Handbook for Arabic Language Teaching Professionals in the 21st Century*,
    edited by Kassem Wahba, Zeinab Taha, and Liz England, 437–446. Mahwah, NJ: Lawrence
    Erlbaum Associates.
Interagency Language Roundtable (ILR) web site: www.govtilr.org.
Iser, Wolfgang. 1978. *The Act of Reading: A Theory of Aesthetic Response*. Baltimore: Johns
    Hopkins University Press.
Ishmael, Aja. 2010. "Studying Abroad in the Arabic-Speaking World: Gender Perspectives." Paper
    presented at the Georgetown University Round Table on Languages and Linguistics (GURT),
    March, 2010.
Jackson, Frederick H., and Marsha A. Kaplan. 2005. "Theory and Practice in Government Lan-
    guage Teaching." Unpublished paper.
Jackson, Fredrick H., and Margaret E. Malone. 2009. "Building the Foreign Language Capacity
    We Need: Toward a Comprehensive Strategy for a National Language Framework." Retrieved
    from www.cal.org/resources/flcapacity.html.
Jackson, Fredrick H., and Eva Zeoli. 2011. "Online and Blended Learning Environments: Review
    of Good Practices in Language Teaching and Learning." November 2, 2011. Unpublished paper.
Kenny, Dallas. 1992. "Arab-Americans Learning Arabic: Motivation and Attitudes." In *The Arabic
    Language in America*, edited by Aleya Rouchdy, 119–161. Detroit: Wayne State University
    Press.
Khalil, Aziz. 2003. "Assessment of the Use of Language Learning Strategies of American Learners
    of Arabic as a Foreign Language," *Al-Arabiyya* 36:27–47.
Kincheloe, Joe L. 2008. *Critical Pedagogy*, 2nd ed. New York: Peter Lang.
Kissling, Elizabeth. 2012. *The Effect of Phonetics Instruction on Learners' Perception and Pro-
    duction of L2 Sounds*. Dissertation, Georgetown University.
Klapper, John. 2001. "Training Graduate Teachers and Foreign Language Assistants in UK
    Universities: A Reflective Approach." In *Mentoring Foreign Language Teaching Assistants,
    Lecturers and Adjunct Faculty*, edited by Benjamin Rivkin, 143–165. Boston: Heinle &
    Heinle.
Koda, Keiko. 1992. "The Effects of Lower-Level Processing Skills on FL Reading Performance:
    Implications for Instruction." *Modern Language Journal* 76:4:502–512.
_____. 2010. The Role of Reading in Fostering Transcultural Competence. *Reading in a Foreign
    Language* 22:supp. 1:5–10.
Kowarski, Ilana. 2010. "Colleges Help Students to Translate Benefits of Study Abroad." *The
    Chronicle of Higher Education*, July 22, 2010. At http://chronicle.com/article/Colleges-help-
    students-to/123653/?sid=at&utm_source=at&autm_medium=en.
Kramsch, Claire. 1985. "Literary Texts in the Classroom: A Discourse." *Modern Language
    Journal* 69:4:356–366.
_____. 1993. *Context and Culture in Language Teaching*. Oxford: Oxford University Press.
_____. 1998. *Language and Culture*. Oxford: Oxford University Press.
_____. 2000. "Second Language Acquisition, Applied Linguistics, and the Teaching of Foreign
    Languages." *Modern Language Journal* 84:3:311–326.
_____. 2010. "The Symbolic Dimensions of the Intercultural." *Language Teaching* 44:3:354–367.
Krashen, Stephen D. 1981. *Second Language Acquisition and Second Language Learning*. Oxford:
    Pergamon.
_____. 1985. *The Input Hypothesis: Issues and Implications*. London: Longman.
_____. 1990. "How Reading and Writing Make You Smarter, or, How Smart People Read and
    Write." *Georgetown University Round Table on Languages and Linguistics 1990*, edited by
    James E. Alatis, 364–376. Washington, DC: Georgetown University Press.

____. 1991. "The Input Hypothesis: An Update." *Georgetown University Round Table on Languages and Linguistics 1991*, edited by James E. Alatis, 409–431. Washington, DC: Georgetown University Press.

____. 1993. "Some Unexpected Consequences of the Input Hypothesis." In *Georgetown University Round Table on Languages and Linguistics 1993*, edited by James E. Alatis, 6–21. Washington, DC: Georgetown University Press.

Krashen, Stephen D., and Tracy D. Terrell. 1983. *The Natural Approach: Language Acquisition in the Classroom*. Hayward, CA: Alemany Press/Oxford: Pergamon Press.

Kuntz, Patricia, and R. Kirk Belnap. 2001. "Beliefs about Learning Held by Teachers and Their Students at Two Arabic Programs Abroad." *Al-Arabiyya* 34:91–113.

Lafford, Barbara A., ed. 2009. *Technology in the Service of Language Learning: Update on Garrett (1991) Trends and Issues. Modern Language Journal* 93: Focus Issue.

Lahlali, El-Mustapha. 2008. *Advanced Media Arabic*. Washington, DC: Georgetown University Press.

____. 2009. *How to Write in Arabic*. Edinburgh: Edinburgh University Press.

Lampe, Jerry. 2007. "Cultural Dimensions of Oral Proficiency in Arabic." Interagency Language Roundtable (ILR) presentation, March 23, 2007.

Lancioni, Giuliano. 2009. "Formulaic Models and Formulaicity in Classical and Modern Standard Arabic." In *Formulaic Language: vol. 1: Distribution and Historical Change*, edited by Roberta Corrigan, Edith Moravcsik, Hamid Ouali, and Kathleen M. Wheatley, 219–238. Amsterdam: John Benjamins.

Lang, James M. 2012. "Metacognition and Student Learning." *The Chronicle of Higher Education* online, January 17, 2012. Accessed January 18, 2012.

Larcher, Pierre. 2001. "Moyen arabe et arabe moyen." *Arabica* 48: 578–609.

Larkin, Margaret. 1995. "The Role of Close Reading in the Elementary Arabic Curriculum." In *The Teaching of Arabic as a Foreign Language*, edited by Mahmoud Al-Batal, 157–173. Provo, UT: American Association of Teachers of Arabic.

Larson, Phyllis. 2006. "The Return of the Text: A Welcome Challenge for Less Commonly Taught Languages." *Modern Language Journal* 90:2:255–258.

Larson-Freeman, Diane. 1983. "Training Teachers or Educating a Teacher." *Georgetown University Round Table on Languages and Linguistics 1983*, edited by James E. Alatis, H. H. Stern, and Peter Strevens, 264–274. Washington, DC: Georgetown University Press.

____. 1990. "On the Need for a Theory of Language Teaching." *Georgetown University Round Table on Languages and Linguistics 1990*, edited by James E. Alatis, 261–270. Washington, DC: Georgetown University Press.

____. 2002. "The Grammar of Choice." In *New Perspectives on Grammar Teaching in Second Language Classrooms*, edited by Eli Hinkel and Sandra Fotos, 103–118. Mahwah, NJ: Lawrence Erlbaum.

____. 2003. *Teaching Language: From Grammar to Grammaring*. Boston: Thomson-Heinle.

Larson-Freeman, Diane, and Marti Anderson. 2011. *Techniques and Principles in Language Teaching*. Oxford: Oxford University Press.

Laufer, Batia. 1997. "The Lexical Plight in Second Language Reading: Words You Don't Know, Words You Think You Know, and Words You Can't Guess." In *Second Language Vocabulary Acquisition*, edited by James Coady and Thomas Huckin, 20–34. Cambridge: Cambridge University Press.

Leaver, Betty Lou. 1997. "Content-Based Instruction in Foreign Language Education: An Overview." Presentation at Georgetown University, October 2, 1997.

Leaver, Betty Lou, and Boris Shekhtman. 2002. "Principles and Practices in Teaching Superior-Level Language Skills: Not Just More of the Same." In *Developing Professional-Level Language Proficiency*, edited by Betty Lou Leaver and Boris Shekhtman, 3–33. Cambridge: Cambridge University Press.

Leaver, Betty Lou, and Stephen B. Stryker. 1989. "Content-Based Instruction for Foreign Language Classrooms." *Foreign Language Annals* 22:3:269–275.

____, eds. 1997. *Content-Based Instruction in Foreign Language Education*. Washington, DC: Georgetown University Press.

Leeman, Jennifer, Lisa Rabin, and Esperanza Roman-Mendoza. 2011. "Identity and Activism in Heritage Language Education." *Modern Language Journal* 95:4:481–495.

Leonardi, Vanessa. 2010. *The Role of Pedagogical Translation in Second Language Acquisition: From Theory to Practice*. Bern: Peter Lang.

Lentin, Jérôme. 2008. "Middle Arabic." In *Encyclopedia of Arabic Language and Linguistics*, vol. 3, edited by Kees Versteegh, 215–224. Leiden: Brill.

Levine, Glen S., Charlotte Melin, Corinne Crane, Monika Chavez, and Thomas A. Lovik. 2008. "The Language Program Director in Curricular and Departmental Reform." *Profession 2008*, 240–254.

Lightbown, Patsy M., and Nina Spada. 2006. *How Languages Are Learned*, 3rd ed. Oxford: Oxford University Press.

Lipski, John M. 2007. "Which Spanish(es) to Teach?" *ADFL Bulletin* 41:2:48–59.

Liskin-Gasparro, Judith. 1996. "Assessment: From Content Standards to Student Performance." In *National Standards, a Catalyst for Reform*, edited by R. C. Lafayette, 169–196. Lincolnwood, IL: National Textbook Company.

Little, David. 1994. Words and Their Properties: Arguments for a Lexical Approach to Pedagogical Grammar." In *Perspectives on Pedagogical Grammar*, edited by Terence Odlin, 99–122. Cambridge: Cambridge University Press.

Little, Greta D., and Sara L. Sanders. 1989. "Classroom Community: A Prerequisite for Communication." *Foreign Language Annals* 22:3:277–281.

Loewen, Shawn, and Hayo Reinders. 2011. *Key Concepts in Second Language Acquistion*. Houndsmills, Basingstoke, Hampshire: Palgrave McMillan.

Long, Michael, and Peter Robinson. 1998. "Focus on Form: Theory, Research, and Practice." In *Focus on Form in Classroom Second Language Acquisition*, edited by Catherine Doughty and Jessica Williams, 15–41. Cambridge: Cambridge University Press.

Loewen, Shawn, and Jenefer Philp. 2006. "Recasts in the Adult English L2 Classroom: Characteristics, Explicitness, and Effectiveness." *Modern Language Journal* 90, vol. 4:536–555.

Lutz, Richard. 1990. "Classroom Shock: The Role of Expectations in an Instructional Setting." In *Georgetown University Round Table on Languages and Linguistics 1990*, edited by James E. Alatis, 144–156. Washington, DC: Georgetown University Press.

Lyons, John. 1990. "Linguistics: Theory, Practice and Research." *Georgetown University Round Table on Languages and Linguistics 1990*, edited by James E. Alatis, 11–30. Washington, DC: Georgetown University Press.

Mackey, Alison, and Jenefer Philp. 1998. "Conversational Interaction and Second Language Development: Recasts, Responses, and Red Herrings?" *Modern Language Journal* 82:3:338–356.

Malone, Margaret. 2009. "How Language Testing Can (Help) Save Your Language Program." http://nclrc.org/teaching_materials/assessment/testing_tips.html, pages 12–13 of 20. Accessed October 3, 2011.

____. 2010. "What Does It Take to Be Accepted as a Professional in the Language Testing Field?" http://nclrc.org/teaching_materials/assessment/testing_tips.html, page 10 of 20. Accessed October 3, 2011.

Malti-Douglas, Fedwa. 1996. *PMLA* Forum: Interdisciplinarity in Literary Studies. *PMLA* 111, no. 2:311.

Matson, Susan, Gloria Flynn, and Yasmine Bia. 2011. "Notetaking: The Critically Overlooked Skill." Presentation at the NAFSA (Association of International Educators) 2011 convention, Vancouver, BC, May, 2011. Accessed August 1, 2012 at http://proposals.nafsa.org/abstract_uploads/2715.61212.GS180.pdf.

McCarus, Ernest, and Raji Rammuny. 1979. *Programmed Course in Modern Literary Arabic Phonology and Script*. Troy, MI: International Book Centre, Inc.

Middle East Centre for Arab Studies (MECAS). 1950. *The First Thousand Words: A Basic Vocabulary for Foreigners (Awwal alf kalima fī l-lugha l-ʕarabiyya li-l-ṭullāb al-ajānib)*. Beirut: American Press.

____. 1959. *A Selected Word List of Modern Literary Arabic*. Beirut: Dar Al-Kutub.

____. 1965. *The M.E.C.A.S. Grammar of Modern Literary Arabic*. Beirut: Khayats.

____. 1967. *The Way Prepared (Al-Ṭarīq al-mumahhad): A Reading Book in Modern Arabic*. Beirut: Khayats.

Mildenberger, Kenneth W. 1959. Bulletin 3: Language and Area Centers: The Curriculum. Language Development Section, U.S. Office of Education.Washington, DC.

Miller, Jim, and Regina Weinert. 1998. *Spontaneous Spoken Language: Syntax and Discourse*. Oxford: Clarendon Press.

Mitchell, T. F. 1962. *Colloquial Arabic*. London: Teach Yourself Books.

____. 1990. *Pronouncing Arabic*, vol.1. Oxford: Clarendon Press.

Modern Language Association (MLA) Ad Hoc Committee on Foreign Languages. 2008. "Transfoming College and University Foreign Language Departments." *Modern Languages Journal* 92, no. 2:284–312.

Modern Language Association (MLA). 2001. Final report: MLA Ad Hoc Committee on Teaching. *Profession 2001*, 225–238.

____. 2007. "Ad Hoc Committee on Foreign Languages. Foreign Languages and Higher Education: New Structures for a Changed World." *Profession 2007*: 234–245.

Moore, John. 1990. "Doubled Verbs in Modern Standard Arabic." In *Perspectives on Arabic Linguistics II*, edited by Mushira Eid and John McCarthy, 55–93. Amsterdam: John Benjamins.

Mora, Raimundo. 1995. "Silence, Interruptions, and Discourse Domains: The Opportunities to Speak." *Applied Language Learning* 6, no. 1&2:27–39.

Morely, Joan. 1990. "Trends and Developments in Listening Comprehension: Theory and Practice." *Georgetown University Round Table on Languages and Linguistics 1990*, edited by James E. Alatis, 317–337. Washington, DC: Georgetown University Press.

Moseley, William G. 2009. "Area Studies in a Global Context." *Chronicle of Higher Education*, November 29, 2009.

Mughazy, Mustafa A. 2000. "Pragmatics of the Evil Eye in Egyptian Arabic." *Studies in the Linguistic Sciences* 30:2:147–157.

____. 2005–2006. "Reading Despite Ambiguity: The Role of Metacognitive Strategies in Reading Arabic Authentic Texts." *Al-Arabiyya* 38–39: 57–74.

Al-Munjid al-abjadī. 1968. 2nd printing. Beirut: Dār al-Mashreq.

Al-Munjid fī l-lugha wa-l-aʕlām. 1994. 34th printing. Beirut: Dār al-Machreq.

Nation, I. S. P. 2001. *Learning Vocabulary in Another Language*. Cambridge: Cambridge University Press.

Nation, Paul, and Robert Waring. 1997. "Vocabulary Size, Text Coverage, and Word Lists." In *Vocabulary: Description, Acquisition and Pedagogy*, eds. Norbert Schmitt and Michael McCarthy, 6–19. Cambridge: Cambridge University Press.

National Capital Language Resource Center (NCLRC). n.d. *Portfolio Assessment in the Foreign Language Classroom*. Washington, DC: National Capital Language Resource Center.

National Standards in Foreign Language Education Project. 2006. *Standards for Foreign Language Learning in the 21st Century*. Lawrence, KS: Allen Press, Inc.

Nattinger, J., and J. DeCarrico. 1989. "Lexical Phrases, Speech Acts, and Teaching Conversation." In *Vocabulary Acquisition. AILA Review 6*, edited by P. Nation and R. Carter, 118–39. Amsterdam: Free University Press.

Nielsen, Helle Lykke. 1994. "How to Teach Arabic Communicatively: A Preliminary Evaluation of Aims, Achievements and Problems at the Odense TAFL Program." *Al-Arabiyya* 27: 27–50.

_____. 1996. "How to Teach Arabic Communicatively: Toward a Theoretical Framework for TAFL." In *Understanding Arabic*, edited by Alaa. Elgibali, 211–239. Cairo: American University in Cairo Press.

_____. 1997a. "Acquisition Order in Arabic as a Foreign Language: A Cognitive Approach." In *Ethnic Encounter and Culture Change*, edited by M'hammed Sabour and Knut S. Vikør. Bergen: Nordic Society for Middle Eastern Studies.

_____. 1997b. "On Acquisition Order of Agreement Procedures in Arabic Learner Language." *Al-Arabiyya* 30:49–93.

_____. 2009. "Second Language Teaching." *Encyclopedia of Arabic Language and Linguistics*, edited by Kees Versteegh, Volume 4, 146–156. Leiden: Brill.

Norris, John M. 2006. "The Why (and How) of Assessing Student Learning Outcomes in College Foreign Language Programs." *Modern Language Journal* 90, no. 4: 576–583.

Nydell, Margaret. 2006. *Understanding Arabs: A Guide for Modern Times*, 4th edition. Yarmouth, ME: Intercultural Press.

Oller, John W. 1988. Review of *The Input Hypothesis* by Stephen D. Krashen. *Language* 64:171–173.

Oller, John W., and Patricia A. Richard-Amato, eds. 1983. *Methods That Work: A Smorgasbord of Ideas for Language Teachers*. New York: Newbury House/Harper-Collins.

O'Malley, Michael, and Anna Uhl Chamot. 1990. *Learning Strategies in Second Language Acquisition*. New York: Cambridge University Press.

Ortega, Lourdes. 2007. "Second Language Learning Explained? SLA across Nine Contemporary Theories." In *Theories in Second Language Acquisition*, edited by Bill VanPatten and Jessica Williams, 225–250. New York: Routledge/Taylor & Francis.

Owens, Jonathan. 2005. "The Grammatical Tradition and Arabic Language Teaching: A View from Here." In *Investigating Arabic: Current Parameters in Analysis and Learning*, edited by Alaa Elgibali, 103–116. Leiden: Brill.

_____. 2006. *A Linguistic History of Arabic*. Oxford: Oxford University Press.

Oxford, Rebecca L. 1988. "Styles, Strategies, and Aptitude: Important Connections for Language Learners." Working draft of keynote presentation, Interagency Language Roundtable invitational aptitude testing symposium. Arlington, VA, September 14–16, 1988.

_____. 1990. "Missing Link: Evidence from Research on Language Learning Styles and Strategies." *Georgetown University Round Table on Languages and Linguistics 1990*, edited by James E. Alatis, 438–458. Washington, DC: Georgetown University Press.

_____. 1994. "Teaching Learning Strategies and Cross-Culturalism in the Language Classroom." Presentation (handout) from Georgetown University Round Table on Languages and Linguistics, March, 1994.

_____. 1997. "Cooperative Learning, Collaborative Learning, and Interaction: Three Communicative Strands in the Language Classroom." *Modern Language Journal* 81:443–456.

_____. 2011. *Teaching and Researching Language Learning Strategies*. Harlow, UK: Longman/Pearson.

Palmer, Jeremy. 2008. "Arabic Diglossia: Student Perceptions of Spoken Arabic after Living in the Arabic-Speaking World." *Arizona Working Papers in SLA and Teaching* 15:81–95.

Palmer, Parker J. 1998. *The Courage to Teach: Exploring the Inner Landscape of a Teacher's Life*. San Francisco: Jossey-Bass.

Parkinson, Dilworth. 1985. "Proficiency to Do What? Developing Oral Proficiency in Students of Modern Standard Arabic." *Al-Arabiyya* 18:1–2:11–43.

_____. 1991. "Searching for Modern *fuṣḥa*: Real-life Formal Arabic." *Al-Arabiyya* 24:31–64.

_____. 2003. "Verbal Features in Oral *fuṣḥa* Performances in Cairo." *International Journal of the Sociology of Language* 163:27–41.

Peeters, Bert. 2008. "Cross-Culturally Speaking, Speaking Cross-Culturally." Conference announcement, Linguist List 19.2761, September 10, 2008.

Pennington, Martha C. 2002. "Grammar and Communication: New Directions in Theory and Practice." In *New Perspectives on Grammar Teaching in Second Language Classrooms*, edited by Eli Hinkel and Sandra Fotos, 77–98. Mahwah, NJ: Lawrence Erlbaum.

Pennington, Martha C., and Jack C. Richards. 1986. "Pronunciation Revisited." *TESOL Quarterly* 20:2:207–225.

Perkins, David N. 2009. *Making Learning Whole: How Seven Principles of Teaching Can Transform Education*. San Francisco: Jossey-Bass.

Philips, June K. 1991. "An Analysis of Text in Video Newscasts: A Tool for Schemata Building in Listeners." *Georgetown University Round Table on Languages and Linguistics 1991*, edited by James E. Alatis, 343–354. Washington, DC: Georgetown University Press.

Pienemann, Manfred. 1989. "Is Language Teachable? Psycholinguistic Experiments and Hypotheses" *Applied Linguistics* 10:1:52–79.

____. 1998. *Language Processing and Second Language Development: Processability Theory.* New York: John Benjamins.

____. 2003. "Language Processing Capacity." In *The Handbook of Second Language Acquisition*, edited by Catherine J. Doughty and Michael H. Long, 679–714. Malden, MA: Blackwell.

____. 2007. "Processability Theory." In *Theories in Second Language Acquisition*, edited by Bill VanPatten and Jessica Williams, 137–154. New York: Routledge/Taylor & Francis.

Pratt, Mary Louise. 2003. "Building a New Public Idea about Language." In *Profession 2003*, edited by Rosemary G. Feal, 110–119. New York: Modern Language Association.

Pullum, Geoffrey. 2012: "Ferment and Befuddlement." *The Chronicle Review, Chronicle of Higher Education*, February 24, 2012, B2.

Pullum, Geoffrey K., and András Kornai. 2012. "Mathematical Linguistics." *Oxford International Encyclopedia of Linguistics*. Oxford: Oxford University Press. Accessed 2/22/2012 from www.kornai.com/MathLing/index.html.

Rammuny, Raji. 1980. *Advanced Arabic Composition Based on Literary Texts and Audio-Visual Materials (al-inshā? al-ʕarabiyy li-l-marHala l-mutaqaddima min khilāl nuṣūṣ adabiyya wa-mawādd samʕiyya - baṣariyya)*. Ann Arbor: Department of Near Eastern Studies, University of Michigan.

____. 1986. "A Model of Proficiency-Based Oral Achievement Testing for Elementary Arabic." *Foreign Language Annals* 19: 4: 321–331.

____. (1987), 1993. *Advanced Business Arabic (Al-lugha l-ʕarabiyya li-l-aʕmāl wa-l-shuʔūn l-tijāriyya)*. Troy, MI: International Book Centre.

____. 1994a. *Advanced Standard Arabic through Authentic Texts and Audiovisual Materials. Part One, Textual Materials (Al-lugha l-ʕarabiyya li-l-marāħil al-mutaqaddima min khilāl nuṣūṣ wa-mawādd samʕiyya baṣariyya aṣīla. Al-juzʔ al-awwal)*. Ann Arbor: University of Michigan Press.

____. 1994b. *Advanced Standard Arabic through Authentic Texts and Audiovisual Materials. Part Two, Audiovisual Materials. (Al-lugha l-ʕarabiyya li-l-marāħil al-mutaqaddima min khilāl nuṣūṣ wa-mawādd samʕiyya baṣariyya aṣīla. Al-juzʔ al-thānī)*. Ann Arbor: University of Michigan Press.

Rardin, Jennybelle P., Daniel D. Tranel, Patricia Tirone, and Bernard D. Green. 1988. *Education in a New Dimension: The Counseling-Learning Approach to Community Language Learning.* East Dubuque, IL: Counseling-Learning Publications.

Reynolds, Rachel R., Kathryn M. Howard, and Julia Deak. 2009. "Heritage Language Learners in First-Year Foreign Language Courses: A Report of General Data Across Learner Subtypes." *Foreign Language Annals* 42:2:250–269.

Richards, Jack C., and Willy A. Renandya, eds. 2002. *Methodology in Language Teaching: An Anthology of Current Practice*. Cambridge: Cambridge University Press.

Richards, Jack C., and Richard Schmidt. 2010. *Dictionary of Language Teaching and Applied Linguistics*, 4th ed. London: Longman.

Ristad, Eric Sven. 2012. "Recognition Complexity." *Oxford International Encyclopedia of Linguistics.* Oxford: Oxford University Press. Accessed 2/22/2012 from www.kornai.com/MathLing/index.html.

Rivkin, Benjamin, ed. 2001. *Mentoring Foreign Language Teaching Assistants, Lecturers and Adjunct Faculty.* Boston: Heinle & Heinle.

Robinson, Peter, and Nick C. Ellis. 2008. "An Introduction to Cognitive Linguistics, Second Language Acquisition, and Language Instruction." In *Handbook of Cognitive Linguistics and Second Language Acquisition*, edited by Peter Robinson and Nick C. Ellis, 3–24. New York: Routledge.

Rosenbaum, Gabriel M. 2000. "*Fuṣḥāmiyya:*" Alternating Style in Egyptian prose. *Zeitschrift für Arabische Linguistik* 38: 68–87.

Rubin, Joan. 1994. "A Review of Second Language Listening Comprehension Research." *Modern Language Journal* 78, no. 2:199–221.

———. 2006. "Developing Listening Comprehension Skills." Handout. National Capital Language Resource Center workshop, George Washington University, Washington, DC, June 29, 2006.

Ryding, Karin C. 1990. *Formal Spoken Arabic: Basic Course.* Washington, DC: Georgetown University Press.

———. 1991. "Proficiency despite Diglossia: A New Approach for Arabic." *Modern Language Journal* 75:2:212–218.

———. 1993. "Creating a Learning Community: Community Language Learning for the Nineties." *Georgetown University Round Table on Languages and Linguistics 1993*, edited by James E. Alatis, 137–147. Washington, DC: Georgetown University Press.

———. 2005. *A Reference Grammar of Modern Standard Arabic.* Cambridge: Cambridge University Press.

———. 2006. "Teaching Arabic in the United States." In *Handbook for Arabic Language Teaching Professionals in the 21st Century*, edited by Kassem Wahba, Zeinab Taha, and Liz England, 13–20. Mahwah, NJ: Lawrence Erlbaum Associates.

———. 2010. "Media Arabic as a Regional Standard." In *Arabic and the Media: Linguistic Analyses and Applications*, edited by Reem Bassiouney, 219–228. Leiden: Brill.

———. 2012. "Critical Languages and Critical Thinking: Reframing Academic Arabic Programs." In *Arabic Language and Linguistics*, edited by Reem Bassiouney and E. Graham Katz, 189–200. Washington, DC: Georgetown University Press.

———. 2013. "Arabic Second Language Acquisition." In *Oxford Handbook of Arabic Linguistics*, edited by Jonathan Owens. Oxford: Oxford University Press.

Ryding, Karin C., and David J. Mehall. 2005. *Formal Spoken Arabic: Basic Course*, 2nd ed. Washington, DC: Georgetown University Press.

Ryding, Karin, and Barbara Stowasser. 1997. "Text Development for Content-Based Instruction in Arabic." In *Content-Based Instruction in Foreign Language Education*, edited by Steven Stryker and Betty Lou Leaver, 107–118. Washington, DC: Georgetown University Press.

Ryding, Karin, and Abdelnour Zaiback. (1993) 2005. *Formal Spoken Arabic: FAST Course.* Georgetown University Press.

Ryding-Lentzner, Karin. 1978. "The Community Language Learning Approach to Arabic: Theory and Application." *Al-Arabiyya* 11:10–14.

Samy, Waheed. 1999. *Arabic Writing for Style (Al-Kitāba wa-l-uslūb).* Cairo: American University in Cairo Press.

———. 2006. "Instructional Media and Learning Arabic." In *A Handbook for Arabic Language Teaching Professionals in the 21st Century*, edited by Kassem Wahba, Zeinab Taha, and Liz England, 263–273. Mahwah, NJ: Lawrence Erlbaum Associates.

Sato, Kazuyoshi, and Robert C. Kleinsasser. 1999. "Communicative Language Teaching (CLT): Practical Understandings." *Modern Language Journal* 83, no. 4:494–517.

Saussy, Haun. 2005. "Language and Literature on the Pedagogical Continuum; or, Life Begins After Proficiency." *ADFL Bulletin* 36, no. 2:17–21.

Savignon, Sandra J. 1985. "Evaluation of Communicative Competence: The ACTFL Provisional Proficiency Guidelines." *Modern Language Journal* 69, no. 2:129–134.

_____. 1990. "Communicative Language Teaching: Definitions and Directions." In *Georgetown University Round Table on Languages and Linguistics 1990*, edited by James Alatis, 207–217. Washington, DC: Georgetown University Press.

Sawaie, Mohammed. 2012. "Review of *An Introduction to Moroccan Arabic and Culture*, by Abdellah Chekayri." *Modern Language Journal* 96, no. 1:141–143.

Schmidt, Richard W. 1994. "Deconstructing Consciousness in Search of Useful Definitions for Applied Linguistics." In *AILA Review* 11: 11–26.

_____. 1996. "Developmental Issues in Interlanguage Pragmatics." *Studies in Second Language Acquisition* 18:149–169.

Scholfield, Phil. 1997. "Vocabulary Reference Works in Foreign Language Learning." In *Vocabulary: Description, Acquisition and Pedagogy*, edited by Norbert Schmitt and Michael McCarthy, 279–302. Cambridge: Cambridge University Press.

Schultz, Ekehard, Günther Krahl, and Wolfgang Reuschel. 2000. *Standard Arabic: An Elementary-Intermediate Course*. Cambridge: Cambridge University Press.

Schultz, Renate A. 2007. "The Challenge of Assessing Cultural Understanding in the Context of Foreign Language Instruction." *Foreign Language Annals* 40, no. 1:8–26.

Scollon, Ron, and Suzanne Wong Scollon. 1995, 2001. *Intercultural Communication*. 2nd ed. Malden, MA: Blackwell.

Segalowitz, Norman. 2000. "Automaticity and Attentional Skill in Fluent Performance." In *Perspectives on Fluency*, edited by H. Riggenbach, 200–219. Ann Arbor: University of Michigan Press.

Selinker, Larry. 1972. "Interlanguage." *International Review of Applied Linguistics* 10: 209–231. Reprinted 1983 in *Second Language Learning: Contrastive Analysis, Error Analysis, and Related Aspects*, edited by Betty Wallace Robinett and Jacquelyn Schachter, 173–196. Ann Arbor: University of Michigan Press.

Shea, Christopher. 1997. "Political Scientists Clash over Value of Area Studies." *The Chronicle of Higher Education*, January 10, 1997, A13–A14.

Shohamy, Elana. 2011. "Assessing Multilingual Competencies: Adopting Construct Valid Assessment." *Modern Language Journal* 95:3:418–429.

Shumway, Nicolas. 2000. "Preparing Graduate Students to Teach in the Major: Two Modest Proposals." *PMLA* 115:5:1193–1195.

Single, Pes Boyle. 2009. "What the Research Says." *Inside Higher Education*, November 2, 2009, www.inside highered.com/layout/set/print/advice/dissertation/single6.

Skinner, B. F. 1953. *Science and Human Behavior*. New York: The Free Press.

Sohn, Sung-Ock, and Sang-Keun Shin. 2007. "True Beginners, False Beginners and Fake Beginners: Placement Strategies for Korean Heritage Speakers." *Foreign Language Annals* 40, no. 3:407–418.

Spolsky, Bernard. 2000. "Language Testing in *The Modern Language Journal*." *Modern Language Journal* 84, no. 4:536–552.

Stansfield, Charles W., and Chip Harman. 1987. *ACTFL Proficiency Guidelines for the Less Commonly Taught Languages*. Washington, DC: Center for Applied Linguistics, and Hastings-on-Hudson, NY: American Council on the Teaching of Foreign Languages.

Stevick, Earl W. 1980. *A Way and Ways*. Boston: Newbury House.

_____. 1982. "The Power Gauge in Language Teaching." In *Innovative Approaches to Language Teaching*, edited by Robert W. Blair, 115–117. Boston: Newbury House.

_____. 1985. "Curriculum Development at the Foreign Service Institute." In *Teaching for Proficiency, the Organizing Principle*, edited by Theodore V. Higgs, 85–112. Lincolnwood IL: National Textbook Company.

_____. 1990. *Humanism in Language Teaching: A Critical Perspective*. Oxford: Oxford University Press.

_____. 1996. *Memory, Meaning & Method*, 2nd. ed. Boston: Heinle & Heinle.

Suleiman, Yasir. 1991. "Affective and Personality Factors in Learning Arabic as a Foreign Language: A Case Study." *Al-Arabiyya* 24: 83–110.

_____. 2011. *Arabic, Self and Identity: A Study in Conflict and Displacement*. Oxford: Oxford University Press.

Swaffar, Janet. 1999. "The Case for Foreign Languages as a Discipline." *Profession 1999*, 155–167. New York: Modern Language Association.

Swaffar, Janet, Katherine Arens, and Heidi Byrnes. 1991. *Reading for Meaning: An Integrated Approach to Language Learning*. Englewood Cliffs, NJ: Prentice Hall.

Takač, Višnja Pavičić. 2008. *Vocabulary Learning Strategies and Foreign Language Acquisition*. Clevedon: Multilingual Matters, Ltd.

Tannen, Deborah. 1984. "Cross-cultural Communication." *CATESOL Occasional Papers* 10 (Fall 1984):1–16.

Teachingworks. 2012. "High-Leverage Practices." Accessed February 3, 2012 at www.teaching-works.org/work-of-teaching/high-leverage-practices.

Terrell, Tracy D. 1982. "A Natural Approach." In *Innovative Approaches to Language Teaching*, edited by Robert W. Blair, 160–173. Boston: Newbury House.

_____. 1985. "The Natural Approach." Talk and handout presented at the Foreign Service Institute March 20, 1985.

_____. 1991. "The Role of Grammar Instruction in a Communicative Approach." *Modern Language Journal* 75, no. 1:52–63.

Terrell, Tracy D., Jeanne Egasse, and Wilfried Voge. 1982. "Techniques for a More Natural Approach to Second Language Acquisition and Learning." In *Innovative Approaches to Language Teaching*, edited by Robert W. Blair, 174–175. Boston: Newbury House.

Thompson, Richard. 1989. "Oral Proficiency in the Less Commonly Taught Languages: What Do We Know about It?" In *Georgetown University Round Table on Languages and Linguistics 1989*, edited by James E. Alatis, 228–234. Washington, DC: Georgetown University Press.

Tomlin, Russell S., and Victor Villa. 1994. "Attention in Cognitive Science and Second Language Acquisition." *Studies in Second Language Acquisition* 16: 183–203.

Tomlinson, Brian, ed. 1998a. *Materials Development in Language Teaching*. Cambridge: Cambridge University Press.

_____. 1998b. "Introduction." In *Materials Development in Language Teaching*, edited by Brian Tomlinson, 1–24. Cambridge: Cambridge University Press.

Trofimovitch, Pavel, and Elizabeth Gatbonton. 2006. "Repetition and Focus on Form in Processing L2 Spanish Words: Implications for Pronunciation Instruction." *Modern Language Journal* 90, no. 4:519–535.

Tweissi, Adel I. 1990. "Foreigner Talk in Arabic: Evidence for the Universality of Language Simplification." In *Perspectives on Arabic Linguistics II*, edited by Mushira Eid and John McCarthy, 296–326. Amsterdam: John Benjamins.

Tyler, Andrea. 2008. "Cognitive Linguistics and Second Language Instruction." In *Handbook of Cognitive Linguistics and Second Language Acquisition*, edited by Peter Robinson and Nick C. Ellis, 456–488. New York: Routledge.

Ur, Penny. 1988, 2007. *Grammar Practice Activities: A Practical Guide for Teachers*. Cambridge: Cambridge University Press.

US Department of State. 1973. "Expected Levels of Absolute Speaking Proficiency in Languages Taught at the Foreign Service Institute." Handout. Washington, DC: Foreign Service Institute. School of Language Studies.

_____. 2004. *Language Continuum*. Washington, DC: Foreign Service Institute, School of Language Studies, George P. Schultz National Foreign Affairs Training Center.

Van Lier, Leo. 1996. *Interaction in the Language Curriculum: Awareness, Autonomy and Authenticity.* New York: Longman.

____. VanPatten, Bill. 1985. "The ACTFL Proficiency Guidelines: Implications for Grammatical Accuracy in the Classroom?" *Studies in Second Language Acquisition* 8: 56–67

____. 2007. "Input Processing in Adult Second Language Acquisition." In *Theories in Second Language Acquisition*, edited by Bill VanPatten and Jessica Williams, 115–136. New York: Routledge/Taylor & Francis.

VanPatten, Bill, and Alessandro G. Benati. 2010. *Key Terms in Second Language Acquisition.* London: Continuum.

VanPatten, Bill, and Jessica Williams, eds. 2007a. *Theories in Second Language Acquisition.* New York: Routledge/Taylor & Francis.

____. 2007b. "Early Theories in Second Language Acquisition." In *Theories in Second Language Acquisition*, edited by Bill Van Patten and Jessica Williams, 17–35. New York: Routledge/Taylor & Francis.

Wahba, Kassem. 2006. "Arabic Language Use and the Educated Language User." In *A Handbook for Arabic Language Teaching Professionals in the 21st Century*, edited by Kassem Wahba, Zeinab Taha, and Liz England, 139–156. Mahwah, NJ: Lawrence Erlbaum Associates.

Al-Warraki, Nariman Naili, and Ahmed Taher Hassanein. 1994. *Adawāt al-rabt fī l-ʕarabiyya l-muʕāṣira. (The Connectors in Modern Standard Arabic).* Cairo: American University in Cairo Press.

Wehr, Hans. 1994. *Arabic-English Dictionary: The Hans Wehr Dictionary of Modern Written Arabic*, edited by J. M. Cowan. 4th ed. Ithaca, NY: Spoken Language Services.

Weigert, Astrid, and Susanne Rinner. 2005. "Integrating Diverse Content Courses Via Genre: From Sports to the EU Economy." Presentation at Georgetown University Round Table on Languages and Linguistics, March 14, 2005.

White, Lydia. 2007. "Linguistic Theory, Universal Grammar, and Second Language Acquisition." In *Theories in Second Language Acquisition*, edited by Bill VanPatten and Jessica Williams, 37–55. New York: Routledge/Taylor & Francis.

Whitney, Heather M. 2011. "Simple Post-Its for Teaching Improvement." *Chronicle of Higher Education* online, September 14, 2011. Retrieved from www.chronicle.com/blogs/profhacker/simple-post-its-for-teaching-improvement.

Widdowson, H. G. 1992. "Perspectives on Communicative Language Teaching: Syllabus Design and Methodology." *In Georgetown University Round Table on Languages and Linguistics 1992*, edited by James Alatis, 501–507. Washington, DC: Georgetown University Press.

Willis, David. 2003. *Rules, Patterns and Words: Grammar and Lexis in English Language Teaching.* Cambridge: Cambridge University Press.

Wilmsen, David. 2006. "What Is Communicative Arabic?" In *A Handbook for Arabic Language Teaching Professionals in the 21st Century*, edited by Kassem Wahba, Zeinab Taha, and Liz England, 125–138. Mahwah, NJ: Lawrence Erlbaum Associates.

Winke, Paula M., and Rajaa Aquil. 2006. "Issues in Developing Standardized Tests of Arabic Language Proficiency." In *A Handbook for Arabic Language Teaching Professionals in the 21st Century*, edited by Kassem Wahba, Zeinab Taha, and Liz England, 221–235. Mahwah, NJ: Lawrence Erlbaum Associates.

Wittgenstein, Ludwig. 2008. *Philosophical Investigations: The German Text, with a Revised English Translation*, 3rd ed. Translated by G. E. M. Anscon. London: Blackwell.

Wong, Rita. 1985. "Does Pronunciation Teaching Have a Place in the Communicative Classroom?" Paper presented at the 1985 Georgetown University Round Table on Languages and Linguistics in Washington, DC.

Wood, D., S. Jerome Bruner, and G. Ross. 1976. "The Role of Tutoring in Problem Solving." *Journal of Child Psychology and Psychiatry* 17: 89–100.

Wright, William. (1859) 1967. *A Grammar of the Arabic Language*, 3rd ed., 2 vols., rev. W. Robertson Smith and M. J. de Goeje. Cambridge: Cambridge University Press.

Yankelovich, Daniel. 2005. "Ferment and Change: Higher Education in 2015." *The Chronicle Review, Chronicle of Higher Education*, November 25, 2005. http://chronicle.com/weekly/v52/ i14b00601.htm.

Younes, Munther A. 2001. *Hikāyāt kalīla wa-dimna (Kalila and Dimna: For students of Arabic)*. Ithaca, NY: Spoken Language Services.

Ziadeh, Farhat J. 1964. *A Reader in Modern Literary Arabic*. Princeton: Princeton University Press.

Ziadeh, Farhat J., and R. Bayly Winder. 1957. *An Introduction to Modern Arabic*. Princeton, NJ: Princeton University Press.

Index

Weinert, R., 183
Whitney, H., 106
Widdowson, H., 73
Williams, J., 22, 24
Willis, D., 197, 198
Wilmsen, D., 75
Winder, R., 42
Wittgenstien, L., 139, 147
Wong, R., 174
Wood, D., 114
Word stress, 174, 176nn11–12
Writing, and pronunciation, 122
Writing, in Arabic
  about, 187
  analyzing compositions, 192–193
  and close reading, 191–192

dictation exercises, 189
handwriting, 189–190
and literacy, 191
notetaking, 191
process and product, 192
sound and script, 187–188
steps in teaching, 188–189

Y
Yankelovich, D., 1, 228n6

Z
Zeoli, E., 85
Ziadeh, F., 42
Zone of proximal development
  (ZPD), 115, 132

6/20